EUROPEAN HUMAN RIGHTS JUSTICE AND PRIVATISATION

With the decline of public funding and new strategies pursued by interest groups, foreign private foundations and donors have become growing contributors to the European human rights justice system. These groups have created their own litigation teams, have increasingly funded NGOs litigating the European Courts, and have contributed to the content and supervision of European judgments, all of which has had direct effects on the growth and procedure of human rights. *European Human Rights Justice and Privatisation* analyses the impacts of this private influence and its effects on international relations between states, including the orientation of European jurisprudence towards Eastern countries and the promotion of private and neoliberal interests. This book looks at the direct and indirect threat posed by this private influence to the independence of European justice and to the protection of human rights in Europe.

GAËTAN CLIQUENNOIS works as a senior fellow in the field of human rights. He is currently a permanent Research Fellow at the CNRS/DCS, Law and Social Change, University of Nantes, and has been a visiting scholar at the University of Cambridge and the London School of Economics and Political Science.

EUROPEAN HUMAN RIGHTS JUSTICE AND PRIVATISATION

The Growing Influence of Foreign Private Funds

GAËTAN CLIQUENNOIS
Université de Nantes, France

CAMBRIDGE
UNIVERSITY PRESS

Shaftesbury Road, Cambridge CB2 8EA, United Kingdom

One Liberty Plaza, 20th Floor, New York, NY 10006, USA

477 Williamstown Road, Port Melbourne, VIC 3207, Australia

314–321, 3rd Floor, Plot 3, Splendor Forum, Jasola District Centre, New Delhi – 110025, India

103 Penang Road, #05–06/07, Visioncrest Commercial, Singapore 238467

Cambridge University Press is part of Cambridge University Press & Assessment, a department of the University of Cambridge.

We share the University's mission to contribute to society through the pursuit of education, learning and research at the highest international levels of excellence.

www.cambridge.org
Information on this title: www.cambridge.org/9781108739450
DOI: 10.1017/9781108683869

© Gaëtan Cliquennois 2020

This publication is in copyright. Subject to statutory exception and to the provisions of relevant collective licensing agreements, no reproduction of any part may take place without the written permission of Cambridge University Press & Assessment.

First published 2020
First paperback edition 2022

A catalogue record for this publication is available from the British Library

Library of Congress Cataloging-in-Publication data
Names: Cliquennois, Gaëtan author.
Title: European human rights justice and privatisation : the growing influence of foreign private funds / Gaëtan Cliquennois, Université de Nantes, France.
Description: Cambridge, United Kingdom ; New York, NY, USA : Cambridge University Press, 2020. | Includes bibliographical references and index.
Identifiers: LCCN 2020009123 (print) | LCCN 2020009124 (ebook) | ISBN 9781108497053 (hardback) | ISBN 9781108739450 (paperback) | ISBN 9781108683869 (epub)
Subjects: LCSH: Human rights–Europe–Cases. | Human rights advocacy–Europe. | Charitable uses, trusts, and foundations–Political activity–Europe. | Non-governmental organizations–Europe–Influence.
Classification: LCC KJC5132 . C55 2020 (print) | LCC KJC5132 (ebook) | DDC 342.408/5–dc23
LC record available at https://lccn.loc.gov/2020009123
LC ebook record available at https://lccn.loc.gov/2020009124

ISBN 978-1-108-49705-3 Hardback
ISBN 978-1-108-73945-0 Paperback

Cambridge University Press & Assessment has no responsibility for the persistence or accuracy of URLs for external or third-party internet websites referred to in this publication and does not guarantee that any content on such websites is, or will remain, accurate or appropriate.

CONTENTS

List of Tables ix
Foreword by x
LISA MCINTOSH SUNDSTROM
Acknowledgments xii

Introduction 1

PART I The Procedural Aspect of the Growing Influence of Private Foundations on the European Human Rights Justice System 7

1 The Increasing Influence of Private Foundations in the Realm of Justice 9
  1.1 The Rise of Interest Groups and Foreign Private Foundations in Justice 9
  1.2 The Impacts of Foreign Private Funds on National Courts: US and Irish Justice 14
  1.3 Why Could the European Courts Be Targeted by Private Donors? 15
    1.3.1 The Increasing Power of the European Court of Human Rights and the Court of Justice of the European Union 16
    1.3.2 The Increasing Role of NGOs in Litigation and Third Party Intervention 29
    1.3.3 The Role of the Economic Crisis of 2007 and the Crucial Need for Litigation Funding 30

2 The Creeping Private Influence on the Inputs of the ECtHR and the CJEU 33
  2.1 The Creation and Development of a Litigation Team by the OSF 33
  2.2 The Private-Sector Funding of Applications Taken by NGOs to the ECtHR and the CJEU 36
    2.2.1 The Funding of NGOs by Private Foundations for Their Litigation Activities 37
    2.2.2 The Role Played by the Main Private Donors 61
  2.3 The Co-funding of NGOs and Private Organisations by Some CoE Member States 65

CONTENTS

3 The Influence of Private Foundations on the Outputs of the ECtHR and the CJEU   66

     3.1 Judicial Results Obtained by Private Foundations and NGOs Financed by Them   67
         3.1.1 Pilot Judgments   68
         3.1.2 Judgments Obtained under Article 46 and Imposing General Measures on Condemned Member States   76
         3.1.3 Other Landmark Judgments   102
     3.2 Documents and Reports by NGOs and Private Foundations as Evidence Applied by the ECtHR and the CJEU   136
     3.3 The Increased Involvement of Private Foundations and NGOs in the Monitoring of the Execution of Human Rights Judgments by Member States   140

4 The Growing Influence Exerted by the Private Sector on the Reform and Structure of the ECtHR and the CJEU   144

     4.1 Contribution of Private Foundations and NGOs to Redesign and Reform of the ECtHR through Advocacy   144
         4.1.1 Reform of the ECtHR, the Process of Execution of Judgments and Claims for an Increase in the ECtHR Budget   144
         4.1.2 NGO Influence on the Rules of the ECtHR on the Treatment of Classified Documents   155
         4.1.3 Research Conducted by NGOs and Private Foundations on the ECtHR's Pilot Judgments Procedure and Fact-Finding Processes   156
     4.2 Private Influence on Nominations of European Judges   158
     4.3 A Broader Approach to Third Party Interventions Submitted by Private Foundations and NGOs   162
     4.4 The Introduction of Private-Sector Management Techniques at the ECtHR and the CJEU Favouring NGOs and Private Foundations   163

PART II   The Substantive Dimension of the Growing Influence of Private Foundations on European Human Rights Justice   171

5 Effects of the Growing Influence of Private Interests on the Orientation of European Case Law   173

     5.1 Orientation of Litigation towards Specific Policy Areas   173
     5.2 Litigation against Specific Countries: Eastern Europe and Russia   175
         5.2.1 Structural Flows of the Constitutional Systems of Eastern Countries and Their Domestic Remedies   179

5.2.2 The Difference that Private Foundations and NGOs Make Concerning the Overrepresentation of Eastern Countries 182

5.3 Reduced Protection of Human Rights in Certain Countries and Policy Areas: Countries and Cases Ignored by NGOs and Private Foundations 187

    5.3.1 Countries Ignored by Private Litigation 188

    5.3.2 Cases and Issues Neglected by Private Foundations: Absence of Real European Judicial Control over Austerity Policies and Their Effects 189

6 Effects of Private Litigation on Domestic Policies and International Relations: The Rise of Tensions between the EU, the US and Eastern Countries 200

6.1 How ECtHR Judgments Transform National Policies, Are Politicised and Expose Nationalist Regimes in Eastern Countries 200

    6.1.1 The Ananyev, Neshkov and Varga Cases: Bulgaria, Hungary and Russia as 'Garrison States' 201

    6.1.2 The Catan Case: Russia as an 'Aggressive, Authoritarian and Nationalist' State that Oppresses Minorities 205

    6.1.3 The Khashiyev and Akayeva and Tagayeva Cases: Russia as a 'Terrorist and Violent State' 208

    6.1.4 Russia and Azerbaijan as 'Oppressive and Corruptive States that Do Not Allow Political Opposition' 212

    6.1.5 The Al Nashiri and Abu Zaybah Cases: Poland and Romania as 'Secret States Running Illegal Counterterrorist Operations' 215

    6.1.6 The Horváth and Kiss and D. H. Judgments: Hungary and the Czech Republic as 'Racist States' 216

6.2 The Eastern and Russian Reactions to European Judicial Condemnations 221

    6.2.1 Bans on Foreign Private Foundations and NGOs in Russia, Hungary and Azerbaijan and Control over NGOs in Poland 221

    6.2.2 New Powers Given to the Russian Supreme Court 228

6.3 The Rise of Political Tensions between Russia and the EU Backed by the US 231

6.4 Towards a New Cold War? 236

7 The Relationships between Litigation Funded by Private Foundations and the Economic and Political Interests They Pursue 241

7.1 The Fight against Nationalism as Part of the Promotion of Borderless Neoliberalism and Free Trade 241

    7.1.1 The Identity and Profile of Board Members of Private
           Foundations: Businessmen, Not Philanthropists   242
    7.1.2 Litigation Impacts in Terms of Economy and Market: Making
           Business in a More Discreet Way through Policy and Regime
           Change   251
  7.2 How and Why Private Foundations Promote Cultural Liberalism and
       Globalism   256
  7.3 The Interests of Certain CoE Member States   258

Conclusion: Towards a Privatised Capture of Human Rights?   260

Select Bibliography   264
Index of Authors   277
General Index   281

TABLES

2.1 Main private foundations, NGOs and their funding 62
5.1 NGOs and their litigation activities, 2000–2018 177
5.2 Total number of applications per country, 1959–2017 178
5.3 Numbers of ECtHR judgments and ECHR violations by Russia (1998–2017) and by main CoE member states (1959–2017) 179

FOREWORD

LISA MCINTOSH SUNDSTROM
Associate Professor of Political Science, University of British Columbia

Private charitable foundations – such as the Open Society, Ford, MacArthur, and Oak Foundations – generously provide funding to NGOs around the world to support their efforts to litigate violations of human rights in international courts. So what is wrong with that? In this book, Gaëtan Cliquennois provides a thought-provoking answer. In doing so, he makes a significant contribution to literatures on international courts, legal mobilisation, privatisation of state functions, and the politics of NGOs and their funding sources. As such, this book is at the cutting edge of questions to which new scholars of litigation in international courts are turning.

Focusing on two major European regional courts, the European Court of Human Rights (ECtHR) and the Court of Justice of the European Union (CJEU), Cliquennois deftly links the efforts of private foundations to encourage litigation by NGOs against European states in these courts to the neoliberal agendas of private foundation leaders. He draws together a number of patterns that some other authors have observed: the classic observation that better resourced litigants with repetitive experience before a court hold considerable advantage in winning victories in them; the disproportionate focus of foundations and these courts on particular kinds of human rights violations, especially in the Eastern portion of the European Union and the Council of Europe; and recent reforms at the ECtHR and CJEU that filter and reduce the number of cases that make it to the stage of admissibility.

By adding a novel focus on the involvement of private foundations in particular, Cliquennois reveals the roles of private foundations in influencing the activities of those individual activists and NGOs that litigate at the ECtHR and CJEU. In addition, he tracks how private foundations 'capture' these courts internally in other respects: for instance, through 'revolving door' relationships between judges appointed to the ECtHR after working for NGOs funded by private foundations or for the foundations themselves; and through the courts' reliance on information from foundation-funded NGOs as case evidence and their roles in monitoring post-judgment implementation.

For those who would ask my initial question – what could be wrong with private foundations supporting the human rights work of activists where violations are occurring? – Cliquennois points out how foundations have exhibited considerable emphases and blind spots in their support. He documents how they have generally ignored certain types of rights violations, such as socio-economic rights and inequalities caused by government economic austerity programmes. He argues that this could be explained by the economic interests of foundation benefactors and founders themselves. Moreover, according to Cliquennois, the emphases of private foundations represent an effort to stigmatise the governments of certain Eastern European countries and Russia, branding them as dangerously authoritarian and nationalist. Their goal is to dismantle nationalist regimes in order to smooth the way for a neoliberal global economy where borders are not barriers to economic exchange.

The argument is extremely provocative and will inspire more research by scholars who follow in his footsteps. Most valuably, Cliquennois cautions us that we must not allow our normative goals of advancing human rights to blind us to the instrumental goals of particular actors who are supporting international human rights advocacy.

ACKNOWLEDGMENTS

I would like to warmly thank Katia Barragan, Brice Champetier, Daphne Ten Kloosterand Elisabeth Lambert for their very useful help and Rafal Encinas de Munagoori, Agustín José Menéndez and François Laffarge for their great support. I would also thank the University of Strasbourg, the University of Nantes, Cambridge University Press and their anonmymous reviewers who have evaluated my book proposal for their very helpful comments.

My ever thoughts go to Sophie, Tristan and Arthur.

Introduction

This book aims to contribute to the analysis of European human rights justice, and in particular of the case law of the European Court of Human Rights (ECtHR) and the Court of Justice of the European Union (CJEU), from what seems to me an unexplored perspective. In a nutshell, I not only consider the case law of the ECtHR and the CJEU as a given and fixed output but also pay attention to the role played by inputs in the form of petitions brought before the Strasbourg and Luxembourg judges by repeated players (and the litigation strategies that underpin them) in making the case law of the ECtHR and the CJEU.

To put it differently, instead of a narrow reconstruction of this or that ruling of the ECtHR and the CJEU, or an analysis of the techniques and methods of interpretation of the court, I consider how the case law of the European Courts comes to be made, both in terms of inputs (complaints and applications) and outputs (execution and politicisation of judgments) and in terms of the process and architecture of the Courts. The repeated players on which I focus are a set of private foundations and non-governmental organisations (NGOs) that have become specialists in bringing cases before the ECtHR and the CJEU. For a long time, their role has been neglected in the literature and in public discussion, although NGOs have integrated litigation into their strategy along with advocacy (McCrudden 2015). The relatively ample public funding for such NGOs in the past might have led to the conclusion that they play a merely facilitating role in individual petitions. Nevertheless, it has been the case since the 2000s that a considerable source of funding for many of these NGOs was a relatively small set of private donors.

Furthermore, austerity policies have made it impossible to ignore the clout that donors have over NGOs. Budgetary cuts have resulted in declining levels of public funding, precisely at a time when the number of potential complaints before the ECtHR and the CJEU has increased, given the proliferation of alleged breaches of fundamental rights resulting from 'austerity policies' justified in the name of 'fiscal emergencies'. But less public funding for NGOs translates into more room for private donors to turn funding into influence. This phenomenon renders it imperative to consider the relationship between output, input and process in the making of the jurisprudence of the ECtHR and the CJEU, and in particular, the structural and substantive political agendas of private donors, or what amounts to the same thing, the ways in which they try to influence the ECtHR and the CJEU through both strategic litigation and strategic funding of NGOs litigating before them. To put it in more scientific terms: by taking seriously the extent to which private donors litigate in the European Courts and fund NGOs, and how they can make use of that funding to shape the agenda behind NGOs' litigation strategies, we can consider how the origin of the financial resources that make it possible to bring cases before the European Courts influence and even capture the structure and the substance of the jurisprudence of the ECtHR and the CJEU.

In this regard, and drawing on economic theories of regulatory and state capture (Hellman et al. 2003; Levine and Forrence 1990; Stigler 1971), movement capture can be used to analyse how private funders operate like interest groups or private firms to buy influence over the goals and strategies pursued by civil servants (Devaux 2019), activists and cause lawyers. The concept of movement capture refers to the process by which private funders leverage their financial resources to exert pressure on cause lawyers and influence the decision-making processes of civil rights organisations (Francis 2018).

The book thus analyses the creeping influence of private funds on European human rights justice in Europe while administration and decision-making stay in the hands of public institutions. The relevance and accuracy of this topic is confirmed by the very recent public debates in Russia, Hungary and Azerbaijan on the role played in the human rights sector by private foundations.[1] While this phenomenon affects 820 million Europeans in forty-seven member states of the Council of Europe (CoE), until now the topic has been neglected in the academic literature. The trend has indeed been overlooked by legal and socio-legal scholars, who have paid attention mainly to alternative dispute resolution in the human rights sector (Mc Gregor 2015; Samuel 2004) and to the

---

[1] See for instance http://budapestbeacon.com/featured-articles/breaking-and-bad-hungarian-parliament-passes-controversial-ngo-law/, www.businessinsider.com/afp-russia-bans-undesirable-khodorkovsky-ngos-2017-4?IR=T and www.theguardian.com/world/2015/nov/30/russia-bans-two-george-soros-foundations-from-giving-grants.

privatisation of public sector services (such as water, education, healthcare, security and prisons) achieved by international and regional human rights jurisdictions (de Feyter and Gómez Isa 2005; de Wolf 2011; Nowak 2017). Although some international research studies have analysed the strategies pursued by US conservative groups (including faith-based NGOs) to promote their convictions by engaging in transnational advocacy and litigation (McCrudden 2015), scant attention has been paid until now to the potential capture and even privatisation of the European Courts through the influence of private foundations. This trend is reported here for the first time, and the impacts of this potential privatisation on justice and society deserve to be analysed.

In this regard, the book addresses the way foreign and private money affects European justice and thus European states. Irish justice, along with the UK, France, Germany, Italy, Spain, Hungary and Poland,[2] could constitute the first national case in point to be influenced by foreign private interests. Nevertheless, this process of foreign private influence on justice seems to be more developed at the European level, although such complaints must first exhaust domestic remedies unless it can be demonstrated that these are unavailable or ineffective. In this respect, the European Courts may be at the forefront of the trend, as their rulings affect and impact a larger number of people than those of a domestic tribunal.

With the decline of public funding (partly due to the economic crisis) and new strategies pursued by interest groups, foreign private foundations and donors have become growing contributors to European human rights justice. The creation of their own litigation teams, their increasing funding of NGOs and applications before the European Courts, and their contribution to the content, evidence and supervision of the judgments delivered by these Courts have direct effects on human rights. From this perspective, the book also analyses the impacts of private influence on European jurisprudence and on international relations between states, thus questioning the direct and non-direct threat this influence poses for the independence of European justice and for the protection of human and fundamental rights in Europe. Private influence on the inputs, outputs (non-direct threat) and structures (direct threat) of the European Courts could orient European jurisprudence towards certain countries (considered to be enemies of wealthy financiers) and

---

[2] Open Society Justice Initiative, *Litigation Report 2015*, pp. 11–12, 14, 50.

the promotion of private interests (such as free-market capitalism and the promotion of competition and free market in a liberal and international society) pursued by private foundations. Consequently, litigants which are not considered by private foundations to be a priority might end up with no real access to the European Courts or to judicial protection of their human rights. At any rate, for citizens not belonging to the countries involved or covered by the issues litigated by private foundations, access to justice and protection of their human rights could be made harder.

While administration and decision-making stay in the hands of public judicial institutions, this private influence also raises issues about the potential capture and privatisation of European human rights justice. Privatisation in this sense is the growing private ownership of European jurisprudence and judicial protection of human rights, as landmark judgments are mainly obtained and monitored by private foundations and NGOs supported by private foundations. As the judiciary contributes in a more significant way over time to the protection of human rights, we might wonder whether traditional judicial independence, notably characterised by free election of judges (Vauchez and Willemez 2006) and by public funding, is threatened by private interests and whether judicial protection of human rights is becoming partly privatised and owned by private foundations. Could human rights (the way their content and protection are interpreted by the European Courts) be considered to be fully under the influence of private foundations through these mechanisms? As this is a completely new field of research, this book will raise awareness and give a new perspective on the human rights justice system. It offers a different understanding of the issues at stake and of the relationships between litigation strategies, advocacy, private funding and European case law with a view to fostering a societal debate about the growing influence of private actors on European human rights justice.

To demonstrate this assumption, I apply a socio-legal method that considers European jurisprudence as partly the result of direct and third party litigation and its funding. In a nutshell, and as I said above, not only do I consider the case law of the ECtHR and the CJEU as a given and fixed output, I also pay attention to the role played by inputs, in the form of the petitions brought before the Strasbourg and Luxembourg judges by repeated players (and the litigation strategies that underpin them), in the making of the case law of the ECtHR and the CJEU. To this end, the book contains a socio-legal analysis of the landmark judgments obtained by private foundations. It also draws on twenty years of empirical data on CJEU and ECtHR litigation and decision-making and the mobilisation of transnational NGOs and private foundations in the EU and the CoE. It uses qualitative and quantitative data on litigation funding and landmark cases delivered by the Courts and obtained by private foundations and NGOs (financed by private foundations) through litigation efforts. It also analyses internal litigation documents, annual and financial reports of private foundations and NGOs litigating in the European Courts and archives collected at the Rockefeller Archives Center (which hosts the Ford Foundation Archives) in New York and at the Open Society Foundation (OSF) in Budapest. Such documents are rarely applied and analysed by legal scholars or in the socio-legal literature, even though they tend to reveal why and how private foundations are interested and invested in matters of justice. As a complement to these archives and official documents, I have conducted informal interviews with heads of NGOs and officials working for the CoE and the EU.

My aim in this book is therefore to contribute to the analysis of the protection of human and fundamental rights in Europe from an unexplored perspective. The first objective of the book is to investigate the creeping influence exerted by foreign private funds on the main aspects (inputs and outputs, content of judgments and structures of the European Courts) of European and national human rights jurisprudence. The second aim of the book is to investigate the effects of this private influence on the protection of human and fundamental rights in Europe and to analyse the relationships between litigation activities carried out by private donors and their political and economic interests. In this regard, the book also raises the issue of how this private influence could have an impact on international relations between states. Finally, the book questions whether this private influence threatens the independence of European justice and may even lead to its potential privatisation. More precisely, Part I will study the procedural aspect of the creeping influence exerted by private foundations on European human and fundamental rights justice, analysing three main indicators of this private influence. Part II will analyse the substantive dimension of this increasing influence in terms of its impacts on the protection of human rights. In this respect, private funding tends to orient applications towards specific countries and domains and potentially contributes to the capture (by private foundations) and even the privatisation of the European human rights system.

PART I

The Procedural Aspect of the Growing Influence of Private Foundations on the European Human Rights Justice System

This first part of the book analyses the procedural dimension of the growing influence of private foundations and groups on European and national justice systems. In particular, we consider why private foundations are interested in investing in litigation before the European Courts and whether such private influence amounts to a partial capture of European jurisprudence (Chapter 1). In this regard, there are three main indicators of a creeping private capture of the European human rights justice system: inputs (Chapter 2), outputs (Chapter 3) and structures of the European Courts (Chapter 4).

1

The Increasing Influence of Private Foundations in the Realm of Justice

This first chapter focuses on the general influence of foreign private money at the European and national judicial level. Drawing on the sparse literature on this issue, this chapter addresses why and how foreign private donors are interested in investing in litigation before the European human rights justice system, which has become more attractive to them over time.

1.1 The Rise of Interest Groups and Foreign Private Foundations in Justice

The legal and socio-legal literature has mainly paid attention to alternative dispute resolution in the human rights sector (McGregor 2015; Samuel 2004) and to the privatisation of public sector services (such as water, education, healthcare, security and prisons) achieved by international and regional human rights jurisdictions (de Feyter and Gómez Isa 2005; de Wolf 2011; Nowak 2017). Until now, scant attention has been paid to the potential privatisation of European human rights justice under the growing influence exerted by private foundations. Several scholars have remarked on the privatisation of justice; for instance, Trevor C. W. Farrow has shown how the privatisation of civil justice occurs without any democratic debate under a widespread ethos of efficiency and cost-saving-based civil justice reform. However, scholars have yet to address European justice and the role played by private foundations in this process.

Analyses of the case law of the ECtHR and the CJEU tend to consist of either black-letter reconstructions of the jurisprudence of the ECtHR or analyses of the techniques and methods of interpretation to which the Strasbourg and Luxembourg judges resort. In the latter regard, it is usually assumed that the ECtHR has developed fundamental rights standards mobilising a range of interpretative methods, which simultaneously reflect the fundamental objectives pursued by the judges and the contextual constraints imposed upon them (Torres Pérez 2009). Although the discretion involved in judicial interpretation (and the use to which discretion is put, i.e. the extent to which it is used to foster socially desirable outcomes) is widely acknowledged to be highly relevant, not much attention has been paid to how litigants try to influence the ECtHR and the CJEU. As several authors have stressed, we lack scholarship analysing the litigant's impact on the substantive content of the case law of European courts beyond specific cases.

It is only recently that the difference made by litigation undertaken by NGOs before international (Lohne 2019) and regional courts (Ahmed 2011; Hitoshi Mayer 2011), and their growing presence at the international level and notably at the International Criminal Court (Lohne 2019), has begun to be studied (Mertus 1999). Kjersti Lohne has shown that NGOs have become central to the 'fight against impunity' for international crimes (Lohne 2017) and for sexual offences (Bringedal Houge and Lohne 2017). In this regard and more generally, important studies have reported the centrality and capacity of NGOs to influence courts and their agenda-setting (Glasius 2006; Lohne 2019), and to foster both judicial and political changes through litigation (Cichowski 2007; Lohne 2019; McIntosh Sundstrom 2014; Vajic 2005) and amicus curiae (Bürli 2017; Collins 2018; van den Eynde 2013). Even though most of these studies were undertaken by US scholars who did not focus on the European Courts, some of their findings seem to us to be relevant in the European context.

First, the socio-legal literature has identified the influence of social movements and defence lawyers as essential to understanding the development of human rights jurisprudence (Sarat and Scheingold 1998, 2001 and 2006), although it has not dealt with and is not really concerned with the influence of donors. The ability of these groups to contribute to the implementation of human rights by courts depends on the national culture of law for each state, which international instruments, legislation and case law can recognise and in which they can enshrine more or fewer human rights. Some authors have, however, challenged the overall impact of such litigation strategies by noting that in the US they need to be supported by ample judicial precedent for bold action, by the legislative and executive branches and by a mix of citizens with little opposition (Cummins and Rhode 2009; Rosenberg 1991).

Second, some socio-legal scholars have stressed that the success of social movements and their political and social influence depend largely on their structures and financial resources (McCann 1995). Fundraising is critical to the operation, professionalisation and survival of rights organisations (Haines 1984; Jenkins and Eckert 1986; McAdam 1982; McCann 1994; McCarthy and Zald 1977; Piven and Cloward 1977). In the same manner, Charles Epp, Marc Galanter and Steven Teles have noted in a positive way and without adopting a critical stance that a judicial lobby and rights litigation can succeed only if rights advocacy organisations, supportive lawyers and important external sources of financing exist (Epp 1998; Galanter 1974; Teles 2008; Tushnet 1987). Only a small number of scholars have challenged this dominant and acritical approach by paying attention to the deceptive underbelly of foundation/grantee relationships related to legal mobilisation (Ferguson 2007, 2013; Francis 2018; Marquez 2003). Through case studies of civil rights organisations, this literature demonstrates that the influence of funders can be subtle and serpentine, as funders have co-opted litigation strategy and attempted to de-radicalise and transform militant black and Latino NGOs into racial liberalism from the top down, with a view to domesticating black and Latino power ideology (Ferguson 2013; Marquez 2003). Despite its significance, this work is insufficiently detailed and still lacks a theoretical framework for understanding the process that has led to greater funder control over the agenda-setting of cause lawyering (Francis 2018).

Third, the NGO-isation theory offers a framework for analysing the consequences of donors providing new funding to NGOs and the way global networks integrate local and national partners (Chahim and Prakash 2013; Choudry and Kapoor 2013; Howell and Pearce 2001; Kamat 2002; Meyers 2016). NGO-isation studies have underlined how grassroots groups are influenced by donors through formalisation and professionalisation processes that significantly alter local groups and alienate members, thus transforming those associations and making them more distant from local needs and closer to their donors (Howell and Pearce 2001).

Fourth, in a rather similar way to the NGO-isation theory, movement capture theory has been applied to the study of the influence and impact that funders have on the development of civil rights legal mobilisation (Francis 2018). Drawing on economic theories of regulatory and state capture (Hellman et al. 2003; Levine and Forrence 1990; Stigler 1971), movement capture is used as a way to analyse how private funders, such as interest groups or private firms, operate to buy influence over the goals and strategies pursued by civil servants (Devaux 2019), activists and cause lawyers. The concept of movement capture refers precisely to the process by which private funders leverage their financial resources to exert pressure on cause lawyers and to influence the decision-making process of civil rights organisations. In this regard, the movement capture framework hinges on the power imbalance between those that own economic resources and those that need them (Francis 2018) and on the power asymmetries embedded in the relationship between community organisations (international and domestic) and funding from NGOs and businesses (Margolis and Walsh 2003). The institutional environment matters, as funders are most likely to increase their influence over civil rights organisations during the early stages of organisational development when funders are scarce or during a period of considerable financial instability, such as the 2007 economic crisis. According to this framework, funders are self-interested agents that can instrumentalise their elevated financial position by linking provision of funds to the achievement of new goals or by shifting the salience of existing agenda issues. In this regard, Megan Ming Francis has illustrated the significance and relevance of capture theory by showing that funders used their financial leverage at a critical juncture in the civil rights movement to reorient the agenda of the NAACP (the National Association for the Advancement of Colored People) away from the issue of racial violence to a specific focus on education (Francis 2018).

Fifth and last, in a study focusing on the Global South, some scholars have asserted that financial support for rights litigation constitutes a minority portion of the relatively small sums devoted to human rights more generally by government development agencies and private foundations that provide financial support for social change (Ron et al. 2016). However, these scholars have demonstrated that funding of local human rights organisations (through international aid) in non-repressive environments is shaped by philanthropic logics of appropriateness (Ron et al. 2016).

With regard to the European context, Rachel Cichowski (2007) revealed the importance of civil society litigation in spurring institutional change and supranational governance, and significant links between civil society (through NGOs), the CJEU and the construction of governance. In the same manner but with regard to the ECtHR, Loveday Hodson (2011) highlighted the impact that NGOs have had on ECtHR case law. In Hodson's view, the dominant role played by NGOs challenges the principle that the objective of litigation is to achieve justice for specific individuals. More recently, Heidi Nichols Haddad (2018) mapped and analysed the differences in NGO participatory roles, frequency and impact on the ECtHR, the Inter-American Human Rights System and the International Criminal Court. She showed that courts can choose strategically to increase their functionality by allowing NGOs to provide necessary information, expertise and services, as well as to shame states for non-cooperation. Through intense participation, NGOs can shape international human rights justice profoundly, but in doing so, may consolidate civil society representation and relinquish their roles as external monitors (Haddad 2018). Lastly, Nicole Bürli (2017) has studied the way that amicus curiae interventions, filed by individuals, NGOs and national governments increasingly over time, influence the jurisprudence delivered by the Strasbourg Court. In this regard, Bürli has shown that three different types of intervention play different roles in the administration of justice: amicus curiae interventions by organisations with a virtual interest in the case, which increase the ECtHR's legitimacy; member state interventions that reinforce state sovereignty; and actual third party interventions by citizens involved in the facts of a case and who are trying to protect their own legal interests (Bürli 2017).

While this body of literature has overlooked the impact that private foundations have had on the development of judicial standards of rights and the creeping privatisation of human rights, their findings regarding the ways in which NGOs try to exert influence are extremely relevant, especially in terms of the specific 'game' of repeated litigation before courts (Albiston 1999; Duffy 2018). In particular, international research studies have analysed the litigation strategies pursued by some American interest law groups, including conservative ones (some of them faith-based NGOs) that promote their convictions by engaging in transnational advocacy and litigation (Duffy 2018; McCrudden 2015).

Other scholars have focused on the very significant influence of private-foundation funding on the economy (Holcombe 2018), international relations and foreign aid (Berman 1983; Bremner 1988; Parmar 2012; Scott-Smith 2014; Tournès 2010), religion, humanitarian reform and social services (Bremner 1988), war (Parmar 2014), health (Brown 1979), medical research and culture (Nielsen 2002), education (Reckhow 2013) and research policy (Arnove 1980; Condliffe Lagemann 1999; Curti and Nash 1965; Fischer 1983; Guilhot 2007; Krige and Rausch 2012; Parmar 2015; Scott-Smith 2012), artistic endeavours (Nielsen 2002), public and legal policy (Dowie 2002; Roelofs 2003; Scott-Smith 2012), racial policy (Willoughby-Herard 2015), political campaigns (Goulden 1971) and international law (Rietzler 2014) and civil rights in the US (Francis 2018; Witt 2019; Zunz 2012). Such academic research on private foundations is not uniform but divided into three main streams.

The first stream is a liberal one that insists on the positive outcomes of private foundations and their very large contribution to democracy and pluralism (Zunz 2012). The second stream stresses the international network applied by private donors and the US domination and hegemony in which American private foundations participate (Berman 1983; Parmar 2012). In particular, Inderjeet Parmar (2012) has defined the role played by private foundations as 'transnational groups which have culturally, intellectually and financially penetrated society and government by providing significant impetus in socialising some of their elements'. In this manner, and again according to Parmar (2012), private foundations are among those who contribute through their funding to US hegemony. In the same perspective, Nicolas Guilhot has shown that the international movement for democracy and human rights contributes to that power itself. Guilhot (2005) demonstrated how the US government, the World Bank, NGOs, think tanks and various international organisations have appropriated the movement for democracy and human rights to export neoliberal policies throughout the world. The third and last stream relies on an economic and sometimes Marxist approach to show that private foundations represent unregulated and unaccountable concentrations of power and wealth (Arnove 1980; Berman 1983; Fischer 1983; Roelofs 2003) that conduct business activities (Cordes and Steuerle 2009). In terms of their economic ideologies, private foundations are seen as applying specific strategies (Brown 1979) and market-based policies (Reckhow 2013) to spread capitalism and even neoliberalism widely in many sectors and policies, and to advance the elite's agenda behind a mask of pluralism (Berman 1983; Roelofs 2003).

While these findings regarding the ways in which private foundations and NGOs try to exert influence are extremely relevant and useful, and can indeed be applied to any specific, repeated litigation, this body of literature has overlooked the impact that private foundations have had on European human rights justice. The academic literature on private foundations has neglected the political and judicial effects of private funding on the European judicial and fundamental rights systems.

1.2 The Impacts of Foreign Private Funds on National Courts: US and Irish Justice

Very little research has analysed the influence of private foundations on justice, and the only existing study is a national one focusing on the US Supreme Court. Joan Roelofs (2003) analysed the impacts of private foundations on the jurisprudence of the US Supreme Court, emphasising that landmark Supreme Court decisions were obtained by private foundations (through their funding), meeting their expectations in three ways:

- The result orientation of Court decisions was a method of directing social change from the elite and not from below. In this way, the jurisprudence of the Supreme Court coincides with elite interests in upholding civil rights (the fight against racism and discrimination and for gender balance and gay rights) and abortion rights to the detriment of economic and social rights, which are neglected.
- The centralising trend in Court decisions reflects both American Law Institute models for making state law uniform and the ideology of private foundations that supported public administration and planning organisations.
- The distinction between public and private became increasingly blurred. Private foundations provided much of the substance of Supreme Court decisions by their support for (1) an ideology promoting social engineering, (2) law school innovations, (3) social science data and (4) public interest law firms.

Roelofs concluded that judicial activism can be seen as a channel for elite demands obtained and developed though a 'policy formation' process (Roelofs 2003).

One national study also analysed the strategies pursued by US conservative groups (including faith-based NGOs) that promote their convictions by engaging in transnational advocacy and litigation (McCrudden 2015). For instance, Kornhaber's 'People's Court' and the study of the introduction of the Irish abortion ban have been entirely funded and lobbied by US conservative groups, which switched off some women's rights in the country. In this regard, Irish justice constitutes another national case in point that has been influenced by foreign private interests. Nonetheless, this process of foreign private influence on justice seems to be more developed at the European level, which has been neglected up to now by scholars.

1.3 Why Could the European Courts Be Targeted by Private Donors?

There are at least three factors pushing private donors to invest in European human rights justice: (1) the growing power and influence of the ECtHR and the CJEU on the member states, (2) the increasing role played by NGOs in litigation and third party intervention before the Strasbourg Court and (3) the economic crisis of 2007, which generated a significant need for litigation funding.

1.3.1 The Increasing Power of the European Court of Human Rights and the Court of Justice of the European Union

Human rights are transnational in nature and could allow foreigners to intervene in national policies for the protection of people whose human rights are violated. As private foundations are themselves transnational, they fit very well with human rights. On this score, the European Courts could be at the forefront of this private trend (Cliquennois and Champetier 2016). Nicolas Guilhot has already pointed out how the US government, the World Bank, NGOs, think tanks and various international organisations financed and invested the movement for democracy and human rights in order to export neoliberalism throughout the world. He identified the various symbolic, ideological and political meanings that have developed around human rights and democracy movements (Guilhot 2005). In this regard, private donors could be interested in influencing the ECtHR's jurisprudence, as the European Court deals with human rights in forty-seven member states by monitoring human rights violations committed by national states.

1.3.1.1 The European Court of Human Rights

The attractiveness of the European Court for private donors is reinforced by the growth of its influence over member state governments since 1998, when the ECtHR's powers over them was greatly increased. The influence of the ECtHR is growing in four main domains:

The Transformation of the ECtHR's Architecture into a Quasi-Constitutional Court Historically, as is well known, the 'ordinary' enforcement mechanism of the ECHR was until the late seventies the intergovernmental European Commission of Human Rights. The Court was set up only in 1959 and remained a rather dormant institution for some years. While the ECtHR accepted the first third party intervention (from NGOs) in 1979 by acknowledging a certain public interest in its decision-making (Bürli 2017), the historical and sociological literature shows that the design and actual workings of the Commission and the Court were heavily influenced by the Cold War context (Alkema 2000; Bates 2010; Christoffersen and Madsen 2011). The binding character of ECtHR rulings (which had and continue to have the force of res judicata) may well have played a role in delaying the establishment and effective activation of the Court (Christoffersen and Madsen 2011; Sadurski 2009; Sharpe 2010). It was indeed only at the end of the Cold War, coinciding with the Russian ratification to the ECHR in 1998, that the ECtHR became fully active and developed the key contours of what is now taken to be the ECHR acquis.

Decisively, it was indeed the end of the Cold War that prompted a fully fledged redesign of the Court. Protocol No. 11, which came into force in 1998, created a single permanent court with full jurisdiction and set up a full quasi-constitutional review structure with a Grand Chamber (which renders leading judgments) and the right for complainants to appeal against first-instance decisions.[1] It is far from an overstatement to conclude that the Court has come to play a role akin to that of a constitutional court competent to review legislation by reference to the yardstick of the ECHR (as fleshed out in its case law; see below). But even though the ECtHR has become a constitutional court, it is a peculiar one. Contrary to what is still largely assumed in most public discussions, the standard litigants before the ECtHR are not individuals seeking justice in individual cases, but – as Hodson has shown – individuals who are supported by repeat players (mostly NGOs). Thus, litigation is not oriented exclusively to the redress of an individual breach of a convention right in a concrete case, but is also part of a long-term litigation strategy aimed at shaping the overall development of the case law of the ECHR in a given direction (Hodson 2011). Indeed those opposing the constitutionalisation trend do so in the very name of preserving the right of the individual to seek redress before the ECtHR (Lambert Abdelgawad 2011). Some scholars consider the increasing constitutionalisation of the ECtHR to be one of the biggest threats and hindrances to the right of individual petition enshrined by Article 24 ECHR,[2] in particular for the most vulnerable groups involving prisoners, migrants and foreigners (Lambert Abdelgawad 2011).

---

[1] Protocol No. 11 to the Convention for the Protection of Human Rights and Fundamental Freedoms on the Restructuring of the Control Mechanism Established by the Convention, Strasbourg, 11 May 1994, ETS No. 155 ratification by parties and entry into force on 1 November 1998.

[2] Reinforced by Resolution CM/Res(2010)25 on Member States' Duty to Respect and Protect the Right of Individual Application to the European Court of Human Rights.

The power of the ECtHR was further reinforced in January 2011 by the establishment of a new single-judge filtering section, following a suggestion made at the Interlaken Conference. The entry into force of Protocol No. 14, which has resulted in single judges (crucially guided more than assisted by the lawyers at the Registry) having more leeway to 'filter' cases at registration,[3] allows the ECtHR to concentrate on 'systemic' issues (Føllesdal et al. 2013). This can be seen as introducing a peculiar form of certiorari (Lambert Abdelgawad 2016), thus fostering the transformation of the ECtHR into a pan-European 'US Supreme Court' (Bond 2012). The selection of cases by the new single-judge filtering section of the ECtHR registry so far, coupled with an amendment to the ECtHR's rules in June 2009 concerning the order in which it deals with cases,[4] has oriented the ECtHR's priority away from individual cases and toward wider systemic issues, including:

- urgent complaints related to the right to life or health (Article 2 of the Convention), to the risk of torture or inhuman and degrading treatment (Article 3) and to the right to legal detention (Article 5);
- complaints with the potential to affect the Convention's effectiveness or which raise questions of general interest;
- complaints arising from pilot/leading judgments (see below for a definition), such as repetitive and systemic violations of human rights resulting in large-scale systemic breaches of the Convention owing to non-compliant legislation or practices in the member states (Cameron 2013).

This priority policy is of such influence that, based on similar priorities to judgments requiring urgent individual measures, pilot judgments and other cases characterised by significant and/or complex structural issues may give rise to numerous repetitive cases. Such policy is applied at the stage of the supervision and execution of judgments by the Committee of Ministers (Lambert Abdelgawad 2013). The CoE Parliamentary Assembly, which has also become more involved in the supervision process, gives priority to pilot judgments and cases raising major structural problems.[5]

---

[3] Protocol No. 14 to the Convention for the Protection of Human Rights and Fundamental Freedoms, 1 June 2010.
[4] See www.echr.coe.int/Documents/Priority_policy_ENG.pdf.
[5] Parliamentary Assembly (2006), Implementation of Judgments of the European Court of Human Rights, Resolution 1516, 2 October 2006; Parliamentary Assembly (2006), Implementation of Judgments of the European Court of Human Rights, Recommendation 1764, 2 October 2006.

Whether as an intended or unintended consequence, the constitutionalisation of the ECtHR, which was reinforced by Protocols No. 15 (which inserts references to the principle of subsidiarity and the margin of appreciation enjoyed by national states into the Convention's preamble and thus gives more importance to the ECtHR landmark judgments) and No. 16 (which allows the highest domestic courts and tribunals to request the ECtHR to give advisory opinions on questions of principle relating to the interpretation or application of the rights and freedoms defined in the ECHR), increases the salience of NGOs funded by donors with deep pockets (Hodson 2011). A more selective policy implies a better technical quality of complaints taken to the ECtHR and thus a professionalisation of litigation to the detriment of individual cases.

The Power of the ECtHR to Deliver Pilot and Quasi-Pilot Judgments since 2004 As part of the constitutionalisation trend, pilot and quasi-pilot judgments were introduced in 2004 to allow the Court to achieve greater unity among its member states, to facilitate the execution of ECtHR judgments and to put an end to human rights violations caused by an underlying systemic and structural issue.⁶ Pilot and quasi-pilot judgments bring together groups of similar cases (in general from 80 to 300 cases) of human rights violations linked to structural and systemic problems.⁷ The implementation of pilot judgments is also a convenient way to reduce the backlog of the Court.

This specific proceeding favours NGOs (as repetitive litigants) with deep pockets, as pilot judgments require the ability to collect and gather many cases of the same nature and to lodge them with the Court in an appropriate way. This ability belongs not to individuals but to structures that are well financed and are repetitive players before the Court. Reciprocally, the ECtHR is now more dependent on the technical quality of the complaints lodged before it, and therefore on NGOs, as good technical quality facilitates the selection of cases on which to render pilot judgments. This goes a long way to render credible the claims of barristers and representatives of NGOs that European judges would hint on a regular basis to NGOs and private foundations that their cases would be welcomed as the basis of pilot judgments of the ECtHR (Leach 2014).

---

⁶ Council of Europe, Resolution (2004) 3 of the Committee of Ministers on Judgments Revealing an Underlying Systemic Problem, 12 May 2004, available at https://wcd.coe.int/ViewDoc.jsp?id=743257&Lang=fr.
⁷ Ibid.

Furthermore, through this specific proceeding, the ECtHR has become progressively more involved in the execution of its judgments by recommending and even by ordering member state governments to take general measures and to implement corrective legislative and/or administrative measures (Lambert Abdelgawad 2013: 278–279). The measure must be reported in action plans submitted by member states to the Committee of Ministers of the Council of Europe.[8] The European Court, along with the Committee of Ministers, is thus able to impose on CoE member states substantial and procedural obligations fostering important changes in both their domestic legislation and their judicial and political systems (Leach 2013). This quite obviously increases the degree of abrasiveness of the ECHR and the potential for private foundations to influence member states through the Strasbourg Court.

The ECtHR's Increased Use of a Wide Range of Bold Interpretation Techniques The use of these techniques enlarges and expands the scope of obligations on the CoE member states. Since the *Marckx v. Belgium* case, these obligations are positive as well as negative;[9] the ECtHR has extended the obligations of the member states to include not only negative obligations (e.g. to refrain from breaching human rights) but also positive obligations, requiring them to take steps to protect the human rights covered by the whole ECHR (Tulkens 2007). These positive obligations have enabled the ECtHR to strengthen, and sometimes extend, the substantive requirements of the ECHR and to link them to procedural obligations. While substantial obligations require the adoption of legal, administrative and judicial measures, procedural obligations refer to the organisation and effectiveness of domestic proceedings (such as the implementation of effective domestic remedies) with a view to protecting the Convention and compensating human rights violations (Tulkens 2014). This in turn has led to legal, administrative, judicial and practical changes to enforce the implementation of the ECHR (Popelier et al. 2011), which means that the ECHR's universality has been exemplified at the national level (Andenas and Bjorge 2013). Again, the Court has thus been rendered significantly more attractive to private investors.

---

[8] Council of Europe, Resolution (2004) 3 of the Committee of Ministers on Judgments Revealing an Underlying Systemic Problem. Strasbourg, 12 May 2004.
[9] Case 6833/74, *Marckx v. Belgium* [13 June 1979] ECtHR.

The Increased Spread of ECtHR Judgments across Europe and Beyond

The ECtHR has intensified over time its interactions with the Council of Europe bodies (Lambert Abdelgawad 2013), in particular with the Committee of Ministers concerning the interpretation and execution of final judgments. Protocol No. 11 gave the ECtHR the right to offer advisory opinions on the interpretation of its rulings and of the Convention when so requested by the Committee of Ministers. With regard to the execution of judgments, including pilot judgments, the proceeding requires special notification of any judgment containing indications of the existence of a systemic problem and of the source of this problem, not only to the Committee of Ministers but also to the Parliamentary Assembly, the Secretary General of the Council of Europe and the Council of Europe Commissioner for Human Rights. In this regard, the Parliamentary Assembly has become progressively more involved in supervising the execution of judgments by adopting a recommendation and/or a resolution on pilot judgments to the Committee of Ministers. The Parliamentary Assembly has also been given the power to open a monitoring procedure and to consider suspending the credentials of a national state if the state intentionally does not execute a judgment.[10] In this manner, the ECtHR case law process has allowed more organs to become more influential, while giving more power to the Strasbourg Court in the filtering process and the execution of judgments.

The Court has also increased its relations with the Committee for the Prevention of Torture (CPT), whose reports of its visits to member states are increasingly used by the Court to gather and provide evidence of human rights violations (Morgan and Evans 2002; van Zyl Smit and Snacken 2009). Reciprocally, the CPT applies in its reports some portion of ECtHR case law to establish its standards towards national states and to make recommendations to them (Cliquennois and Snacken 2018).

The ECtHR and the Council of Europe have also cooperated to an increasing extent with European Union bodies,[11] which, for instance, echo the judgments rendered by the ECtHR by making

---

[10] Parliamentary Assembly, Resolution 1226 (2000) on the Execution of Judgments of the European Court of Human Rights; Parliamentary Assembly, AS/Jur (2009), 36, Committee on Legal Affairs and Human Rights, Implementation of Judgments of the European Court of Human Rights Progress Report, 31 August 2009.

[11] See Recommendation 1743 (2006) 1 Memorandum of Understanding between the Council of Europe and the European Union Adopted by the Assembly on 13 April 2006 (14th Sitting) and the Assembly debate on 13 April 2006 (14th Sitting), Doc. 10892, Report of the Political Affairs Committee, Rapporteur: Mr Kosachev.

recommendations,[12] reports,[13] and funding programmes to improve the implementation of ECtHR case law and European human rights standards.[14] The EU judicial organ, the CJEU, has itself relayed and given more strength to the protection of fundamental rights (and more precisely the right to dignity) and the requirements imposed by the Strasbourg Court through a judgment in Joined Cases Aranyosi and Căldăraru delivered by the CJEU on 5 April 2016.[15] In this way, the CJEU not only endorses the ECtHR criteria on bad and degrading treatments but also gives more power to the ECtHR judgments in the case of systemic and structural issues by putting an end to the principle of cooperation and mutual trust (recognised by the European Council) between the EU member states in penal matters.[16]

The intensification of relations with the CoE bodies and the EU has led to ECtHR rulings spreading gradually across member states and being imposed on them (Mayerfeld 2011) as a 'common European law on human rights'. While the Court has paradoxically at the same time reinforced the principle of subsidiarity (Spano 2014) and the margin of appreciation given to condemned states to reform their legislation and administrative practices (Arai-Tahakashi 2013), the reinforcement of the role played by the Court and of its impacts on national states could attract private donors.

Furthermore, the ECtHR has increased its power beyond Europe; the African Court on Human and People's Rights[17] and the Inter-American Court of Human Rights are influenced by it, as they cite ECtHR case law in their own jurisprudence on a regular basis (Bertoni 2009). The spread of ECtHR judgments over other regional courts and their case law is

---

[12] See, for instance, European Parliament, Recommendation on 24 February 2004 on the Rights of Prisoners in the EU, Report A5-00094/2004, Rapporteur: Maurizio Turco.

[13] See, for instance, European Parliament, Report for the Committee on Civil Liberties, Justice and Home Affairs Delegation to Italy on the Situations of Prisons and Correction Centres, 9 April 2014.

[14] Criminal justice and human rights programmes funded by the Directorate-General for Justice of the European Commission. For example, JUST/2013/JPEN/AG/4554 funds the implementation of a suicide prevention system in several European countries, in accordance with the case law of the ECtHR and CPT standards.

[15] Case C 404/15 and C 659/15 PPU, *Aranyosi–Căldăraru* [5 April 2016] CJEU.

[16] Ibid.

[17] The influence of the Strasbourg Court is perceptible in many cases delivered by the African Court, among which are Case 040/2016, *Maria Kouma and Ousmane Diabaté v. Republic of Malo* [21 March 2018] §39; Case 005/2013, *Alex Thomas v. United Republic of Tanzania* [20 November 2015] §97, 118–120 and 130; Case 004/2013, *Lohe Issa Konate v. Burkina Faso* [5 December 2014].

another factor making the Strasbourg Court more central and more attractive to private investors.

1.3.1.2 The Court of Justice of the European Union

The CJEU was established in 1952 by the Treaty of Paris of 1951 as the judicial side of the European Coal and Steel Community and grew over time. Its main mission initially was to interpret EU law and to ensure that it was applied equally by all EU member states and institutions (de Búrca and Weiler 2001). In this regard, the main CJEU remit was to settle legal disputes between national governments and EU institutions.

Like the ECtHR, the CJEU took more power through significant changes to its structures and architecture, and through the enlargment of its competences and remit in the field of fundamental rights.

Changes to the CJEU's Structures and Architecture With the creation of the European Union in 1993, the power of the CJEU was designed by the Community pillar (the first pillar). The Amsterdam Treaty and the Lisbon Treaty gave more power to the Court to apply EU law across the EU. Its architecture evolved over time to cope with this increase in power and caseload through a continual increase in jurisdiction, budget and number of judges (except from 2013 to 2017;[18] see below).

As the backlog of the CJEU became more and more substantial over time, it was decided in 1988 to establish the Court of First Instance, later named the General Court (GC), with a view to reducing and rationalising the caseload of the European Court. The GC was afforded to rule on actions for annulment taken by individuals, companies and, in some cases, EU governments. In practice, the GC deals mainly with competition law, state aid, trade, agriculture and trademarks. Nevertheless, the caseload of the GC also quickly became unmanagable owing to the growing number of cases, fed in part by new accessions to the EU, the inflation of EU legislation, the increasing dissemination of CJEU case law (through annual EU meetings attended by EU and national judges,[19] seminars held at the CJEU,[20] contributions intended for national judges in the context of European judicial associations or networks,[21] placement

---

[18] CJEU, Annual Report of 2017: The Year in Review, p. 45.
[19] Ibid., pp. 37–39.
[20] Ibid., p. 41.
[21] Ibid., p. 42.

of national judges in the CJEU chambers of a member,[22] official visits from national judges, prosecutors and representatives of member states to the CJEU,[23] trainee lawyers,[24] an open day at the CJEU for EU citizens and legal professionals)[25] and the development of litigation for advocacy purpose. In addition, the adoption of the Charter of Fundamental Rights of the European Union in 2000, the legal complexity of cases brought before the Court and the fact-finding function the GC had to fulfil have also contributed to the backlog (Weiler 2016). For these reasons, the system of chambers, a Grand Chamber (which sits when a member state or an institution of the Union that is party to the proceedings so requests) and a Full Court (which sits for cases brought before it pursuant to Article 228(2), Article 245(2), Article 247 or Article 286(6) of the Treaty on the Functioning of the European Union) was revamped to reinforce the power and the consistency of the Court.[26] Moreover, in 2004, following the Treaty of Nice, the Civil Service Tribunal was created with a view to reducing the caseload and to serve as a model of a specialised tribunal over civil matters.

Despite these reforms, the growth in the caseload (the number of cases before the CJEU increased from 398 in 2000 to 912 in 2014) and the excessive duration of proceedings before the GC remained a persistent issue that made room for further reform of the EU judicial structure.[27] The reform was adopted with the aim of reducing within a short time both the volume of pending cases (caused by the pervasiveness and complexity of EU law) and the excessive duration of proceedings before the GC, and to reinforce legal certainty.[28] Rather than creating several specialised tribunals as provided for in Article 257 of the Treaty on the Functioning of the European Union, it was finally decided in 2015 to reform the EU judicial structure by increasing the number of sitting judges on the GC from twenty-eight to fifty-six, in addition to the

---

[22] CJEU, Annual Report of 2016: The Year in Review, p. 35.
[23] CJEU, Annual Report of 2017: The Year in Review, p. 41; CJEU, Annual Report of 2016: The Year in Review, p. 34.
[24] CJEU, Annual Report of 2017: The Year in Review, p. 42.
[25] Ibid., p. 40; CJEU, Annual Report of 2016: The Year in Review, p. 33.
[26] Article 16 of the Protocol on the Statute of the Court of Justice SN 1248/1/01 REV1, 14 February 2001.
[27] Regulation (EU, Euratom) 2015/2422 of the European Parliament and of the Council of 16 December 2015 amending Protocol No. 3 on the Statute of the Court of Justice of the European Union. OJ: JOL_2015_341_R_0002, 24 December 2015, L341/14.
[28] Ibid.

twenty-eight judges sitting on the Court of Justice,[29] (after a staff reduction for a period of five years, as part of the recovery of posts imposed by the budgetary authority in 2013),[30] and by abolishing the Civil Service Tribunal. Its juridiction was transferred immediately to the enlarged GC on 1 September 2016.[31]

Enlargement of the CJEU's Competences and Remit in the Field of Fundamental Rights Regarding its remit, the CJEU gives rulings on cases brought before it. The scope of the most common remits have been enlarged over time owing to the ratification of new treaties and the use of bold intepretation techniques (Torres Pérez 2009). The competence of the Court covers the following areas:

- Interpretation of EU law (preliminary rulings) and treaties, as national courts of EU countries are required to ensure EU law is properly applied and implemented but courts in different countries might interpret it differently. In this respect, if national courts are confused about the interpretation or validity of an EU law, they can ask the Court to clarify the meaning of EU law. The same mechanism can be applied to determine whether a national law or practice is compatible with EU law.
- Enforcement of EU law (infringement proceedings) against a national government that has failed to comply with EU law. The complaint can be lodged by the European Commission or by another EU country. If the country is found to be at fault, it must comply with EU law or risk being taken to the Court a second time and required to pay a fine.
- Annulment of EU legal Acts (actions for annulment) if an EU Act is believed to violate EU treaties or fundamental rights. In this situation, the Court can be asked to annul the Act by an EU government, by the Council of the EU, by the European Commission or (in some cases) by the European Parliament.
- Annulment of an EU legal Act on behalf of private indviduals who are directly affected by it.
- Actions for failure to act with a view to ensuring the EU takes action. The Parliament, Council and Commission must make certain decisions

---

[29] Ibid.
[30] CJEU, Annual Report of 2017: The Year in Review, p. 45.
[31] Regulation (EU, Euratom) 2015/2422 of the European Parliament and of the Council of 16 December 2015 amending Protocol No. 3 on the Statute of the Court of Justice of the European Union. OJ: JOL_2015_341_R_0002, 24 December 2015, L341/15.

under certain circumstances. If they refrain from making such decisions, cases can be brought before the Court by EU governments, other EU institutions or (under certain conditions) individuals or companies.
- Actions for damages sanctioning EU institutions. Any person or company who has had their interests harmed by the action or inaction of the EU or its staff can take their case to the Court. The GC can thus, in such circumstances, be seized at first instance by individuals, companies or organisations (including NGOs) taking action against an EU institution if their rights are infringed by it. A large proportion of the litigation brought before the GC is related to economic domains such as intellectual property (EU trademarks and designs), competition, state aid, and banking and financial supervision.[32]
- Appeals limited to points of law against decisions made by the GC, a remedy allowing the Court of Justice to quash the decision of the GC.[33]
- Decisions on 'restrictive measures' (such as arms embargoes, freezing of assets, prohibitions on entering and travelling through the territory of the European Union, or bans on imports and exports) are a foreign policy instrument by which the EU seeks to obtain a change of policy or behaviour from a non-member country. Restrictive measures may target governments, companies, natural persons, or groups and organisations (such as terrorist groups). The Court of Justice and the GC have handed down a certain number of cases concerning restrictive measures in relation to Afghanistan, Belarus, Côte d'Ivoire, Egypt, Iran, Libya, Russia, Syria, Tunisia, Ukraine and Zimbabwe.[34]

Thanks in part to these new competences, the Court has acquired a growing international role and profile to the extent that its judgments have effect not only on the parties concerned in a given case but also on non-member countries.

With regard to the human rights sphere, the Court has only recently endorsed its role as a fundamental rights tribunal, even though the Court has made reference on a regular basis since the early 1970s to fundamental rights as general principles of law and to provisions of the European Convention on Human Rights (Weiler and Lockhart 1995; Weiler 2009). For a long time the CJEU remained inexperienced in the field of

---

[32] CJEU, Annual Report of 2017: The Year in Review, p. 34.
[33] Ibid., p. 32. For instance, in 2017, 22 per cent of the decisions made by the General Court were appealed before the Court of Justice.
[34] CJEU, Annual Report of 2017: The Year in Review, p. 29.

fundamental rights, especially compared to the ECtHR. Several factors have contributed to the CJEU progressively becoming a human rights tribunal: (1) the coming into force of the European Charter of Fundamental Rights, (2) the progressively expanding scope of EU powers, (3) the implementation of the Lisbon Treaty, which greatly extended the Court's jurisdiction and (4) and a potential enlargement of third party interventions, which could still extend the scope and volume of litigation on fundamental rights before the Court (see Section 1.3.2 for this last factor).

First, the new competence in human rights adjudication has coincided with the coming into force of the Charter of Fundamental Rights of the European Union. Inspired, among other developments, by the ECHR and the European Social Charter, the Charter of Fundamental Rights of the European Union was proclaimed on 7 December 2000 by the European Parliament, the Council of Ministers and the European Commission. It enshrines the very large scope of political, social and economic rights that had bound the European Union and the member states since 1 December 2009.[35] More precisely, the implementation, application and interpretation of the Charter of Fundamental Rights is a competence of the CJEU. In this regard, the binding EU Charter of Fundamental of Fundamental Rights has indeed impacted the competence of the Court, as shown by the growing number of cases in which a provision of the Charter was cited or argued before the Court and the increasing engagement of the Court with the Charter argument in a growing number of these cases (de Búrca 2013). In such cases, the Court has given prominence to the Charter, which has thus expanded the role of the Court in the field of fundamental rights. The implementation of the Charter has widened the CJEU's fundamental rights role not just by increasing the set of rights provisions that it is empowered to enforce, but also by expanding the scope of the Court's jurisdiction over new areas and domains of law such as immigration, asylum, privacy, security, terrorism and prison custody.

The growth of the Court's role as a fundamental rights adjudicator is also an effect of the continual expansion of the scope of EU law (de Búrca 2013) and new directives. A significant portion of the EU's legislative corpus now integrates immigration and asylum, security and privacy

---

[35] Article 6(1) of the Treaty on European Union.

within its scope to such an extent that it represented 15.25 per cent of the matters dealt with by the Court in 2017.[36] This new area of freedom, security and justice stands alongside the more traditional fields of EU policy covered by the CJEU, such as market regulation (10.75 per cent), consumer protection (5 per cent), taxation (15.5 per cent), intellectual and industrial property (15 per cent) and competition and state aid (21.5 per cent).[37] These new developments are channelled by a pervasiveness of the EU as lawmaker that may contrevene and infringe fundamental rights law in many respects. In this regard, a massive increase in the number and variety of legal acts of the institutions, bodies, offices and agencies of the Union, as well as in the volume and complexity of the cases brought before the GC, must be highlighted.[38]

In this regard, the role of the Lisbon Treaty must be highlighted, as it has increased the likely extent of the CJEU's case law on fundamental rights issues in at least two ways. First, the Treaty gives a mandate to the Court to scrutinise the areas of security, freedom, justice and immigration, and more particularly the acts of EU agencies such as Frontex and the European Asylum Support Office. Second, the Treaty reinforces the application of the accelerated procedure and the urgent preliminary ruling procedure for detainees (Carrera et al. 2012). Beyond the Lisbon Treaty, the CJEU has also extended its own jurisdiction into domains of social regulation that are, or ought to be, the prerogative of the member states (Weiler 2009).

Subsequently, the evolution of the Court towards a powerful fundamental rights tribunal has rendered it much more attractive to private donors interested in the human rights realm. More generally, both the CJEU (McCown 2009) and the ECtHR create an internal structural incentive to litigate, in that repetitive and well-funded litigators tend to come out ahead, not only owing to the development of new structures and new powers but also owing to the creation of legal precedent. This attractiveness is demonstrated and reinforced through the increasing role played by NGOs in litigation and third party intervention before both Courts.

---

[36] CJEU, Annual Report of 2017: The Year in Review, p. 33.
[37] Ibid., p. 33.
[38] Regulation (EU, Euratom) 2015/2422 of the European Parliament and of the Council of 16 December 2015 amending Protocol No. 3 on the Statute of the Court of Justice of the European Union. OJ: JOL_2015_341_R_0002, 24 December 2015, L341/14.

1.3.2 The Increasing Role of NGOs in Litigation and Third Party Intervention

For a case to reach the Courts, it is necessary not only that it can be argued that one or several rights has/have been breached but also that the plaintiff has the necessary resources to make their case. Given the 'filtering' system now in force (through which most cases are rejected as 'plainly inadmissible') and the tendency of both Courts to focus on a reduced number of 'relevant' cases, even more economic and intellectual resources are needed to win a case. In this respect, the new role played by the CJEU in fundamental rights adjudication potentially gives rise to an increase in third party interventions before it and enhances opportunities for private litigation by individuals, interest groups and firms (Conant 2002; Kelemen 2011). Such enlargement could extend the scope and volume of litigation before the CJEU and could result in landmark judgments and significants improvements in the case law.

However, up to now, third party litigation has been much more limited than in the ECtHR, as the CJEU only accepts amicus briefs in direct actions from EU institutions or a member state or in certain circumstances in which a third party 'can establish an interest in the result of a case submitted to the Court of Justice'.[39] While the statute of the CJEU does not allow third party interventions other than from specified institutions, agencies or member states,[40] third party briefs can be submitted in cases where the third party has already been granted rights of intervention before the domestic court from which the reference was made. But third party briefs remain quite rare in practice (de Búrca 2013).

For its part, the ECtHR and its successive transformations increase the salience of NGOs that are well funded by donors, in particular given the reinforcement of filtering policies and the introduction of pilot judgments seen above. These changes favour NGOs that are repetitive litigants and that have an excellent knowledge and know-how of the case law, the formal conditions, the proceedings and the litigation techniques to be applied before the ECtHR. Conversely the ECtHR is now more dependent on the technical quality of complaints brought before it, in particular in pilot judgment proceedings (as that facilitates the selection of the cases on which to render pilot judgments). The relationships between the ECtHR and NGOs have thus been strengthened as the

---

[39] Article 40 of the Statute of the Court of Justice.
[40] Article 23 of the Statute of the Court of Justice.

ECtHR looks for complaints that could be sources of pilot and landmark judgments.

Similarly, amicus curiae briefings, which allow third parties to intervene in pending litigation, have become more relevant (see also Chapter 4). NGOs are among the typical actors filing such briefs.[41] The Strasbourg Court considers that the particular expertise and knowledge of NGOs entitles them to act in such a capacity,[42] and indeed that vulnerable persons without representatives can be defended by NGOs as interveners.[43] This process therefore increases the likelihood of NGOs influencing the ECtHR. Lastly, NGOs have been associated since 2006 with the execution of judgments delivered by the ECtHR. NGOs were allowed at that time to send communications to the CoE's Committee of Ministers (CM) about the execution of the ECtHR judgments under Article 46 §2 ECHR. During the supervision process in which national states indicate to the CM the measures planned and or taken in an 'action plan' to comply with the final judgment, NGOs and national institutions prompting and protecting human rights can submit communications to the CM denouncing the failure of a state to execute a judgment.[44]

1.3.3 The Role of the Economic Crisis of 2007 and the Crucial Need for Litigation Funding

Historically, NGOs have always come in different types and sizes. Public funding of the activities of NGOs was justified in terms of ensuring that these organisations were motivated in their actions and decisions by public concerns, perhaps particularly when acting as litigators before courts. Litigation is cost-intensive and time-consuming, as it relies on legal advice given by qualified lawyers and implies significant preparation for each case through documentation, research and empowerment of communities and individuals.[45] Furthermore, to be successful, litigation

---

[41] Article 36 of the European Convention on Human Rights (third party interventions).
[42] See for instance Case 55721/07, *Al-Skeini and Others* v. *United Kingdom* [7 July 2011] ECtHR, available at http://hudoc.echr.coe.int/eng?i=001-105606.
[43] Case 47848/08, *The Centre for Legal Resources on Behalf of Valentin Câmpeanu* v. *Romania* [17 July 2014] ECtHR.
[44] Rule 9.2 of the Rules of the Committee of Ministers for the Supervision of the Execution of Judgments and of the Terms of Friendly Settlements (Adopted by the Committee of Ministers on 10 May 2006 at the 964th Meeting of the Ministers' Deputies), available at https://wcd.coe.int/ViewDoc.jsp?id=999329.
[45] OSJI, *Global Human Rights Litigation Report 2017*, p. 5.

must often be undertaken in conjunction with advocacy efforts, which are themselves expensive (Epp 1998).

Funding is especially relevant to litigation before the ECtHR, given that judicial expenses cannot be fully refunded and that there is no legal aid system that could cover the costs incurred by NGOs (Cliquennois and Champetier 2016). In this regard, awards and reimbursement of costs and expenses (to the victims of human rights violations), as well as the granting of legal aid by the ECtHR, remain vague, ambiguous, case by case and too low for applicants, especially for the most vulnerable ones (Susanu 2016). In practice, the amount reimbursed by the ECtHR depends on the quality of the barrister's submission, the number and complexity of legal issues dealt with by the Court, and the volume of documents and observations prepared by the barristers (Susanu 2016: 56). Likewise, legal aid is granted to the applicant by the ECtHR only in cases involving complex issues of fact and law (such as the length of proceedings, the non-execution of judgments, especially by Moldova, Russia and Ukraine, and certain categories of cases concerning expropriation issues) and not in cases of a repetitive nature.[46] As complex matters require a high degree of legal competence, they are dealt with as a priority by very experienced lawyers and NGOs. These criteria therefore favour professional organisations and wealthy applicants to the detriment of the poorest ones.

Furthermore, the manifold crises that have hit European states since 2007 have resulted in austerity policies that have both increased the number of potential complaints on breaches of human rights (generated by austerity policies) filed by NGOs (not only before courts but also before other institutions guarding fundamental rights, such as ombudsmen, human rights commissions and equality bodies; see Chapter 5) and, at the same time, reduced their ability to do so, as public subsidies to NGOs have themselves been reduced as part of the austerity drive.[47] Cuts in funding throughout the NGO sector have led an increasing number of

---

[46] Rules 10 et seq. of the European Court of Human Rights.
[47] The Council of Europe Commissioner (2013). Safeguarding Human Rights in Times of Economic Crisis. Issue Paper published by the Council of Europe Commissioner for Human Rights, Commissioner for Human Rights, Issue Paper (2013), available at https://rm.coe.int/safeguarding-human-rights-in-times-of-economic-crisis-issue-paper-publ/1680908dfa, p. 2. Fundamental Rights Agency (2013). The European Union as a Community of Values: Safeguarding Fundamental Rights in Times of Crisis, available at http://fra.europa.eu/en/publication/2013/european-union-community-values-safeguarding-fundamental-rights-times-crisis.

individuals to seek help and redress from NGOs.[48] In that regard, it is revealing that in 2014 the NGO Interights, a very significant player before the ECtHR, was forced to close down because of a lack of funding in the aftermath of the economic crisis.[49]

As their need for financial support has increased and their public funding has decreased, NGOs have become increasingly dependent on private donors and a mixture of foreign public–private actors for funding and for their growing litigation activities. As a result, the most important and influential NGOs litigating before the Strasbourg and Luxembourg Courts are massively dependent on funds which as a matter of fact come from private foundations established mostly in the USA. This is perhaps best illustrated by considering the funding structure of the NGOs that are repeat litigants (see Chapter 2).

In summary, the evolution of the Court into a powerful fundamental rights tribunal has made it much more attractive to private donors interested in human rights. More generally, both the CJEU and the ECtHR have established an internal structural incentive to litigate, in that well-funded repetitive litigators tend to come out ahead, not only because of the development of new structures and new powers but also because of the creation of legal precedent. This attractiveness is reinforced through the increasing role played by NGOs in litigation and third party intervention before both Courts. In addition, austerity policies have made it impossible to ignore the clout donors have over NGOs. Budgetary cuts have resulted in declining levels of public funding, precisely at a time when the number of potential complaints before the ECtHR and the CJEU has increased, given the multiplication of alleged breaches of fundamental rights resulting from 'austerity policies' justified in the name of 'fiscal emergency'. But less public funding for NGOs translates into more room for private donors to turn funding into influence. This renders it imperative to consider the relationship between output, input and process in the making of the jurisprudence of the ECtHR and the CJEU, and the ways in which private foundations try to influence the ECtHR and the CJEU through their own litigation activities and their strategic funding of NGOs litigating before it.

---

[48] See for instance 2012 Annual Report of the AIRE Centre (2013), p. 1, available at www.airecentre.org/data/files/resources/13/2012-AIRE-Annual-Report.pdf.

[49] See www.interights.org/home/index.html: 'Interights closed down on 27 May 2014', available at https://wcd.coe.int/ViewDoc.jsp?id=2130915.

2

The Creeping Private Influence on the Inputs of the ECtHR and the CJEU

In this chapter, we analyse the creeping private power over the inputs of the European Courts: the growing participation of private donors in the litigation process that they undertake, fund and support. We present the main private litigation teams, including the one created by the Open Society Foundations (OSF), and the source of their funding, and we analyse the litigation documents brought by private foundations and NGOs backed by private donors over twenty years (before and after the economic downturn). We show that litigation activities undertaken by private foundations and those carried out by the most important NGOs before the European Courts are fully funded and supported by a limited roster of foreign private donors.

2.1 The Creation and Development of a Litigation Team by the OSF

In 2004, one private foundation, the OSF, set up its own litigation team, which brings cases before the ECtHR, the CJEU and also domestic courts to obtain landmark judgments and pilot judgments against national states.[1] This direct intervention in litigation in addition to its funding of NGOs (which also litigate the European Courts) makes the OSF quite distinctive from other private foundations. It reflects the larger, dual judicial and political role played by the OSF, which is both one of the most private donors funding many NGOs in Europe and a powerful think tank that intervenes in groups of NGOs and interest groups and lobbies the CoE and the EU directly. Its lobby relies on its own experts or on the knowledge produced by the NGOs it finances (Calligaro 2018).

Historically, the Open Society Institute (OSI) was set up in 1979 in New York by George Soros, a very well-known financier and speculator

---

[1] See for instance www.opensocietyfoundations.org/reports/global-human-rights-litigation-report.

who became an American citizen and has been world-famous (Slater 2009) since his successful speculation against sterling in September 1992. Soros has invested a significant portion of the money he gained from speculations made by his hedge fund (located in Curaçao) in the development and funding of his foundations, notably with a view to avoiding taxes (Slater 2009). Soros' foundations became the OSF in 1993 and recruited as president Aryeh Neier, former leader of Human Rights Watch and the American Civil Liberties Union and a member of the US Council on Foreign Relations.[2] The OSF expanded its influence and power over time to become the second-largest private philanthropy network in the United States.[3] Its main aims are to frame and shape public policy to promote open and liberal societies, good governance, human rights, and economic, legal and social reform.

With regard to its role in the field of human rights, in 2004 the OSF created a specific judicial and human rights programme, called the Open Society Justice Initiative (OSJI), which funds many of the NGOs litigating the ECtHR and the CJEU. Meanwhile, the OSJI is also engaged in strategic litigation before national[4] and regional courts (including the European Courts) and the UN Human Rights Committee,[5] applying 'a strategy of filing mass or iterative cases rather than only seeking a single landmark judgment'.[6] Since 2004, the OSJI has indeed taken no fewer than forty-seven cases to the ECtHR and two cases to the CJEU,[7] in combination with out-of-court advocacy efforts, pilot projects, documentation, research into human rights issues and institutional and human capacity building.[8]

In this regard, legal cases are not only conceived by the OSJI as a way of 'obtaining individual redress but also as a means of achieving a broader effect by setting an important precedent or otherwise reforming official policy and practice'.[9] The complaints brought by the OSJI before

---

[2] Council on Foreign Relations, 'Board list', available at www.cfr.org/about/membership; for the Open Society Foundation, 'People', available at www.opensocietyfoundations.org/people/george-soros.
[3] See www.opensocietyfoundations.org/about/history.
[4] OSJI, *Global Human Rights Litigation Report*, 2017, available at www.opensocietyfoundations.org/sites/default/files/litigation-global-report-20180428.pdf.
[5] OSJI, *Global Human Rights Litigation Report*, October 2013, p. 1.
[6] OSJI, *Strategic Litigation Impacts. Insights from Global Experience*, 2018, pp. 19–20.
[7] OSJI, *Global Human Rights Litigation Report*, 2017, pp. 23–29. See also www.justiceinitiative.org/litigation/.
[8] OSJI, *Global Human Rights Litigation Report*, October 2013, pp. 3–5.
[9] Ibid., p. 1.

the European Courts relate to counterterrorism and security policies (extraordinary rendition, torture, arbitrary detention),[10] police custody,[11] citizenship[12] and statelessness,[13] political opposition,[14] human rights activists and whistle blowers,[15] the ban on the veil and ethnic profiling,[16] political, religious, educational and police discrimination,[17] and racism against minorities, including Roma,[18] forced labour,[19] freedom of assembly,[20] expression and information,[21] the right to truth in

---

[10] Case no 39630/09, *El-Masri* v. *Macedonia* [13 December 2012] ECtHR; Case no 28761/11, *Al Nashiri* v. *Poland* [24 July 2014] ECtHR; Case no 33234/12, *Al Nashiri* v. *Poland* [31 May 2018]; Case no 33234/12, *Al Nashiri* v. *Romania* [31 May 2018] ECtHR; *HRMI (Human Rights Monitoring Institute)* v. *Lithuania* [20 December 2012] ECtHR, see www.right2info.org/cases/plomino_documents/briefs-hrmi-v.-lithuania/getfile?filename=hrmi-v.pdf; Case nos 58170/13, 62322/14 and 24960/15, *Big Brother Watch and Others* v. *United Kingdom* [13 September 2018] ECtHR (third party intervention).

[11] Case no 74016/12, *Etxbarria Caballero* v. *Spain* [7 October 2014] ECtHR (third party intervention).

[12] Case no 38590/10, *Biao* v. *Denmark* [24 May 2016] ECtHR (with third party intervention submitted with AIRE); Case no 59135/09, *Emin Huseynov* v. *Azerbaijan* [7 May 2015] ECtHR.

[13] Case no 64372/11, *Nazari* v. *Denmark* [6 September 2016] ECtHR; Case no 26828/06, *Kurić* v. *Slovenia* [26 June 2012] ECtHR (third party intervention); Case no 29627/16, *Sentsov and Kolchenko* v. *Russia* [19 November 2018].

[14] Case no 59135/09, *Emin Huseynov* v. *Azerbaijan* [7 May 2015] ECtHR.

[15] Case no 32631/09 53799/12, *Magnitskiy and Others* v. *Russia* [27 August 2019] ECtHR.

[16] Case no 43835/11, *S. A. S.* v. *France* [1 July 2014] ECtHR, in which Liberty also intervened as third party; Case no 34085/17, *Zeshan Muhammad* v. *Spain* [14 December 2018] ECtHR; Case nos 55762/00 and 55974/00, *Timishev* v. *Russia* [13 December 2005] ECtHR.

[17] *Seydi and Others* v. *France* [8 May 2016] ECtHR, available at www.justiceinitiative.org/uploads/e1df6986-b799-41d4-ba27-d598855f5512/litigation-echr-seydi-france-eng-20170523.pdf; Case no 65840/09, *Ouardiri* v. *Switzerland* [28 June 2011] ECtHR; Case no 55607/09, *H. P.* v. *Denmark* [13 December 2016] ECtHR; Case nos 27996/06 and 34836/06, *Sejdić and Finci* v. *Bosnia and Herzegovina* [22 December 2009] ECtHR.

[18] Case no 53461/15, *Kosa* v. *Hungary* [21 November 2017] ECtHR (third party intervention); Case nos 43577/98 and 43579/98, *Nachova* v. *Bulgaria* [6 July 2005] ECtHR; Case no 57325/00, *D. H.* v. *Czech Republic* [13 November 2007] ECtHR; Case nos 27996/06 and 34836/06, *Sejdić and Finci* v. *Bosnia and Herzegovina* [23 December 2009] ECtHR; Case no 20546/07, *Makhashevy* v. *Russia* [31 July 2012] ECtHR; Case C-83/14 *Nikolova* v. *Romanian CEZ Electricity* [16 July 2015] CJEU; *E. C.* v. *Italy* [8 June 2015] CJEU; Case no 19841/06, *Bagdanovicius and Others* v. *Russia* [11 October 2016] ECtHR; *Mikhaj and Others* v. *Russia* ECtHR, see www.justiceinitiative.org/litigation/mikhaj-and-others-v-russia.

[19] Case no 21884/15, *Chowdury and Others* v. *Greece* [30 March 2017] ECtHR.

[20] Application no 18079/15, *Bumbes* v. *Romania* [28 February 2019] ECtHR.

[21] Case no 11751/03, *Romanenko* v. *Russia* [8 October 2009] ECtHR; Case no 38224/03, *Sanoma Uitgevers* v. *The Netherlands* [14 September 2010] ECtHR; Case no 22385/03, *Kasabova*

history,[22] the right to information,[23] press freedom,[24] and the right to reputation.[25] The massive costs to small newspapers and NGOs of libel suits have also been denounced and attacked through litigation before the ECtHR.[26] The OSJI has also lodged complaints with the ECtHR concerning the way certain Eastern European countries limit NGO funding and its own advocacy and litigation efforts through national legislation that explicitly targets Soros and the OSJI's network of private foundations and NGOs.[27]

Along with its strategic litigation efforts, the OSJI works with governments to transform policies that cause human rights violations, advocates with decision-makers for change, uses the media to bring attention to issues and builds the capacity of civil society to improve and foster litigation.[28]

In summary, the OSJI plays a dual judicial role as a real litigant before the European Courts and as one of the most private donors that funds many NGOs to bring cases before the European Courts. The question that arises is thus how the OSJI and other private foundations identify and select NGOs for litigation purposes.

2.2 The Private-Sector Funding of Applications Taken by NGOs to the ECtHR and the CJEU

In addition to litigating in the European Courts themselves, private foundations are increasingly financing NGOs that litigate intensively and lodge complaints with the ECtHR and the CJEU.

---

v. *Bulgaria* [19 April 2011] ECtHR; Case no 3111/10, *Yildirim* v. *Turkey* [18 December 2012] ECtHR; Case no 50376/09, *Girleanu* v. *Romania* [26 June 2018] ECtHR.

[22] Case no 55508/07 and 29520/09, *Janowiec* v. *Russia* [21 October 2013] ECtHR.

[23] Case no 63898/09, *Bubon* v. *Russia* [7 February 2017] ECtHR; *HCLU* v. *Hungary* ECtHR.

[24] OSJI, *Global Human Rights Litigation Report*, 2017, pp. 23–29; Case no 37374/05, *Társaság a Szabadságjogokért* v. *Hungary* [14 April 2009] ECtHR.

[25] Case no 18310/06, *Pauliukene and Pauliukas* v. *Lithuania* [5 November 2013] ECtHR.

[26] Case no 39401/04, *MGN Ltd* v. *United Kingdom* [18 January 2011] ECtHR (third party intervention).

[27] *OSI-Budapest* v. *Hungary* [12 September 2018] ECtHR available at www.justiceinitiative.org/uploads/ef281023-a31d-4e40-a808-d9350a827d34/litigation-osibudapest-hungary-20180924.pdf; Application nos 74288/14 and 64568/16, *Democracy and Human Rights Resource Centre and Others* v. *Azerbaijan* [29 May 2018] ECtHR.

[28] OSJI, *Strategic Litigation Impacts. Insights from Global Experience*, 2018, p. 20.

2.2.1 The Funding of NGOs by Private Foundations for Their Litigation Activities

Prior to the turn of the century, collective litigation was conducted mainly by two British NGOs, JUSTICE and Liberty, and by the International Commission of Jurists (ICJ) without any financial funding from private foundations. This situation has changed radically since the 2000s with the emergence of many NGOs financed by private foundations for their litigation activities.

2.2.1.1 An Historical Perspective

Although prior to the turn of the century most collective litigation was conducted by JUSTICE, Liberty and the ICJ without any financial support from private foundations,[29] the Centre for the Independence of Judges and Lawyers, which was created by the ICJ, had been the only structure financed since 1978 by the Rockefeller Brothers Fund and the Ford Foundation.[30] At that time, among the main landmark cases obtained before the ECtHR by these NGOs were the judgments in *McCann and Others* v. *United Kingdom*[31] and *Thynne, Wilson and Gunnell* v. *United Kingdom*,[32] both concerning the right to life and its prevention. This litigation was, then, quite limited both in terms of quantity and influence.

Liberty (formerly the National Council for Civil Liberties) was founded in 1934 by Ronald Kidd and Sylvia Scaffardi, and supported by H. G. Wells, Vera Brittain, Dr Edith Summerskill, Clement Attlee, Kingsley Martin and Professor Harold Laski, to oppose brutal police attempts to stop people protesting peacefully in hunger marches against legislation that caused poverty. Liberty included public figures such as E. M. Forster as its president and Attlee, Aneurin Bevan, Havelock Ellis, Aldous Huxley, J. B. Priestley, Bertrand Russell, and Wells among its vice presidents. Liberty has campaigned on a significant range of issues over

---

[29] Unlike in the US, where the Ford Foundation financed groups undertaking litigation and participated in the promotion of civil rights, particularly for minorities, from the mid-1960s (*Ford Foundation Grantees and The Pursuit of Justice*, 2000, available at www.fordfoundation.org/media/1707/2000-ford-foundation-grantees-and-the-pursuit-of-justice.pdf, p. 8).

[30] CIMA, Bulletin no. 6, October 1980.

[31] Case no 18984/91, *McCann and Others* v. *United Kingdom* [27 September 1995] ECtHR.

[32] Case nos 11787/85, 11978/86 and 12009/86, *Thynne, Wilson and Gunnell* v. *United Kingdom* [25 October 1990] ECtHR.

the last eighty years, from fighting fascism, mass surveillance, internment and abuse of police power to defending free speech, the right to demonstrate and demanding equal rights for all. In this fight, Liberty has provided legal advice and supported groundbreaking cases through test case litigation since 1934. The main judgments obtained by Liberty before the ECtHR relate to child trafficking,[33] the right to manifest religious beliefs in a non-discriminatory manner,[34] discrimination in the field of sexual orientation,[35] discrimination in the workplace due to trade union membership,[36] collective trade union rights,[37] freedom of assembly and association,[38] and the violation of the right to respect for private and family life,[39] notably caused by MI5 surveillance,[40] the British Terrorism Act 2000 (the broad police power to stop and search without suspicion),[41] British electronic surveillance programmes[42] and the retention of communications data,[43] and the use of fingerprints and DNA samples.[44] Other significant fields of litigation concern the right to life and investigation into deaths (in the Al-Skeini case, third party comments were sent in conjunction with the European Human Rights Advocacy Centre [EHRAC], Human Rights Watch, Interights, the International

---

[33] Case no 77587/12, *VCL v. United Kingdom* [5 March 2018] ECtHR.
[34] Case nos 48420/10, 59842/10, 51671/10 and 36516/10, *Eweida and Others v. United Kingdom* [15 January 2013] ECtHR; Case no 43835/11, *S. A. S. v. France* [1 July 2014] ECtHR, see the written submission on behalf of Liberty available at www.libertyhumanrights.org.uk/sites/default/files/SAS%20v%20France%20-%20Written%20Subs.pdf; Case no 4619/12; *Fouzia Dakir v. Belgium* [11 July 2017] ECtHR, see the third party intervention submitted by Liberty available at www.libertyhumanrights.org.uk/sites/default/files/Liberty%20submissions%20as%20filed%2015%2011%2027.pdf.
[35] Case no 40016/98, *Karner v. Austria* [24 July 2003] ECtHR.
[36] Case no 2962/11, *Terence Brough v. United Kingdom* [30 August 2016] ECtHR.
[37] Case nos 30668/96, 30671/96 and 30678/96, *Wilson, National Union of Journalists and Others v. United Kingdom* [2 July 2002] ECtHR.
[38] Case no 31045/10, *National Union of Rail, Maritime and Transport Workers v. United Kingdom* [8 April 2014] ECtHR.
[39] Case nos 33985/96 and 33986/96, *Smith and Grady v. United Kingdom* [25 July 2000] ECtHR.
[40] Case no 20317/92, *Hewitt and Harman v. United Kingdom* [1 September 1993] ECtHR.
[41] Case no 4158/05, *Gillan and Quinton v. United Kingdom* [12 January 2010] ECtHR.
[42] Case no 58243/00, *Liberty and Others v. United Kingdom* [1 July 2008] ECtHR; Case nos 58170/13, 62322/14 and 24960/15, *Big Brother Watch and Others v. United Kingdom* [13 September 2018] ECtHR.
[43] Case C-203/15 and C-698/15, *Tele2 Sverige AB v Post-och telestyrelsen* and *Secretary of State for the Home Department v Tom Watson and others* [21 December 2016] CJEU.
[44] Case nos 30562/04 and 30566/04, *S. and Marper v. United Kingdom* [4 December 2008] ECtHR; Case no 32968/11, *Sabure Malik v. United Kingdom* [30 June 2016] ECtHR.

Federation for Human Rights and the Law Society),[45] the right to liberty,[46] the legality of detention,[47] and the right to dignity in detention.[48]

JUSTICE was founded in 1957 by a group of lawyers to promote and enforce the rule of law. In 1958, JUSTICE became the UK section of the ICJ.[49] Historically, JUSTICE has contributed to the release of many wrongfully convicted prisoners and has denounced systematic failures in the British criminal justice system. In 1983, it established a working group on human rights to bring international human rights standards into domestic law. It has acted in appeals to the ECtHR and assisted in the first case in which that court allowed third party intervention. JUSTICE mainly litigates in the European Courts in the realms of counterterrorism,[50] criminal justice,[51] prison,[52] and detention.[53] It also takes cases to the ECtHR concerning the lack of effective domestic remedies in relation to torture.[54]

Last but not least, the ICJ,[55] which was founded in 1952, is a very well-known international organisation with consultative status at the CoE, the United Nations and other international organisations. The ICJ, which is composed of judges, barristers and lawyers, files complaints and makes third party interventions before the ECtHR, notably in the fields of rendition/secret detention,[56] detention,[57] sexual discrimination,[58] and freedom of expression.[59]

---

[45] Case no 18984/91, *McCann and Others* v. *United Kingdom* [27 September 1995] ECtHR; Case no 55721/07, *Al-Skeini* v. *United Kingdom* [7 July 2011] ECtHR.
[46] Case nos 11787/85, 11978/86 and 12009/86, *Thynne, Wilson and Gunnell* v. *United Kingdom* [25 October 1990] ECtHR; Case no 27021/08, *Al-Jedda* v. *United Kingdom* [7 July 2011] ECtHR.
[47] Case no 3455/05, *A.* v. *United Kingdom* [19 February 2009] ECtHR.
[48] Case no 61498/08, *Al-Saadoon and Mr Khalef Hussain Mufdhi* v. *United Kingdom* [2 March 2010] ECtHR.
[49] See https://justice.org.uk/about-us/history-achievements/.
[50] Case no 22414/93, *Chahal* v. *United Kingdom* [15 November 1996] ECtHR.
[51] Case no 24888/94, *V.* v. *United Kingdom* [16 December 1999] ECtHR, Case nos 26766/05 and 22228/06, *Al Khawaja and Tahery* v. *United Kingdom* [15 December 2011] ECtHR.
[52] Case no 9787/82, *Weeks* v. *United Kingdom* [2 March 1987] ECtHR.
[53] Case no 7021/08, *Al Jedda* v. *United Kingdom* [7 July 2011] ECtHR; Case no 8139/09, *Othman* v. *United Kingdom* [17 January 2012]; Case no 46295/99, *Stafford* v. *United Kingdom* [28 May 2002] ECtHR.
[54] Case nos 34356/06 and 40528/06, *Jones* v. *United Kingdom* [14 January 2014] ECtHR.
[55] www.icj.org/.
[56] Case no 28761/11, *Al Nashiri* v. *Poland* [24 July 2014] ECtHR; Case no 33234/12, *Al Nashiri* v. *Romania* [31 May 2018] ECtHR; Case no 39630/09, *El-Masri* v. *Former Yugoslav Republic of Macedonia* [13 December 2012] ECtHR.
[57] Case no 42337/12, *Suso Musa* v. *Malta* [23 July 2013] ECtHR.
[58] Case no 51362/09, *Taddeucci and McCall* v. *Italy* [30 June 2016] ECtHR.
[59] Case no 29492/05, *Kudeshkina* v. *Russia* [26 February 2009] ECtHR; Case no 1813/07, *Vejdeland* v. *Sweden* [9 February 2012] ECtHR.

2.2.1.2 The Growing Private Funding of Litigation since the 2000s

This situation has changed since the end of the 1990s, following the accession of many Eastern European countries to the ECHR and the EU and the establishment of many NGOs (such as EHRAC, see below) that litigate in the European Courts. In particular, human rights groups working in Eastern and Central Europe have developed lawsuits that aim to enforce ECHR rulings in their own countries. As more countries in post-communist Europe have joined the CoE, they have ratified the ECHR, which has become applicable in their domestic law. As a first step, these groups have tried to vindicate the norms of the ECHR in their national courts. When those efforts have failed, the groups have lodged complaints with the ECtHR (Hershkoff and McCutcheon 2000) under the influence of their former private funders, the Ford Foundation. This strategy is exemplified in the regional work of the Budapest-based European Roma Rights Centre (ERRC, see below), which has been funded since 1998 by the Ford Foundation to take important cases to the ECtHR (Hershkoff and McCutcheon 2000). At that time, the most important case litigated by ERCC was the Assenov case (see Chapter 3).[60]

While historically some Eastern European NGOs (including the ERRC) were financed by the Ford Foundation to litigate for the first time by the end of the 1990s, a second major change has occurred since the 2000s with the growing funding of litigation (undertaken by NGOs) by more recent private foundations such as the OSF, the MacArthur Foundation, the Oak Foundation (Cliquennois and Champetier 2016) and the Sigrid Rausing Trust. In this regard, the 2000s saw a considerable increase in private funding of litigation. For instance, Liberty has received significant funding since 2007 from the OSF, the Oak Foundation and the Sigrid Rausing Trust.[61] For its part, JUSTICE has increasingly been financed by the OSF (2013–2014),[62] the Sigrid Rausing Trust (2012),[63] the Joseph Rowntree Charitable Trust (2012, 2015 and 2016),[64] the Nuffield Foundation (2012–2013),[65] the Evan Cornish Foundation

---

[60] Case no 24760/94, *Assenov* v. *Bulgaria* [28 October 1998] ECtHR.
[61] Liberty, *A Year in Review*, 2014, p. 21; Liberty, *Director's Report and Financial Statements for the Year Ending 31 December 2016*, p. 14.
[62] JUSTICE, *Annual Report 2013–2014*, p. 14.
[63] JUSTICE, *Annual Review 2012*, p. 28.
[64] JUSTICE, *Annual Report 2015–2016*, p. 16; JUSTICE, *Annual Report 2014–2015*, p. 16; JUSTICE, *Annual Review 2012*, p. 28.
[65] JUSTICE, *Annual Review 2013*, p. 24; JUSTICE, *Annual Review 2012*, p. 28.

(2017 and 2018) and the Allen & Overy Foundation (2017 and 2018).[66] Lastly, the ICJ has been progressively funded since the 2000s by the OSF,[67] the Sigrid Rausing Trust,[68] the Ford Foundation,[69] the MacArthur Foundation,[70] and the Oak Foundation.[71]

Private funding takes place directly but also through regular calls for proposals launched by private foundations (see Chapter 5), which seem to be an efficient way of influencing the content of cases brought by NGOs before the European Courts.[72] Furthermore, financing NGOs is a way for private foundations to intervene more selectively in litigation and to focus on certain countries by relying on local knowledge and competences on the ground acquired and possessed by NGOs.[73] According to the OSJI, efficient litigation needs to empower communities, to use a mix of civil society techniques and to work with strong national partners such as civil society groups or an NGO coalition.[74] Conversely, funding and standard procedures for case management stemming from private foundations are of interest for NGOs.[75]

A considerable number of cases against member states are brought to the ECtHR and the CJEU by a reduced number of NGOs that have this as one of their key purposes, if not their only purpose. Moreover, a very high number of the ECtHR rulings that find countries in breach of the ECHR result from petitions brought by these NGOs or are given in cases in which these NGOs have acted as amicus curiae. In the rest of this section, we consider which NGOs these are, how many and what kinds of cases they have brought before the ECtHR and the CJEU, and who the main funders of their activities are.

European Human Rights Advocacy Centre (EHRAC) EHRAC is an international NGO launched in 2003 by barrister Bill Bowring with funding from the EU[76] through the European Initiative for Democracy

---

[66] JUSTICE, *Annual Report 2017–2018*, p. 19; JUSTICE, *Annual Report 2017–2016*, p. 17.
[67] See www.sigrid-rausing-trust.org/Grantees/International-Commission-of-Jurists; ICJ, *Annual Report 2017*, p. 49; ICJ, *Annual Report 2012*, p. 70.
[68] ICJ, *Annual Report 2017*, p. 49.
[69] ICJ, *Annual Report 2012*, p. 70.
[70] Ibid.
[71] Ibid.
[72] See for instance www.opensocietyfoundations.org/search?q=grants+results.
[73] See for instance OSJI, *Global Human Rights Litigation Report*, 2013, p. 5.
[74] OSJI, *Global Human Rights Litigation Report*, 2017, p. 5.
[75] OSJI, *Global Human Rights Litigation Report*, 2015, p. 5.
[76] E. Gilligan, 'Chechen victims can get money, but a tribunal would be even better', *Chicago Tribune*, 20 March 2005, available at http://articles.chicagotribune.com/2005-03 20/news/0503200193_1_chechencivilians-european-court-chechnya-and-ingushetia.

and Human Rights scheme.[77] EHRAC has also been a university centre of litigation as part of the law school at Middlesex University (London) since 2013. EHRAC exclusively targets Russia, Ukraine, Georgia, Azerbaijan and Armenia at the ECtHR. Its main funders are the Oak Foundation, the OSF, the Sigrid Rausing Trust, the (US) National Endowment for Democracy and the MacArthur Foundation; the said donors account for 93 per cent of EHRAC's income.[78] Other donors have included ACAT Suisse, Avaaz, the Allan and Nesta Ferguson Charitable Trust, the Foreign and Commonwealth Office (2005, 2006, 2007–2009, 2016), the Netherlands Helsinki Committee (2009–2010), the Oakdale Charitable Trust and the Persula Foundation.[79] EHRAC is assisted in its litigation efforts by the US-based East-West Management Institute (EWMI).[80] In particular, the EWMI is responsible for a new five-year human rights and justice support programme funded by the United States Agency for International Development (USAID)[81] entitled Promoting Rule of Law in Georgia (PROLoG) with a view to reinforcing the justice system in Georgia and increasing its judicial independence, due

---

[77] The European Initiative for Democracy and Human Rights (EIDHR) is a European instrument promoting assistance for democracy, human rights and civil society in Russia, a focus country for 2002–2004. The EIDHR can fund NGOs and international organisations promoting human rights, democratisation and conflict prevention activities. In Russia, projects with NGOs, the UN High Commissioner for Human Rights and the CoE are at present under implementation, covering a wide range of areas such as promotion of independent media, strengthening the independence of the judiciary, a humane prison system, and assistance for victims of human rights violations in the northern Caucasus. See http://eeas.europa.eu/russia/docs/02-06_en.pdf.

[78] EHRAC, *Annual Report 2018*, available at http://ehrac.org.uk/wp-content/uploads/2019/07/EHRAC-Annual-Report-2018.pdf, p. 23; EHRAC, *Strategic Plan 2013–2023*, available at www.ehrac.org.uk/about-us/annual-reports/.

[79] See http://ehrac.org.uk/about-us/our-supporters/.

[80] The EWMI brings together government, civil society, and the private sector to transform post-Soviet societies and institutions. It is notably funded by the OSF, the Rockefeller Brothers Fund, the American Jewish World Service, Asian Development Bank, the Charles Stewart Mott Foundation, the European Commission, the Balkan Trust for Democracy of the German Marshall Fund, the International Finance Corporation, Norwegian People's Aid, the Swedish Program for ICT in Developing Regions (SPIDER), the United Nations Industrial Development Organization, the UK Department for International Development, the US Department of State, USAID and the World Bank. In addition, one of the EWMI Board Directors is the former Director of International Operations for the Open Society Institute. See https://ewmi.org/BODandStaff.

[81] USAID carries out US foreign policy by expanding stable, free societies, creating markets and trade partners for the US and promoting broad-scale human rights. See www.usaid.gov/who-we-are.

process and the protection of human rights.[82] EHRAC is also assisted in advocacy by the International Partnership for Human Rights (IPHR), an NGO financed by the OSF, the Swedish International Development Cooperation Agency, the EU and the National Endowment for Democracy that monitors, documents and reports on human rights violations in the former Soviet Union in light of international standards and lobbies international institutions on human rights issues.[83]

EHRAC is headed by the professor of law and barrister Philippe Leach and has twelve members of staff (including a Director, Programme Manager, Case and Project Support Officer, PR and Development Officer, Programme and Finance Adviser, Senior Lawyer and Legal Officer).[84] In addition, EHRAC uses external lawyers and runs an internship programme (with thirteen interns) in its office at Middlesex University to recruit students, postgraduates and professionals for litigation.[85] More broadly, EHRAC assists and helps NGOs and lawyers in Russia, the South Caucasus and Ukraine in taking cases to the ECtHR. As part of this assistance, EHRAC supports and litigates with lawyers at the Memorial Centre (see below), the Georgian Young Lawyers' Association and the Ukrainian Helsinki Human Rights Union.[86]

Thanks to these cooperations and the money that it devotes to human rights litigation and advocacy (which accounts for more than half of its budget),[87] EHRAC is currently working on 330 cases taken to the ECtHR against Russia, Ukraine, Georgia, Azerbaijan and Armenia, notably in collaboration with the Memorial Centre. From 2003 to 2018, EHRAC has contributed to litigation leading to 160 ECtHR judgments (out of over 300 complaints); in 96 per cent of these cases, the ECtHR found that ECHR rights had been breached.[88] Most cases concern Russia and are related to the Beslan school siege,[89] the ongoing political conflicts in

---

[82] EHRAC, *Annual Report 2016*, available at http://ehrac.org.uk/wpcontent/uploads/2017/07/EHRAC-Annual-Report-2016.pdf.
[83] See http://iphronline.org/about/who-we-are.
[84] EHRAC, *Annual Report 2018*, p. 21; EHRAC, *Annual Report 2014*, available at http://ehrac.org.uk/about-us/annual-reports/.
[85] See http://ehrac.org.uk/about-us/jobs-listing/.
[86] EHRAC, *Annual Report 2018*, pp. 20–21; EHRAC, *Annual Report 2017*, p. 2.
[87] EHRAC, *Annual Report 2018*, p. 23.
[88] EHRAC, *Annual Report 2014*, p. 9.
[89] Case no 26562/07 and six other applications, *Tagayeva and Others v. Russia*, 13 April 2017.

Chechnya,[90] Ukraine,[91] Dagestan,[92] Abkhazia, Nagorno-Karabakh, Crimea[93] and the contested region of South Ossetia,[94] and the territorial dispute with Georgia.[95] Through these cases, EHRAC has denounced many instances of torture, extrajudicial killing and enforced disappearance, arbitrary arrest and detention[96] and the disproportionate use of military force in these regional conflicts.[97] Litigation has also concerned unlawful restrictions on the rights to freedom of expression and association, challenges to the ban on foreign NGOs adopted by the Russian authorities[98] (see Chapter 5), the right not to be discriminated against, the right to demonstrate, the right to a fair trial, the right to a healthy environment, excessive surveillance,[99] the protection of journalists and human rights advocates, the rights of detainees and of people subject to an extradition process, and the right to freedom of movement.[100] More recently, state corruption,[101] religious freedom, women's

---

[90] Since 2005, over 200 ECtHR judgments have been passed down in cases taken by EHRAC/Memorial concerning Chechnya. See for instance Case nos 57942/00 and 57945/00, *Khashiyev and Akayeva* v. *Russia* [24 February 2005] ECtHR; Case nos 57947/00, 57948/00 and 57949/00, *Isayeva, Yusupova and Bazayeva* v. *Russia* [24 February 2005] ECtHR.

[91] 'Following Russia's annexation of Crimea in April 2014, and the ensuing armed conflict in the Donbas region, EHRAC has been working in partnership with the Ukrainian Helsinki Human Rights Union (UHHRU) to litigate related cases of human rights violations at the European Court of Human Rights.' 'EHRAC supporting cases at the European Court of Ukrainians detained in Russia', 11 November 2015, available at www.ehrac.org.uk/news/ehrac-supporting-cases-at-the-european-court-ofukrainians-detained-in-russia/.

[92] Case no 23445/03, *Esmukhambetov and Others* v. *Russia* [29 March 2011] ECtHR; Case no 41437/10, *Abdurakhman Abdurakhmanov* v. *Russia* [22 September 2015] ECtHR.

[93] Tatar Mejlis against Russia lodged with the ECtHR, 30 March 2017.

[94] Regarding the Ossetian conflict, EHRAC in partnership with the Georgian Young Lawyers' Association has submitted thirty-two pending cases to the European Court and is currently waiting for its judgments, see EHRAC, 'Our cases', available at http://www.ehrac.org.uk/about-our-work/human-rights-litigation/cases/.

[95] See for instance Application no 3963/18, *Matkava and Others* v. *Russia* [11 January 2018] ECtHR; EHRAC, *Annual Report 2018*, p. 9.

[96] See for instance Case no 8516/08, *Barakhoyev* v. *Russia* [17 January 2017] ECtHR.

[97] EHRAC, 'EHRAC 10 Year Review: a decade of human rights litigation', 1 December 2013, available at www.ehrac.org.uk/about-us/annual-reports/.

[98] Application no 9988/13, Ecodefence and Others against Russia and 48 Other Applications [22 March 2018] ECtHR. See also EHRAC, *Annual Report 2018*, p. 10 and *Annual Report 2017*, p. 26

[99] Case no 47143/06, *Roman Zakharov* v. *Russia* [4 December 2015] ECtHR.

[100] See EHRAC, *Annual Report 2014*.

[101] See EHRAC, *Annual Report 2018*, p. 26.

rights,[102] and LGBTI rights[103] have been integrated into the main domains of litigation covered by EHRAC. As part of its litigation efforts, EHRAC also advocates for the effective implementation of European Court judgments.[104]

Memorial Human Rights Centre Memorial Human Rights Centre, established in 1991, is one of the leading human rights NGOs based in the Russian Federation. It is funded and supported by the Global Fund of Conflict prevention (Embassy of Great Britain), the Embassy of Netherlands and France, the UNHCR Management of the UN High Commissioner for Refugees, the European Commission, EHRAC, the OSF, the National Endowment for Democracy (NED), the Norwegian Helsinki Committee (NHC) and the MacArthur Foundation.[105] Memorial, which has fifty-eight branches across the Russian Federation, focuses on breaches of human rights in the Ukrainian, Chechen and Ossetian conflicts.[106] It says its aim is to foster human rights through international mechanisms, namely the ECtHR and the UN. Since 2000, Memorial has sued Russia before the ECtHR for violations of human rights, mainly those of civilians during armed conflict in the Chechen Republic.[107]

---

[102] See Application no 11467/15, *S. N. against Russia* Lodged with the ECtHR on 20 February 2015; Application no 33056/17, *Taliko Tkhelidze against Georgia* Lodged with the ECtHR on 13 April 2017.

[103] Application no 76797/13, *Ilupin and Others* v. *Russia* [12 November 2018] ECtHR; Case nos 67667/09, 44092/12 and 56717/12, *Bayev and Others* v. *Russia* [20 June 2017] ECtHR; Case nos 4916/07, 25924/08 and 14500/09, *Alekseyev* v. *Russia* [21 October 2010] ECtHR. See EHRAC, *Annual Report 2018*, pp. 12–13.

[104] EHRAC, 'EHRAC 10 Year Review: a decade of human rights litigation', 1 December 2013, available at www.ehrac.org.uk/about-us/annual-reports/.

[105] Олег Орлов, о работе Правозащитного центра 'Мемориал' Выступление на встрече с донорами 18 апреля 2012 года [Oleg Orlov, the work of the Human Rights Centre 'Memorial' Speech at a meeting with donors 18 April 2012], available at https://memohrc.org/ru/specials/oleg-orlov-o-rabote-pravozashchitnogo-centra-memorial.

[106] Правозащитный центр 'Мемориал', 'Между перемирием и войной' – доклад 'Мемориала' оситуации на востоке Украины [Between truth and war: report of 'Memorial' about the situation in eastern Ukraine], 2015, available at http://memohrc.org/#programs; 'Они начинают любить своего дракона'. Доклад 'Чеченцы в России' ['They begin to love your dragon.' The report 'The Chechens in Russia'], 2014, available at http://memohrc.org/#programs.

[107] Защита прав человека с использованием международных механизмов [Protection of human rights by using international mechanisms], 2015, available at https://memohrc.org/ru/content/zashchita-prav-cheloveka-s-ispolzovaniem-mezhdunarodnyh-mehanizmov.

Lawyers working for Memorial took eleven cases in 2011 and more than thirty cases in 2012 to the ECtHR.[108] In addition, because Memorial and EHRAC began collaborating in 2000, from 2000 to 2014 the ECtHR issued eighty-seven positive rulings on 101 complaints filed by Memorial and EHRAC.[109] Of these, sixty-one rulings were handed down covering fifty-one complaints by residents of Chechnya asserting violations by Russian security forces during armed conflict and counterterrorism operations (extrajudicial executions, non-selective bombings, disappearances, torture and destruction of private households).[110] Other cases deal with protection of victims of torture and ill treatment in police and pre-trial detention, protection of the rights of persons exposed to discrimination and/or violence on ethnic, racial and/or sexual grounds, protection of the rights of foreigners and of freedom of expression and assembly in the Russian Federation, protection from environmental pollution and protection of the right to private and family life.[111] Memorial and EHRAC are also involved in the execution stage of ECtHR rulings. They train lawyers, specialists and students by giving them qualified help on business management.[112] Since 2011, alongside other Russian NGOs, Memorial has been vocal regarding the reform of the ECtHR, pleading for increased efficiency on the part of the ECtHR in the name of the protection of applicants' interests.[113] Memorial was deemed a 'foreign agent' by the Russian Justice Ministry in July 2014, following a decision by the St Petersburg Court, which ruled in 2013 that this human rights group was obliged to register as a 'foreign agent' organisation (we return to this characterisation of 'foreign agent' and its implications in

---

[108] Ibid.
[109] EHRAC, '101 EHRAC & Memorial cases at the European Court of Human Rights', 2015, available at www.ehrac.org.uk/news/101-ehrac-memorial-cases-at-the-european-court-of-human-rights/.
[110] Ibid.
[111] Ibid.
[112] Ibid. For instance, following the condemnation of Russia in *Fadeyeva* v. *Russia* (Case no 55723/00, [9 June 2005] ECtHR), Memorial and EHRAC consider the measures adopted by the Russian authorities (which have installed new equipment at the company to reduce harmful emissions in order to comply with the obligations imposed by the ECtHR) insufficient for the improvement of the environmental situation in Cherepovets.
[113] Защита прав человека с использованием международных механизмов [Protection of human rights using international mechanisms], 2015, available at https://memohrc.org/ru/content/zashchita-prav-cheloveka-s-ispolzovaniem-mezhdunarodnyh-mehanizmov.

Chapter 6).[114] Memorial has brought a case to the ECtHR contesting this decision;[115] in the meantime, it has reinforced its cooperation with EHRAC.

International Protection Center (IPC) The International Protection Center (IPC) is a Russia-based NGO created in 1994 after Russia ratified the Human Rights Committee Mechanism with the Optional Protocol to the International Covenant on Civil and Political Rights. Once Russia had ratified the ECHR, the IPC used it to litigate against Russia.[116] The IPC is mainly funded by the NED, the MacArthur Foundation, the OSF and the Oak Foundation.[117] Since 1999, the IPC has been the Russian office of the ICJ, which rallies professional lawyers and other professionals in the field of protection of human rights protection. The main activity of the centre is providing legal assistance to the victims of human rights violations, especially when pleading before international bodies (notably the ECtHR and the Human Rights Committee of the UN in Geneva). The IPC takes on average thirty cases per year against Russia to the ECtHR (mostly on the basis of Articles 2, 3, 5 and 6 ECHR). The IPC also pursues educational programmes directly supported by the MacArthur Foundation oriented towards training in litigation and bringing complaints before the ECtHR.[118] The majority of programme participants are representatives of public and human rights organisations such as the Nizhny Novgorod Committee against torture and the Moscow Helsinki Group (see below).[119] Since the end of 2012, the IPC has been targeted by 'the Russian law on foreign agents' (see Chapter 6), which is a major obstacle to their obtaining funds from foreign sources.

Nizhny Novgorod Committee against Torture The Nizhny Novgorod Committee against Torture was founded in 2000 by a number of well-known human rights advocates (including the present NGO head, Igor Kalyapin). This NGO is funded mainly by the European Commission,

---

[114] Case no 2-1835/13, *Prosecutor of the Admiralty District of St Petersburg* v. *ADC Memorial* [December 12,2013] Leninsky District Court of St Petersburg.
[115] ADC Memorial, 'Memorial takes its case to the European Court of Human Rights', 15 July 2014, available at http://adcmemorial.org/www/9544.html?lang=en.
[116] See www.icj.org/women-profiles-karinna-moskalenko/.
[117] IPC Annual Reports 2005, 2009 and 2011, retrieved from www.ip-centre.ru, website no longer available, on file with the author.
[118] IPC Annual Report 2009, website no longer available, on file with the author.
[119] Ibid.

the UK Foreign and Commonwealth Office, the Embassy of the Netherlands, the OSF, the NED and the MacArthur Foundation.[120] The Committee was created as a human rights organisation with the purpose of monitoring torture, abuses and violent treatment in Russia, its mission defined as the granting of professional legal and medical aid to victims of torture. Since 2000, the Committee has filed complaints regarding torture and inhuman or degrading treatment. In the context of such applications, the Committee carries out public investigations, represents the victim's interests before courts and investigation bodies, and provides assistance with a view to obtaining compensation. Between 2000 and 2014, the Committee foundation launched 1,402 applications dealing with human rights violations, conducted hundreds of public investigations and succeeded in making the Russian state pay millions of roubles in compensation to people who suffered from unlawful actions on the part of law enforcement agents. Committee lawyers have also obtained the conviction of more than seventy law enforcement agents in torture cases. From 2000 to 2010, the Committee prepared and filed sixty-seven applications to the ECtHR.[121] In the best known case launched by the Committee, *Mikheyev* v. *Russian Federation*, concerning torture in police custody, the ECtHR ruled in favour of the applicant, establishing that Russia had breached the ECHR.[122] The Committee also brought *Lyapin* v. *Russia*, a case concerning ill treatment by police, leading to a judgment grouping 135 complaints.[123]

Stichting Russian Justice Initiative (SRJI) The Stichting Russian Justice Initiative (SRJI) was established in Moscow in late 2001 (originally under the name Stichting Chechnya Justice Initiative, with its present name being used since 2004). The main driver of the initiative was Diedrich Lohmann, former director of Human Rights Watch, which is funded mostly by the OSF. The SRJI was intended to provide legal assistance to the civilians of the Chechen conflict. Anna Kornilina, a young Russian law graduate, played a key role in persuading victims to bring their cases before the ECtHR. With seed funding from the Dutch

---

[120] Committee Against Torture (Nizhny Novgorod), 'General information. Support', available at www.pytkam.net/web/index.php?go=Content&id=279.
[121] Committee Against Torture (Nizhny Novgorod), 'Cases', available at www.pytkam.net/web/index.php?go=Content&id=285.
[122] Case no 77617/01, *Mikheyev* v. *Russia* [26 January 2006] ECtHR.
[123] Case no 46956/09, *Lyapin* v. *Russia* [24 July 2014] ECtHR.

government, the Stichting Chechnya Justice Initiative opened offices not only in Moscow and the Netherlands but also in Ingushetia.[124] The SRJI has established itself as one of the leading legal representation and litigation projects in Russia. Funding comes from the OSF, the Dutch and Norwegian Ministries of Foreign Affairs, the Swedish Helsinki Committee, the United Nations High Commissioner for Refugees and the United Nations Voluntary Fund for Victims of Torture.[125] The SRJI resorts to domestic and international legal mechanisms to seek justice for grave human rights violations in regional and armed conflicts involving the North and South Caucasus. It has represented over 2,000 clients in over 300 cases lodged at the ECtHR. According to statements from a lawyer at the Court and information from other legal representatives, more than 400 cases regarding grave human rights abuses in Chechnya and Ingushetia and other North Caucasus republics had been submitted to the Court by December 2013, with some successful results.[126] The SRJI represented clients from North Caucasus in almost 290 of those cases. From 2001 to 2011, it represented more than 1,500 applicants from Chechnya, Ingushetia, Kabardino-Balkaria and Dagestan, and since mid-2008 over 400 from Georgia and South Ossetia.[127] By the end of 2013, the SRJI had won 149 cases at the ECtHR, leading to rulings finding Russia responsible for grave violations of human rights in both Chechnya and Ingushetia. Over the past ten years, the SRJI's successful litigation has set precedents in the areas of the right to life (in missing persons cases), standards for effective investigations, the suffering of relatives of missing persons, and the use of force in counterterrorism operations. The SRJI, in cooperation with Human Rights Watch, was also behind the leading ruling (followed by many others) on torture and abduction in Chechnya.[128] It has taken sixty-six applications relating to the conflict in Georgia to the ECHR on behalf of more than 400 beneficiaries.[129] The

---

[124] Gilligan, 'Chechen victims can get money, but a tribunal would be even better', *Chicago Tribune*, 20 March 2005.
[125] SRJI, *Ten Years 2001–2011 Report*, available at www.srji.org/en/about/annual/, p. 18.
[126] See for instance Case no 60272/00, *Estamirov and Others* v. *Russia* [12 October 2006] ECtHR; Case no 41840/02, *Sadykov* v. *Russia* [7 October 2010] ECtHR.
[127] SRJI, *Ten Years 2001–2011 Report*, p. 5.
[128] Ibid., p. 4.
[129] For a list of ECHR cases related to the Georgia–Russia war, see the Georgian Young Lawyers' Association (GYLA), Submission to the National Institute for Human Rights (NIHR) and Human Rights Priority 1 for Consideration at the 113th Session of the Human Rights Committee (16 March–2 April 2015) Russian Federation Russia's Responsibility for Human Rights in Occupied Regions of Georgia, available at http://

SRJI's work encompasses all stages of domestic and international litigation, including implementation of European Court judgments.[130] In particular, it strives to ensure ECtHR judgments on the North Caucasus result in more thorough and effective investigations at the domestic level, leading where possible to prosecutions of perpetrators, and in reforms of law enforcement practices and legal norms that perpetuate systemic abuses and investigative shortcomings. The SRJI works closely with the Amsterdam International Law Clinic, the Chechnya Advocacy Network, EHRAC, Memorial, Human Rights Watch, the International Helsinki Federation for Human Rights, the Moscow Helsinki Group, the Nizhny Novgorod Committee against Torture, the NHC and the Protection of Individual Rights in the Russian Federation.[131] In August 2007 the American Bar Association recognised the work of the SRJI with a special award.

AIRE (Advice on Individual Rights in Europe) Centre The AIRE (Advice on Individual Rights in Europe) Centre is a London-based charity created in 1993 to provide free legal advice on European human rights law and European Union law. AIRE is funded by the Diana, Princess of Wales Memorial Fund (2012), the AB Charitable Trust (2013–2014), the Allen & Overy Foundation (2013–2014), the Baring Foundation (2012–2014), the Centre for Democracy and Human Rights in Montenegro (2013–2014), the Evan Cornish Foundation (2013–2014), Freshfields Bruckhaus Deringer (2013–2014), the Hadley Trust (2013–2014), the Joseph Rowntree Charitable Trust (2013–2014), the OSF (2013–2014), the Pilgrim Trust (2013–2014), the Ptarmigan Trust (2013–2014), the Sigrid Rausing Trust (2013–2014), the Strategic Legal Fund (2013–2014), Unbound Philanthropy (from 2012–2014), the London Legal Support Trust, the Shade Foundation, Migration Work CIC, the Esmée Fairbairn Foundation, Zennström Philanthropies, the Trust for London, Comic Relief, the CoE, the European Commission, the Fundamental Rights Agency, Harvard Law School, and the European Programme for Integration and Migration. AIRE also receives financial

nihr.freeuni.edu.ge/.../Submission%20from%20NIHR; European Commissioner for Human Rights, Monitoring of Investigations into Cases of Missing Persons during and after the August 2008 Armed Conflict in Georgia, Commission for Human Rights (2010) 35, 29 September 2010, available at https://wcd.coe.int/ViewDoc.jsp?id=1675137#P163_27305.

[130] SRJI, 'Implementation of judgments', available at www.srji.org/en/implementation/.
[131] Ibid.

support from the UK Foreign and Commonwealth Office (via British Embassies in Podgorica, Sarajevo and Belgrade), the CoE, the Organisation for Security and Cooperation in Europe (OSCE), the Friedrich Ebert Foundation, the Konrad Adenauer Foundation and the OSF for sustaining rule of law projects and strengthening law reform with government institutions and NGOs in the Western Balkans.[132] One of the main aims pursued by AIRE is tackling breaches of fundamental European rights through litigation.[133] Since 1993, AIRE has taken more than 100 cases to the ECtHR and the CJEU to assist marginalised and vulnerable individuals, such as migrants, prisoners, children and victims of human trafficking and discrimination, to assert their human rights and to promote awareness of European law rights.[134] The main cases litigated by AIRE have therefore involved the rights of migrants,[135] but they also cover fair trials, extradition,[136] international protection, family law, children's rights,[137] prisoners' rights and in particular their right to vote,[138] cross-border

---

[132] AIRE Centre, *2013-2014 Annual Report*, available at www.airecentre.org/annual-report, p. 26.

[133] AIRE Centre, *Strategic Plan 2019 to 2024*, p. 9.

[134] AIRE Centre, *Directors and Trustees' Report and Accounts for the Year Ended 31st March 2018*, p. 2; *2013-2014 Annual Report*, pp. 16-17.

[135] Case no 47287/15, *Ilias and Ahmed* v. *Hungary* [14 March 2017] ECtHR related to push backs from Hungarian transit zones; Case no 19951/16, *H. A. and Others* v. *Greece* [28 February 2019] ECtHR on issues affecting migrant and asylum-seeking children (detention of nine unaccompanied minors aged between 15 and 18 from Syria, Iraq, and Morocco in Greek police stations); Application no 42902/17 *M. A. and Others* v. *Poland* [3 August 2017] ECtHR, third party intervention (along with ICJ) concerning children and families and the duty to accept asylum request; Case no 14165/16, *Sh. D and Others* v. *Greece* [13 June 2019] ECtHR, written submissions from AIRE along with the European Council of Refugees (ECRE) and ICJ, which relates to five undocumented children of Afghan nationality subject to detention and/or closed reception measures in Greece; Case no 8675/15 8697/15, *N. D. and N. T.* v. *Spain* [3 October 2017] ECtHR, third party intervention along with Amnesty International and ICJ on Spain's pushback policy in Melilla. See also AIRE Centre, *Annual Report 2012*, available at www.airecentre .org/data/files/resources/13/2012-AIRE-Annual-Report.pdf, p. 1.

[136] Case no 2947/06, *Ismoilov* v. *Russian Federation* [24 April 2008] ECtHR.

[137] Case 93/18, *Bajratari* v. *SSHD* [2 October 2019] CJEU; Case C-129/18, *S. M.* v. *Entry Clearance Officer, United Kingdom Visa Section* [26 March 2019] CJEU; Case no 28481/12, *Oller Kaminska* v. *Poland* [18 January 2018] ECtHR on violation of the applicant's right to respect for her family life on account of the Polish authorities' inability to swiftly reunite her with her daughter; Application no 47287/17, *Trawalli and Others* v. *Italy* [11 January 2018] ECtHR; Application no 5797/17, *Darboe and Camara* v. *Italy* [14 February 2017] ECtHR.

[138] Case no 74025/01, *Hirst* v. *United Kingdom* (No 2) [6 October 2005] ECtHR. In this case, AIRE intervened as a third party to put an end to the blanket ban on convicted prisoners in the United Kingdom voting in elections.

criminal justice,[139] human trafficking,[140] ill treatment by state authorities,[141] discrimination,[142] and accountability[143] of state authorities.[144] The most important cases obtained by AIRE concern discrimination and migrants. In *O'Donoghue v. United Kingdom*,[145] a ECtHR pilot judgment that was initially litigated with Law Centre Northern Ireland, AIRE represented a couple with children who were prevented from marrying due to the operation of the UK Certificate of Approval scheme, which restricted the rights of foreigners to marry unless they married in the Church of England. In *Sejdić and Finci v. Bosnia and Herzegovina*,[146] litigated by the OSJI (see Section 2.1), AIRE intervened as a third party in this case concerning the denial to members of certain ethnic minorities (Jews and Roma) the right to stand for elected office in Bosnia and Herzegovina. Finally, AIRE was involved as a third party intervener (along with Amnesty International and Human Rights Watch) before the ECtHR as regards the principle of non-refoulement and return of migrants to their country of departure,[147] and before the CJEU in judgments

[139] Case no 63019/10, *E. B.* v *United Kingdom* [20 May 2014] ECtHR, third party intervention from AIRE together with Fair Trials International.

[140] Case no 25965/04, *Rantsev v. Cyprus and Russia* [7 January 2010] ECtHR (third party intervention); Case no 49113/09, *L. R. v. United Kingdom* [14 June 2011] ECtHR; Case no 63019/10, *E. B. v. United Kingdom* [20 May 2014] ECtHR, litigation from AIRE, together with Fair Trials International, about the theory and practice of the European Arrest Warrant (EAW) and the human rights issues that it raises; Case no 30696/09, *M. S. S. v. Belgium and Greece* [21 January 2011] ECtHR.

[141] Case nos 27715/95 and 30209/96, *Berlinski v. Poland* [20 June 2002] ECtHR; Case C-357/09, *Saïd Shamilovich Kadzoev v. Direktsia 'Migratsia' pri Ministerstvo na vatreshnite* [30 November 2009] CJEU; Case no 56437/07, *Kadzoev v. Bulgaria* [1 October 2013] ECtHR. The Kadzoev case was litigated by the AIRE Centre together with the Legal Clinic for Refugees and Immigrants, which represented the applicant, who was held in solitary confinement while his claim for asylum was under review, as he risked prohibited ill treatment in case of return to Russia.

[142] Case no 33290/96, *Salgueiro da Silva Mouta v. Portugal* [21 December 1999] ECtHR; Case no 50231/13, *Sabalić v. Croatia* [6 March 2017] ECtHR. In these cases, AIRE represented the applicants and fought discrimination against homosexuals and lesbians. In Case no 47159/08, *Solomon v. Spain* and *B. S. v. Spain* [24 July 2012] ECtHR, AIRE also acted as a third party in conjunction with the University of Columbia Sexuality and Gender Law Clinic to represent a black prostitute, lawfully resident in Spain, on the ground that she was discriminated against by Spanish police on the basis of her race and gender (Article 14) and that her right to dignity was violated (Article 3).

[143] Case no 23452/94, *Osman v. United Kingdom* [28 October 1998] ECtHR; Case no 29392/95, *Z. and Others v. United Kingdom* [10 May 2001] ECtHR.

[144] See www.airecentre.org/Pages/Category/our-key-cases.

[145] Case no 34848/07, *O'Donoghue v. United Kingdom* [14 December 2010] ECtHR.

[146] Case nos 27996/06 and 34836/06, *Sejdić and Finci v. Bosnia and Herzegovina* [22 December 2009] ECtHR.

[147] Case no 27765/09, *Hirsi Jamaa and Others v. Italy* [23 February 2012] ECtHR.

related to the return of asylum seekers from the UK to Greece,[148] the rights of Turkish workers in the UK,[149] the rights of entry and residence of other (extended) family members of immigrants,[150] and the right for pregnant women to retain the status of worker under EU law and to access state support.[151]

Other NGOs funded by the OSF, the MacArthur Foundation and the Oak Foundation Other NGOs that have brought cases before the ECtHR and the CJEU include Fair Trials;[152] Promo-Lex, which obtained twenty-six judgments against Moldova and one against Russia (the famous Catan case, see Chapter 3) between 2006 and 2018;[153] Rechters voor Rechters;[154] Open Russia, the NGO that manages the largest charitable projects financed by Oil Company Yukos, owned by Mikhail Khodorkovsky;[155] the Public Verdict Foundation;[156] Lawyers for Human Rights[157] (which was created in 1979 to fight human rights violations under apartheid and is mainly funded by the OSF, the Ford Foundation, the Sigrid Rausing Trust, Atlantic Philanthropies and the US Bureau of Population, Refugees and Migration);[158] the Association of Russian Lawyers for Human Rights (which is notably involved in the important Adam Osmayev and Ilya Pyanzin case concerning an 'assassination attempt on Putin's life');[159] the Russian NGO Lawyers for Constitutional Rights and Freedoms (JURIX);[160] and

---

[148] Case C-411/10, *R (NS) v. Secretary of State for the Home Department* [22 September 2011] CJEU.
[149] Case C-186/10, *Oguz v. SSHD* [21 July 2011] CJEU.
[150] Case C-83/11, *Secretary of State for the Home Department v. Rahman* [5 September 2012] CJEU.
[151] Case C-507/12, *Jessy Saint Prix v. Secretary of State for Work and Pensions* [19 June 2014] CJEU.
[152] www.fairtrials.org/who-are-fair-trials?funders.
[153] https://promolex.md/category/ctedo/hotarari/?lang=en.
[154] www.rechtersvoorrechters.nl/english/.
[155] Open Russia's Human Rights Team submitted five appeals to the ECtHR in connection with demonstrations that took place throughout Russia in 2017. See www.khodorkovsky.com/human-rights/.
[156] http://en.publicverdict.org/.
[157] www.lhr.org.za.
[158] www.lhr.org.za/funders.
[159] See http://eng.rusadvocat.com/node/118.
[160] JURIX, which was created in 2003, combines litigation, legal advocacy, legal expertise and dissemination of legal knowledge. It focuses its efforts on such fields as constitutionalism, independence of the judiciary, the legal profession, legal education, and anti-discrimination in Russia. JURIX gives priority in strategic litigation to the following

Accept,[161] an NGO that defends gay rights in Romania. These NGOs are all funded by private foundations including the OSF, the MacArthur Foundation and the Oak Foundation (except for Lawyers for Human Rights, which is not financed by the Oak Foundation) to litigate in the European Courts, with a major focus on Eastern European countries. Lastly, Article 19, which was founded in 1987 by Aryeh Neier (from the OSF), Martin Ennals, J. Roderick MacArthur and Greg MacArthur (director of the MacArthur Foundation), is a British human rights organisation that defends freedom of information and expression (even for certain sects)[162] around the world through advocacy (namely lobbying governments to pass laws that comply with international standards of freedom of expression) and litigation.[163] In this regard, Article 19 submits expert opinions through amicus briefs to national and regional courts, including the ECtHR. Article 19 mostly files suits before the ECtHR against Eastern European countries[164] and Turkey.[165] It is financed mainly by the OSF, the Ford Foundation, the MacArthur Foundation, the William and Flora Hewlett Foundation, the NED, the Netherlands Ministry of Foreign Affairs, and the UK Foreign and Commonwealth Office.[166]

The Helsinki Committees Following the Helsinki Conference on Security and Cooperation in Europe, which was attended by the heads of all European countries (except Albania) as well as by the United States

---

areas: freedom of speech, expression and information; freedom of peaceful assembly; discrimination on ethnic, gender, religious or linguistic grounds; right to property; environmental rights; and rights of small indigenous peoples. See www.linkedin.com/company/lawyers-for-constitutional-rights-and-freedoms-jurix-/.

[161] www.acceptromania.ro.
[162] See for instance Case no 16354/06, *Raël Movement* v. *Switzerland* [13 July 2012] ECtHR.
[163] www.article19.org/law-and-policy/.
[164] Application no 8257/13, *Rabczewska* v. *Poland* [7 September 2017]; case no 11257/16, *Magyar Jeti Zrt* v. *Hungary* [4 December 2018] ECtHR; Case no 11915/15, *Endy Gęsina-Torres* v. *Poland* [20 February 2018] ECtHR; Case nos 29580/12, 36847/12, 11252/13, 12317/13 and 43746/14, *Aleksey Navalnyy* v. *Russia* [15 November 2018] ECtHR; Case no 10795/14, *Kharitonov* v. *Russia* [communicated to the Russian authorities on 27 April 2017] ECtHR.
[165] Case no 14305/17, *Selahattin Demirtaş and Others* v. *Turkey* [20 November 2018] ECtHR; Case no 16538/17, *Şahin Alpay* v. *Turkey* [20 March 2018] ECtHR; Case no 13252/17, *Ahmet Hüsrev Altan* v. *Turkey* [20 October 2017] ECtHR; Case no 13237/17, *Mehmet Hasan Altan* v. *Turkey* [20 March 2018] ECtHR; Case no 53413/11, *Ahmet Şık* v. *Turkey* [8 July 2014] ECtHR.
[166] Article 19, *International Annual Report 2017: Defending Freedom of Expression and Information around the World*, p. 65.

and Canada, and the signature of the Final Act of the meeting (called the Helsinki Act)[167] on 1 August 1975 by Russia, including the adoption of a commitment to adhere to international standards of human rights, Moscow human rights defenders Yuri Orlov, Andrei Amalric, Valentin Turchin and Anatoly Sharansky suggested the creation of associations independent of governments to monitor the implementation of the humanitarian Articles of the Act.[168] The Helsinki Committees were therefore established in all Eastern European countries (Poland, Romania, Bulgaria and Russia) to control the effectiveness of the Act. These structures became independent over time and were transformed into NGOs watching and challenging human rights violations in their own countries through advocacy, training and litigation before domestic Courts and the ECtHR, with an average of fifteen ECtHR cases a year.

The Bulgarian Helsinki Committee (BHC) was established in 1992 to protect human rights in Bulgaria. It is financed by the Oak Foundation, the OSF, the Solon Foundation, the Leon Levy Foundation, the European Commission, the German Marshall Fund of the United States, the Royal Dutch Embassy in Bulgaria and the Dutch Ministry of Foreign Affairs (through the Matra programme), USAID and the Westminster Foundation for Democracy.[169] The BHC offers free legal help to the victims of human rights violations and litigates before the domestic and regional courts. It takes cases on the grounds of discrimination (ethnicity and religion, gender and sexual orientation, mental illness)[170] and protection of detainees[171] and child victims (with mental disabilities)[172] from state neglect and abuse before the ECtHR, with an average of fifteen cases a year.[173]

---

[167] The Helsinki Final Act was adopted by all the countries of Europe, the US and Canada to reduce tension between the Soviet and Western blocs, with a view to securing their common acceptance of the post-World War II status quo and frontiers in Europe and to respecting human rights and fundamental freedoms.

[168] See www.mhg.ru/history.

[169] See www.bghelsinki.org/en/about-us/funding/.

[170] The leading case obtained by the BHC is Case no 25446/06, *Yordanova and Others v. Bulgaria* [24 April 2012] ECtHR. See BHC, *Annual Report 2013*, available at www.bghelsinki.org/media/uploads/documents/reports/annual_activity_report/bhc-annual-activity-report-2013_en.pdf, p. 13.

[171] BHC, *Annual Report 2014*, available at www.bghelsinki.org/media/uploads/documents/reports/annual_activity_report/bhc-annual-activity-report-2014_en.pdf, p. 10.

[172] BHC, *Annual Report 2015*, available at www.bghelsinki.org/media/uploads/documents/reports/annual_activity_report/bhc-annual-activity-report-2015_en.pdf, p. 10.

[173] BHC, *Annual Report 2016*, available at www.bghelsinki.org/media/uploads/documents/reports/annual_activity_report/bhc-annual-activity-report-2016_en.pdf, p. 12.

The Hungarian Helsinki Committee (HHC) was founded in 1989 with a view to protecting human dignity, in particular by helping refugees, detainees and victims of law enforcement violence. It began providing professional legal assistance in 1994. Despite having only a few members at the time of its establishment, by 2016 the HHC had twenty professionals among its members. The HHC is financed mainly by the OSF (between 35 per cent and more than 40 per cent, depending on the year), the Oak Foundation (between 10 per cent and 15 per cent, depending on the year), the European Commission (17 per cent), and the Dutch Embassy and the Dutch government (1 per cent).[174] Although the HHC has recently invested in new arenas of litigation such as dismissal of public officials without justification, most of the cases litigated by the HHC before the ECtHR and the CJEU concern detention,[175] ill treatment,[176] lack of domestic remedies,[177] and asylum procedures.[178] In line with the strategic litigation it pursues, it has also taken several cases of unlawfully detained asylum seekers[179] and pre-trial prisoners[180] to the ECtHR. One important case litigated by HHC was that in which the

---

[174] www.helsinki.hu/en/about_us/finances/. See also *HHC Annual Report 2016*, available at www.helsinki.hu/wp-content/uploads/Hungarian-Helsinki-Committee-annual-report-2016.pdf, p. 39.

[175] See for instance two landmark judgments and one pilot judgment obtained: Case no 47287/15, *Ilias and Ahmed* v. *Hungary* [14 March 2017] ECtHR; Case no 9912/15, *O. M.* v. *Hungary* [5 July 2016] ECtHR; Case nos 14097/12, 45135/12, 73712/12, 34001/13, 44055/13 and 64586/13, *Varga and Others* v. *Hungary*, [10 March 2015] ECtHR. See also the HHC Annual Report 2016, available at www.helsinki.hu/wp-content/uploads/Hungarian-Helsinki-Committee-annual-report-2016.pdf, p. 1.

[176] www.helsinki.hu/en/european_court_of_human_rights_cases/. In this regard, the HHC provided representation before the ECtHR in the first successful Hungarian case regarding police ill-treatment. See Case no 57967/00, *Kmetty* v. *Hungary* [16 December 2003] ECtHR.

[177] Case no 47287/15, *Ilias and Ahmed* v. *Hungary* [14 March 2017] ECtHR, §§100–101.

[178] For instance, the HHC obtained the ban from the CJEU on the psychological testing of sexual-emotional orientation in asylum procedures as it was considered by the Court to interfere disproportionately with private life. See Case C-473/16, *F v Bevándorlási és Állampolgársági Hivatal* [25 January 2018] CJEU.

[179] Case no 13058/11, *Al-Tayyar Abdelhakim* v. *Hungary* [23 October 2012] ECtHR; Case no 13457/11, *Hendrin Ali Said and Aras Ali Said* v. *Hungary* [23 October 2012] ECtHR; Case no 10816/10, *Lokpo and Touré* v. *Hungary* [20 September 2011] ECtHR; Case no 62116/12, *Nabil and Others* v. *Hungary* [22 September 2015] ECtHR.

[180] Case no 33292/09, *A. B.* v. *Hungary* [16 April 2013] ECtHR; Case no 59196/08, *Baksza* v. *Hungary* [23 April 2013] ECtHR; Case no 50130/12, *Bandur* v. *Hungary* [5 July 2016] ECtHR; Case no 19547/07, *Darvas* v. *Hungary* [11 January 2011] ECtHR; Case no 19325/09, *Ferencné Kovács* v. *Hungary* [20 December 2011] ECtHR; Case no 50255/12, *Süveges* v. *Hungary* [5 January 2016] ECtHR; Case no 43888/08, *X. Y.* v. *Hungary* [19 March 2013] ECtHR; Case no 71747/11, *Zsak* v. *Hungary* [19 November 2013] ECtHR.

Grand Chamber of the ECtHR ruled for the first time that the ECHR protects the right of access to information, and that the HHC's right to freedom of expression was breached when police refused to disclose the names of ex officio defence counsels and the number of cases in which they were appointed in a given year.[181]

On behalf of Romanian anti-communist dissidents, the Association for the Defence of Human Rights in Romania – the Helsinki Committee (APADOR-CH) was established in 1990, supported by the League for the Defence of Human Rights in Romania (headquartered in Paris) and the International Helsinki Federation. The main mission pursued by APADOR-CH is to take action and litigate for the protection of human rights, in particular for vulnerable persons (arrestees, detainees, drug addicts, minors, sex workers, gays and lesbians) when they are in danger or their rights are infringed.[182] To fulfil this mission, APADOR-CH is financed by the OSI's Human Rights and Governance Programme, the OSF, the Foundation for Civil Society (through its civil society and civic innovation programme), the Balkan Trust for Democracy (created in 2003 by the German Marshall Fund of the United States, USAID and the Charles Stewart Mott Foundation),[183] the European Commission, the Dutch Embassy and the Fund for Bilateral Relations within the Norwegian Financial Mechanism.[184] Former donors include the Trust for Civil Society in Central and Eastern European countries, the Swiss Embassy, the ERRC and the ICCO/Church in Action (a Protestant movement based in the Netherlands).[185] The main priorities set by APADOR-CH are the monitoring of police abuses, regulations and practices in the field of national security with an impact on human rights, and regulations and practices related to deprivation of liberty.[186] In addition, freedom of

---

[181] Case no 18030/11, *Magyar Helsinki Bizottag* v. *Hungary* [8 November 2016] ECtHR. See also HHC, *Annual Report 2016*, available at www.helsinki.hu/wp-content/uploads/Hungarian-Helsinki-Committee-annual-report-2016.pdf, p. 1.

[182] APADOR-CH, *25 Years of Connecting People with Their Rights*, 2016, pp. 1–10.

[183] Other donors are the Compagnia di San Paolo, the Czech Ministry of Foreign Affairs, the British Foreign and Commonwealth Office, the Danish Ministry of Foreign Affairs, the Embassy of the Kingdom of the Netherlands (Belgrade, Serbia), the Greek Ministry of Foreign Affairs, the Norwegian Ministry of Foreign Affairs, Robert Bosch Stiftung, the Rockefeller Brothers Fund, the Swedish International Development Cooperation Agency and the Tipping Point Foundation.

[184] APADOR-CH, *Annual Report 2017*, p. 19; *Annual Report 2016*, p. 27; *Annual Report 2014*, p. 24; *Annual Report 2013*, p. 17.

[185] APADOR-CH, *Annual Report 2008*, available at www.apador.org/en/raportul-de-activitate-al-apador-ch-2008/.

[186] See www.apador.org/en/despre-apador-ch/.

expression and the press, freedom of conscience (in favour of Jehovah's Witnesses and the yoga organisation called Movement for Spiritual Integration into the Absolute [MISA]) and the protection of minorities including gay people have also become APADOR's main fields of interest.[187] From this perspective, APADOR-CH offers legal representation before the ECtHR in a limited number of cases which are considered to be of strategic importance to the organisation.[188] It takes on cases relating to a breach of one of the following rights prescribed in the ECHR: the right to life (Article 2),[189] prohibition of torture (Article 3),[190] the right to liberty and security (Article 5),[191] the right to respect for private and family life (Article 8),[192] freedom of expression (Article 10),[193] and freedom of assembly and association (Article 11).[194]

---

[187] APADOR-CH, *25 Years of Connecting People with Their Rights*, 2016, pp. 21–28.
[188] Ibid., p. 54.
[189] Case no 2959/11 *Garcea v. Romania* [24 March 2015] ECtHR; Case nos 10865/09, 45886/07 and 32431/08, *Mocanu and Others v Romania* [17 September 2014] ECtHR; Case no 24329/02 *Mugurel Soare v. Romania* [22 February 2011] ECtHR; Case no 45661/99 *Carabulea v. Romania* [13 July 2010] ECtHR; Case no 42344/07, *Predica v. Romania* [7 June 2011] ECtHR; Case no 11273/05, *Csiki v. Romania* [5 July 2011] ECtHR.
[190] Several cases are related to applicants ill-treated by law enforcement officials: Case nos 41138/98 and 64320/01, *Moldovan and Others v. Romania* [13 July 2005] ECtHR; Case no 1454/09, *Doiciu v. Romania* [5 May 2015] ECtHR. Other cases concern applicants beaten by the police: Case no 68842/13, *Serban Marinescu v. Romania* [15 December 2015] ECtHR; Case no 70040/13, *Victor Stanciu v. Romania* [9 January 2018] ECtHR; Case no 37971/02, *Vili Rupa (no. 2) v. Romania* [19 July 2011] ECtHR. Other main cases concern detention conditions, such as Case no 56664/08, *Flămânzeanu v. Romania* [12 April 2011] ECtHR; Case no 65158/09, *Adrian Drăgan v. Romania* [2 February 2016] ECtHR; Application no 48231/13, *Marius Mavroian v. Romania* [4 March 2014] ECtHR; Case no 17044/03, *Cucolas v. Romania* [26 October 2010] ECtHR; Case no 27240/03, *Fane Ciobanu v. Romania* [11 October 2011] ECtHR; Case no 22362/06, *Cucu v. Romania* [13 November 2012] ECtHR; Case no 35972/05, *Iacov Stanciu v. Romania* [24 July 2012] ECtHR; Case no 32800/12, *Rădulescu v. Romania* [1 April 2014] ECtHR. In this matter, one pilot judgment was obtained by APADOR-CH: Case nos 61467/12, 39516/13, 48231/13 and 68191/13, *Rezmives and Others v. Romania* [25 April 2017] ECtHR).
[191] Case no 3584/02, *Daniel Tarau v. Romania* [24 February 2009] ECtHR.
[192] Case no 23022/13, *Cazul D. M. D. v. Romania* [3 October 2017] ECtHR; Case no 40238/02, *Bucur and Toma v. Romania* [8 January 2013] ECtHR.
[193] In Case no 33348/96, *Cumpanu and Mazăre v. Romania* [17 December 2004] ECtHR, two journalists from Cluj, condemned to prison and fined for calumny were represented by APADOR before the ECtHR, which condemned Romania for violating their right to freedom of expression. In *Cauza Roșiianu v. Romania* (Case no 27329/06 [24 June 2014] ECtHR), the Mayor refused to give public information to a journalist. See also Case no 40238/02, *Bucur and Toma v. Romania* [8 January 2013] ECtHR; Case no 17437/03, *Cornelia Popa v. Romania* [29 March 2011] ECtHR.
[194] Case no 42722/02, *Stoica v Romania* [4 March 2008] ECtHR.

The Helsinki Committee in Poland was established under martial law in 1982 by a small group of intellectuals. It was an underground organisation that built a network of alliances throughout Poland and abroad.[195] In 1989, its members created the Helsinki Foundation for Human Rights (HFHR), which is supervised by the Human Rights House Foundation, which notably litigates in Russia and Azerbaijan before the ECtHR[196] and is funded by the Norwegian Ministry of Foreign Affairs, the Ministry of Foreign Affairs of the Czech Republic and the Swiss Federal Department for Foreign Affairs.[197] The HFHR is financed on a general basis by the OSF and the Sigrid Rausing Trust.[198] It is also cofinanced for certain of its projects by the NED (for monitoring the human rights situation in Donbas, for defending human rights defenders and for promoting freedom of association); by the Gere Foundation, the OSF, the Human Rights House Foundation, the Heinrich Böll Foundation, the EU and International Solidarity Fund (for monitoring human rights violations in Crimea and Donbas, for improving the independent local mass media in Crimea, for helping the oppressed and undertaking legal education and legal action at national and international level for human rights in Belarus and in Azerbaijan);[199] by the Netherlands Helsinki Committee, the Polish Ministry of Labour, the Polish Business Roundtable and Religion in Transition (for the promotion of local democracy in Poland, and human rights and activism in Donbas); and the US Department of State (for human rights monitoring in Donbas).[200]

One of the main pillars of the HFHR's activity is litigation before the ECtHR concerning prison conditions, pre-trial detention, disabled persons, juvenile detention, execution of contacts with children, access to abortion, criminal defamation, freedom of press and the monitoring of the implementation of judgments process before the CM of the CoE.[201]

---

[195] www.hfhr.pl/en/helsinki-committee/about-the-committee/.
[196] Human Rights House Foundation, *Annual Report 2017–2018*, pp. 38 and 43.
[197] https://humanrightshouse.org/who-we-are/donors-and-supporters/.
[198] www.hfhr.pl/en/supporters/donations/.
[199] It is financed mainly by the Polish Development Cooperation, USAID, GIZ, EuropeAid, and the governments of Canada and Switzerland.
[200] www.hfhr.pl/en/supporters/wspolfinansowanie-en/.
[201] Helsinki Foundation for Human Rights, *Report on the Implementation of Judgments of the European Court of Human Rights in Poland*, March 2017, available at www.hfhr.pl/wp-content/uploads/2017/03/Raport-implementacja-ETPC-10-03-2017.pdf.

European Roma Rights Centre (ERRC) The European Roma Rights Centre (ERRC) was established in 1996 as a Roma-led international public interest law organisation working to fight anti-Roma racism and human rights abuses through strategic litigation, research and policy development, advocacy and human rights education. Its main goal is to fight discrimination and to achieve equal access to justice, education, housing, healthcare and public services for Roma. The ERCC is financed by the OSF, the Ford Foundation, the Ruben and Elisabeth Rausing Trust, the Charles Stewart Mott Foundation, the UK Foreign and Commonwealth Office Human Rights Project Fund, the Rockefeller Brothers Fund, the British Embassy in Budapest, the Charity Know How Programme of the Allavida Foundation and the EU.[202] With regard to its litigation activities before the ECtHR, in the fifty-five cases it has instructed the ERCC has obtained some positive judgments under Article 14 and the groundbreaking cases of *D. H. and Others v. Czech Republic*,[203] *Moldovan and Others v. Romania*,[204] and *Šečič v. Croatia*[205] in relation to discrimination in access to education and the state response to racially motivated violence.[206]

Interights Interights, which was established in 1982, was an international legal human rights NGO based in London. Most Interights funds came from grants and donations from trusts and foundations in the UK, Europe and the USA.[207] Interights was funded by the Ford Foundation,[208] the OSF, the MacArthur Foundation, the Oak Foundation, the UK Foreign and Commonwealth Office, Allen & Overy, Dechert LLP, Freshfields Bruckhaus Deringer, the Boston College of Law, the International Senior Lawyers Project and TrustLaw. Interights operated worldwide, with a major strategic litigation focus in Africa, Europe (especially South Eastern, Central and Eastern Europe and the former

---

[202] ERCC, *Annual Report 2001–2002*.
[203] Case no 57325/00, *D. H. and Others v. Czech Republic* [13 November 2007] ECtHR.
[204] Case nos 41138/98 and 64320/01, *Moldovan and Others v. Romania* [13 July 2005] ECtHR.
[205] Case no 40116/02, *Šečič v. Croatia* [31 May 2007] ECtHR.
[206] See www.errc.org/what-we-do/strategic-litigation/european-court-cases.
[207] Interights, *Annual Review 2006–2007*, available at www.interights.org/document/139/index.html, p. 22; Interights, *Business Plan 2011–2016*, available at www.interights.org/businessplan2011–2016/index.html.
[208] For instance, the amount received in 2012 was USD 500,000, under the Strengthening Human Rights Worldwide initiative. See Interights, *Business Plan 2011–2016*.

Soviet Union, including the South Caucasus region), and the Middle East and North Africa. It brought 209 filter cases (including 173 cases concerning Russia, leading to several pilot judgments)[209] before the ECtHR from 2004 to 2014.[210] As already mentioned, Interights was obliged to close down in May 2014 as a result of major financial difficulties.

* * *

This roster of significant repeated litigants against Eastern European countries allows us to conclude that a limited number of NGOs have played a key role in defining the input of ECtHR case law. These NGOs have been able to play that role thanks to generous funding from a limited number of private donors, mainly the OSF, the Ford Foundation, the MacArthur Foundation, the Oak Foundation and the Sigrid Rausing Trust (see Table 2.1).

2.2.2 The Role Played by the Main Private Donors

Over the decade from 2006 to 2015, four private foundations (the Ford Foundation, the MacArthur Foundation, the Oak Foundation and the OSF) spent over USD 138 million supporting strategic litigation worldwide.[211] This is why we examine not only the identity of the main private donors but also the nature of their activities and their investment in the field of human rights.

One of the most important donors financing European human rights litigation is the Ford Foundation, which is the second-largest foundation in the United States. It was established in Michigan in 1936 by Edsel Ford (son of Henry Ford, the founder of the Ford Motor Company) and moved in 1953 to New York, becoming one of the most active international organisations in the field of human welfare, with a USD 12 billion endowment including USD 500 million in grants around the world every year.[212] The Ford Foundation has funded litigation since the mid-1960s, supporting the US grantees who used litigation to protect the constitutionally guaranteed rights of disadvantaged minority groups (disabled persons, black and Latino people, etc.) and women suffering

---

[209] 'Sensitive cases' were not mentioned by Interights.
[210] See www.interights.org/our-cases/index.html.
[211] Foundation Center Maps, available at http://foundationcenter.org/gain-knowledge/foundation-maps.
[212] https://philanthropy.com/article/Ford-Foundation-Offers-Buyouts/162571.

Table 2.1 *Main private foundations, NGOs and their funding*

NGO	Main sources of funding
OSJI (Open Society Justice Initiative)	Soros Quantum Fund (hedge fund), USAID
Memorial	Open Society Foundations (OSF), MacArthur Foundation, Embassies of Great Britain, Netherlands and France, the European Commission, National Endowment for Democracy (NED), Norwegian Helsinki Committee (NHC)
EHRAC (European Human Rights Advocacy Centre)	OSF, MacArthur Foundation, Oak Foundation, Sigrid Rausing Trust, NED
International Protection Center (IPC)	OSF, MacArthur Foundation, Oak Foundation, NED
Nizhny Novgorod Committee against Torture (NNCAT)	OSF,, MacArthur Foundation, NED, European Commission,, UK Foreign and Commonwealth Office,, Embassy of the Netherlands
Stichting Russian Justice Initiative (SRJI)	OSF, Royal Netherlands and Norwegian Ministry of Foreign Affairs, Swedish Helsinki Committee, UN High Commissioner for Refugees, UN Voluntary Fund for Victims of Torture
Interights	OSF, Ford Foundation, MacArthur Foundation, UK Foreign and Commonwealth Office, Allen & Overy, Dechert LLP, Freshfields Bruckhaus Deringer, Boston College of Law, International Senior Lawyers Project, TrustLaw
AIRE Centre	Diana, Princess of Wales Memorial Fund (2012), AB Charitable Trust (2013–2014, 2018), Allen & Overy Foundation (2013–2014, 2018), Baring Foundation (2012–2014), Centre for Democracy and Human Rights in Montenegro (2013–2014), Evan Cornish Foundation (2013–2014), Freshfields Bruckhaus Deringer (2013–2014, 2018), Hadley Trust (2013–2014), Joseph Rowntree Charitable Trust (2013–2014), OSF (2013–2014),

Table 2.1 (cont.)

NGO	Main sources of funding
	Pilgrim Trust (2013–2014), Ptarmigan Trust (2013–2014, 2018), Sigrid Rausing Trust (2013–2014), Strategic Legal Fund (2013–2014), Unbound Philanthropy (2012–2014), Simmons & Simmons Charitable Trust (2018), London Legal Support Trust, Shade Foundation, Migration Work CIC, Esmée Fairbairn Foundation, Zennström Philanthropies, Law Society (2018), Trust for London, Comic Relief, CoE, European Commission, Fundamental Rights Agency, Harvard Law School, European Programme for Integration and Migration
Helsinki Committees (Poland, Hungary, Romania, Bulgaria)	OSF,, Sigrid Rausing Trust, USAID
European Roma Rights Centre (ERRC)	OSF, Ford Foundation, Ruben and Elisabeth Rausing Trust, Charles Stewart Mott Foundation, Rockefeller Brothers Fund, Allavida Foundation, UK Foreign and Commonwealth Office Human Rights Project Fund , British Embassy (Budapest), EU
Article 19	OSF, Ford Foundation, MacArthur Foundation, William and Flora Hewlett Foundation, NED, Netherlands Ministry of Foreign Affairs, UK Foreign and Commonwealth Office

acute and systemic discrimination.[213] In the 1970s, the Ford Foundation also began supporting litigation work in Latin America and in South Africa to challenge apartheid and to encourage South Africa's transition to new political regime.[214] Later, at the end of the 1990s, it financed litigation in Eastern countries before the ECtHR (see Chapter 5).

[213] Ibid., p. 11.
[214] Ibid., p. 16.

Another important donor funding human rights litigation before the European Courts is the John D. and Catherine T. MacArthur Foundation, which is the twelfth-largest foundation in the United States, with an endowment of nearly USD 7 billion. It was founded in 1970 by John MacArthur (1897–1978), who developed and owned the insurance firm Bankers Life and Casualty Company and invested in real estate in oil and textiles. At the time of his death, he was one of the three wealthiest men in America.[215] The foundation is headquartered in Chicago.

Another major donor financing NGOs taking cases to the European Courts is the Oak Foundation, a group of charitable and philanthropic organisations established in many countries. The Oak Foundation was founded in 1983 by Alan Parker, a British businessman who worked for DFS Group, a duty-free shopping network, and invested in the hedge funds and high technology that made him a billionaire. Today, the Oak Foundation has its main administrative office in Geneva, Switzerland and a presence in seven other countries: Bulgaria, Denmark, India, Tanzania, the UK, the US and Zimbabwe. Early grants were made in Denmark to organisations supporting single mothers and torture victims in 1983,[216] before the focus moved to Eastern European countries (see Chapter 5).

The Sigrid Rausing Trust is another private donor that finances litigation before the ECtHR and the CJEU. Sigrid Rausing, an Emeritus member of the international board of Human Rights Watch, is a Swedish philanthropist, anthropologist and publisher. Her father, Hans Rausing, was a wealthy Swedish businessman and CEO of the Swedish packaging company Tetra Pak (currently the largest food packaging company in the world),[217] which was co-founded by his grandfather, Ruben Rausing. Sigrid Rausing established the Sea Foundation charitable trust in 1988 and transferred the funds in 1996 to the Ruben and Elisabeth Rausing Trust, named after her grandparents. Renamed the Sigrid Rausing Trust in 2003, by 2014 it had given approximately GBP 208.3 million to human rights organisations globally.[218] It runs ten programmes, including several that focus on advocacy, research and litigation, women's rights, LGBTI rights, and detention, torture and the death penalty.[219]

---

[215] See www.macfound.org/about/#sthash.TJ2t2mGp.dpuf.
[216] See https://oakfnd.org/values-mission-history/.
[217] In the Forbes world ranking for 2011, Rausing had an estimated fortune of USD 10 billion.
[218] See www.sigrid-rausing-trust.org/.
[219] Ibid.

2.3 The Co-funding of NGOs and Private Organisations by Some CoE Member States

NGOs are financed in their litigation activities not only by private foundations but also by a mix of public and private actors. The funding of inputs is backed up by certain member states (including the Netherlands, the UK, Sweden, Norway and Switzerland) that participate in this co-funding through their embassies, as revealed in the Rockefeller Archives and the annual and financial reports of thirty NGOs (see Table 2.1). In addition to the Nizhny Novgorod Committee against Torture, the SRJI, Interights, the ERRC, the various Helsinki Committees and Article 19, which are all cofinanced by foreign embassies (see Table 2.1), Promo-Lex, an NGO that brings many cases before the Strasbourg Court, is financed by the Embassy of the Kingdom of Norway, the Swedish Helsinki Committee for Human Rights, the OSF and the Royal Netherlands Embassy.[220]

Lastly, the NED is another donor and supporter of litigation. The NED is a private, non-profit foundation, although it receives annual funding from the US Congress to support 1,600 NGO projects in more than ninety countries,[221] including in Eastern Europe.[222] The aim of such grants to 'local, independent organisations promoting political and economic freedom' is to foster 'a strong civil society, independent media, human rights, and the rule of law'.[223] The NED's current president is Carl Gershman, formerly Senior Counselor to the United States Representative to the UN, in which capacity he served as the US Representative to the UN's Third Committee, which deals with human rights issues, and also as Alternate Representative of the US to the UN Security Council.[224] EHRAC and the IPC are notably co-funded by the NED (see Table 2.1).

In summary, private funding of litigation to which little public funding is added has influence and impact not only on the inputs but also on the outputs of the ECtHR and the CJEU, starting with their case law and the execution of their judgments.

---

[220] Promo-Lex, annual reports from 2005 to 2015.
[221] See www.ned.org/about/.
[222] See www.ned.org/regions/.
[223] Ibid.
[224] See www.ned.org/experts/carl-gershman/.

3

The Influence of Private Foundations on the Outputs of the ECtHR and the CJEU

This chapter analyses the influence of private foundations on the outputs of the ECtHR and the CJEU. This process refers, on the one hand, to the tendency for both courts to deliver landmark judgments on cases taken by OSJI and the NGOs funded by private foundations and to rely in their judgments on documents and reports made by private foundations and the NGOs. On the other hand, this trend also refers to the increased involvement of private foundations and NGOs in the monitoring of the execution of judgments by member states. Furthermore, a private organisation (Judgment Watch) has recently been created and funded by a private foundation, the OSF, to support, monitor and promote the implementation of the most significant ECtHR judgments litigated by the OSJI and the NGOs.

With regard to the process level that is the topic of this first part of the book, the most convenient way for private foundations to achieve social changes and to have important impacts on national policies through litigation efforts is to take significant cases to the European Courts and to obtain pilot judgments, judgments delivered by the ECtHR under Article 46 ECHR and landmark judgments rendered by the CJEU. Conversely, the analysis of the landmark cases obtained by private foundations reveals the priorities set up and targeted by private foundations. To achieve such objectives, private foundations and NGOs that are financed by them use and conduct strategic litigation. As discussed in Chapter 2, according to the OSJI, efficient and strategic litigation needs to empower communities, use a mix of civil society techniques, and work with strong national partners such as civil society groups or an NGO coalition. Private foundations and NGOs thus cooperate to obtain significant judicial results.

To this end, we analyse and detail the execution of pilot and landmark judgments obtained over fifteen years by NGOs and private foundations. (There are of course many other more ordinary judgments litigated by private foundations that are not analysed in this book owing to lack of space.) Communications that private foundations and NGOs send to the CM about human rights violations committed by certain member states concerning their execution of judgments are also scrutinised.

3.1 Judicial Results Obtained by Private Foundations and NGOs Financed by Them

The establishment of private litigation teams and the financial dependence of NGOs from the private sector have increased the extent to which private donors can shape and influence their own and NGOs' litigation strategies and, thus, European jurisprudence. We show that both private foundations and NGOs are able to obtain the following:

- pilot judgments rendered by the ECtHR that can be identified in terms of the group of identical and repetitive cases they gather and that derive from systemic problems and the same root cause (the dysfunction under national law) of human rights violations. Pilot judgments are characterised by a specific proceeding, such as an action plan that has to be submitted by the condemned state in response to a pilot judgment (see Chapter 1).
- judgments delivered by the ECtHR under Article 46 ECHR that require general measures from the condemned state
- landmark judgments rendered by the ECtHR and the CJEU. Landmark judgments either effect a shift in European jurisprudence or create a new path for future case law and are identified as such by the CJEU in its annual reports.[1]
- key cases that are judgments given priority by the ECtHR.

We hypothesise that such judicial successes (pilot and landmark judgments, and key cases litigated and obtained by private foundations) feed and nurture the phenomenon of capture by private foundations.

In particular and for the very first time, we analyse the legal and judicial arguments and evidence offered by private foundations and NGOs in their litigated cases (and often either provided in their own reports or financed by them). We also scrutinise for the first time the way national states respond legally to judicial condemnations obtained by private foundations and NGOs in order to obtain an insight into their influence on condemned states.

---

[1] See https://curia.europa.eu/jcms/jcms/Jo2_7000/en/.

3.1.1 Pilot Judgments

Private foundations and particularly the OSF have obtained a significant number of pilot judgments in key areas covering political cases, discrimination, counterterrorism and detention policies.

3.1.1.1 Discrimination Policies

Private foundations have made discrimination policies one of the main fields in which they litigate. Through their intervention, they have contributed to an expansion of the scope of discrimination to new areas to such an extent that it concerns and covers core policies conducted by national states that are affected by such litigation.

This is for instance the case in the judgment of *Kurić and Others v. Slovenia*,[2] in which the OSJI (along with the Equal Rights Trust, the Peace Institute – Institute for Contemporary Social and Political Studies, and the Legal Information Centre of Non-governmental Organisations) acted as third party. The Kurić case deals with the problem of the statelessness of more than 18,000 former Yugoslavian citizens who were erased from Slovenian civil registers for having missed the deadline for applying for Slovenian nationality.[3] In this case, the OSJI argued that customary international law there obliges a state to avoid making people stateless and to improve the condition of those who have been left stateless (who were marginalised and vulnerable), especially in cases of state succession.[4] In response, the Grand Chamber of the ECtHR held that the severe effect of the erasure was in breach of the private life (Article 8) of those affected, and that there had been unlawful discrimination against them on account of their nationality (Article 14).[5] The Kurić judgment, which is a pilot judgment, was the very first on statelessness on such scale, and it ordered the state, as a general measure, to set up an ad hoc domestic compensation scheme, which was adopted by Slovenia.[6]

---

[2] Case no 26828/06, *Kurić and Others v. Slovenia* [26 June 2012] ECtHR.
[3] OSJI, 'Written comments', 6 May 2011, available at www.opensocietyfoundations.org/sites/default/files/kuric-written-comments-20110506.pdf.
[4] Case no 26828/06, *Kurić and Others v. Slovenia* [26 June 2012] ECtHR, §§331–335.
[5] Ibid., §§360–362.
[6] Case no 26828/06, *Kurić and Others v. Slovenia* [12 March 2014, just satisfaction] ECtHR, §§137–139.

3.1.1.2 Penal Policies

Traditionally, penal policies constitute one of the fundamental domestic competences exerted by national states. However, certain counterterrorism policies have been fought by NGOs backed by private foundations through serious litigation efforts that have resulted in one pilot judgment that sets limits on the power of Russia in this field.

Counterterrorism Policies and Strategies In the area of counterterrorism policies and strategies, the main judgment is the Khashiyev and Akayeva case[7] (which gathers a group of 221 cases including the Isayeva[8] and Abuyeva[9] cases and the Mayayeva[10] and Askhabova[11] cases, all instructed by EHRAC and Memorial, and the case of *Israilova v. Russia*,[12] in relation to enforced disappearance in Chechnya and litigated by the SRJI). The case was brought by EHRAC and Memorial concerning human rights violations committed in Grozny between December 1999 and January 2000. EHRAC and Memorial alleged that the applicants' relatives had been intentionally killed by federal soldiers, submitting that there existed sufficiently strong, clear and concordant evidence to satisfy the established evidentiary standard.[13] EHRAC also underlined that Russia had failed to conduct an independent, effective and thorough investigation into these deaths and into acts of torture and extrajudicial killings by soldiers; they did so by referring to press cuttings and NGO reports (issued by Human Rights Watch) which, in their view, showed serious hindrances to the proper functioning of the Russian justice system.[14] Lastly, EHRAC and Memorial reported that they had no effective remedies under Articles 2 and 3 ECHR.[15] The arguments raised by EHRAC and Memorial helped the ECtHR to find that 'violent' and 'counterterrorist' Russian operations conducted in Chechnya had

---

[7] Case nos 57942/00 and 57945/00, *Khashiyev and Akayeva v. Russia* [24 February 2005] ECtHR.
[8] Case no 57950/00, *Isayeva v. Russia* [24 February 2005] ECtHR.
[9] Case no 27065/05, *Abuyeva and Others v. Russia* [2 December 2010] ECtHR.
[10] Case no 37287/09, *Mayayeva v. Russia*.
[11] Case no 54765/09, *Askhabova v. Russia* [18 April 2013] ECtHR. In this case, the ECtHR decided to apply Rule 41 of the Rules of Court and to grant priority treatment to the application.
[12] Case no 4571/04, *Israilova and Others v. Russia* [23 April 2009] ECtHR.
[13] Case nos 57942/00 and 57945/00, *Khashiyev and Akayeva v. Russia* [24 February 2005] ECtHR, §§126-127.
[14] Ibid., §§148-151.
[15] Ibid., §181.

violated several ECHR rights (Articles 2, 3 and 13 ECHR). The ECtHR relied partly on fact-finding by Human Rights Watch (see below) and found that subsequently the Russian Federation had breached its conventional obligation to investigate the said human rights violations.[16]

Condemnation in the Khashiyev and Akayeva case led to some changes in Russian practice. Following this ruling and the one in the case of Aslakhanova and others,[17] championed by the SRJI, and more recent ones in the cases of Tsakoyevy,[18] Makhloyev,[19] Kukurkhoyeva,[20] and Yandadeva and others,[21] mainly litigated by the SRJI, Memorial and EHRAC, Russia has adopted general measures and several action plans to comply with the obligations imposed by the ECtHR and its commitment to bring those responsible for human rights violations (enforced disappearances, extrajudicial killings and torture) in the North Caucasus and in Chechnya to justice. In particular, Russia has set up a programme to combat abductions and has created an integrated independent body in charge of searching for persons missing as a result of counterterrorism operations in the North Caucasus, including not only Chechnya but also Ingushetia, Dagestan and North Ossetia-Alania.[22] Russia has also adopted organisational and methodological measures to assist the criminal investigation subdivisions of the Ministry of Internal Affairs so as to bring perpetrators before the courts. A Federal Law on Citizens' Participation in Maintaining Public Order has also been passed to facilitate working with the victims (including specific recognition of their status) and to increase cooperation with civil society institutions and NGOs.[23]

Prison Policies The creation of pilot judgments proceedings has very seriously increased the influence of ECtHR case law (and thus private foundations and NGOs) on domestic prison policies. While the Court previously considered that, in principle, a wide margin of appreciation was given to member states, the use of pilot judgments in the prison

---

[16] Ibid., §§36 and 150.
[17] Case no 2944/06 and 8300/07, 50184/07, 332/08, 42509/10, *Aslakhanova and Others v. Russia* [18 December 2012] ECtHR.
[18] Case no 16397/07, *Tsakoyevy* v. *Russia* [2 October 2018] ECtHR.
[19] Case no 66320/09, *Makhloyev* v. *Russia* [16 October 2018] ECtHR.
[20] Case no 50556/08 and nine others, *Kukurkhoyeva* v. *Georgia* [22 January 2019] ECtHR.
[21] Case no 5374/07 and nine others, *Yandadeva and Others* v. *Russia* [4 December 2018] ECtHR.
[22] Action Plan DH-DD(2014)1431E/21 November 2014.
[23] Updated Action Plan (17/07/2015) DH-DD(2015)773E/24 July 2015.

domain has changed this traditional view. Now, the ECtHR tends (notably in situations of prison overcrowding) to see a circumstance limiting, in the name of the inviolability of the prohibition under Article 3, the margin of appreciation given to member states. In this respect, the ECtHR regards it as incumbent on the respondent government to organise its penitentiary system in a way that ensures respect for the dignity of detainees, regardless of financial or logistical difficulties.[24]

While one of the most important pilot judgments rendered by the ECtHR in the field of prison policies was the Torreggiani case,[25] in which Italy was requested to put an end to its prison overcrowding and its bad detention conditions through new penal and prison policies, many pilot judgments pronounced against Eastern countries have been instructed by NGOs funded by private foundations (see below). This private litigation has resulted in the reform of national penal and prison policies, the fight against prison overcrowding and poor prison conditions, and the implementation of effective domestic remedies (Cliquennois and de Suremain 2018; Cliquennois and Snacken 2018).

In its case law on prisons, mostly obtained by private foundations, the ECtHR has indicated general measures to facilitate the speediest and most effective solutions for recurrent irregularities in prison conditions. According to the ECtHR, the problem of overcrowding must be solved by means of a reduction in the number of prisoners through more frequent use of non-custodial punitive measures,[26] and by minimising the recourse to pre-trial detention.[27] In the same way, the ECtHR has recalled several recommendations of the CM inviting states to encourage prosecutors and judges to use alternatives to detention as much as possible and to reorient their criminal policy towards reduced use of imprisonment in order to put an end to the inflation of the prison population.[28]

In addition, for ECHR violations originating in prison overcrowding, the ECtHR has ruled that the state has an obligation to provide an effective domestic remedy or a combination of remedies both preventive

---

[24] Case no 7064/05, *Mamedova v. Russia* [1 June 2006] ECtHR, §63.
[25] Case nos 43517/09, 46882/09, 55400/09, 57875/09, 61535/09, 35315/10 and 37818/10, *Torreggiani and Others v. Italy* [8 January 2013] ECtHR.
[26] *Norbert Sikorski v. Poland*, §158.
[27] Case nos 42525/07 and 60800/08, *Ananyev and Others v. Russia* [10 January 2012] ECtHR, §197.
[28] See in particular Recommendation No. R (99) 22 and Recommendation Rec(2006)13 of the Committee of Ministers.

and compensatory in nature.[29] In this way, the member states can either amend existing remedies or introduce new ones that guarantee effective redress.[30] The ECtHR has considered specific options for preventive and compensatory remedies, such as reasonable financial compensation and a mitigation of sentence (sentence reduction) for prisoners who have already been subjected to inhumane prison conditions.[31] Furthermore, the ECtHR has reiterated that a measurable reduction in a prison sentence offers satisfactory redress for an ECHR violation in criminal cases,[32] and for poor material conditions of detention.[33]

In this regard, one of the most significant cases obtained by private foundations is the judgment of *Neshkov and Others* v. *Bulgaria*,[34] along with the Kehayov group of cases on Bulgarian prison overcrowding and bad treatment.[35] The Neshkov case is a pilot judgment influenced by the Bulgarian Helsinki Committee (BHC), which both litigated[36] and also intervened in the form of written submission to the Court.[37] In its third party comments to the Court, BHC emphasised the very poor prison conditions, unsuitable living conditions, poor hygiene and overcrowding, and the detrimental effects of prison overcrowding on healthcare, violence, isolation, ill treatment and social activities.[38] Bulgaria was then asked by the ECtHR to decrease its prison overcrowding, to remedy poor detention conditions under Article 3 and to implement new preventive and compensatory domestic remedies under Article 13.[39] In response, on 25 January 2017 the Bulgarian parliament passed the Law on Amendments in the Execution of Punishments and Pre-Trial Detention Act, the

---

[29] Case nos 14097/12, 45135/12, 73712/12, 34001/13, 44055/13 and 64586/13, *Varga and Others* v. *Hungary* [10 March 2015] ECtHR, §110.
[30] See Case no 46347/99, *Xenides-Arestis* v. *Turkey* [22 December 2005] ECtHR, §40.
[31] See Case nos 42525/07 and 60800/08, *Ananyev and Others* v. *Russia* [10 January 2012] ECtHR, §§214–231.
[32] See Case no 64886/01, *Cocchiarella* v. *Italy* [29 March 2006] ECtHR, §77; Case nos 14097/12, 45135/12, 73712/12, 34001/13, 44055/13 and 64586/13, *Varga and Others* v. *Hungary* [10 March 2015] ECtHR, §109.
[33] See Case no 49169/09, *Stella and Others* [25 September 2014] ECtHR, §§59–63; Case nos 14097/12, 45135/12, 73712/12, 34001/13, 44055/13 and 64586/13, *Varga and Others* v. *Hungary* [10 March 2015] ECtHR, §109.
[34] Case no 36925/10, 21487/12, 72893/12, 73196/12, 77718/12 and 9717/13, *Neshkov and Others* v. *Bulgaria* [27 January 2015] ECtHR.
[35] Case no 41035/98, *Kehayov* v. *Bulgaria* [18 January 2005] ECtHR.
[36] Ibid., §2.
[37] Ibid., §8.
[38] Ibid., §§219–224.
[39] Ibid., §§268–291.

Criminal Code and the Criminal Procedure Code, which extended alternatives to prison sentences and early conditional release, and adopted new rules for allocation and transfer of prisoners as well as preventive and compensatory remedies.[40]

In a similar way, in a recent pilot judgment (*Varga and Others v. Hungary*)[41] litigated by the Hungarian Helsinki Committee,[42] the ECtHR found a violation of Article 3 on account of prison overcrowding and poor prison conditions.[43] The Court had previously found the same violation of Article 3 for similar conditions of detention in four cases.[44] Furthermore, in the judgments in the cases of Szél and Hagyó, the ECtHR concluded that there had been a violation of Article 13 on the ground of the absence of any effective domestic remedies for the applicants' complaints about the conditions of their detention.[45] In addition, the ECtHR referred to 450 prima facie meritorious applications against Hungary about inadequate conditions of detention and concluded that there was a recurrent structural problem.[46] This is why the ECtHR obliged Hungary under Article 3 to decrease its prison overcrowding, which was deemed a mass and structural problem, and to establish and put in place an effective domestic remedy.[47] In particular, the ECtHR found that the domestic remedy reported by the government, although accessible, was ineffective in practice, as it did not adequately compensate the applicants for periods of detention characterised by poor detention conditions. Furthermore, the Hungarian government had not provided

---

[40] Communication from Bulgaria Concerning the cases of Kehayov and Neshkov and Others v. Bulgaria, Action Plan (21/12/2017), 1310th Meeting (March 2018) DH-DD (2018)13.
[41] Case nos 14097/12, 45135/12, 73712/12, 34001/13, 44055/13 and 64586/13, *Varga and Others v. Hungary* [10 March 2015] ECtHR.
[42] See also HHC, *Annual Report of 2016*, p. 1, available at www.helsinki.hu/wp-content/uploads/Hungarian-Helsinki-Committee-annual-report-2016.pdf.
[43] Secretariat of the Committee of Ministers, Communication from a NGO (Public Verdict Foundation) (07/10/2013) in the Case of Ananyev and Others against Russian Federation, DH-DD(2014)44, 10 January 2014, available at https://wcd.coe.int/ViewDoc.jsp?id=2146465&Site=CM&BackColorInternet=C3C3C3&BackColorIntranet=EDB021&BackColorLogged=F5D383, pp. 3–12.
[44] Case no 44357/13, *Szél and Others v. Hungary*, [16 September 2014] ECtHR; Case no 15707/10, *István Gábor Kovács v. Hungary* [17 January 2012] ECtHR; Case no 52624/10 *Hagyó* [23 April 2013] ECtHR; Case no 69095/10, *Fehér v. Hungary* [2 July 2013] ECtHR.
[45] *Szél*, §61; *Hagyó*, §58.
[46] Case nos 14097/12, 45135/12, 73712/12, 34001/13, 44055/13 and 64586/13, *Varga and Others v. Hungary* [10 March 2015] ECtHR, §98.
[47] Ibid., §106.

evidence for the existence of a remedy which was likely to improve bad conditions of detention.[48]

Rezmives and Others v. Romania is another pilot judgment litigated and obtained by APADOR-CH regarding prison overcrowding that was in breach of the right to dignity according to the ECtHR.[49] More precisely, the Strasbourg Court found that the applicants' situation was part of a general problem originating in a structural dysfunction specific to the Romanian prison system.[50] The ECtHR therefore requested from Romania measures to fight prison overcrowding and improve the material conditions of detention, as well as to put in place effective domestic remedies (a preventive remedy and a specific compensatory remedy).[51] An innovative system of compensatory measures was thus implemented by Romanian Law 169/2017 for the modification of prison law, granting the right to benefit from conditional release to prisoners who meet the conditions required by the law or who have been housed in improper conditions (defined as a space smaller or equal to 4 m^2 or a space with improper hygiene means).[52] The 2017 law also grants a six-day reduction of a prison sentence for every thirty days served in inappropriate prison conditions.[53]

Prior to this pilot judgment, APADOR-CH intervened as third party in the case of *Iacov Stanciu v. Romania*,[54] also concerning to prison overcrowding and poor conditions of detention, and prepared as a semi-pilot judgment. In the Stanciu case, which followed the Bragadireanu group of cases,[55] the ECtHR held that detention conditions are a recurrent problem in Romanian prisons, and requested that Romania solve the systemic issues[56] underlined by APADOR.[57] While on 27 April 2016 the government approved a memorandum of measures supposed to tackle the issue and to improve detention conditions and the probation system

---

[48] Ibid., §65.
[49] Case no 61467/12, 39516/13, 48231/13 and 68191/13, *Rezmives and Others v. Romania* [25 April 2017] ECtHR.
[50] Ibid., §108.
[51] Ibid., §126.
[52] Law No 169/2017 for Amending and Completing the Law No 254/2013 on the Enforcement of Sentences and of Measures Involving Deprivation of Liberty Ordered by Judicial Bodies during Driminal Proceedings.
[53] Ibid.
[54] Case no 35972/05, *Iacov Stanciu vs. Romania* [24 July 2012] ECtHR.
[55] Case no 22088/04, *Bragadireanu v. Romania* [6 December 2007] ECtHR.
[56] Ibid., §§195–198.
[57] Ibid., §193.

(with plans for the construction of new prisons to be ready by 2023 and a draft law on amnesty and pardoning which is still in the Romanian parliament for debate), none of the measures was implemented immediately. This is why a pilot judgment was delivered by the ECtHR giving the Romanian authorities a six-month deadline to provide 'a precise timetable for the implementation of the general measures'.[58]

In a similar way, the Ciorap group of cases,[59] litigated by Lawyers for Human Rights (an NGO financed by the Atlantic Philanthropies, Fastenopfer, the Ford Foundation, the OSF, the Sigrid Rausing Trust, the EU and the American Bureau of Population, Refugees and Migration), mainly concern poor prison conditions, prison overcrowding and the lack of effective domestic remedies in Moldova. A revised action plan by the government of the Republic of Moldova was submitted in January 2018 and reported the construction of a new modern detention facility to replace the old one, the renovation of other detention facilities and the adoption of the law of 20 July 2017 (on amending and completing certain legislative acts on inadequate conditions of detention and reduction of duration of detention), which covers complaints against the administration of the penitentiary institution on conditions of detention seriously affecting the rights of convicts or detainees.[60]

Ananyev and Others v. *Russia* was another pilot judgment on prison conditions brought by the IPC.[61] The case concerned the poor conditions of detention of applicants in Russian remand centres (article 3ECHR)[62] and the lack of an effective remedy in that respect (Article 13 ECHR). This pilot judgment dealt with an important volume of cases (eighty) and complaints (250). In its ruling, the Strasbourg Court highlighted the structural problems (both legal and logistical in nature) resulting from the malfunctioning of the Russian penitentiary system, as well as the insufficiency of legal and administrative safeguards against ill treatment.

---

[58] Case no 61467/12, 39516/13, 48231/13 and 68191/13, *Rezmives and Others* v. *Romania* [25 April 2017] ECtHR.
[59] Case no 12066/02, *Ciorap* v. *Moldova* [19 June 2007] ECtHR.
[60] Communication from Moldova Concerning the Case of Ciorap, Pladi and Becciev v. Republic of Moldova, Revised Action Plan (11/01/2018), 1310th Meeting (March 2018) DH-DD(2018)33.
[61] Case nos 42525/07 and 60800/08, *Ananyev and Others* v. *Russia* [10 January 2012] ECtHR, §197.
[62] See Russia Legal Information Agency, 'Russia scrambles to improve detainee rights record under ECHR guidance' (9 January 2013), available at http://rapsinews.com/judicial_analyst/20130109/265853623.html.

In particular, the ECtHR considered that the excessive length of pre-trial detention, already notably condemned by the Grand Chamber in the case of *Idalov* v. *Russia* (litigated by the IPC and by Ms N. Lisman, a lawyer practising in Boston for the International Senior Lawyers Project funded by the OSJI and the OSF and cooperating with JURIX),[63] should be addressed by the Russian government, in particular by considering alternative ways of reducing overcrowding in prisons (including provisional arrangements, and eventually leading to the establishment of safeguards against the admission of prisoners in excess of prison capacity). The Russian authorities were also instructed to make available a combination of preventive and compensatory remedies complying with the requirements set out by the Court.[64] The pressing need for comprehensive general measures to tackle inadequate detention conditions (including access to healthcare) in Russian prisons had already been highlighted by the CM in the Kalashnikov group of cases monitored by the Association of Russian Lawyers for Human Rights.[65] Similar concerns had been underlined by a specific project of the Human Rights Trust Fund on 'implementing pilot judgments, "quasi-pilot" judgments and judgments revealing systemic and structural problems in the field of detention on remand and remedies to challenge conditions of detention' for which the Russian Federation is one of the beneficiaries.[66]

3.1.2 *Judgments Obtained under Article 46 and Imposing General Measures on Condemned Member States*

Some important judgments rendered by the ECtHR under Article 46 that imply general measures taken by the condemned state have been litigated by NGOs and private foundations in the field of detention, prison and (im)migration policies, counterterrorism, the organisation of the judiciary, surveillance and political violence committed by national states.

---

[63] Case no 5826/03, *Idalov* v. *Russia* [22 May 2012] ECtHR.
[64] CoE Directorate General Human Rights and Rule of Law, Guide to Good Practice in Respect of Domestic Remedies Adopted by the Committee of Ministers on 18 September 2013, available at www.echr.coe.int/Documents/Pub_coe_domestics_remedies_ENG.pdf, pp. 25–31 and 41–43.
[65] Case no 47095/99, *Kalashnikov* v. *Russia*, 15 July 2002.
[66] HRTF Project No. 18, covering six beneficiary member states, available at www.coe.int/en/web/execution/human-rights-trust-fund.

3.1.2.1 General Detention and Prison and (Im)migration Policies

The judgments obtained under Article 46 are in line with the pilot judgments litigated by NGOs and private foundations and analysed above in the context of general detention and prison and migration policies. Such judgments reinforce the impacts of European case law at national level.

One of the main judgments delivered under Article 46 by the ECtHR was the case of *László Magyar v. Hungary*,[67] which was litigated by the Hungarian Helsinki Committee (HHC) through third party intervention. In line with the previous case law partly set up by the Kafkaris[68] and Vinter[69] judgments, the ECtHR confirmed that the sentence of life imprisonment without the possibility of parole (whole/actual life sentence) imposed upon the applicant was in breach of Article 3 ECHR.[70] The Court also found a breach of the right to a fair trial (Article 6) because of the excessive length (eight years) of the criminal proceedings against the applicant.[71] In this regard, the ECtHR was in line with the HHC, which regarded the possibility of a presidential pardon as not really affecting the length of an actual life sentence in Hungary. The HHC stated that the discretionary nature of the pardon decision, the lack of reasoning given for negative decisions, the lack of guidelines as to the aspects to be taken into account by decision-makers and the lack of publicly available detailed data on decisions granting pardon did not influence positively the possibility of parole, which remained entirely theoretical.[72] The ECtHR suggested under Article 46 that the Hungarian authorities should put in place a legislative reform of the system of review of whole life sentences with a view to guaranteeing 'the examination in every particular case of whether continued detention is justified on legitimate penological grounds and should enable whole life prisoners to foresee, with some degree of precision, what they must do to be considered for release and under what conditions'.[73]

---

[67] Case no 73593/10, *László Magyar v. Hungary* [20 May 2014] ECtHR.
[68] Case no 21906/04, *Kafkaris v. Cyprus* [12 February 2008] ECtHR.
[69] Case no 66069/09 130/10 3896/10, *Vinter and Others v. United Kingdom* [9 July 2013] ECtHR.
[70] Ibid., §§54–59.
[71] Ibid., §§64–66.
[72] Ibid., §41.
[73] Ibid., §71.

In *Piechowicz* v. *Poland*,[74] the Helsinki Foundation for Human Rights (HFHR) submitted in its third party intervention that the cumulative impact of restrictions imposed on 'dangerous detainees' taken together with the common practice of continuing the regime without sufficient grounds amounted to a violation of Article 3.[75] In the same manner, the ECtHR judgment that was delivered under Article 46 (requiring general measures of implementation) underlined the restrictions and the cumulative effects of the 'dangerous detainee' regime on the applicant, and that the length and severity of the measures taken exceeded the legitimate requirements of security in detention and that they were not fully necessary to attain the legitimate objective pursued by the authorities.[76] The ECtHR therefore decided that there was a violation of Article 3 ECHR. In response, in 2015 the Polish government amended the Criminal Enforcement Code to implement the ECtHR judgments in the cases of *Piechowicz* v. *Poland* and *Horych* v. *Poland*.[77] According to the amendment, the 'dangerous detainee' regime might be imposed only on a detainee who had committed a crime of a high degree of social harmfulness.[78] In addition, during the process of extension of the regime of a 'dangerous detainee', the Polish authorities were obliged to take into account factors such as the prisoner's personal conditions, motivation while committing the crime, behaviour in prison and degree of demoralisation.[79]

In the field of healthcare for disabled prisoners, *D. G.* v. *Poland* is the main case litigated by NGOs.[80] In the D. G. judgment, which is part of the Kaprykowski group of cases (decided under Article 46 of the Convention),[81] the HFHR intervened as third party along with the European Disability Forum and the International Disability Alliance.[82] Like the HFHR, the ECtHR underlined that excessive constraints on prison infrastructure and poor conditions of detention for disabled prisoners

---

[74] Case no 20071/07, *Piechowicz* v. *Poland* [17 April 2012] ECtHR.
[75] Ibid., §§154–157.
[76] Ibid., §178.
[77] Case no 13621/08, *Horych* v. *Poland* [17 April 2012] ECtHR.
[78] Act of 10 September 2015 Amending the Criminal Executive Code and Certain Other Acts, Official Journal from 2015 item 1573.
[79] Ibid.
[80] Case no 45705/07, *D. G.* v. *Poland* [12 February 2013] ECtHR.
[81] Case no 23052/05, *Kaprykowski* v. *Poland* [3 February 2009] ECtHR.
[82] Ibid., §4.

constitute a breach of the right to dignity.[83] In response, the Polish authorities developed the medical services available to prisoners, improved sanitary and living standards in detention facilities and introduced dedicated healthcare programmes and new remedies.[84] Their updated action report provided information on a civil compensatory remedy and the right to be detained in conditions respecting one's dignity as personal rights for the infringement of which the state treasury can be held liable.[85]

In *Suso Musa* v. *Malta*,[86] the ICJ intervened as third party to underline the excessive duration of the applicant's detention coupled with the inadequate immigration conditions at the barracks where he was held.[87] The ECtHR was sensitive to the arguments raised by the ICJ,[88] and recommended that Malta take the necessary general measures to improve conditions of immigration detention and to limit detention periods so that they remain connected to the ground of detention applicable in an immigration context.[89] Furthermore, the ECtHR noted that it had found a violation of Article 5 §4 (legality of detention) on the ground that none of the remedies available in Malta could be considered speedy for the purposes of that provision.[90] Thus, the Court requested that Malta adopt appropriate legal and/or other measures in order to secure in its domestic legal order a mechanism that allows individuals taking proceedings to determine the lawfulness of their detention to obtain a determination of their claim within Convention-compatible time limits.[91]

Immigration policies have historically been a state monopoly, a situation that has recently been challenged by the EU and the ECtHR on behalf of NGOs (backed by private foundations). The most famous case is *Hirsi Jamaa and Others* v. *Italy*,[92] delivered under Article 46 and litigated by Human Rights Watch (HRW), the Columbia Law School Human Rights Clinic, the AIRE Centre, Amnesty International (AI) and

---

[83] Ibid., §139-140 and 176-177.
[84] Submission by Poland to the CM, Updated Action Report from 21 June 2016 in the Kaprykowski Group of Cases no. 23052/05 against Poland.
[85] Ibid., p. 15.
[86] Case no 42337/12, *Suso Musa* v. *Malta* [23 July 2013] ECtHR.
[87] Ibid., §5.
[88] Ibid., §123.
[89] Ibid., §123.
[90] Ibid., §122.
[91] Ibid., §122.
[92] Case no 27765/09, *Hirsi Jamaa and Others* v. *Italy* [23 February 2012] ECtHR.

the International Federation for Human Rights (FIDH) through third party interventions. In their interventions, the NGOs stressed that the applicants' transfer to Libya by Italy had violated Articles 3 and 13 ECHR and Article 4 of Protocol No. 4 by referring to the dramatic situation in Libya. In particular, HRW condemned Italy's forced return of irregular migrants to Libya by relying on the statements made by several direct witnesses and by asserting in its reports of 2006 and 2009 that during 2009 Italy had carried out nine operations on the high seas, returning 834 Somali, Eritrean and Nigerian nationals to Libya.[93] HRW argued that irregular migrants were systematically arrested and often subjected to torture and physical violence, including rape, owing to the absence of a national asylum system. In violation of UN guidelines on detention, migrants were often tortured and detained indefinitely in inhuman detention conditions (with no medical assistance) and with no judicial supervision.[94] For their part, AIRE, AI and the FIDH noted that several reports made by HRW over a number of years showed that the human rights situation in Libya was dramatic, notably for refugees, asylum seekers and migrants.[95] The NGO emphasised a 'duty to investigate' (where there was reliable information from diverse sources that detention or living conditions in Libya were incompatible with Article 3 ECHR) that must prevail over commitments arising out of bilateral or multilateral agreements over the fight against clandestine immigration.[96] Lastly, AIRE, AI and the FIDH argued that the individuals who were pushed back as a result of interception on the high seas did not have access to any remedy in the contracting state responsible for the operations, much less any remedy capable of meeting the requirements of Article 13. The NGOs emphasised that when the contracting parties to the ECHR were involved in interceptions at sea resulting in a pushback, their responsibility was to ensure that each of the persons concerned had an effective opportunity to challenge his or her return and to obtain an examination of his or her application.[97] The ECtHR took into account the arguments applied by the NGOs by condemning Italy and enlarging the scope of the non-refoulement principle (derived from the rules for the rescue of persons at sea and those governing the fight against people trafficking)

---

[93] Ibid., §101.
[94] Ibid., §102.
[95] Ibid., §103.
[96] Ibid.
[97] Ibid., §194.

with regard to the risk of torture and inhumane and ill treatment even when the parties concerned had failed expressly to request asylum.[98]

3.1.2.2 The Punishment of Political Opponents, Watchdogs, Human Rights Activists and Whistle Blowers

It is only recently that the punishment of watchdogs, human rights activists and whistle blowers (unlawful arrest and detention, poor detention conditions and right to health) has been challenged by private foundations and NGOs before the ECtHR, which has no prior jurisprudence in the field.

The judgment of *Rasul Jafarov* v. *Azerbaijan*,[99] which was delivered on 17 March 2016 by the ECtHR as part of the Ilgar Mammadov group of cases rendered under Article 46 (Mammadov being an opposition politician detained as a political prisoner in very poor prison conditions),[100] was instructed by EHRAC. EHRAC underlined that there was insufficient evidence and information to establish a 'reasonable suspicion' that Mammadov had committed any of the criminal offences with which he had been charged, including illegal entrepreneurship, large-scale tax evasion and abuse of power, or stemming from the non-registration of the human rights organisation Human Rights Club (HRC).[101] In this regard, EHRAC submitted that the activities of HRC, even in the absence of state registration, could not be considered to be illegal entrepreneurial activities.[102] The HFHR, the Human Rights House Foundation[103] and Freedom Now,[104] which is funded by the OSF, the Oak Foundation, Tom Lantos Foundation, the Bradley Foundation and the Moriah Fund,[105] also intervened as third party to point out the degrading condition of human rights defenders, journalists and activists in Azerbaijan and the

---

[98] Ibid., §§122–138.
[99] Case no 69981/14, *Rasul Jafarov* v. *Azerbaijan* [17 March 2016] ECtHR.
[100] Case no 15172/13, *Ilgar Mammadov* v. *Azerbaijan* [22 May 2014] ECtHR.
[101] Ibid., §87.
[102] Ibid., §§87–96.
[103] The Human Rights House Foundation oversees the work of the HRHF and is registered in Norway.
[104] Freedom Now is a US-based NGO that works to free individual prisoners of conscience through legal, political and public relations advocacy and litigation efforts. See www.freedom-now.org/about/mission/.
[105] See ibid. and Freedom Now, *Annual Report 2018*, available at www.freedom-now.org/wp-content/uploads/2018/12/Freedom-Now-2018-Annual-Report.pdf, p. 23; Freedom Now, *Annual Report 2017*, available at www.freedom-now.org/wp-content/uploads/2019/07/Freedom-Now-2017-Annual-Report.pdf, p. 23.

almost complete shutdown of independent human rights organisations, the striking expansion in scope and severity of specious criminal charges used against civil society leaders, and the adoption of legislation regulating and controlling NGOs.[106] According to these NGOs, Azerbaijan incarcerates human rights defenders, journalists and activists who had cooperated intensively with the CoE and engaged with other international monitoring mechanisms.[107] In particular, in EHRAC's view, the very public support from a number of state officials for the prosecution showed that the measures taken by the authorities had political grounds, since state officials of the highest ranks usually labelled all NGOs receiving grants from abroad as traitors and 'fifth columnists'.[108] The ECtHR was sensitive to these allegations and ruled that the arrest and detention of the famous human rights defender Rasul Jafarov (considered to be an American agent and accused of failing to register grants)[109] was unjustified, and had the aim of punishing him for his human rights activities. Jafarov had also been linked to a targeted repressive campaign against human rights defenders and NGOs, which included disparaging public statements by various high-ranking officials. In this regard, the ECtHR found a violation of Article 18 linked to Article 5 and grounded on the repression of human rights defenders as a result of their human rights activity.[110] The relation established by the ECtHR between Article 5 and Article 18 was made in accordance with the previous, very thin case law of the Court, which began with the case of *Cebotari* v. *Moldova*,[111] litigated by Lawyers for Human Rights,[112] concerning the unlawful detention of the CEO of a private company. A link between Articles 5 and 18 was also made by the ECtHR in the case of *Tymoshenko* v. *Ukraine*,[113] which was partly championed by the OSJI and related to the detention of the leader of the Batkivshchyna political party supported by the OSF, of the Yulia Tymoshenko Bloc and of one of the leaders of the Orange Revolution (and thus a political opponent of the rival presidential candidate Victor Yanukovych).

---

[106] Case no 69981/14, *Rasul Jafarov* v. *Azerbaijan* [17 March 2016] ECtHR, §§107–113.
[107] Ibid., §107.
[108] Ibid., §149.
[109] He is one of the founders of the HRC.
[110] Case no 69981/14, *Rasul Jafarov* v. *Azerbaijan* [17 March 2016] ECtHR, §§153–163.
[111] Case no 35615/06, *Cebotari* v. *Moldova* [13 November 2007] ECtHR.
[112] Ibid., §2.
[113] Case no 49872/11, *Tymoshenko* v. *Ukraine* [30 April 2013] ECtHR.

This landmark judgment echoes the Aliyev case (which concerns a violation of the right to free and fair elections),[114] the Yunusov case (see below) and the case of Mammadli against Azerbaijan[115] (litigated by the HFHR, the Human Rights House Foundation, and Freedom Now through third party interventions),[116] which concern the punishment of human rights defenders. In response, Azerbaijan submitted several action plans,[117] the last of which aimed to improve the operation of penitentiaries, humanise penal policies and extend the application of alternative sanctions and non-custodial procedural measures of restraint.[118] In particular, Azerbaijan set up decriminalisation of certain crimes; provision of alternative sentences to imprisonment; development of grounds for non-custodial measures of restraint and alternative sentences; wider application of institutions of substitution of remainder of imprisonment by lighter punishments, parole and suspended sentences; extension of the application of measures of restraint other than arrest; simplification of rules for amendment of arrest by alternative measures of restraint; and further limitation of grounds for arrest for low-risk or less serious crime.[119] However, these measures were judged to be insufficient by the CM, which launched an infringement procedure against Azerbaijan (see below), denouncing the prolonged unlawful detention of the applicant. In reaction, Azerbaijan cited the decision of the Supreme Court of Azerbaijan, which held that the applicant must be released unconditionally and provided him with the remedy in connection with the pre-trial detention questioned by the ECtHR.[120]

---

[114] Case no 18705/06, *Aliyev* v. *Azerbaijan* [8 April 2010] ECtHR.
[115] Case no 47145/14, *Mammadli* v. *Azerbaijan* [19 April 2018] ECtHR.
[116] Ibid., §4.
[117] Communication from Azerbaijan Concerning the Case of Ilgar Mammadov against Azerbaijan (Application No. 15172/13), 1214th Meeting (2–4 December 2014) (DH) – Action Plan (26/11/2014) – DH-DD(2014)1450 26/11/2014; Communication from Azerbaijan Concerning the Case of Ilgar Mammadov against Azerbaijan (Application No. 15172/13), 1278/H46-1 – Action Plan (14/02/2017), DH-DD(2017)172 15/02/2017.
[118] On 10 February 2017, the President of the Republic of Azerbaijan signed an Executive Order 'On improvement of operation of penitentiary, humanization of penal policies and extension of application of alternative sanctions and non-custodial procedural measures of restraint'.
[119] Communication from Azerbaijan Concerning the Case of Ilgar Mammadov v. Azerbaijan (Application No. 15172/13), 1278/H46-1 – Action Plan (14/02/2017), DH-DD(2017)172 15/02/2017, pp. 1–2.
[120] Rule 8.2a Communication from the Authorities (01/06/2019) in the Case of Ilgar Mammadov v. Azerbaijan (Application No. 15172/13), 1348th Meeting (June 2019) (DH), DH-DD(2019)634 03/06/2019.

This judgment paved the way for the future ECtHR case law on this matter and was preceded by the judgment in *Intigam Aliyev* v. *Azerbaijan*,[121] which was also successfully litigated by EHRAC and delivered by the ECtHR under Article 46. The judgment concerned the arrest and detention of the chairman of the Legal Education Society and human rights activist on charges of illegal entrepreneurship, large-scale tax evasion and abuse of power.[122] EHRAC argued that the applicant was held in appalling conditions in pre-trial detention (in breach of Articles 2 and 3 and with reference to the Varga case discussed above)[123] and that his detention and conviction were politically motivated and aimed at silencing him and punishing him for his human rights activities and not based on legal grounds (in breach of Articles 5 and 18).[124] Third party comments made by the HFHR, the Human Rights House Foundation and Freedom Now concerned the situation of human rights defenders in Azerbaijan and the hindrances faced by NGOs as a result of the recent legislative amendments on NGOs.[125] In line with EHRAC, the ECtHR found a violation of Article 3, stating that the space afforded to the applicant fell far below the required standard of personal space, and that his cell lacked adequate ventilation and sanitary facilities.[126] It also ruled that the arrest and detention of the applicant were unlawful and in breach of Article 5 §1 ECHR, and that he was detained without any 'reasonable suspicion' of having committed a criminal offence.[127] The ECtHR also held that the domestic courts consistently failed to check the existence of reasonable suspicion underpinning Intigam's arrest and detention, as well as the legitimacy of its aim. Thus the ECtHR found a violation of Article 5 §4: 'the role of the domestic courts was limited to automatic endorsement of the prosecution's applications without any genuine or independent review of the "lawfulness" of the applicant's detention'.[128] Turning to the searches of Intigam's home and office and the seizure of his files, the ECtHR found that these measures were not

---

[121] Case no 68762/14 and 71200/14, *Intigam Aliyev* v. *Azerbaijan* [20 September 2018] ECtHR.
[122] The applicant has taken several cases against Azerbaijan to the ECtHR, including cases related to irregularities during the 2010 parliamentary elections.
[123] Ibid., §§102 and 121.
[124] Ibid., §§143–148 and 192–194.
[125] Ibid., §151.
[126] Ibid., §§123–127.
[127] Ibid., §§154–166.
[128] Ibid., §172.

legitimate and concluded that the Azerbaijan government had breached Intigam's right to respect for private and home life (Article 8).[129] In addition, the ECtHR established that 'The totality of the circumstance indicates that the authorities' actions were driven by improper reasons, and the actual purpose of the impugned measures was to silence and punish (Mr Aliyev) for his activities in the area of human rights as well as to prevent him from continuing those activities.' The ECtHR therefore found that his status as a human rights activist had motivated the Azerbaijan authorities to arrest and put him in prison, in breach of Article 18.[130] The ECtHR also stressed that Intigam's case was not an isolated one, but rather one of many systemic reprisals against human rights activists and journalists by the authorities.[131] This why, regarding the general measures taken under Article 46, the ECtHR ordered that Azerbaijan must take action to address this issue: 'the necessary general measures to be taken by the respondent state must focus, as a matter of priority, on the protection of critics of the government, civil society activists and human rights defenders against arbitrary arrest and detention. The measures to be taken must ensure the eradication of retaliatory prosecutions and misuse of criminal law against this group of individuals and the non-repetition of similar practices in the future.'[132]

The last judgment delivered by the ECtHR in this area was the Magnitskiy case,[133] which was litigated by the OSJI. The case concerns a Russian (who was the head of tax practice at the Moscow office of Firestone Duncan, a Moscow-based company providing legal, tax, accounting and audit services to foreign investors in Russia) accused by the Russian authorities of tax evasion and suffering from a denial of medical care that led to his death in pre-trial detention. The so-called 'whistle blower' had denounced a $230 million fraud against the Russian exchequer allegedly perpetrated by senior Russian Interior Ministry officials. In its application, the OSJI claimed that Russia had violated Articles 2, 3, 5, 6 (violation of the principle of the presumption of innocence under Article 6 §2) and 13.[134] More precisely, the OSJI argued that the conditions of Magnitskiy's detention were appalling,[135] that his detention

---

[129] Ibid., §§178–189.
[130] Ibid., §§206–216.
[131] Ibid., §214.
[132] Ibid., §§223 and 226.
[133] Case no 32631/09 53799/12, *Magnitskiy and Others* v. *Russia* [27 August 2019] ECtHR.
[134] Ibid.
[135] Ibid., §180.

lacked justification (owing to an absence of impartiality on the part of the investigating authority that had resulted in a conflict of interest)[136] and that its length was unreasonable and unjustified (based on ill-founded arguments) under Article 5 §3.[137] The OSJI emphasised that the applicant had died because of the absence of medical care in detention and that the criminal proceedings against him had been unfair. Furthermore, the OSJI alleged that the Russian authorities had failed to secure the applicant's life,[138] that the applicant had been ill-treated by prison officers, and that the Russian government had failed to effectively investigate the circumstances and causes of his death.[139] Lastly, the OSJI raised a violation of the principle of the presumption of innocence enshrined in Article 6 §2 concerning his posthumous conviction.[140] With regard to the procedural argument, the OSJI invited the ECtHR under Article 46 to request that Russia set up an independent commission of inquiry into the circumstances of Mr Magnitskiy's death; issue a public apology for the denial of justice; amend the Russian Code of Criminal Procedure in order to ensure the preservation of evidence and effective access to independent medical examinations; and carry out legislative reform preventing posthumous proceedings from taking place against the will of the accused's relatives.[141] The ECtHR embodied the main legal arguments raised by the OSJI in considering that the applicant was detained in severely overcrowded conditions that amounted to inhuman and degrading treatment in breach of Article 3.[142] The ECtHR also found that the applicant's detention was not sufficiently grounded under Article 5 §3,[143] and that by depriving the applicant of important medical care, the Russian authorities unreasonably put his life in danger.[144] The ECtHR also concluded that the investigation into Magnitskiy's death did not comply with the ECHR,[145] and that the posthumous proceedings against the applicant, which ended with his conviction, breached the requirements of Article 6 §1 and §2 on account of their inherent unfairness (due to the

---

[136] Ibid., §197.
[137] Ibid., §208.
[138] Ibid., §§247–249.
[139] Ibid., §227.
[140] Ibid., §276.
[141] Ibid., §291.
[142] Ibid., §193.
[143] Ibid., §§213–223.
[144] Ibid., §§257–265.
[145] Ibid., §§233–236 and 267–272.

violation of the principle of the equality of arms and the guarantees of a fair trial).[146]

3.1.2.3 Counterterrorism Policies

One of the leading cases in the field of counterterrorism policies is the judgment in *Esmukhambetov and Others* v. *Russia* rendered under Article 46 and litigated by EHRAC and Memorial.[147] Both NGOs alleged that an aerial strike on a Chechen village in which the applicants had been living was not justified by any evidence confirming the presence of illegal or terrorist armed groups and that it resulted in the deaths of the family members of several applicants and in the destruction of the houses and property of all the applicants.[148] The NGOs also complained that the legal framework concerning the use of force and firearms by military personnel in Russia, being vague and inadequate, did not provide sufficient safeguards to prevent the arbitrary deprivation of life and to satisfy the requirement of protection 'by law' of the right to life.[149] Lastly, EHRAC and Memorial complained about the moral suffering the applicants had endured in connection with the aerial strike, the lack of an adequate, effective and timely investigation into the events, and the lack of effective remedies in respect of the alleged violations of Articles 2, 3, 8 and 13 ECHR and Article 1 of Protocol No. 1.[150] The ECtHR shared the view of EHRAC and Memorial in condemning the Russian authorities for the lack of a real investigation.[151] The ECtHR also ruled that the Russian state had not demonstrated that the force used by the federal service officers was absolutely necessary (as the Russian authorities did not provide evidence that any unlawful violence committed by terrorists was threatened or likely, or that lethal force was used in an attempt to effect a lawful arrest of any person) and therefore strictly proportionate to the achievement of one of the aims set out in paragraph 2 of Article 2.[152] Furthermore, the Court held that the authorities had neither proved nor considered at all comprehensively the limits and constraints on the use of indiscriminate weapons within a populated area (or how to minimise the risk of deaths) and their disproportion to the purpose of

---

[146] Ibid., §§280–284.
[147] Case no 23445/03, *Esmukhambetov and Others* v. *Russia* [29 March 2011] ECtHR.
[148] Ibid., §133.
[149] Ibid., §135.
[150] Ibid., §3.
[151] Ibid., §§114–130.
[152] Ibid., §141.

effecting the lawful arrest of a person with respect to the risk of loss of lives.[153] More generally, the Court noted the insurmountable hindrances it faced as a result of the state's non-cooperation.[154] The ECtHR therefore found that the Russian state had failed in its obligation to protect the right to life of the applicants.[155]

More recently, the ECtHR rendered one of its most famous judgments on the legality of Russian counterterrorism operations. The case of *Tagayeva and Others* v. *Russia*[156] was delivered under Article 46 and championed by EHRAC and Memorial, who represented 300 of the applicants (out of a total of 409). The case concerned the 2004 Beslan school siege, in which 331 victims (including 186 children) were killed in a terrorist attack committed by Chechen separatists, who held 1,128 people (886 children) hostage in the school for three days. Based on several reports on counterterrorism and on medical forensic expertise they had requested,[157] EHRAC and Memorial argued that the response of the Russian authorities to the Chechen terrorist attack (an assault by Russian security forces that included the use of tanks and flamethrowers) failed seriously and contributed to casualties amongst the hostages.[158] Likewise, the ECtHR found that the assault by the Russian security forces was excessive and amounted to a violation of the right to life.[159]

First, the ECtHR held that the authorities failed to take preventive security measures in the light of prior knowledge of a planned attack in the area at an educational institution,[160] and in breach of Russia's positive obligation to protect the right to life. Second, the ECtHR ruled that the investigation into the Beslan siege failed to establish whether the use of force by the state authorities was justified.[161] In particular, the investigation did not examine how the victims had died, and the Russian authorities failed to properly collect and record evidence before the site was irreparably altered by large machinery and the lifting of the security cordon. Third, the Court also found serious defects in the planning and

---

[153] Ibid., §146.
[154] Ibid., §142.
[155] Ibid., §§150–151.
[156] Case no 26562/07 and 6 other applications, *Tagayeva and Others* v. *Russia* [13 April 2017] ECtHR.
[157] Ibid., §§436–456.
[158] Ibid., §§478–479.
[159] Ibid., §§481–493.
[160] Ibid., §§478–493.
[161] Ibid., §§494–593.

control of the security operation. The absence of formal leadership resulted in significant flaws in in the decision-making process, and impacted the ability of the authorities to coordinate the medical, rescue and firefighting response.[162] The ECtHR also concluded that the security task forces used disproportionately powerful and indiscriminate weapons (including tank cannon, grenade launchers and flamethrowers), which led to hundreds of fatalities and injuries.[163] Fourth and more generally, the ECtHR ruled that Russia failed to establish a 'framework of a system of adequate and effective safeguards against arbitrariness and abuse of force' that created a gap in the regulation of life-threatening situations.[164] The Court held that the Russian government had not brought a 'satisfactory and convincing explanation' that the lethal force used had been no more than absolutely necessary', and such a massive use of explosive and indiscriminate weapons could not be considered as absolutely necessary.[165]

In this perspective, the ECtHR ordered Russia to take steps to implement relevant legal and operational standards, and to deter new violations of the right to life. Russia was asked to collect information and establish the truth; to acknowledge publicly and condemn violations of the right to life in the course of security operations; to improve dissemination of information and training for police; to ensure strict compliance on the part of military and security staff with the relevant international legal standards (as also stated in the case of *Abakarova* v. *Russia*, litigated by EHRAC and concerning the killing of Chechen civilians killed during the attack on a Chechen village in 2000);[166] to establish an appropriate legal framework (which reflects international standards) to prevent similar future breaches; and to investigate the attack (with a view to ensuring proper public scrutiny and allowing the victims access to the key documents) and assess the use of indiscriminate weapons by the state.[167]

3.1.2.4 Changes to the Judiciary

Some NGOs funded by private foundations have been able to obtain landmark judgments that order significant changes to national judiciary

---

[162] Ibid., §§540–574.
[163] Ibid., §§575–611.
[164] Ibid., §599.
[165] Ibid., §§600–610.
[166] Case no 16664/07, *Abakarova* v. *Russia* [15 October 2015] ECtHR.
[167] Ibid., §§640–641.

powers and judicial structures, such as the organisation of judicial institutions, the election of judges and the implementation or reform of new domestic remedies. In this field, and as pointed out above, litigation thus appears to be an efficient way of influencing the national judiciary structures that constitute a traditional competence exerted by national states.

Judicial Institutions and the Election of Judges The field of dismissal of judges is a recent litigation area in which the ECtHR has delivered a jurisprudence that progressively limits the power of national states to dismiss their judges. In this regard, EHRAC took the landmark case of *Volkov* v. *Ukraine* (in which it was also decided to give priority to the application in accordance with Rules 41 and 46 of the Rules of Court)[168] to the ECtHR in order to challenge the applicant's dismissal from the post of judge of the Ukrainian Supreme Court. In particular, EHRAC alleged under Article 6 ECHR that (i) the case had not been considered by an 'independent and impartial tribunal', on account of the composition of the Higher Administrative Court and the High Council of Justice (HCJ), the subordination of its members to other state bodies and the personal bias of some of its members in the applicant's case; (ii) the proceedings before the HCJ had been unfair and had not provided significant procedural safeguards, including limitation periods for disciplinary penalties; (iii) Parliament had reached a decision on the applicant's dismissal at a plenary meeting without any proper examination of the case and by abusing the electronic voting system; (iv) the case had not been heard by a 'tribunal established by law'; (v) the decisions in the case had been made without a proper assessment of the evidence, and important arguments raised by the defence had not been properly addressed; (vi) the lack of sufficient competence on the part of the Higher Administrative Court to review the acts adopted by the HCJ had badly affected his 'right to a court'; and (vii) the principle of equality of arms had been violated.[169] In addition, EHRAC submitted that this case showed fundamental systemic problems in the Ukrainian legal system arising from the state's failure to respect the principle of the separation of powers. In this way, EHRAC argued that the issues reflected the necessity of amending the relevant area of domestic legislation. In particular, and according to EHRAC, amendments had to be introduced to the

---

[168] Case no 21722/11, *Oleksandr Volkov* v. *Ukraine* [9 January 2013], ECtHR.
[169] Ibid., §§28–29 and 83.

Constitution and the HCJ Act 1998 concerning the principles of composition of the HCJ and the procedures for the appointment and dismissal of judges, and to the Code of Administrative Justice with regard to the jurisdiction and powers of the HAC.[170]

In response, the ECtHR established a number of criteria for examining whether the HCJ as a disciplinary body of judges complied with the requirements of independence and impartiality. First, the Court underlined the need for substantial representation of judges within such a body by considering that where at least half of the membership of a tribunal was composed of judges, including the chairperson with a casting vote, this would be a strong indicator of impartiality.[171] Second, with a view to reducing the influence of political organs on the composition of the disciplinary body, it was necessary to evaluate the manner in which judges were appointed to that body, having regard to the authorities that delegated them and the role played by the judicial community in that process.[172] Third, the ECtHR decided to establish whether the members of the disciplinary body worked on a full-time basis or continued to work and receive a wage independently; given that the latter situation would thus involve their material, hierarchical and administrative dependence on their primary employers, this would thwart their independence and impartiality.[173] Fourth, the ECtHR paid particular attention to the participation of representatives of the prosecution authorities in the composition of the disciplinary body for judges by considering that the inclusion of the Prosecutor General ex officio and the other members delegated by the prosecution authorities raised concerns as to the impartiality of the disciplinary body of judges in view of the functional role of prosecutors in domestic judicial proceedings.[174] Fifth, where the members who play a role in the preliminary inquiry in a disciplinary case cannot participate in the determination of the same case by the disciplinary body, such a duplication of functions could cast doubt on the impartiality of those members.[175]

With regard to those criteria that were violated, for the very first time the ECtHR ordered a government to ensure a judge's reinstatement.[176]

---

[170] Ibid., §196.
[171] Ibid., §109.
[172] Ibid., §112.
[173] Ibid., §113.
[174] Ibid., §114.
[175] Ibid., §115.
[176] Ibid., §§207 and 208.

The ECtHR also found systemic issues with judicial independence, notably concerning the HCJ,[177] and ordered legislative reform related to judicial discipline.[178] Furthermore, the intervention by the legislative body, the Ukrainian parliament, did not remove the structural defects of a lack of 'independence and impartiality' but rather increased the politicisation of the procedure and contributed to its inconsistency with the principle of the separation of powers.[179] In this regard, the judgment emphasised the unacceptability of politicians having control over the appointment and dismissal of judges (through the HCJ),[180] which required amendments to the Ukrainian Constitution and legislative reform involving the restructuring of the institutional basis of the Ukrainian judicial system.[181] In this perspective, the Law of 12 February 2015 'On ensuring the right to fair trial' amended the Law 'On the High Council of Justice' by providing for a mechanism of public appointment of HCJ members. A new legislation entitled 'On Amending the Constitution of Ukraine Regarding the Judiciary' was also passed on 2 June 2016 with the aim of improving the independence and impartiality of the Ukrainian judicial system and its accountability, and of guaranteeing protection of judges from violations and arbitrary actions when taking disciplinary measures. The judicial reform resulted in structural simplification of the Ukrainian court system, implementing a three-tier judicial system, with a reformed Supreme Court as the highest level of jurisdiction. The reform strengthens the powers and the institutional capacity of the HCJ to cope with issues of judicial discipline and careers of judges.[182] This legislation held in particular that the majority of the HCJ shall be judges elected by their peers.[183] Furthermore, a new law was passed on 21 December 2016 to remove the political component from the judicial branch and to exclude Parliament from the mechanisms of the

---

[177] Ibid., §117.
[178] Ibid., §200.
[179] Ibid., §118.
[180] Ibid., §§120–122.
[181] Ibid., §200.
[182] 1318th Meeting (June 2018) (DH) – Action plan (07/03/2018) – Communication from Ukraine Concerning the Cases of Oleksandr Volkov and Salov v. Ukraine (Applications No. 21722/11, 65518/01) DH-DD(2018)275 19/03/2018, p. 3.
[183] Action Report (19/10/2016) – Communication from Ukraine Concerning the Case of Oleksandr Volkov against Ukraine (Application No. 21772/11) 1273rd Meeting (6–8 December 2016) (DH) – DH-DD(2016)1162 21/10/2016, pp. 3–4.

appointment and dismissal of judges.¹⁸⁴ In addition, in the Action Plan of 7 March 2018, the Ukrainian authorities informed the CM that prosecutors are no longer engaged in proceedings concerning the disciplinary liability and careers of judges.¹⁸⁵ The new legislation thus seems to be in adequacy with the ECtHR ruling and with a CoE project aimed at 'Strengthening the system of judicial accountability in Ukraine'. The measures outlined in the Volkov judgment also provide a roadmap for national representatives working in the field of justice reform in Armenia, Georgia and Moldova, under the CoE's guidance.¹⁸⁶

The Volkov case paved the way for successful litigation on the election of judges. In this regard and following the Volkov judgment, the case of *Kulykov and Others* v. *Ukraine* was also litigated by EHRAC to obtain a judgment of the unlawfulness of the dismissal of eighteen Ukrainian judges.¹⁸⁷ All eighteen of the applicants were domestic court judges who were dismissed between 2008 and 2013 because of proceedings brought against them for 'breach of oath', as established by the HCJ. In this regard, the ECtHR found a violation of the right to a fair trial (Article 6 §1) concerning the state's breach of the principles of independence and impartiality as underlined by EHRAC.¹⁸⁸ In finding a violation of the right to respect for private life (Article 8), the Court was in line with its findings in the Volkov judgment and with EHRAC's allegations.¹⁸⁹ As a result, it held that the applicants' dismissal constituted an interference with their private life and that such interference does not comply with the requirements of 'quality of law' and was thus unlawful.¹⁹⁰ The ECtHR required the government to secure the applicants' reinstatement.¹⁹¹

---

¹⁸⁴ 1280th Meeting (7–9 March 2017) (DH) – Communication from the Authorities (20/01/2017) in the Case of Oleksandr Volkov and Salov Group against Ukraine (Application No. 8794/04), DH DD(2017)81 23/01/2017, p. 3.
¹⁸⁵ 1318th Meeting (June 2018) (DH) – Action Plan (07/03/2018) – Communication from Ukraine Concerning the Cases of Oleksandr Volkov and Salov against Ukraine (Applications No. 21722/11, 65518/01) DH-DD(2018)275 19/03/2018.
¹⁸⁶ 1280th meeting (7–9 March 2017) (DH) – Communication from the Authorities (20/01/2017) in the case of Oleksandr Volkov and Salov Group against Ukraine (Application No. 8794/04), DH DD(2017)81 23/01/2017, p. 3.
¹⁸⁷ Case nos 5114/09 and 17 others, *Kulykov and Others* v. *Ukraine* [19 January 2013] ECtHR.
¹⁸⁸ Ibid., §135.
¹⁸⁹ Ibid., §138.
¹⁹⁰ Ibid.
¹⁹¹ Ibid., §148.

Changes to the Judicial Structure: Introduction and Implementation of Effective Domestic Remedies and Official Investigation Some evolving jurisprudence that progressively limits states' discretion has also been obtained by private foundations and NGOs concerning the introduction and implementation of effective domestic remedies and the conduct of official investigations.

For instance, the lack of effective domestic remedies in the Czech Republic with regard to Article 5 ECHR was condemned by the ECtHR in the case of *Cervenka v. Czech Republic*.[192] In this case, which concerned the applicant's placement in a social care home without sufficient guarantees against arbitrariness, third party interventions were made by the Centre for Disability Law and Policy (CDLP),[193] funded by Atlantic Philanthropies, which is led by Chuck Feeney, who has devoted USD 8 billion of his wealth (stemming from duty-free shops) to 'philanthropy'.[194] In its third party submission, the CDLP alleged that it would be fully in adequacy with ECtHR case law and in compliance with the UN Convention on the Rights of Persons with Disabilities if the Court stated that deprivation of legal capacity and involuntary institutionalisation had occurred because the Czech state had failed to make reasonable accommodation for persons with disabilities.[195] The CDLP alleged that such a failure constituted a discriminatory interference with the rights guaranteed by Articles 5 and 8 in addition to a lack of effective remedy available for disabled persons in this area.[196] The ECtHR was sensitive to the legal arguments raised by the CDLP in considering that the applicant was not offered an effective domestic remedy and that the deprivation of the applicant's liberty was therefore not justified by Article 5 §1[197] and §4.[198] As a remedy, the Czech authorities adopted an amendment to the Act on Social Services and to the Act on Special Court Proceedings that came into force on 1 August 2016. The amendment laid down conditions under which a guardian of a person restricted in her legal capacity can resort to the assignment of the individual in a social care institution. The conditions are derived from ECtHR case law,[199] and they include the

---

[192] Case no 62507/12, *Cervenka v. Czech Republic* [13 October 2016] ECtHR.
[193] See www.nuigalway.ie/centre-disability-law-policy/.
[194] See www.atlanticphilanthropies.org/our-story.
[195] Case no 62507/12, *Cervenka v. Czech Republic* [13 October 2016] ECtHR, §101.
[196] Ibid.
[197] Ibid., §§102–124.
[198] Ibid., §§131–136.
[199] See Case no 36760/06, *Stanev v. Bulgaria* [17 January 2012] ECtHR.

presence of a mental illness, grave risk to the life or health of the person concerned and/or persons in her surroundings, and the principles of necessity and subsidiarity. Furthermore, and in addition to the stricter conditions for the placement of a person in a social care institution, the new legislation provides for judicial review of the placement.[200]

Lastly, APADOR-CH intervened as third party, along with the European arm of the International Lesbian, Gay, Bisexual, Trans and Intersex Association (ILGA-Europe) and the AIRE Centre, in the case of *M. C. and A. C. v. Romania*,[201] claiming lack of effective remedy after two members of a gay parade in Bucharest were brutalised by civilians. The ECtHR condemned the failure of the Romanian authorities to investigate the potential criminally homophobic grounds of the attack, which took place after the applicants had left a police-protected LGBTI rally, and found violation of Article 3 in conjunction with Article 14.[202] In response to the CM, the Romanian Ministry of Justice communicated that the application ECRIS allows the collection of statistical data related to criminal cases in which the court held the commission of the offence to be motivated by hate, as regulated by Article 77 of the New Romanian Criminal Code (the NRCC). The Romanian authorities were also obliged to improve access to justice for victims of hate crimes and to train in a more efficient way judges and professionals working for the judiciary.[203]

Regarding legal representation, the leading case in this matter is *Valentin Câmpeanu v. Romania*,[204] in which the Centre for Legal Resources (created in 1998 and financed by the OSF) was instructed.[205] The case concerned the failure of the authorities to protect the right to life of a young man of Roma origin, orphaned, HIV-positive and diagnosed with profound intellectual disability. Third party comments were

---

[200] Communication from the Czech Republic Concerning the Case of Cervenka v. Czech Republic (Application No. 62507/12) to the CM of the CoE, 1340th Meeting (March 2019) (DH), Action Report, 29 January 2019, available at https://search.coe.int/cm/Pages/result_details.aspx?ObjectId=090000168092099b, p. 2.

[201] Case no 12060/12, *M. C. and A. C. v. Romania* [12 April 2016] ECtHR, cited above.

[202] Ibid., §§105–126.

[203] Communication from Romania Concerning the Case of M. C. and A. C. v. Romania (Application No. 12060/12), 1324th Meeting (September 2018) (DH-DD(2018)808), Revised Action Plan, 24 August 2018, available at https://search.coe.int/cm/Pages/result_details.aspx?ObjectId=09000016808d2981.

[204] Case no 47848/08, *Centre for Legal Resources on Behalf of Valentin Câmpeanu v. Romania* [17 July 2014] ECtHR.

[205] Centre for Legal Resources, *Annual Report 2017. Justice. Dignity. Equality*, p. 3, available at www.crj.ro/wp-content/uploads/2018/10/CLR-Annual-report-2017.pdf.

made by HRW, the Mental Disability Advocacy Center and the BHC, arguing that a locus standi before courts has to be given to NGOs because of the factual or legal inability of individuals with intellectual disabilities to have access to justice and the state's impunity for violations of their rights.[206] The ECtHR sitting in Grand Chamber ruled that Romanian authorities had breached Article 2 ECHR in relation to severe shortcomings in the social and medical care afforded to the applicant before his death at a psychiatric hospital. In particular, the ECtHR noted that the failure of the authorities to appoint a legal guardian or other representative resulted in the absence of representation for Mr Câmpeanu's protection and of representations on his behalf to the national courts or the ECtHR.[207] In the exceptional circumstances that prompted it to allow the CLR to complain on behalf of Mr Câmpeanu,[208] the ECtHR also found a violation of Article 13 taken in conjunction with Article 2 on account of the state's failure to secure and implement an appropriate legal framework that would have enabled complaints related to Mr Câmpeanu's allegations to have been examined by an independent authority.[209] Considering the existence of a wider problem calling for general measures for the execution of its judgment, the ECtHR recommended under Article 46 that Romania adopt the general measures necessary to ensure that mentally disabled persons are allowed independent representation, enabling them to have Convention complaints relating to their health and treatment examined before a court or other independent body.[210] In their response to the CM, the Romanian authorities undertook to amend the Mental Health Act and to regulate its implementation, and to establish a new investigation mechanism, an Ethics Council, a Commission for the analysis of deaths, a petitioning mechanism responsible for monitoring the respect of patient rights and a Council for Monitoring the implementation of the UN Convention on the Rights of Persons with Disabilities.[211]

---

[206] Case no 47848/08, *Centre for Legal Resources on Behalf of Valentin Câmpeanu v. Romania*, note 420, §§94–95.
[207] Ibid., §111.
[208] Ibid., §112.
[209] Ibid., §§150–153.
[210] Ibid., §161.
[211] Communication from Romania Concerning the Case of Centre for Legal Resources on Behalf of Valentin Câmpeanu against Romania, Revised Action Plan (02/01/2017), 1280th Meeting (7–9 March 2017) DH-DD(2017)30-rev.

3.1.2.5 States as 'Watching States'

NGOs also litigate cases related to surveillance exerted by national states that has been recently challenged by the ECtHR. One of the most well-known judgments is the Roman Zakharov case,[212] in which Russia was considered to be a 'watching state' by EHRAC and Memorial, who instructed this case on surveillance of mobile phones by the Russian authorities. In a groundbreaking Grand Chamber judgment, the ECtHR held that Russian legislation on surveillance of mobile telephones failed to provide 'adequate and effective guarantees against arbitrariness and the risk of abuse'.[213] The judgment was delivered under Article 46 and is therefore under the closed supervision of the CM along with the case of Alexei Navalnyy and Peter Ofitserova (for 'Kirovlesu').[214]

3.1.2.6 Political Violence Committed by National States and Violation of the Right to Demonstrate for Political Opponents and LGBT People

In connection with the issue of 'watching states', NGOs have litigated cases on political violence committed by national states (especially Russia) in relation to the right to demonstrate, and particularly in the context of the Russian presidential election.

In a groundbreaking judgment instructed by EHRAC and Memorial, the ECtHR ruled in *Frumkin* v. *Russia* that the Russian authorities had failed in their obligation to protect freedom of assembly by not taking adequate measures to ensure that the Bolotnaya Square protest of 6 May 2012 (against what was perceived by some political opponents such as Alexei Navalnyy as 'rigged presidential elections') was conducted peacefully.[215] Specifically, the Court found that, by failing to communicate with the leaders of the rally, the authorities were unable to prevent disorder and to guarantee the safety of all citizens involved. For the first time, the responsibility of state authorities was established for having failed to preserve the security and safety of demonstrators.

---

[212] Case no 47143/06, *Roman Zakharov* v. *Russia*, ECtHR, 4 December 2015.
[213] See http://ehrac.org.uk/news/journalist-wins-decision-establishing-arbitrary-and-abusive-secret-mobile-phone-surveillance-in-russia/.
[214] Case nos 46632/13 and 28671/14, *Alexei Navalnyy and Peter Ofitserova* v. *Russia*, ECtHR, 23 February 2016.
[215] Case no 74568/12, *Frumkin* v. *Russia* [5 January 2016] ECtHR.

The Frumkin judgment was followed by the case of *Akimenkov v. Russia*,²¹⁶ championed by IPC, which alleged that the applicant had been prosecuted for participation in mass disorder at Bolotnaya Square and that his arrest and pre-trial detention had not been based on relevant and sufficient reasons.²¹⁷ The ECtHR proved the IPC right in condemning Russia for breach of Article 5 §3 as the detention of the applicant was no longer justified after his pre-trial detention, which covered the specific offence imputed to the applicant, namely shouting political slogans and throwing a flagpole that hit a police officer but caused no lasting harm.²¹⁸

In the further case of *Navalnyy v. Russia* litigated by IPC and Article 19,²¹⁹ both NGOs complained that the arrest of the applicant, a political opponent, at public events on seven occasions had violated his right to freedom of peaceful assembly and right to liberty, and alleged that his arrest, detention and the administrative charges brought against him had pursued the aim of undermining his right to freedom of assembly for political reasons. The ECtHR agreed with the NGOs and held in a judgment delivered under Article 46 that there had been breaches of Article 11 on account of all seven episodes complained of; breaches of Article 5 §1 on account of the applicant's arrest on seven occasions and his pre-trial detention on two occasions; and breaches of Article 6 §1 as regards six sets of administrative proceedings. In particular, the ECtHR considered under Article 46 that

> Russia should take appropriate legislative and/or other general measures to secure in its domestic legal order a mechanism requiring the competent authorities to have due regard to the fundamental character of the freedom of peaceful assembly and show appropriate tolerance towards unauthorised but peaceful gatherings causing only a certain disruption to ordinary life not going beyond a level of minor disturbance.²²⁰

The ECtHR stated that prevention of similar breaches in the future should be addressed in the appropriate legal framework, in particular ensuring that the national legal instruments pertaining to the restrictions and the modalities of the exercise of the right to freedom of assembly do

---

[216] Case no 2613/13 50041/14, *Akimenkov v. Russia* [6 February 2018] ECtHR.
[217] Ibid., §3.
[218] Ibid., §§102–106.
[219] Case no 29580/12, *Navalnyy v. Russia* [15 November 2018] ECtHR.
[220] Ibid., §186.

not represent a hidden obstacle to the freedom of peaceful assembly protected by Article 11.[221]

Following the cases of *Genderdoc-M* v. *Moldova*[222] (instructed by Genderdoc-M, which is mainly funded by the Soros Foundation-Moldova, the OSF, the Sigrid Rausing Trust and the American Bar Association,[223] and with the third party intervention of the ICJ) and *Alekseyev* v. *Russia*,[224] monitored by the ILGA and Coming Out and concerning repeated bans on demonstrations promoting tolerance and respect for the human rights of LGBT persons that were condemned by the ECtHR under Articles 11 (right to peaceful assembly), 13 and 14, the ECtHR delivered a recent judgment under Article 46 in *Bayev* v. *Russia*.[225] Third party interventions were made by the Family and Demography Foundation (which alleged that protection of children would be incomplete without a ban on 'homosexual propaganda' among children)[226] and Interights. They were joined by ILGA-Europe, Coming Out and the Russian Lesbian, Gay, Bisexual and Transgender (LGBT) Network, which claimed a rise in discrimination and violence against LGBT people in Russia, in hate crimes, in bullying and harassment of LGBT children, and in pressure on same-sex couples and the children they are raising and on LGBT advocacy organisations.[227] The ECtHR, which was sensitive to the arguments raised by the NGOs, found violations of the right to freedom of expression (Article 10) and discrimination (Article 14) on account of fines imposed on the applicants for promoting homosexuality among minors through banners in violation of the regional laws prohibiting such 'propaganda', adopted in several regions since 2006, and followed in 2013 by a nationwide law to similar effect.[228] In response, an action plan was submitted to the CM by Russia that passed a new Code of Administrative Offences in 2015 to comply with international standards and ECtHR case law. In particular the Code allows organisers and

---

[221] Ibid., §186.
[222] Case no 9106/06, *Genderdoc-M* v. *Moldova* [12 June 2012] ECtHR.
[223] Genderdoc-M (2015) *Five Years Activity Report (2010–2014)*, available at www.gdm.md/files/untitled%20folder/Five%20years%20report%20GDM%202010_2014%20eng.pdf, p. 45.
[224] Case nos 4916/07, 25924/08 and 14599/09, *Alekseyev* v. *Russia* [21 October 2010] ECtHR.
[225] Case no 67667/090, *Bayev* v. *Russia* [20 June 2017] ECtHR.
[226] Ibid., §58.
[227] Ibid., §§59–60.
[228] Ibid., §§61–84 and 87–92.

participants of gay events to take their cases to court under new improved procedures for protection of their violated or challenged rights, freedom and legitimate interests.[229]

3.1.2.7 The Right to a Healthy Environment

Violations by member states of the right to a healthy environment constitute another realm litigated by private foundations and NGOs. The case of *Fadeyeva* v. *Russia* is one of the leading judgments delivered by the ECtHR in this field.[230] The case was brought by EHRAC and Memorial, which alleged that the operation of a steel plant in close proximity to the applicant's home was a risk to her health and well-being owing to the pollution generated and that it breached Article 8 ECHR.[231] The ECtHR held that in order to fall within the scope of Article 8, complaints relating to environmental nuisances have to show, first, that they interfere with the applicant's private sphere, and, second, that they attain a certain level of severity.[232] In this case, the very strong combination of indirect evidence and presumptions made it possible to conclude that the applicant's health had deteriorated as a result of her prolonged exposure to the industrial emissions from the steel plant and that it had adversely affected her quality of life at home.[233] In addition, the Court ruled that the Russian authorities were in a position to assess the pollution hazards and to take adequate measures to prevent or reduce them, and that such a position raised an issue of the state's positive obligation under Article 8.[234] The Court concluded that, despite the wide margin of appreciation left to the state, Russia had failed to strike a fair balance between the interests of the community and the applicant's effective enjoyment of her right to respect for her home and her private life under Article 8, since the state had both failed to resettle the applicant and to regulate private industry.[235]

---

[229] Action plan (22/10/2018) 331st Meeting (December2018) (DH) Item Reference: A Communication from the Russian Federation Concerning the Cases of Alekseyev and Bayev and Others against Russian Federation.
[230] Case no 55723/00, *Fadeyeva* v. *Russia* [9 June 2005] ECtHR.
[231] Ibid., §§64–65 and 71–73.
[232] Ibid., §§68–70.
[233] Ibid., §§79–88.
[234] Ibid., §§89–93.
[235] Ibid., §§116–134.

The Fadeyeva case paved the way for successful litigation in this area, including the cases of *Tatar v. Romania*,[236] which was litigated by APADOR, and *Jugheli and Others v. Georgia*,[237] which was taken by both the Georgian Young Lawyers Association and EHRAC. In the latter case, the NGOs complained that a thermal power plant in close proximity to the applicants' homes had endangered their health and well-being (because of the air pollution as well as the noise and electromagnetic pollution emanating from the thermal power plant) in breach of Article 8.[238] The ECtHR agreed with such claims and condemned Georgia for not succeeding in striking a fair balance between the interests of the community in having an operational thermal power plant and the applicants' effective enjoyment of their right to respect for their home and private life, owing to the defective regulatory framework at the material time and the passive attitude adopted by the government in the face of the air pollution emanating from the thermal power plant.[239] As a remedy, Georgia introduced in June 2017 an amendment to the Law on Environmental Protection, which envisages the necessity of an environmental assessment procedure: 'an environmental impact assessment shall be carried out before the issuance of environmental impact permits in order to identify and examine potential impacts on the environment in accordance with the Environmental Assessment Code'.[240] Furthermore, on 24 April 2018, the Georgian Ministry of Environment and Agriculture set up mobile automatic stations for monitoring atmospheric air quality.[241] Lastly, on 27 July 2018, a Green Economy Development Strategy defined two priorities: to neutralise the results of previous careless environmental management (including improving the quality of atmospheric air) and to preserve existing natural resources.[242]

---

[236] Case no 67021/01, *Tatar v. Romania* [27 January 2009] ECtHR.
[237] Case no 38342/05, *Jugheli and Others v. Georgia* [13 July 2017] ECtHR.
[238] Ibid., §§3–4 and 56–59.
[239] Ibid., §§73–78.
[240] Communication from Georgia Concerning the Case of Jugheli and Others v. Georgia (Application No. 38342/05), 1324th Meeting (September 2018) (DH) – Action Plan (03/08/2018), DH-DD(2018)769, 8 August 2018, available at https://search.coe.int/cm/Pages/result_details.aspx?ObjectId=09000016808cc8a0.
[241] Ibid.
[242] Ibid.

3.1.3 Other Landmark Judgments

Other landmark judgments litigated by private foundations are judgments rendered by the Grand Chamber of the Strasbourg Court and the CJEU in the fields of discrimination and of penal, prison, immigration and detention policies.

3.1.3.1 Discrimination

Discrimination and the defence of minorities (ethnic, sexual and others) have constituted one of the main litigation domains for the OSJI and for NGOs financed by private foundations. Through their litigation efforts, NGOs and private foundations have obtained an enlargement of the scope covered by discrimination law to new groups of people (defined by their racial, religious, gender, sexual, national, social or political characteristics), new situations (such as indirect discrimination) and new fields (including police discrimination and discrimination in terms of economics, education, family, sexuality, religion, private life and politics).

Police Discrimination Police discrimination against minorities has been particularly litigated by private foundations and NGOs. One of the most famous cases is the judgment of *Nachova v. Bulgaria*.[243] It was brought by the OSJI, the European Roma Rights Centre and Interights as third party,[244] and concerned police discrimination against two unarmed Roma conscripts who were shot by police in Bulgaria. The European Roma Rights Centre pointed out in its third intervention that while 'high levels of racially motivated violence and repeated calls on the part of international bodies, such as the UN Committee against Torture, for the establishment of "an effective, reliable and independent complaint system" and for adequate investigation of police abuse, the authorities had failed to act'.[245] In parallel, Interights criticised the ECtHR's 'beyond reasonable doubt' standard as erecting insurmountable hindrances to establishing discrimination and stressed that 'international practice supported the view that in discrimination cases the burden of proof should

---

[243] Case no 43577/98 and 43579/98, *Nachova v. Bulgaria* [6 July 2005] ECtHR.
[244] Ibid., §8.
[245] Ibid., §139.

shift to the respondent upon the claimant establishing a prima facie case'.[246] For its part, the OSJI argued the procedural obligation of states, in international and comparative law, to investigate racial discrimination and violence as necessary to ensure effective protection of substantive rights. In addition, in accordance with the prevailing European and international practice, racial motivation was an aggravating circumstance in criminal law and, as a result, subject to investigation. According to the OSJI, states consequently had a duty to investigate acts of racial violence.[247] The Grand Chamber of the Court followed the OSJI's third party intervention by finding that the Bulgarian authorities had failed in their duty under Article 14 of the Convention taken in conjunction with Article 2 to take all possible steps to investigate whether or not discrimination may have played a role in the events. The ECtHR ruled therefore and for the first time that there had been a violation of Article 14 (prohibition of discrimination) taken in conjunction with Article 2 in its procedural aspect.[248]

Economic Discrimination Private foundations have applied the concept of discrimination to the economic field and pushed the idea of economic discrimination through intense litigation. The CJEU was sensitive to such a concept of economic discrimination in the case of *Nikolova v. Romanian CEZ Electricity*.[249] The OSJI represented the applicant in this landmark judgment, which is the very first in which the CJEU had to decide on discrimination against a district of residents, and the most important ruling to date dealing with the EU's Race Equality Directive. The CJEU's powerful interpretation of the scope of the Directive in the Nikolova case significantly enhances the protection available to racial or ethnic minorities under EU law. In its submissions to the CJEU, the OSJI was in favour of an inclusive and effective interpretation of the EU Racial Equality Directive 2000/43 and the EU Fundamental Rights Charter. According to the OSJI, the concept of 'discrimination based on racial or ethnic origin' in EU race equality law should be interpreted to include discrimination grounded on race, colour, descent, national or ethnic origin, and membership of a national minority, and forbids discrimination based on Roma origin. A practice

---

[246] Ibid., §§140–141.
[247] Ibid., §143.
[248] Ibid., §168.
[249] Case C-83/14, *Nikolova v. Romanian CEZ Electricity* [16 July 2015] CJEU.

based on the racial or ethnic origin of persons living in a specific district is forbidden even when some of the people living in the district are not from the minority group. In the view of the OSJI, any individual affected by such a practice can claim to be a victim of discrimination on the basis of racial or ethnic origin. The threshold for discrimination should target any measure which results in less favourable treatment or in a disadvantage that is capable of amounting to discrimination. It is not necessary for the applicant to show that there was particularly serious or demonstrably significant disadvantage. The OSJI argued that 'direct discrimination' refers to the practice of explicitly focusing on actual or perceived 'Roma districts', and so the electricity company had the burden of proving that their choice to place electricity meters out of the reach of consumers was not 'based on' the consumers' Roma racial or ethnic origin. According to the OSJI, even though the company's choice of district was grounded exclusively on considerations other than racial or ethnic origin, the practice inevitably promotes racist assumptions against Roma people in a way that violates the founding principles of the EU and thus is not reasonably and objectively justified. In the OSJI's view, any legitimate concerns about theft by consumers should be dealt with on a case-by-case basis, in a reasonable and proportionate way, rather than by stigmatising entire Roma communities.[250]

The CJEU was sensitive to the OSJI's view and held that the EU Race Equality Directive prohibition on discrimination on the basis of race or ethnic origin also applies to anyone who suffers less favourable treatment or a particular disadvantage caused by a discriminatory measure. The CJEU stated that CEZ Electricity's practice constituted indirect discrimination, as it put Roma people at a particular disadvantage compared to people living in districts where the meters are at a normal height. Indirect discrimination occurs if actions cannot be properly justified on the ground of the legitimate aims of preventing and combatting fraud and abuse and ensuring the security and quality of the energy network.[251] Following the CJEU judgment, CEZ adopted a plan to pilot alternative metering for affected Roma communities and began replacing meters in Dupnitsa and Ihtiman, installing accessible 'smart meters' in more than 900 households. In two other Roma communities, in Sofia and Byala Slatina, CEZ also planned to pilot secure boxes accessible only to customers, each with twenty-five smart meters inside. More broadly, CEZ

---

[250] See www.opensocietyfoundations.org/litigation/nikolova-v-cez-electricity.
[251] *Nikolova v. Romanian CEZ Electricity*; cited above, §§46–128.

planned to relocate the remaining meters with affected Roma communities.

Educational Segregation and Discrimination Education constitutes another realm in which NGOs and private foundations have tried to push the idea of discrimination. In particular, several cases on educational segregation were taken by the OSJI as counsel together with the European Roma Rights Centre with a view to expanding ECtHR case law on discrimination to cover indirect discrimination. The cases of *Horváth and Kiss* v. *Hungary*,[252] and *Orsus and Others* v. *Croatia*,[253] both litigated by the OSJI and the European Roma Rights Centre, of *Sampanis and Others* v. *Greece*,[254] and *Lavida and Others* v. *Greece*,[255] both championed by the Greek Helsinki Monitor, and of *D. H.* v. *Czech Republic*,[256] in which third party comments were submitted by the International Step by Step Association (financed by the OSF, the Jacobs Foundation and the Bernard Van Leer Foundation),[257] the Roma Education Fund (created and financed by the OSF and the World Bank),[258] Interights and HRW, Minority Rights Group International (founded and financed by the Ford Foundation),[259] the European Network Against Racism (financed by amongst others the OSF, the Sigrid Rausing Trust and the Joseph Rowntree Charitable Trust), and the International Federation for Human Rights, all concerned the educational segregation of Roma children who were disproportionately sent to 'special schools' for children with minor mental disabilities and given a sub-standard education, according to the OSJI. The Grand Chamber of the Strasbourg Court found that such segregation was not justified and constituted an indirect discrimination against the school children in the provision of education, a breach of Article 14 and Article 2 of Protocol No. 1 (the right to education). The ECtHR held that disproportionate assignment of Roma children to

---

[252] Case no 11146/11, *Horváth and Kiss* v. *Hungary* [29 January 2013] ECtHR.
[253] Case no 15766/03, *Orsus and Others* v. *Croatia* [16 March 2010] ECtHR. Third party comments were also submitted by Interights and Greek Helsinki Monitor.
[254] Case no 32526/05, *Sampanis and Others* v. *Greece* [5 June 2008] ECtHR.
[255] Case no 7973/10, *Lavida and Others* v. *Greece* [30 May 2013] ECtHR.
[256] Case no 57325/00, *D. H.* v. *Czech Republic* [13 November 2007] ECtHR.
[257] ISSA, *Annual Report 2017*, available at www.issa.nl/sites/default/files/u327/ISSA%20Annual%20Report%202017%20-%20LR.pdf, p. 38.
[258] Roma Education Fund, *2017 Annual Report*, available at www.romaeducationfund.org/sites/default/files/publications/ref_2017_annualreport_2.pdf, p. 105.
[259] See https://minorityrights.org/about-us/our-history/.

special schools was not reasonably and objectively justified by the Czech and Hungarian authorities and constituted unlawful discrimination.

Familial and Sexual Discrimination, Freedom of Religion and Respect for Private Life NGOs and private foundations have also tried to push the limits of discrimination in the fields of family, sexuality, religion and private life. For instance, in *O'Donoghue v. United Kingdom*,[260] AIRE represented couples (composed of an immigrant and a national) with children who were prevented from marrying by the operation of the UK Certificate of Approval scheme, which limited the rights of foreigners to marry unless they married in the Church of England. The ECtHR found that the UK Certificate of Approval scheme was discriminatory on the grounds of religion under Article 12 (the right to marry),[261] of its blanket prohibition on the exercise of the right to marry on all persons in a specified category,[262] and of the level of the fee charged that impaired the right to marry.[263] The scheme was then amended under the pressure of AIRE's litigation.

With regard to the more specific freedom of religion that constitutes another field of litigation for NGOs and private foundations, the most famous case is the judgment of *Lautsi v. Italy* rendered by the ECtHR Grand Chamber.[264] Third party interventions were submitted by the ICJ, Interights and HRW, which argued that the compulsory display of religious symbols such as the crucifix in state school classrooms was incompatible with the principle of neutrality and the rights guaranteed to pupils and their parents under Article 9 of the Convention and Article 2 of Protocol No. 1. Educational pluralism was an established principle, upheld not only in the Court's case law but also in the case law of a number of supreme courts and in various international instruments. Furthermore, ECtHR case law supported a duty of state neutrality and impartiality among religious beliefs in the provision of public services, including education.[265] In particular, the NGOs considered that, as several supreme courts had held, state neutrality among religious beliefs was particularly significant in the classroom because, school being

---

[260] Case no 34848/07, *O'Donoghue v. United Kingdom* [14 December 2010] ECtHR.
[261] Ibid., §§91–92.
[262] Ibid., §89.
[263] Ibid., §90.
[264] Case no 30814/06, *Lautsi and Others v. Italy* [18 March 2011] ECtHR.
[265] Ibid., §54.

compulsory, children could be subjected to indoctrination there.[266] However, the ECtHR did not follow the arguments raised by the NGOs, and instead pointed out the importance of the Christian legacy in Italy and the essentially passive nature of the crucifix.[267] The ECtHR thus considered that the crucifix in Italian classrooms cannot lead to indoctrination of pupils and that the Italian state has not exceeded its margin of appreciation.[268]

In the field of same-sex marriages, one of the landmark judgments is the case of *Adrian Coman, Robert Clabourn Hamilton and NGO Accept v. Romania*,[269] which was litigated before the CJEU by the Romanian NGO Accept. The case concerned the refusal of the Romanian authorities to recognise the same-sex marriages of migrant EU citizens with third-country nationals. In their initial third party intervention, the ICJ, the AIRE Centre, the European Commission on Sexual Orientation Law (ECSOL), FIDH and ILGA-EUROPE (financed by the Arcus Foundation, the Sigrid Rausing Trust, the government of the Netherlands and Freedom House) argued before the Romanian Constitutional Court that such refusal is in breach of relevant EU law and the ECHR.[270] In an additional intervention, the five NGOs made supplementary written submissions to the Constitutional Court of Romania in light of the ECtHR judgment in the case of *Taddeucci and McCall v. Italy*,[271] in which third party comments were made by the ICJ, ILGA-Europe, ECSOL and the Network of European LGBT Families (NELFA) with a view to seeking a declaration of discrimination on the ground of sexual orientation as regards the exercise of the right of freedom of movement within the EU.[272]

---

[266] Ibid.
[267] Ibid., §§71–72.
[268] Ibid., §76.
[269] C-673/16, *Adrian Coman, Robert Clabourn Hamilton and NGO Accept v. Romania* [5 June 2018] CJEU.
[270] See www.icj.org/romania-icj-intervenes-before-the-constitutional-court-of-romania-in-case-concerning-entitlement-to-residence-permit-on-the-basis-of-same-sex-marriage/.
[271] Case no 51362/09, *Taddeucci and McCall v. Italy* [30 June 2016] ECtHR. The ECtHR decided that, at the material time, by deciding to treat homosexual couples – for the purposes of granting a residence permit for family reasons – in the same manner as heterosexual couples who had not regularised their situation, the state violated the applicants' right not to be discriminated against on the basis of sexual orientation in the enjoyment of their rights under Article 8 §98.
[272] Ibid.

The application lodged with the CJEU and supported by Accept was grounded on the directive on the exercise of freedom of movement, which allows the spouse of an EU citizen to join his husband in the member state in which the husband is living. Asked to rule on an objection of unconstitutionality raised in those proceedings, the Romanian Constitutional Court asked the Court of Justice if the applicant may be regarded as the 'spouse' of an EU citizen who has exercised his right to freedom of movement and must therefore be granted a permanent right of residence in Romania when Romania does not recognise homosexual marriage.

In response, the CJEU stressed that in the directive on the exercise of freedom of movement, the word 'spouse', which means an individual married to another person, is gender-neutral and may therefore entail the same-sex spouse of an EU citizen.[273] In this regard, public policy, which is applied to justify restrictions to the right to freedom of movement, must be interpreted strictly. The scope of the right to freedom of movement cannot be defined unilaterally by each member state without any oversight by the EU.[274] The Court held that freedom of movement for persons may be restricted independently of the nationality of the persons concerned, if the restrictions are grounded on objective public interest considerations and are proportionate to a legitimate aim pursued by national law.[275] The CJEU found that recognition by a member state of a homosexual marriage concluded in another member state in accordance with the law of that state for the sole purpose of granting a derived right of residence to a national of a non-EU state does not threaten the institution of marriage in the first member state. According to the CJEU, that obligation does not oblige a member state to legalise homosexual marriage. Furthermore, an obligation to recognise such marriages for the sole purpose of granting a derived right of residence to a national of a non-EU state does not undermine the national identity or pose a threat to the public policy of the member state.[276] Lastly, the CJEU observed that restrictions to the exercise of freedom of movement for persons may be justified only where such a measure is consistent with the fundamental

---

[273] C-673/16, *Adrian Coman, Robert Clabourn Hamilton and NGO Accept v. Romania* [5 June 2018] CJEU, §35.
[274] Ibid., §44.
[275] Ibid., §41.
[276] Ibid., §§45–46.

rights guaranteed by the EU Charter of Fundamental Rights.[277] The CJEU argued that it is also apparent from ECtHR case law that the relationship of a homosexual couple may fall within the right to respect for 'private life' and 'family life' (guaranteed by the Charter) in the same way as a relationship of a heterosexual couple in the same situation.[278]

In the same way, in *F. v. Bevándorlási és Állampolgársági Hivatal*, the HHC obtained from the CJEU a ban on the psychological testing of sexual-emotional orientation in asylum procedures.[279] The CJEU ruled that the procedures, should recourse be had in that context to an expert's report, must be in line with other relevant EU law provisions, and in particular with the fundamental rights guaranteed by the Charter, such as the right to respect for human dignity, enshrined in Article 1 of the Charter, and the right to respect for private and family life guaranteed by Article 7 thereof.[280] The CJEU also found that the examination of the application for international protection must cover an individual assessment of that application and has to include all relevant facts as they relate to the country of origin of the applicant at the time of taking a decision on the application, the relevant statements and documentation presented by him, and his individual position and personal circumstances.[281] Where necessary, the competent authority must also take account of the explanation provided regarding a lack of evidence, and of the applicant's general credibility.[282] The CJEU concluded that Article 4 of Directive 2011/95 must be interpreted as meaning that

> the determining authority cannot base its decision solely on the conclusions of an expert's report that must be consistent with, in particular, the fundamental rights guaranteed by the Charter (including the right to respect for private and family life), and that that authority cannot, a fortiori, be bound by those conclusions when assessing the statements made by an applicant relating to his sexual orientation.[283]

---

[277] Ibid., §§47–49.
[278] Ibid., §50
[279] Case C-473/16, *F. v. Bevándorlási és Állampolgársági Hivatal* [25 January 2018] CJEU.
[280] See Case C-148/13 to C-150/13, *A., B. and C. v. Staatssecretaris van Veiligheid en Justitie* [2 December 2014] CJEU, §53.
[281] Case C-473/16, *F. v. Bevándorlási és Állampolgársági Hivatal* [25 January 2018] CJEU, §41.
[282] See, by analogy, case C-472/13, *Shepherd v. Bundesrepublik Deutschland* [26 February 2015] CJEU, §26, and Case C-560/14, *M. v. Irish Minister for Justice and Equality* [9 February 2017] CJEU, §36.
[283] Case C-473/16, *F. v. Bevándorlási és Állampolgársági Hivatal* [25 January 2018] CJEU, §42.

With regard to fundamental rights specifically, the psychological report was considered by the CJEU to interfere disproportionately with private life.[284]

In another case litigated by Accept, the Asociaţia Accept judgment,[285] the CJEU examined the adequate way for European courts to punish anti-gay harassment under the EU law barring anti-gay discrimination in employment.[286] The case was about the refusal of Romanian tycoon George Becali and his football club, Steaua Bucharest, to recruit a gay footballer. Under Romanian law, sanctions for discrimination include a fine of up to €1,800 and community service. However, the Romanian anti-discrimination council gave only a written warning, because by the time it reached its decision more than six months had passed since Becali's statements. The court ruled that such an interpretation of Romanian law was not in compliance with the requirement to have a regime of 'effective, proportionate and dissuasive sanctions', where this results in a lack of meaningful penalty. Romanian law did not allow for a damages claim where there was no identifiable victim, and a written warning appeared to relate generally to minor offences. The court therefore cast doubt on whether it would be effective to limit the 'penalty' to such a warning, even if widely publicised. The CJEU also rejected the idea that the club would have had an impossible task in disproving discrimination. The club had the option of publicly denying that Becali's statements reflected its views and proving that it had a policy of equal opportunity in recruitment; in fact, the club's lawyer had allegedly affirmed that Becali's approach was unwritten club policy. The CJEU also ruled that anti-gay direct discrimination can be found without any identifiable victim. It ruled that Directive 2000/78 allows Romanian laws to give legal standing to NGOs to challenge homophobic harassment and discrimination where there is no such victim.

Political and Ethnic Discrimination   NGOs and private foundations have also extended their litigation focused on discrimination to the political realm with a view to obtaining a wider scope and definition of discrimination from the ECtHR. For instance, in *Sejdić and Finci*

---

[284] Ibid.
[285] Case C-81/12, *Asociaţia ACCEPT* v. *Romania* [25 April 2013] CJEU.
[286] Directive 2000/78/EC of 27 November 2000 Establishing a General Framework for Equal Treatment in Employment and Occupation.

v. *Bosnia and Herzegovina*,[287] AIRE and the OSJI intervened as third party in this case concerning the denial to members of certain ethnic minorities (Jews and Roma) the right to stand for elected office in Bosnia and Herzegovina. Under the constitutional provision adopted following the Dayton Agreement, only members of the three main ethnic groups can stand for office. The AIRE Centre and the OSJI's intervention dealt with the limitations on standing for office in European countries since World War II, where such restrictions have generally been imposed only as a punishment for a criminal offence of affiliation with a discredited regime. In particular, the OSJI argued that restrictions on political rights (which allow social bonds to be maintained), particularly on the suspect basis of race and ethnicity, were not only discriminatory but thwarted the meaning of citizenship itself. The OSJI underlined the effect of the ethnic conflict, where legally entrenched distinctions grounded on ethnicity could increase tensions, rather than fostering the constructive and sustainable relations between all ethnicities that were necessary to a viable multi-ethnic state.[288] The ECtHR Grand Chamber took up the arguments made in the intervention in its judgment in which it found for the first time a violation of Article 14 in this field.[289]

3.1.3.2 The Right to Legal Abortion

The right to legal abortion has been particularly invested and promoted by NGOs and private foundations as a gendered right for women (see Chapter 5), partly through litigation efforts. In particular, the case of *P. and S. v. Poland*,[290] in which the HFHR and AI intervened as third party, is one of the three most important ECtHR judgments on access to legal abortion in Poland. In all three cases,[291] the ECtHR followed the same line of argument raised by HFHR and AI (which underlined significant barriers faced by pregnant women to abort)[292] by considering that the

---

[287] Case no 27996/06 & 34836/06, *Sejdić and Finci v. Bosnia and Herzegovina* [22 December 2009] ECtHR.
[288] Ibid., §37.
[289] Ibid., §50.
[290] Case no 57375/08, *P. and S. v. Poland* [30 October 2012] ECtHR
[291] Case no 5410/03, *Tysiac v. Poland* [20 March 2007] ECtHR was litigated by Interights, and third party comments were made by the Center for Reproductive Rights (based in New York) and the Polish Federation for Women and Family Planning, together with the Polish Helsinki Foundation for Human Rights, Warsaw, the Forum of Polish Women (Gdańsk) and the Association of Catholic Families; Case no 27617/04, *R. R. v. Poland* [26 May 2011] ECtHR.
[292] Ibid., §§58–59 and 77.

rights of the applicants were violated under Articles 3 and 8 because of the practical hindrances they experienced in exercising their right to legal abortion.[293] With a view to implementing these judgments fully, the ECtHR asserted that the Polish authorities must take steps to guarantee not only theoretical but also practical access to abortion.[294] On 21 September 2017, the CM asked the Polish government to provide information on the guarantees of effective access to legal procedures for termination of pregnancy. In June 2018, the Polish government presented a report to the CM stating that some general measures aimed at the implementation of the ECtHR judgments would be introduced in the draft law on the amendment of the Patient Rights and Patient Rights Ombudsman Law of 6 November 2008.[295]

The case of *A., B. and C. v. Ireland*,[296] another landmark judgment delivered by the ECtHR, was litigated by the Irish Family Planning Association, which is partly financed by the OSF, the Summit Foundation and the HRA Pharma Foundation.[297] The latter complained for health and well-being reasons under Article 8 about the prohibition of abortion in Ireland and the alleged failure to implement the constitutional right to an abortion in Ireland in the case of a risk to the life of the woman.[298] In addition, third party comments were sent by the Center for Reproductive Rights (an NGO partly financed by OSF, the Ford Foundation and the MacArthur Foundation)[299] and the International Reproductive and Sexual Health Law Programme (which collaborates with the OSF),[300] which both considered that denying a lawful abortion to protect a woman's physical and mental health contradicted international law and comparative standards that recognised that the state

---

[293] Ibid., §§100–112, 128–137 and 157–169.
[294] Ibid., §111.
[295] Communication (22/06/2018) from Poland Concerning the Case of P. and S. v. Poland, Information Made Available under Rule 8.2a of the Rules of the Committee of Ministers for the Supervision of the Execution of Judgments and of the Terms of Friendly Settlements, 1324th Meeting (September 2018) DH-DD(2018)659.
[296] Case no 25579/05, *A., B. and C. v. Ireland* [16 December 2010] ECtHR.
[297] Irish Family Planning Association, *Director's Report and Financial Statement for the Year Ended 31 December 2018*, p. 25; *Director's Report and Financial Statement for the Year Ended 31 December 2016*, p. 9; *Annual Report of 2008*, p. 10.
[298] Case no 25579/05, *A., B. and C. v. Ireland* [16 December 2010] ECtHR, §3.
[299] Center for Reproductive Rights, *2011–2012 Annual Report*, p. 56; *2006 Annual Report*, p. 36.
[300] International Reproductive and Sexual Health Law Programme, *2012 Annual Report*, pp. 5, 7, 16.

should aim to protect prenatal interests through proportionate means that give due consideration to the rights of pregnant women, such that restrictive criminal abortion laws and harsh penalties were excessively burdensome on women and abortion providers.[301] While the ECtHR rejected the argument that Article 8 conferred a right to abortion,[302] it found that Ireland had violated the ECHR by failing to provide an accessible and effective procedure by which a woman can have it established whether she qualifies for a legal abortion under current Irish law.[303]

3.1.3.3 Victims of Human Trafficking and Sexual Offences

In the human trafficking realm, which constitutes in general a field completely underlitigated by NGOs and private foundations, the only important case is *Rantsev v. Cyprus and Russia*,[304] in which the AIRE Centre and Interights intervened as third party, providing the Court with information on the obligation of states to protect victims of trafficking. The AIRE Centre asserted that the case law of international supervisory bodies against trafficking had yet to address fully the extent and content of positive obligations owed by states in the circumstances arising in the current case. With regard to ECtHR jurisprudence, AIRE argued that while the ECtHR had already considered the extent of the application of Article 4 in a trafficking case, that case had dealt exclusively with the failure of the state to put in place adequate criminal law provisions to prevent and punish the perpetrators.[305] Similarly, the ECtHR held that trafficking constitutes a violation of Article 4 (prohibition of slavery, servitude, and forced and compulsory labour) and applied for the first time the principle of the positive obligation of states to the protection to be afforded to trafficking victims,[306] referring to the growth in human trafficking that has been made easier in part by the collapse of the former Communist bloc.[307]

---

[301] A Case no 25579/05, *A., B. and C. v. Ireland* [16 December 2010] ECtHR, §§206–211.
[302] Ibid., §§216–242.
[303] Ibid., §§243–268.
[304] Case no 25965/04, *Rantsev v. Cyprus and Russia* [7 January 2010] ECtHR.
[305] Ibid., §271.
[306] Ibid., §§293, 298, 308–309.
[307] Ibid., §278.

Sexual offences are also a domain underlitigated by private foundations and NGOs. The only cases litigated by NGOs in this area are *M. C. v. Bulgaria*,[308] in which Interights intervened as third party, and *S. N. v. Russia*,[309] which was championed by EHRAC and Memorial. With regard to the M. C. case, Interights argued that over the past two decades the traditional definition of rape had been reformed in civil and common law jurisdictions and in international law (including the International Criminal Tribunals for Rwanda and the former Yugoslavia, and the Statute of the International Criminal Court and its draft Rules). Interights stressed that the reform of rape law, in both international and national law,[310] reflected a shift from a 'historical approach' to the 'equality approach' to the issue of consent that considered rape as an offence against a woman's autonomy.[311] A central concern underlying reforms in rape law had been to clarify that it was not obligatory to establish that the accused had overcome the victim's physical resistance in order to provide the evidence for the lack of consent.[312] Interights complained that in this case the approach of the Romanian authorities to rape originated in defective legislation and reflected a predominant practice of prosecuting rape perpetrators only on evidence of significant physical resistance.[313] The ECtHR shared the same view as Interights, although not in such general terms, and ruled that there had been a violation of the respondent state's positive obligations and a lack of investigation under both Articles 3 and 8 in that particular case.[314]

In the S. N. case, EHRAC and Memorial alleged that the Russian authorities failed in their positive obligation to conduct an effective investigation into a Dagestani minor's complaints of rape and to ensure adequate protection of her private life. In particular, EHRAC and Memorial complained that the investigators had appeared to blame the applicant and to focus on her behaviour and that of her family instead of paying more attention to the alleged perpetrators.[315] The ECtHR agreed with EHRAC and Memorial and found violations of the state's positive obligation to effectively investigate and punish rape under the

---

[308] Case no 39272/98, *M. C. v. Bulgaria* [4 December 2003] ECtHR.
[309] Case no 11467/15, *S. N. v. Russia* [20 November 2018] ECtHR.
[310] Case no 39272/98, *M. C. v. Bulgaria* [4 December 2003] ECtHR, §§129–147.
[311] Ibid., §§126–127.
[312] Ibid., §127.
[313] Ibid.
[314] Ibid., §§169–187.
[315] Ibid., §45.

prohibition of torture, inhuman and degrading treatment (Article 3) and the right to private life (Article 8).[316] In this regard, the ECtHR acknowledged that there are still inherent obstacles in investigating sex crimes in Russia.[317]

3.1.3.4   Penal, Prison, Immigration and Detention Policies

As already underlined, unlawful detention and poor conditions of detention have been invested by NGOs and private foundations as an important and specific domain of litigation and a way of influencing and even orienting national penal, prison, counterterrorism and immigration policies.

Unlawful Detention   In the domain of unlawful detention, one of the most important cases is the judgment of *Merabishvili* v. *Georgia* delivered by the ECtHR and instructed by EHRAC on the unlawful detention of the former prime Minister of Georgia.[318] This is a landmark judgment that resets the Court's case law on politically motivated proceedings and on Article 18 ECHR.[319] In the judgment, the ECtHR considered for the first time that Article 18 prohibits the CoE member states from restricting the rights and freedoms enshrined in the ECHR for purposes not prescribed by the ECHR, and to this extent it is autonomous,[320] contrary to an older and more limited approach to Article 18. In line with EHRAC, the Grand Chamber argued that political motivations were behind the extended pre-trial detention of former Prime Minister and Interior Minister Vano Merabishvili (one of the Rose Revolution's protagonists in Georgia). According to the ECtHR, pre-trial detention was overused by the Georgian Dream coalition to put political pressure on him in violation of Article 5 §3,[321] despite the applicant's role, in his capacity as Minister of Internal Affairs, in the alleged cover-up of a 2006 murder implicating high-ranking officers of the Ministry and the applicant's wife.[322] His detention was no longer justified and was used to

---

[316] Ibid., §§48–53.
[317] Ibid., §52.
[318] Case no 72508/13, *Merabishvili* v. *Georgia* [28 November 2017] ECtHR.
[319] Article 18 held that 'The restrictions permitted under [the] Convention to the said rights and freedoms shall not be applied for any purpose other than those for which they have been prescribed.'
[320] Case no 72508/13, *Merabishvili* v. *Georgia* [28 November 2017] ECtHR, §§289–288.
[321] Ibid., §§231–235.
[322] Case no 25091/07, *Enukidze and Girgvliani* v. *Georgia* [April 2011] ECtHR, §§15–22.

exert pressure on him, in breach of Article 18, the object and purpose of which is 'to prevent the misuse of power'.[323] In its judgment, the ECtHR held that it will closely scrutinise the explanations of states about incarceration of political actors and draw inferences from indirect evidence, as it has done in this case.

According to EHRAC, the Grand Chamber has paved the way for individual victims of politically motivated detentions and prosecutions across Europe to challenge state abuse of power in a more effective way.[324] In response, some constitutional amendments have been adopted to make the Prosecutor's Office (which will be elected by the Parliament) an independent and separate constitutional institution. The Georgian Parliament also adopted on 21 July 2018 the law on State Inspector's Service in order to investigate cases concerning alleged violations of Articles 2 and 3.[325]

Another landmark case is that of *Ilias and Ahmed v. Hungary*,[326] which was litigated by the HHC along with the AIRE Centre.[327] Both NGOs argued that confinement in transit zones in Hungary must be considered as unlawful detention under Article 5 and violation of the right to dignity under Article 3. The ECtHR held for the first time in this case that confinement in transit zones in Hungary must be considered to be unlawful detention under Articles 3, 5 and 13,[328] and it obliged the Hungarian authorities to take interim measures to avoid several asylum-seeking children from being deported to and detained in the transit zones.[329]

In the landmark case of *O. M. v. Hungary*,[330] the HHC also obtained an enlargement of the scope of Article 5 to categories other than prisoners. In this judgment, the ECtHR considered that the detention of a gay asylum seeker was unlawful and verged on arbitrariness under Article 5.[331] The ECtHR judgment echoed the third party comments made by the

---

[323] Case no 72508/13, *Merabishvili v. Georgia* [28 November 2017] ECtHR, §§320–354.
[324] See http://ehrac.org.uk/news/former-georgian-prime-ministers-detention-politically-motivated-says-european-court/.
[325] Communication from Georgia concerning the cases of Merabishvili v. Georgia, Action Plan (26/10/2018), 1331st meeting (December 2018) DH-DD(2018)1056.
[326] Case no 47287/15, *Ilias and Ahmed v. Hungary* [14 March 2017] ECtHR.
[327] AIRE Centre (2018), *Directors and Trustees' Report and Accounts for the Year Ended 31st March 2018*, p. 4.
[328] Ibid., §§58–69, 73–77, 98–101 and 117–125.
[329] Ibid.
[330] Case no 9912/15, *O. M. v. Hungary* [5 July 2016] ECtHR.
[331] Ibid., §§45–54.

AIRE Centre, the European Council on Refugees and Exiles (ECRE), ILGA-EUROPE and the ICJ, which pointed out some inconsistencies between Hungarian laws and practices related to immigration detention and the principles developed by the UNHCR and the EU.[332] The ECtHR relied notably on the case of *Blokhin* v. *Russia*,[333] in which it was decided that detention in a temporary detention centre for juvenile offenders was unlawful because of the inhumane conditions there. This previous judgment had been obtained by the Mental Disability Advocacy Center financed by the OSF and the EU.[334]

Life Sentences The ECtHR reiterated and developed its jurisprudence on life sentences (previously set up in the cases of Kafkaris, Vinter and László Magyar litigated by NGOs, see above) in the *T. P. and A. T.* v. *Hungary* case,[335] in which the HHC intervened as third party. The HHC underlined in particular that the new review mechanism introduced by the Hungarian legislator did not comply with the standards set by the Court in *Vinter and Others* v. *United Kingdom* as it did not provide any real prospect of release. In addition, the final decision in the new mandatory pardon procedure was still made by the President of Hungary and was by law discretionary, and thus raised several concerns.[336] In line with the HHC, the ECtHR held that, irrespective of the new 'mandatory pardon procedure' introduced for whole lifers by the Hungarian parliament to comply with the requirements imposed by the ECtHR in the László Magyar case, Hungarian rules on life imprisonment without parole still violate Article 3. Hungary then submitted in 2018 an action plan that pointed out the inconsistency of the ECtHR's jurisprudence and the inner coherence of the system of punishments under Hungarian law which made the swift implementation of the judgment impossible.[337]

Torture and Ill Treatment by State Authorities In the immigration domain, the case of *Kadzoev* v. *Bulgaria* was the result of a litigation undertaken by the AIRE Centre, together with the Legal Clinic for

---

[332] Ibid., §§38–39.
[333] Case no 47152/06, *Blokhin* v. *Russia* [23 March 2016] ECtHR.
[334] www.mdac.info/en/test/donors.
[335] Case nos 37871/14 and 73986/14, *T. P. and A. T.* v. *Hungary* [4 October 2016] ECtHR.
[336] Ibid., §§33–34.
[337] Communication from Hungary Concerning the Case of Lázló Maygar v. Hungary, Action Plan (29/03/2018), 1318th Meeting (June 2018) DH-DD(2018)350.

Refugees and Immigrants in Bulgaria.[338] The NGOs represented the applicant, who was held in solitary confinement whilst his claim for asylum was under review, as he risked prohibited ill treatment in case of return to Russia (which refused to recognise his Russian nationality and thus to provide the necessary travel documents for removal). During 2009, the legality of his ongoing detention was referred for the first time by the Bulgarian courts to the CJEU concerning the EU Returns Directive, which was subjected for the very first time to a ruling.[339] In its judgment, the CJEU stressed that the aim of Article 15 §§5–6 of the Directive was to guarantee in any event that detention for the purpose of removal must not exceed eighteen months. The CJEU held that those provisions imposed that the maximum length of detention laid down in them had to include a period of detention completed in connection with a removal procedure begun before the rules in the Directive became applicable. It ruled more particularly that the period during which enforcement of a deportation order had been suspended because the person concerned had challenged it by way of judicial review was to be taken into account in calculating the period of detention for the purpose of removal, where the person concerned was in detention during that procedure. The CJEU also held that Article 15 §4 of the Directive meant that only a real prospect that removal could be executed successfully, having regard to the periods laid down in Article 15 §5 and §6, corresponded to a reasonable prospect of removal, and that such a reasonable prospect was not established if it appeared unlikely that the person concerned would be admitted to a third country, having regard to those periods.[340] Regarding his complaint before the ECtHR, the applicant raised violations of Articles 3, 5, 8, 13 and 14 concerning attempts to remove him to Russia, the effectiveness of Bulgaria's asylum procedures at the material time, the length and legality of his immigration detention, and the ill treatment and discrimination he alleged that he had suffered while in immigration detention. However, his application was struck out of the list of cases by the ECtHR because of his unwillingness to pursue his case.[341]

---

[338] Case no 56437/07, *Kadzoev* v. *Bulgaria* [1 October 2013] ECtHR.
[339] Case C-357/09, *Saïd Shamilovich Kadzoev* v. *Direktsia 'Migratsia' pri Ministerstvo na vatreshnite raboti* [30 November 2009] CJEU.
[340] Ibid.
[341] Case no 56437/07, *Kadzoev* v. *Bulgaria* [1 October 2013] ECtHR.

In the field of torture in police custody in which NGOs and private foundations also try to limit and even challenge the traditional power exerted by national states, in 1998 the ERRC obtained, through a third party intervention made with AI,[342] a landmark judgment in the already mentioned Assenov case on alleged ill treatment by the police and unlawful pre-trial detention.[343] In its third party intervention, the ERRC stressed that the Assenov case was the first ECtHR judgment involving applicants from the Roma ethnic group from Central or Eastern Europe. The ERRC also underlined 'the broader context of discrimination and disadvantage which Roma face throughout Bulgaria and much of Europe' and the necessity of extending ECHR protection to Europe's most vulnerable minorities.[344] Lastly, the ERRC emphasised the absence of investigation of police ill treatment police of Romani individuals in Bulgaria and adequate remedies required by circumstances where significant injuries have been caused to an individual at a time when he is in custody after apprehension by the police, particularly where the individual's vulnerability is increased by age, association with a disadvantaged minority group, or other factors under Article 3 ECHR.[345] The ECtHR, which was sensitive to such a third party intervention, found that the medical evidence and Mr Assenov's testimony raised a reasonable suspicion that the injuries from which the applicant suffered might have been inflicted by the police.[346] The ECtHR ruled that the Bulgarian government violated Assenov's rights by subjecting him to torture and degrading treatment (Article 3) while he was in police custody, and also by failing to investigate the incident officially. In the light of the judgment in the case of *McCann and Others* v. *United Kingdom*,[347] in which AI, Liberty,

---

[342] Case no 24760/94, *Assenov* v. *Bulgaria* [28 October 1998] ECtHR, §§97–98 and 101 §5. European Roma Rights Centre, *Written Comments to the European Court of Human Rights in the Assenov Case*, 29 April 1998, available at www.errc.org/uploads/upload_en/file/assenov%20brief%20-%20final.pdf.
[343] Case no 24760/94, *Assenov and Others* v. *Bulgaria* [28 October 1998] ECtHR.
[344] European Roma Rights Centre, *Written Comments to the European Court of Human Rights in the Assenov Case*, 29 April 1998.
[345] Ibid.
[346] Case no 24760/94, *Assenov* v. *Bulgaria* [28 October 1998] ECtHR, §§97–98 and 101.
[347] Case no 18984/91, *McCann and Others* v. *United Kingdom* [27 September 1995] ECtHR. In the McCann case, the ECtHR condemned the UK for not having taken effective measures to prevent the risk associated with counter-terrorist operations that led to the applicant's death, in circumstances where the state authorities knew or ought to have known of the risk that they would be carried out.

Inquest and British–Irish Rights Watch submitted a third party intervention,[348] the ECtHR held that Bulgaria was in breach of Article 3, which was read together with the state's Article 1 duty to 'secure to everyone within their jurisdiction the rights and freedoms in the Convention' that require an effective official investigation, capable of leading to the identification and punishment of those responsible.[349] The ECtHR assessed the investigation in the light of the above criteria, finding that it was insufficient and ineffective for the purposes of Article 3. The ECtHR also ruled in light of Article 13 that Bulgaria did not offer an effective domestic remedy able to challenge violations under Article 3.[350] In this regard, the ruling broadened the scope of international law by making the right to an investigation and to a domestic remedy part of the right to be free of official torture and mistreatment.

More recently, the case of *Sergei Ryabov* v. *Russia*,[351] which is in continuity with the Assenov case, concerned an applicant who was sentenced for murder to eighteen years in prison and had complained of ill treatment by the police and of unfair trial, which caused self-incrimination as a result of beatings. The applicant in the ECHR was represented by lawyers of the IPC and a member of the Moscow Helsinki Group. The ECtHR found a violation of Article 3 and concluded that the Russian authorities had failed to conduct effective investigations into violations alleged by Ryabov.[352] In addition, the ECtHR found a breach of Article 6, as the verdict of the Russian court was grounded on the applicant's self-incrimination as a result of ill treatment.[353] This landmark ECtHR judgment called for a change to judicial practice in Russia for a confession by referring to the concept of an unfair trial, even though a similar line of reasoning was followed by the ECtHR in *Tangiyev* v. *Russia*,[354] instructed by the SRJI.[355] The ECtHR ruled that the confession of the accused and evidence obtained through torture and inhumane treatment used to establish the relevant facts in criminal proceedings make the trial as a whole unfair.[356]

---

[348] Ibid., §5 and §161.
[349] Case no 24760/94, *Assenov* v. *Bulgaria* [28 October 1998] ECtHR, §102.
[350] Ibid.
[351] Case no 2674/07, *Sergei Ryabov* v. *Russia* [17 July 2018] ECtHR.
[352] Ibid., §§38–52.
[353] Ibid., §§57–60.
[354] Case no 27610/05, *Tangiyev* v. *Russia* [11 December 2012] ECtHR.
[355] Ibid., §2.
[356] Case no 2674/07, *Sergei Ryabov* v. *Russia* [17 July 2018] ECtHR, §§57–60.

Control over National Counterterrorism Policies As outlined above, NGOs and private foundations try through litigation to increase control over counterterrorism policies conducted by Eastern European states. In this regard, the OSJI intervened as counsel in landmark judgments against Macedonia,[357] Poland,[358] and Romania,[359] regarding their counterterrorism policies and their extraordinary rendition and secret detention programmes run with the US Central Intelligence Agency (CIA). The HFHR, the ICJ and AI also sent third party comments to the ECtHR in the Al Nashiri case.[360] Interights, Redress, the ICJ and AI intervened as third party in the El Masri case.[361] A similar and simultaneous case, *Husayn (Abu Zubaydah) v. Poland*,[362] was instructed by Interights and third party comments were sent by the ICJ and AI.[363] All the NGOs argued in these cases that acts of cooperation by officials of contracting parties in renditions or secret detentions by the agents of a foreign state leading to arbitrary detention, enforced disappearances, torture (notably caused by unauthorised and harsh interrogation methods) or other ill treatment engage the Convention responsibility of the member states.[364] Furthermore, the NGOs denounced the absence of effective measures (such as effective investigation) to prevent such operations, in circumstances where the state authorities knew or ought to have known of the risk that these would be carried out.[365] In all these rulings and in line with the allegations made by the NGOs, the ECtHR ruled that the secret detention programme violates Article 5 and that unauthorised interrogation methods inflicted on the applicants constituted torture.[366] In addition, the ECtHR also held that collaboration with the CIA rendition and secret detention programme is fully prohibited on the main ground of Articles 3, 5 and 8 and Article 6 in the Abu Zubaydah case,[367] and that member states must be accountable for CIA torture.[368] In response, the Polish government passed the Anti-Terrorism Act on

---

[357] Case no 39630/09, *El-Masri v. Macedonia* [13 December 2012] ECtHR.
[358] Case no 28761/11, *Al Nashiri v. Poland* [24 July 2014] ECtHR.
[359] Case no 33234/12, *Al Nashiri v. Romania* [31 May 2018] ECtHR.
[360] Case no 28761/11, *Al Nashiri v. Poland* [24 July 2014] ECtHR, §7.
[361] Case no 39630/09, *El-Masri v. Macedonia* [13 December 2012] ECtHR.
[362] Case no 7511/13, *Husayn (Abu Zubaydah) v. Poland* [24 July 2014] ECtHR.
[363] Ibid., §7.
[364] Case no 28761/11, *Al Nashiri v. Poland*, ECtHR, 24 July 2014, §447–450.
[365] Ibid., §449.
[366] Ibid., §511–516.
[367] Case no 7511/13 *Husayn (Abu Zubaydah) v. Poland*, ECtHR, 24 July 2014, §§546–561.
[368] Ibid., §517–519.

10 June 2016, which provided the special security services with new competences.[369]

The same line of reasoning was applied by the ECtHR in the case of *Al Nashiri v. Romania*,[370] litigated by the OSJI and with APADOR-CH, AI and ICJ intervening as third party, to claim that the Romanian authorities failed to conduct an effective investigation into the alleged secret CIA detention centres in Romania.[371] With consideration to the inadequacy of the parliamentary inquiry and deficiencies in the criminal investigation, the ECtHR held that Romania failed to comply with the requirements of a 'prompt', 'thorough' and 'effective' investigation for the purposes of Article 3 ECHR.[372]

3.1.3.5 Political Rights for Prisoners

NGOs and private foundations push an agenda oriented towards the recognition of political rights for prisoners. For instance, the case of *Hirst v. United Kingdom* was litigated by the AIRE Centre (third party intervention) and concerned the blanket ban on convicted prisoners in the UK voting in elections.[373] The AIRE Centre's intervention highlighted the connection between the normalisation of life in prison and successful reintegration into society on release. It looked at the role of voting in reintegration.[374] The Court found a violation of Article 3 of Protocol No. 1 to the Convention. The Court emphasised the role of universal suffrage in democratic society and held that any interference with the right to vote must be proportionate, that is there must be a link between the offence committed and issues relating to elections and democratic institutions.[375] This landmark judgment, which paved the way for the following pilot judgment of *Greens and M. T. v. United Kingdom*,[376] and for the judgment of *Anchugov and Gladkov v. Russia*,[377] which condemned Russia for its disenfranchisement and ban on

---

[369] Polish Act of 10 June 2016 on Anti-terrorist Activities and on the amendments to other acts, available at www.legislationline.org/download/id/6361/file/Poland_Act_on%20_anti-terrorist%20_activities_2016_en.pdf.
[370] Case no 33234/12, *Al Nashiri v. Romania* [31 May 2018] ECtHR.
[371] Ibid., §§630–635.
[372] Ibid., §§642–656.
[373] Case no 74025/01, *Hirst v. United Kingdom* [6 October 2005] ECtHR.
[374] Ibid., §54.
[375] Ibid., §62, 72–85.
[376] Case no 60041/08 and 60054/08, *Greens and M. T. v. United Kingdom* [23 November 2010] ECtHR.
[377] Case no 11157/04 and 15162/05, *Anchugov and Gladkov v. Russia* [4 July 2013] ECtHR.

prisoners' voting rights, was delivered by the Grand Chamber in October 2005 but as of yet the UK has failed to implement it.

Freedom of the Press and Pluralism, Liberty of Expression and Journalism, and Limits on Institutional Reputation Freedom of the press and liberty of expression and journalism is another domain in which NGOs and private foundations litigate. In this regard, the case of *Romanenko v. Russia* is a landmark judgment,[378] litigated by the Jurists for Constitutional Rights and Freedoms (JURIX, a Russia NGO that was financed by the OSF,[379] and worked with the OSJI)[380] and in which the OSJI and the Moscow Media Law and Policy Institute intervened as third party. In its intervention, OSJI pointed out that if the reputation or rights of public authorities were to be protected by Article 10 §2, this would expose journalists to a constant risk of harassment through lawsuits and would threaten the media's ability to act as a watchdog of public administration. With consideration to that danger, the OSJI argued that many courts thwarted public authorities from suing journalists and citizens in defamation by referring to the necessary openness of such authorities to uninhibited public criticism and relying on the American jurisprudence on freedom of press.[381] Using American case law again, the OSJI, which underlined that public officials could not substitute themselves for their respective institutions in taking legal action,[382] also stressed that journalists should not be exposed to liability for defamation when they accurately publish statements contained in non-confidential government documents.[383] The ECtHR judgment followed that line of reasoning, set limits on government agencies suing to defend their reputation, and cast doubt on whether they can benefit from protection of institutional reputation.[384] In this respect, the ECtHR found a breach of the right to freedom of expression recognised by Article 10.

Prior to this landmark judgment, the ECtHR delivered several judgments litigated by JURIX (which intervened as third party) on freedom of

---

[378] Case no 11751/03, *Romanenko and Others v. Russia* [8 October 2009] ECtHR.
[379] Its website was www.jurix.ru.
[380] See for instance JURIX and OSJI, *Ethnic Profiling in the Moscow Metro*, 2016, available at www.justiceinitiative.org/uploads/90298695-6f7d-47dc bc27d9926ea96024/metro_20060613.pdf.
[381] Ibid., §32.
[382] Ibid., §33.
[383] Ibid., §34.
[384] Ibid., §§46–48.

expression given to journalists. In the case of *Filatenko v. Russia*,[385] JURIX argued that the protection of expression on core subjects of politics and government in the middle of an election campaign is so crucial that, in libel actions, the Court should pay particular attention to whether a statement made by a journalist asserts an actionable false fact or is understood as political speculation, conjecture or hyperbole. Without such scrutiny, there is a risk of abusive litigation against the media by political elites over statements inherently not capable of being proved true or false.[386] In particular, questions, speculations or conjectures should be estimated as value judgments, and courts cannot impose on the media defendants to prove their truth, especially when such statements, which belong to the media coverage of an election campaign, are made in the heat of political debate.[387] Relying partly on the same arguments, the ECtHR found that the judicial interference of the Russian political power in media coverage was not justified and proportionate to the legitimate aim of the protection of the reputation of others,[388] and that that the Russian courts overstepped the narrow margin of appreciation allowed to them for restrictions on debates of public interest.[389] Considering the vital importance of free political debate in a democratic society in the context of free elections or the wider limits of criticism that politicians should be faced with and tolerate,[390] the ECtHR held that there has been a violation of Article 10. This case echoed the case of *Dyuldin and Kislov v. Russia*,[391] in which JURIX also intervened as third party to underline the chilling impact of defamation on free speech if public institutions could sue their critics, and that the free flow of information is crucial to vigorous political discourse,[392]

Kasabova v. Bulgaria is another significant case in which the OSJI intervened as third party.[393] The case concerns a journalist who published an investigation of alleged corruption in the Burgas school system and was prosecuted for the criminal offence of defamation. The OSJI considered that the presumption of falsity, especially in criminal libel

---

[385] Case no 73219/01, *Filatenko v. Russia*, ECtHR, 6 December 2007.
[386] Ibid., §34.
[387] Ibid., §35.
[388] Ibid., §45.
[389] Ibid., §49.
[390] Ibid., §48.
[391] Case no 25968/02, *Dyuldin and Kislov v. Russia*, ECtHR, 31 July 2007.
[392] Ibid., §34.
[393] Case no 22385/03, *Kasabova v. Bulgaria* [19 April 2011] ECtHR.

cases, was as such contrary to Article 10 and that under that provision all elements of the offence of defamation had to be proved by the complainant to the criminal standard. The OSJI also emphasised the presumption's potential chilling effect, especially when combined with strict liability in respect of libel.[394] The ECtHR decided that a reporter could not be required to bear the same burden as the prosecution in a bribery case and that her sentence was disproportionate.[395] The main aim pursued by the OSJI was to limit the use of defamation to silence journalists exposing corruption.[396]

Another landmark judgment is the case of *Centro Europa 7* v. *Italy*,[397] which was delivered by the Grand Chamber of the ECtHR and influenced by the OSJI under third party intervention. The main goal of the OSJI was to 'strengthen structural elements of the free "market of ideas" and ensure an enabling environment for both traditional journalism and free speech on the Internet'.[398] The OSJI relied mainly on the European 'Guiding Principles on Broadcast Media Pluralism' standards, which recognised that the duty to ensure pluralism and competition required limits on media ownership, especially in broadcasting.[399] In its third party submission, the OSJI also noted that the circumstances of the case were to be contextualised historically and broadly in the Italian broadcasting and information sector, which was dominated by a political leader and a political party, unlike other EU member states.[400] Lastly, the OSJI submitted that the ECtHR should order Italy to implement measures of a general and systemic nature in order to guarantee the pluralism of its broadcasting system.[401] The ECtHR agreed with the OSJI, ruling that

> the legislative framework, as applied to the applicant company, which was unable to operate in the television-broadcasting sector for more than ten years despite having been granted a licence in a public tendering procedure, did not satisfy the foreseeability requirement under the Convention

---

[394] Ibid., §48.
[395] Ibid., §§50–73.
[396] OSJI, *Global Human Rights Litigation Report*, October 2013, p. 4.
[397] Case no 38433/09, *Centro Europa 7* v. *Italy*, ECtHR, 7 June 2012.
[398] OSJI, *Human Rights Litigation Report, 2015*, pp. 23–27.
[399] Case no 38433/09, *Centro Europa 7* v. *Italy*, ECtHR, 7 June 2012, §126.
[400] Ibid., §§127–128.
[401] Ibid., §128.

and deprived the company of the measure of protection against arbitrariness required by the rule of law in a democratic society.[402]

The ECtHR emphasised the reduced competition in the audio-visual sector resulting from such shortcomings. It found then a failure by the Italian state to comply with its positive obligation to put in place an appropriate legislative and administrative framework to guarantee effective media pluralism and competition under Article 10.[403]

3.1.3.6 Watchdogs and Human Rights Activists: Right to Information, Freedom of Expression, Unlawful Arrest, Poor Detention Conditions and Right to Health

The protection of human rights activists in relation to the right to information, freedom of expression, the right to health, unlawful arrest and poor detention conditions has been a significant area of litigation for NGOs backed by private foundations.

Human Rights Activists Ill-Treated, Unlawfully Arrested and Detained in Russia, Azerbaijan and Hungary in Poor Detention Conditions-
One of the landmark judgments in the field of human rights activists is the case of *Yunusova and Yunusov* v. *Azerbaijan*,[404] which was litigated by EHRAC. EHRAC alleged that the applicants (activists) had not been provided with the requisite medical assistance in detention and that they had been unable to get effective medical care, which had subjected them to severe physical and mental suffering. EHRAC also argued that their conditions of detention had not been adapted to their state of health.[405] In addition, EHRAC complained that there had been no effective domestic remedies in respect of their complaints relating to their medical treatment in detention and the compatibility of their state of health with their conditions of detention.[406] The judgment, which echoed the arguments submitted by EHRAC, was the first case against Azerbaijan where the Court found a lack of adequate medical treatment in a prison (where human rights activists were held) to be in violation of the Convention.[407] Another important finding is a breach of Article 34 in relation to the

---

[402] Ibid., §156.
[403] Ibid., §§144–158.
[404] Case no 59620/14, *Yunusova and Yunusov* v. *Azerbaijan* [2 June 2016].
[405] Ibid., §134.
[406] Ibid., §124.
[407] Ibid., §§141–151.

government's failure to provide information on the health situation of the applicants.[408]

Another significant judgment is the case of *Orlov and Others v. Russia*,[409] litigated by EHRAC and Memorial. The applicants alleged under Articles 3, 5 and 13 ECHR and Article 1 of Protocol No. 1 to the ECHR that as journalists and a human rights activist (the Chairman of Memorial at that time), they had been abducted and subjected to ill treatment amounting to torture by state agents in Ingushetia on the eve of a protest meeting against abuse of authority by the security forces.[410] EHRAC and Memorial complained that the Russian authorities failed to effectively investigate the issue,[411] and that they were ill-treated by state agents who were running a special operation.[412] In its decision, the ECtHR, which was in line with the NGOs, relied on the leading case of *Suleymanov v. Russia* (also championed by EHRAC and Memorial)[413] on ill treatment of a member of illegal armed groups, where the Court found that the authorities failed to conduct an effective, independent and timely investigation under Article 3.[414] However, contrary to the Suleymanov judgment, the ECtHR ruled in the Volkov case that state agents were responsible for abducting, ill-treating and punishing the applicants in breach of the substantial aspect of Article 3.[415]

Right to Information and Freedom of Expression One of the most significant judgments in this area is the case of *TASZ v. Hungary*,[416] which was litigated by the OSJI before the ECtHR concerning the Hungarian Civil Liberties Union (HCLU), which was denied access to a copy of the complaint filed by a Hungarian member of parliament with the Constitutional Court about Hungary's drug laws. The OSJI third party intervention emphasised the right to information in European law and practice compared to other regional human rights systems. In particular, the OSJI refers in its submission to the ruling Claude Reyes v Chile of the Inter-American Court of Human Rights, which was also

---

[408] Ibid., §§113–120.
[409] Case no 5632/10, *Orlov and Others v. Russia* [14 March 2017] ECtHR.
[410] Ibid., §90.
[411] Ibid., §81.
[412] Ibid., §90.
[413] Case no 32501/11, *Suleymanov v. Russia* [22 January 2013] ECtHR.
[414] Ibid., §§140–150.
[415] Case no 5632/10, *Orlov and Others v. Russia* [14 March 2017] ECtHR, §§92–98.
[416] Case no 37374/05, *Társaság a Szabadságjogokért v. Hungary* [14 April 2009] ECtHR.

litigated by the OSJI.[417] The ECtHR held that this refusal violated the right of an NGO to access information that was needed for them to carry out their role as a public watchdog under Article 10.[418] The judgment delivered by the Strasbourg Court constituted a groundbreaking ruling recognising the fundamental nature of the right to information that can be used by campaigners and the public alike in Europe.

Another important case litigated by the HHC (in addition to third party intervention made by the HCLU and Fair Trials) was the case of *Magyar Helsinki Bizottság v. Hungary*, in which the Grand Chamber of the ECtHR ruled for the first time that the Court has to protect the right of access to information under Article 10 concerning the processing of personal data.[419] In this landmark case, the Hungarian authorities refused to provide the HCC, which was conducting a survey partly funded by the OSF, with the names of public defenders and the number of their appointments.[420] In particular, the ECtHR found that the HHC's right to freedom of expression was breached when the police refused to disclose the names of ex officio defence counsels and the number of cases in which they were appointed in a given year.[421] In this regard, the ECtHR was sensitive to the arguments raised by the HHC concerning access to information that is a condition for the effective exercise of the right to freedom of expression. The HCC and other NGOs argued that access to information was inherent in the right to freedom of expression, since rejecting access to data impeded the enjoyment of that freedom.[422]

3.1.3.7 Changes to the Judiciary and Access to Justice

In the field of changes to the judiciary, a landmark judgment, *Denisov v. Ukraine*, in line with the Volkov ruling and concerning the dismissal of the President and judge of the Kyiv Administrative Court of Appeal, was recently instructed by EHRAC and delivered by the Grand Chamber of

---

[417] OSJI, *Written Comments on the Case of Társaság a Szabadságjogokért v. Hungary*, September 2008, available at www.opensocietyfoundations.org/sites/default/files/hungary_20080901.pdf.

[418] Case no 37374/05, *Társaság a Szabadságjogokért v. Hungary* [14 April 2009] ECtHR, §§35–39.

[419] Case no 18030/11, *Magyar Helsinki Bizottság v. Hungary* [8 November 2016] ECtHR.

[420] Ibid., §§11–20.

[421] Ibid. See also HHC, *Annual Report of 2016*, available at www.helsinki.hu/wp-content/uploads/Hungarian-Helsinki-Committee-annual-report-2016.pdf, p. 1.

[422] Case no 18030/11, *Magyar Helsinki Bizottság v. Hungary* [8 November 2016] ECtHR, §68 and §§104–116.

the ECtHR.[423] A third party intervention was made by ICJ,[424] which submitted that the principle of the independence of the judiciary necessarily required security of tenure in the office of court president.[425] With a view to ensuring such security of tenure and to maintaining both the independence of individual court presidents and their capacity to uphold the independence of judges in their courts, proceedings for removal from the position of court president had to guarantee independence and fairness like those for removal from the office of judge.[426] The ECtHR held that the way that the High Court of Justice had first dismissed Mr Denisov as president of the court owing to managerial inefficiency and the way that the Higher Administrative Court had later reviewed that decision were affected by similar defects and issues as in the case of *Volkov* v. *Ukraine*.[427] The first body had been neither independent nor impartial and the second had been unable to remedy the defects of the first set of proceedings. The ECtHR therefore found a violation of the right to a fair trial.[428]

The same line of reasoning was applied in the ECtHR Grand Chamber case of *Baka* v. *Hungary*,[429] in which third party interventions were made by the HHC, the HCLU, the Eötvös Károly Institute, the HFHR based in Poland and the ICJ.[430] In its third party submission, the ICJ provided the ECtHR with (a) an analysis in relation to the role of court presidents in the self-governance of the courts and in maintaining judicial independence; (b) international standards in relation to security of tenure of judges and court presidents; (c) the significance of procedural safeguards, including under Article 6 §1 ECHR, in decisions affecting the career and tenure of court presidents and (d) in light of international standards and principles, the extent to which a disciplinary measure such as removal from the position of president of a court may be in breach of the right to respect for private life as protected by Article 8.[431] In addition, the ICJ argued that court presidents in most European jurisdictions play an important role in the self-governance and impartiality of the judiciary.

---

[423] Case no 76639/11, *Denisov* v. *Ukraine* [25 September 2018] ECtHR.
[424] Ibid., §7.
[425] Ibid., §42.
[426] Ibid.
[427] Ibid., §68.
[428] Ibid., §81–82.
[429] Case no 20261/12, *Baka* v. *Hungary* [23 June 2016] ECtHR.
[430] Ibid., §9.
[431] Ibid., §98.

In this way, the ICJ emphasised that upholding the independence of the judiciary imposes that court presidents should, in the discharge of these functions, be independent from the executive, as well as from other powerful interests. The ICJ stressed that the nature of the court president role impacts the application of Convention rights to measures affecting their judicial career, including removal from the role of court president.[432] The NGOs even turned to Viviane Reding, Vice-President of the European Commission, and to the Venice Commission, arguing that the transformation of the Supreme Court into Curia had not led to such significant changes in the Court's duties that would have justified the dismissal of its President and that the rule of law was violated.[433] The ECtHR agreed with the ICJ's view and found that the premature end of Mr Baka's mandate violated Article 6 (the right of access to a tribunal) on the ground of his inability to challenge the termination of his mandate. In a similar way to the NGOs,[434] the ECtHR also held that the dismissal and the adoption of new rules to exclude Mr Baka from being re-elected were not motivated by a justified restructuring of the supreme judicial authority in Hungary but were directly caused by the views and criticisms that he had publicly expressed in his professional capacity on the legislative reforms of the new Fidesz-led government. His right to freedom of expression was therefore also violated. In condemning Hungary, the ECtHR notably relied on a CJEU judgment that found in April 2014 that by prematurely putting an end to the term served by its Data Protection Commissioner, Hungary had breached its obligations under EU law.[435] In response, the Hungarian government considered that 'no general measures were found necessary because the violation found by the Court resulted from a one-time constitutional reform of the Hungarian judicial system'.[436]

In the case of *Kudeshkina v. Russian Federation*,[437] in which the IPC acted for the applicant, the ECtHR found that the applicant's dismissal

---

[432] Ibid., §98–99.
[433] See https://helsinki.hu/wp-content/uploads/HHC-HCLU EKINT_3rd_party_intervention_Baka_v_Hungary.pdf.
[434] Ibid.
[435] Case C-288/12, *Commission v. Hungary* [8 April 2014] CJEU.
[436] CoE Committee of Ministers, 1280th Meeting (7–9 March 2017) (DH) – Action Report (14/12/2016) – Communication from Hungary Concerning the Case of Baka against Hungary (Application No. 20261/12), p. 2.
[437] Case no 29492/05, *Kudeshkina v. Russia* [26 February 2009] ECtHR.

from the judiciary in 2004 was in breach of Article 10 ECHR. In particular, both the IPC and the ECtHR noted and insisted that the sanctions were imposed on the applicant because of her critical comments about the Russian judiciary.[438] The applicant was obliged to resign from her office early as the relevant court was abrogated from the judge's rank. In the ECtHR's view, these sanctions were disproportionately severe and capable of having a 'chilling effect on judges who wish to participate in the public debate on the effectiveness of judicial institutions'.[439] In particular, the ECtHR ruled that the domestic authorities had failed to find the right balance between the need to protect the authority of the judiciary and the protection of the reputation or rights of others, on the one hand, and the need to protect the applicant's right to freedom of expression, on the other hand.[440] In response, the Russian Supreme Court gave explanations in its Plenum Resolution of 27 June 2013 'On Application by the Courts of General Jurisdiction of the Convention for the Protection of Human Rights and Fundamental Freedoms of 4 November 1950 and the Protocols thereto' and in a recent judgment to the Russian courts on the features of examination of cases on the protection of honour, dignity and business reputation by taking into account the ECtHR jurisprudence and international principles and standards.[441] In addition, in 2013, Article 12.116 of the Russian Law of 26 June 1992 (no. 3132-1) 'On Status of Judges in the Russian Federation' ('the Law on Status of Judges') was amended.to integrate a new disciplinary sanction in form of reproof, as an alternative to early termination of office.[442] Lastly, Plenary Resolution of the Supreme Court of the Russian Federation of 14 April 2016 no. 13 'On the judicial practice for application of the law governing the issues of disciplinary liability of judges' was adopted to provide detailed explanations to the courts about the procedure and grounds for bringing judges to disciplinary liability.[443] In response, the IPC informed the CM that, in its opinion, the Russian authorities have neither offered the

---

[438] Ibid., §§60–64.
[439] Ibid., §§79–102.
[440] Ibid., §101.
[441] CoE Committee of Ministers, 1310th Meeting (March 2018) (DH) – Action Report (22/01/2018) – Communication from the Russian Federation Concerning the case of Kudeshkina v. Russian Federation (Application No. 29492/05), pp. 3–4.
[442] Ibid., p. 6.
[443] Ibid., p. 7.

applicant any redress nor discussed the execution of the Kudeshkina judgment.[444]

Changes to Criminal Investigations In the field of criminal investigation, the case main judgment is the case of *Tsechoyev v. Russia*,[445] which was litigated by EHRAC and Memorial.[446] The applicant's brother had been detained because of his suspected participation in the kidnap of the older brother of a top-level oil company executive. He was detained for around ten months in various facilities before being taken from his cell in a pre-trial facility by four men carrying falsified documents, allegedly to transfer him to another facility. The applicant's brother was later found dead, and a criminal investigation was instituted. EHRAC and Memorial considered that the criminal investigation was ineffective and that domestic remedies were lacking under Article 2.[447] The ECtHR held that insufficient evidence was provided to show that the men who kidnapped and murdered the applicant's brother were state agents, or that there was a foreseeable, real and immediate risk to his life when he was transferred to those men. Consequently, and partly relying on the case of *Medova v. Russia*, which was also litigated by EHRAC and Memorial,[448] the ECtHR found a breach of the procedural limb of Article 2 given the ineffectiveness of the investigation following the death of the applicant's brother. The Court underlined that, in questioning state officials poorly, the investigation had not pursued an obvious aim of enquiry effectively and should have brought crucial evidence about the circumstances of the case and the identity of the kidnappers.[449]

Extradition and the Right to a Fair Trial In the domain of extradition and the right to a fair trial, the landmark case is the Ismoilov judgment against the Russian Federation.[450] The AIRE Centre and HRW submitted a third party intervention in this case.[451] The Ismoilov judgment

---

[444] CoE Committee of Ministers, 1331st Meeting (December 2018) (DH) – Rule 9.1 Communication from the Applicant (29/08/2018) in the Case of Kudeshkina v. Russian Federation (Application No. 29492/05).
[445] Case no 39358/05, *Tsechoyev v. Russia* [15 March 2011] ECtHR.
[446] Ibid., §2.
[447] Ibid., §§112 and 144.
[448] Case no 25385/04, *Medova v. Russia* [15 January 2009] ECtHR.
[449] Case no 39358/05, *Tsechoyev v. Russia* [15 March 2011] ECtHR, §§152–153.
[450] Case no 2947/06, *Ismoilov v. Russia* [24 April 2008] ECtHR.
[451] Ibid., §5.

concerned the extradition to Uzbekistan of individuals who alleged that they were at risk of torture and an unfair trial, that there had been no effective judicial review of their detention, that their right to be presumed innocent had been violated, and that the diplomatic assurances were inadequate safeguards against ill treatment offered by a state with such a record of serious systemic human rights violations.[452] The third parties, HRW and the AIRE Centre, underlined the growing consensus among governments and international experts (the UN and the CPT) on the inadequate safeguard (through diplomatic assurances) against torture and other ill treatment in Uzbekistan.[453] They also cite in their third party intervention the case of *Shamayev and Others v. Georgia and Russia*,[454] which was litigated by Interights, to point out the risk of torture in case of extradition to Russia.[455] In its Ismoilov judgment, which was sensitive to the arguments raised by AIRE and HRW (and to a previous ECtHR judgment litigated by AI, JUSTICE and Liberty in conjunction with AIRE,[456] in which the Court cautioned against reliance on diplomatic assurances against torture from a state where torture is endemic or persistent),[457] the ECtHR ruled for the first time that Article 6 (the right to a fair trial) could in some cases apply to extradition proceedings as well as applying extra-territorially to the trial that would take place.[458]

Political and Military Conflicts between States The case of *Sargsyan v. Azerbaijan* is a groundbreaking judgment rendered by the Grand Chamber of the ECtHR and litigated by EHRAC and Legal Guide (an Armenian NGO) on the wider context of the old Nagorno-Karabakh conflict (which ended in 1992) between Azerbaijan and Armenia.[459] In this case, the ECtHR highlighted the responsibility of the two states to find a political resolution to the conflict. In June 2015, the ECtHR held that the Azerbaijani government was responsible for violating the property rights of the Sargsyan family, whose home was destroyed by heavy

---

[452] Ibid., §4.
[453] Ibid., §111.
[454] Case no 36378/02, *Shamayev and Others v. Georgia and Russia* [12 April 2005] ECtHR.
[455] Case no 2947/06, *Ismoilov v Russia* [24 April 2008] ECtHR, §113.
[456] Case no 22414/93, *Chahal v. United Kingdom* [15 November 1996] ECtHR.
[457] Ibid., §105.
[458] Case no 2947/06, *Ismoilov v Russia* [24 April 2008] ECtHR.
[459] Case no 40167/06, *Sargsyan v. Azerbaijan* [16 June 2015 and 12 December 2017] ECtHR.

bombing in a region located in the conflict zone. In this regard, the ECtHR called for a property restitution mechanism.[460] A parallel case (*Chiragov v. Armenia*)[461] also found Armenia responsible for breaching the property rights of a group of Azerbaijani refugees who were displaced during the conflict. In the 2015 judgment, the ECtHR held that the family's inability to return to the village or to be compensated for the loss of their land and property was in breach of their property rights (Article 1 of Protocol No. 1 of the ECHR) and their right to respect for their family life and home (Article 8). The family's inability to visit their relatives' graves in the village was also in breach of Article 8.[462] Sticking to the legal arguments applied by EHRAC,[463] the ECtHR also found that Azerbaijan had failed both to create and implement a property restitution mechanism and an effective domestic remedy which would allow the Sargsyan family to have their property rights restored (Article 13).[464]

Another significant case is *Catan and Others v. Moldova and Russia*,[465] which was brought before the Grand Chamber of the ECtHR by Interights and Promo-Lex. The background of the case concerned the conflict between Russia and Moldova over the territory of the non-recognised Moldavian Republic of Transdniestria (hereafter, MRT). The said territory, although claimed by the Moldovan republic, was de facto under the control of a Russian-supported 'independent' administration. Before the ECtHR, Interights and Promo-Lex questioned Russian jurisdiction (on the basis of Article 1 ECHR) over the applicants, a group of 170 Moldovan nationals (children of school age, their teachers and parents) living in the MRT.[466] Another question at stake was the unlawfulness of the decision taken by Transdniestrian authorities to close all the schools providing education in the Moldovan/Romanian language (to the extent that this was said to breach Article 8 ECHR and Article 2 of Protocol No. 1 to the Convention).[467] In addition, Interights and Promo-Lex argued that the intimidation, harassment, discrimination and

---

[460] Ibid., §241.
[461] Case no 13216/05, *Chiragov v. Armenia* [16 June 2015] ECtHR.
[462] Case no 40167/06, *Sargsyan v. Azerbaijan* [16 June 2015 and 12 December 2017] ECtHR, §§259–261.
[463] Ibid., §§44–45, 121–122, 154–162, 206–208, 244–246 and 263–266.
[464] Ibid., §§271–274.
[465] Case nos 43370/04, 8252/05 and 18454/06, *Catan and Others v. Moldova and Russia* [19 October 2012] ECtHR.
[466] Ibid., §§83–88.
[467] Ibid., §§125–130.

detention of ethnic Moldovans, on the basis of their non-compliance with the 1994 law banning and criminalising the use of Latin script in Transdniestrian schools (and requiring that the Moldovan language be written in the Cyrillic script), constituted a violation of Article 14 ECHR. 'Ethnic' Moldovans were registered and went to schools using the Latin script in defiance of the MRT's attempts to further isolate the Moldovan community in Transdniestria.[468]

The arguments raised by the NGOs were considered to be worthy by the ECtHR, which condemned Russia, ruling that it had effective jurisdiction and control over Transdniestria from 2002 to 2004, not only through its military but also through political and economic assistance to the MRT,[469] which it was found could not have survived without such assistance. The ECtHR also found Russia responsible for the violation of the applicants' right to education under Article 2 of Protocol No. 1 of the Convention, as it was de facto the effective holder of power in the territory.

3.1.3.8 States as 'Watching States'

In addition to the Zakharov case (see Chapter 2), another landmark judgment on watching states is the case of *Bucur and Toma v. Romania*.[470] The ECHR ruled in favour of the applicants, who were represented by APADOR-CH. Romania was condemned by the ECtHR for illegal phone surveillance and for sanctioning a former intelligence officer who made the surveillance public. APADOR alleged in particular that the Law of 1991 no. 51 does not guarantee against arbitrary surveillance as this law does not mention the categories of information that can be registered and kept. APADOR referred to the case of *Rotaru v. Romania*,[471] in which the ECtHR found some defects of the law of 1992 no. 14 concerning the organisation and the functioning of the Romanian Information Service.[472] In particular, and in line with its previous jurisprudence and notably its judgment in *Guja v. Moldova*,[473] which was litigated by the NGO Lawyers for Human Rights and

---

[468] Ibid., §157.
[469] Ibid., §§11–123.
[470] Case no 40238/02, *Bucur and Toma v. Romania* [8 January 2013] ECtHR.
[471] Case no 28341/95, *Rotaru v. Romania* [4 May 2000] ECtHR.
[472] Case no 40238/02, *Bucur and Toma v. Romania* [8 January 2013] ECtHR, §161.
[473] Case no 14277/04, *Guja v. Moldova* [12 February 2008] ECtHR.

concerned a breach of the right to freedom of expression under Article 10,[474] the ECtHR found violations of Article 38 (the obligation to cooperate with the Court),[475] of Article 6 (the right to a fair trial),[476] of Article 10 (the right to freedom of expression),[477] of Article 8 (the right for respect for private and family life)[478] and of Article 13 (the right to effective appeal).[479]

To obtain such pilot and landmark judgments, private foundations and NGOs often rely on former judgments they have litigated and on their own documents and reports that they brought to the European Courts with a view to asserting their claims and allegations.

3.2 Documents and Reports by NGOs and Private Foundations as Evidence Applied by the ECtHR and the CJEU

In many rulings and as highlighted above in our analysis of the cases litigated by private foundations and NGOs, the ECtHR and the CJEU rely partly on previous judgments obtained by NGOs and private foundations. For instance, in the O'Donoghue case (litigated by AIRE), the ECtHR cited the Hirst judgment (also instructed by AIRE) and the case of *Frasik v. Poland* (third party intervention from the HFHR)[480] to condemn the United Kingdom, stating that 'a general, automatic and indiscriminate restriction on a vitally important Convention right fell outside any acceptable margin of appreciation' given to member states.[481] In the case of *Rantsev v. Cyprus and Russia*, the ECtHR relied on the Nachova judgment (in which the OSJI, the European Roma Rights Centre and Interights had intervened), the judgment of *Paul Edwards v. United Kingdom* (litigated by Liberty) and the Medova case (instructed by EHRAC and Memorial)[482] to condemn both Cyprus and Russia.

---

[474] In particular, the right to impart information, as a result of the dismissal of the applicant from the Prosecutor General's Office for divulging two documents which in his opinion disclosed interference by a high-ranking politician in pending criminal proceedings.
[475] Case no 40238/02, *Bucur and Toma v. Romania* [8 January 2013] ECtHR, §§67–73.
[476] Ibid., §§126–132.
[477] Ibid., §§95–120.
[478] Ibid., §§162–165.
[479] Ibid., §§169–173.
[480] Case no 22933/02, *Frasik v. Poland* [5 January 2010] ECtHR.
[481] Case no 34848/07, *O'Donoghue v. United Kingdom* [14 December 2010] ECtHR, §89.
[482] Case no 25385/04, *Medova v. Russia* [15 January 2009] ECtHR.

On the other hand, the ECtHR uses evidence gathered and provided by NGOs (backed by private foundations) to condemn national states in certain cases. For example, some ECtHR rulings against Romania (such as the cases of *Ahmad Ali* v. *Romania*, *Vasilescu* v. *Romania*, and *Necula and Mihăilă* v. *Romania*, see above) quoted APADOR-CH reports. In the same way, the ECtHR cited the report by the HHC in the case of *Ilias and Ahmed* v. *Hungary*.[483] In *Ismailov* v. *Russia*,[484] the ECtHR relied partly on the reports on Uzbekistan[485] made by both AI and HRW to condemn Russia.[486] In a similar manner, in the Catan judgment some reports made by the International Crisis Group[487] were applied by the ECtHR to condemn Russia.[488]

In the Jafarov judgment (see above), the ECtHR even cited statements made by the grant donors of an applicant who was the director of the HRC. In these statements, the grant donors (including notably the NED, the Royal Norwegian Embassy in Baku, the British Embassy in Azerbaijan, the OSF, the Assistance Foundation, and the Fritt Ord Foundation) provided the ECtHR with details of the relevant grants and donations awarded to the HRC. The ECtHR noted that the applicant had regularly provided the relevant donor with the necessary accounting information related to the expenditure of the funds, and underlined that the donor organisations and embassies had every confidence that the funds had been used properly for the projects and initiatives for which they had been awarded.[489]

---

[483] Case no 47287/15, *Ilias and Ahmed* v. *Hungary*, cited above, §45.
[484] Case no 20110/13, *Ismailov* v. *Russia* [17 April 2014] ECtHR.
[485] Human Rights Watch, *World Annual Report*, chapter on Uzbekistan, January 2013; AI, *Annual Report*, chapter on Uzbekistan, May 2013; AI, *Return to Torture: Extradition, Forcible Returns and Removals to Central Asia*, 2013. In addition, the ECtHR also cited the AI Report of 20 September 2005, *Uzbekistan: Lifting the Siege on the Truth about Andija* and the AI report of 10 May 2006, *Uzbekistan: Andijan – Impunity Must Not Prevail*.
[486] Case no 20110/13, *Ismailov* v. *Russia* [17 April 2014] ECtHR, §§65–68.
[487] The NGO International Crisis Group is financed by the Open Society Foundations and counts Georges Soros as member of the Board of Directors, Trustee and funder, and Richard Armitage and Zbigniew Brzezinski as Senior Advisers). See International Crisis Group, *Crisis Group Senior Advisor Report*, available at www.crisisgroup.org/en/about/board/crisis-groupsenior-advisers.aspx.
[488] Case nos 43370/04, 8252/05 and 18454/06, *Catan and Others* v. *Moldova and Russia* [19 October 2012] ECtHR, §§71–72.
[489] Case no 69981/14, *Rasul Jafarov* v. *Azerbaijan* [17 March 2016] ECtHR, §§32–34.

In the same way, HRW, which is fully financed by the OSF,[490] the Ford Foundation and the Oak Foundation,[491] makes reports that are regularly cited and used by the ECtHR in its judgments to show breaches of human rights committed by national states. The main cases documented by HRW were those of *Fatullayev* v. *Azerbaijan*,[492] litigated by EHRAC/Memorial and related to the Nagorno-Karabakh conflict; *Al Nashiri* v. *Poland*, instructed by the OSJI; *Abu Zubaydah* v. *Poland*, litigated by Interights concerning rendition programmes run by the CIA in cooperation with the Polish authorities; and *Ismoilov and Others* v. *Russia*, concerning potential extradition to Uzbekistan that involved a risk of ill treatment and of an unfair trial. HRW also sends third party comments to the ECtHR in certain cases, such as in *Ismoilov and Others* v. *Russia*, which was litigated by EHRAC and Human Watch. In this last case, HRW referred in its third party intervention to several cases it had documented (thanks to funding from the OSF) on individuals extradited on the basis of diplomatic assurances who were subsequently tortured by Uzbekistan officials.[493] Instructed by EHRAC and Memorial, the Khashiyev and Akayeva pilot judgment, including the Isayeva and Abuyeva case, was delivered by the ECtHR against Russia, notably on the basis of an enquiry conducted by HRW[494] about human rights violations committed in Grozny between December 1999 and January 2000.[495]

The same process applies for AI, on whose reports the ECtHR relies to condemn certain member states. For instance, in *Al Nashiri* v. *Poland*, *Al Nashiri* v. *Romania*, and *Husayn (Abu Zubaydah)* v. *Poland*, the ECtHR used, among other evidence, several reports on secret detention facilities

---

[490] See www.opensocietyfoundations.org/newsroom/soros-and-open-society-foundations-give-100-million-human-rights-watch.
[491] See www.hrw.org/fr/about/partners.
[492] Case no 40984/07, *Fatullayev* v. *Azerbaijan* [22 April 2010] ECtHR.
[493] Ibid., §113. See Case no 36378/02, *Shamayev and Others* v. *Georgia and Russia* [12 April 2005] ECtHR.
[494] See activities undertaken by Human Rights Watch at the ECtHR at www.hrw.org/tag/european-court-human-rights.
[495] Case nos 57942/00 and 57945/00, *Khashiyev and Akayeva* v. *Russia* [24 February 2005] ECtHR, §§36 and 150.

by AI,[496] HRW,[497] and the HFHR[498] to condemn Poland.[499] In a similar way, the Human Rights Project and AI provided reports on numerous incidents of alleged racial violence against Roma in Bulgaria (including by law enforcement agents) to obtain the condemnation of the Bulgarian authorities in the Nachova case.[500] Two reports by AI ('Punjab Police: Beyond the Bounds of the Law' and 'India: Determining the Fate of the "Disappeared" in Punjab') were also applied by the ECtHR in the Chahal judgment litigated by AI, Justice and Liberty in conjunction with AIRE through third party intervention.[501] Consequently, some important NGOs (including AI and HRW), which are financed by private foundations, are able to document their litigation activities substantially through the reports on human rights that they make on behalf of private foundations.

Regarding the influence of national governments on evidence used by the ECtHR, the Sargsyan case shows that the ECtHR relied on information brought by the American Association for the Advancement of Science (AAAS, funded by the US government)[502] in the framework of its 'Geospatial Technologies and Human Rights Programme'. The AAAS is also notably financed by the Ford Foundation, the Oak Foundation and the OSF.[503] The ECtHR also applied the AAAS report on trafficking in persons[504] in the Rantsev case to condemn Cyprus and Russia.

As a complement to litigation efforts in combination with their own documents and reports, private foundations are increasingly investing and increasing their involvement in the monitoring of the execution of human rights judgments by the CoE member states.

---

[496] See for instance the Amnesty International report, *Unlock the Truth: Poland's Involvement in CIA Secret Detention*, June 2013.
[497] Human Rights Watch, *Statement on US Secret Detention Facilities in Europe*, 6 November 2005.
[498] International Helsinki Federation for Human Rights, *Anti-Terrorism Measures, Security and Human Rights: Developments in Europe, Central Asia and North America in the Aftermath of September 11*, April 2003.
[499] Case no 28761/11, *Al Nashiri v. Poland*, ECtHR, 24 July 2016, §§176 and 217–228.
[500] Case no 43577/98 and 43579/98, *Nachova v. Bulgaria*, ECtHR, 6 July 2005, §59.
[501] Case no 22414/93, *Chahal v. United Kingdom*, cited above, §§55–56.
[502] AAAS Annual Report, *Meeting Global Challenges: Discovery and Innovation*, 2014, p. 48. AAAS, *2017 Donor List*, p. 16.
[503] AAAS, *Annual Report 2014*, pp. 47–48. AAAS, *2017 Donor List*, pp. 15–16.
[504] US State Department, *Report on Trafficking in Persons*, June 2008.

3.3 The Increased Involvement of Private Foundations and NGOs in the Monitoring of the Execution of Human Rights Judgments by Member States

According to the OSJI, proper implementation of judgments has to be a matter of concern from the beginning of the litigation and the selection of cases.[505] Litigation does not suffice in itself if the European judgments are not implemented by the condemned states. The full implementation of judgments is indeed a significant part of litigation efforts and a real objective pursued by private foundations and NGOs, as the OSJI puts it:

> Litigation and advocacy often continue well beyond the final decision of a Court. OSJI acts to ensure that the judgments are fully implemented. This involves promoting the decision within the affected community, monitoring the situation on the ground to establish whether changes have been made, engaging in advocacy to clear political blockages to reform, and where necessary challenging the failure to implement by re-litigating the issue.[506]

With consideration to implementation, OSJI has made several reports with a view to improving the execution of judgments and increasing its own participation in the process. In this regard, the report 'From Judgment to Justice' highlighted poor compliance with decisions of European human rights systems.[507] The OSJI report 'From Rights to Remedies' examined the development of new models of national implementation in certain countries that could inspire the European Courts.[508] In the same way, the OSJI has conceived a mechanism to orient political resources towards better and more efficient execution of ECtHR judgments.[509]

Historically and as pointed out above, NGOs as well as national institutions for the promotion and protection of human rights were not involved in the execution of judgments. This situation changed in 2006, when NGOs were allowed under Rule 9.2 of the Rules of the CM to send communications to the CM concerning the lack of execution of final

---

[505] OSJI, *Global Human Rights Litigation Report, 2015*, p. 5.
[506] OSJI, *Global Human Rights Litigation Report, 2013*, p. 5.
[507] OSJI, *From Judgment to Justice. Implementing International and Regional Human Rights Decisions*, 2010.
[508] OSJI, *From Rights to Remedies. Structures and Strategies for Implementing International Human Rights Decisions*, 26 May 2013.
[509] Ibid.

judgments by their member states.⁵¹⁰ This recent mechanism has allowed NGOs and private foundations to monitor the execution of judgments by national states and to inform the CM about their potential lack of compliance with ECtHR judgments.

In practice, private foundations and NGOs have made intensive use of this new possibility. Nearly all the landmark judgments obtained by the OSJI and the NGOs funded by private foundations are monitored by them with regard to the execution stage. For instance, in *D. H. v. Czech Republic*, the OSJI has cooperated with several Czech NGOs to provide lawmakers with information on reforms to the education law that are necessary to make domestic practice in compliance with the ECtHR judgment.⁵¹¹ More globally, the OSJI has used other regional mechanisms to obtain full implementation of the ECtHR ruling by asking the European Commission to launch infringement proceedings against the Czech authorities on the ground of a breach of the EU Racial Equality Directive. In response, the EU Commission launched the process. In the meantime, the OSJI has engaged the Human Rights Commissioner and organised many briefings for the CM prior to each meeting at which the D. H. case is evoked. It has also brought local activists to testify the non-implementation on the ground and made numerous written submissions to the CM in response to the Czech government's claim. In the Kurić judgment, the OSJI also assisted the applicants in their efforts to ensure the full implementation of the Grand Chamber judgment before the CM of the Council of Europe.⁵¹²

More generally, interventions by NGOs allow them to influence the process of execution of judgments and to denounce repetitive human rights violations committed by their national states, in particular Russia and Eastern countries (see Chapter 6).⁵¹³ For instance, the execution of

---

[510] Council of Europe, Rules of the Committee of Ministers for the Supervision of the Execution of Judgments and of the Terms of Friendly Settlements Adopted by the Committee of Ministers on 10 May 2006 at the 964th Meeting of the Ministers' Deputies and Amended on 18 January 2017 at the 1275th Meeting of the Ministers' Deputies.
[511] OSJI, *Justice Initiative Human Rights Litigation Report*, July 2015, p. 7.
[512] See www.opensocietyfoundations.org/litigation/kuric-v-slovenia.
[513] For instance in 2016, the HFHR brought to the attention of the CM that concerning the D. G. case, the Polish authorities did not provide adequate environmental and technical accommodations for disabled prisoners. See Communication from 1 September 2016 of the Helsinki Foundation for Human Rights in the Case of D. G. v. Poland (Kaprykowski Group), available at http://hudoc.exec.coe.int/eng#{%22EXECIdentifier%22:[%22DH-DD(2016)986E%22]}.

the Ananyev judgment was monitored by the Public Verdict Foundation,[514] Penal Reform International,[515] and the Association of Russian Lawyers for Human Rights.

Other NGOs, which are also financed by the OSF but which litigate less than others in terms of quantity, intervene in this monitoring process. This applies for instance to AI, which sends observations along with AIRE, and ECRE, and the Italian, Dutch, Swedish, Norwegian and United Kingdom governments in the *Tarakhel* v. *Switzerland* case.[516] For its part, HRW has monitored the execution of important judgments delivered against Russia, including the Isigova, Bazorkina, Tsechoyev, Akhmadov, Isayeva and Abuyeva cases. HRW also intervened along with Liberty in the case of *A., B. and C.* v. *Ireland* on abortion by citing its own report 'A State of Isolation – Access to Abortion for Women in Ireland'.[517]

In addition, two private organisations, Judgment Watch[518] and the European Implementation Network (EIN)[519] based in Strasbourg have recently been created and funded by the OSF to support, monitor and promote the execution and implementation of human rights judgments, in particular those delivered by the ECtHR.[520] The Oak Foundation has also financed EIN to reinforce the role of civil society in the implementation of ECtHR judgments.[521] An analysis of this task shows that EIN focuses particularly on the execution of judgments that concern Eastern European countries.[522] More specifically, EIN organises events and lectures about topics of interest to litigants and diplomats; briefs on

---

[514] Secretariat of the Committee of Ministers, Communication from an NGO (Public Verdict Foundation) (07/10/2013) in the Case of Ananyev and Others against Russian Federation, DH-DD(2014)44, 10 January 2014, available at https://wcd.coe.int/ViewDoc.jsp?id= 2146465&Site=CM&BackColorInternet=C3C3C3&BackColorIntranet=EDB021&BackColor Logged=F5D383, pp. 3–12.

[515] Secretariat of the Committee of Ministers, Communication from an NGO (Penal Reform International PRI) (27/09/2012) in the Case of Ananyev and Others against Russian Federation', DH-DD(2012)1026, 6 November 2012, available at https://wcd.coe .int/ViewDoc.jsp?id=2000467&Site=CM&BackColorInternet=C3C3C3&BackColorIntra net=EDB021&BackColorLogged=F5D383.

[516] Case no 29217/12, *Tarakhel* v. *Switzerland* [4 November 2014] ECtHR.

[517] Case no 25579/05, *A., B. and C.* v. *Ireland* [16 December 2010] ECtHR.

[518] https://twitter.com/judgmentwatch?lang=fr.

[519] www.einnetwork.org/.

[520] OSJI, *Q & A: Reform of the ECtHR* (April 2012) Briefing Paper 4, available at www .opensocietyfoundations.org/briefing-papers/q-reform-european-court-human-rights.

[521] http://oakfnd.org/grant-database-ihr.html.

[522] www.einnetwork.org/case-briefing-2/.

persistent problems in geographic areas and specific countries (especially Russia and Azerbaijan); holds 'brown bag' lunches gathering activists from various regions to talk about their challenges; and orchestrates advocacy drives at the CoE Parliamentary Assembly with regard to non-implemented cases.[523]

Private foundations and some NGOs have also used new approaches to persuade states to implement ECtHR judgments. In this regard, several NGOs (including EHRAC, the HFHR and Freedom Now) argued in the case of *Mammadov v. Azerbaijan* for the initiation of infringement proceedings, which requires a two-thirds majority vote from all forty-seven member states and allows the CM to refer a case back to the ECtHR where a state has failed to comply with a judgment.[524]

In sum, private foundations and the NGOs they fund have not only obtained judicial success (pilot judgments, judgments delivered under Article 46 and landmark judgments) thanks to their litigation efforts but are also able to influence the case law of the European Courts through the use of evidence partly brought by them and by their active participation in the supervision of ECtHR judgments. This influence on the inputs and the outputs of the Courts is sufficiently great for us to wonder to what extent private foundations and NGOs have captured the case law of the European Courts. Private foundations and NGOs have also been progressively associated with the reform of the architecture of the European Courts, which is another way of capturing the Courts and their case law.

---

[523] OSJI, *Q & A: Reform of the ECtHR* (April 2012) Briefing Paper 4.
[524] See http://echrblog.blogspot.com/2019/05/first-infringement-proceedings-judgment.html.

4

The Growing Influence Exerted by the Private Sector on the Reform and Structure of the ECtHR and the CJEU

This chapter sheds light on the latest significant indicator of the growing capture by private foundations of the European justice system as private foundations are increasingly involved in the reform and structure of the European Courts. To provide evidence of this trend, we rely on internal and advocacy documents drafted by the European Courts, NGOs and private foundations about the successive reforms of the European human rights justice system.

4.1 Contribution of Private Foundations and NGOs to Redesign and Reform of the ECtHR through Advocacy

Private foundations and NGOs have increased their participation in the redesign and reform of the ECtHR thanks to advocacy efforts.

4.1.1 Reform of the ECtHR, the Process of Execution of Judgments and Claims for an Increase in the ECtHR Budget

We have argued, particularly in Chapter 3, that NGOs aim to exert and do actually exert judicial influence through repeated litigation and submissions to the CM relating to the execution of judgments. However, the very point of repeated litigation is not only to shape case law, but to do so in ways that reflect and are reflected by public policy in a wider sense (for more details on this aspect, see Chapter 6). On the one hand, public advocacy not only complements litigation but is in many ways a necessary precondition for successful litigation, as it generates better judicial and political conditions for litigation purposes (Bouwen and McCown 2007) as emphasised by the OSF itself. On the other hand, advocacy may increase the chances of NGOs persuading the CoE to devote more human and financial resources to the ECtHR with a view to reinforcing the monitoring of specific countries and areas (see Chapter 5). Meanwhile, private foundations make advocacy efforts to reform the structures of the ECtHR, to increase the influence of the ECtHR and the pervasiveness of its case law, and to reinforce the execution of its judgments in order to sustain and develop long-term litigation strategies and bolster their social and policy impacts.

4.1.1.1 More Budget for the ECtHR

Private foundations push for enhancing the power of the ECtHR through more budget and for more influence of its own litigation on the way it deals with applications.[1] The OSF constitutes a very clear example in this regard. It finances the CoE through voluntary contributions, funding that goes hand in hand with attempts to influence the evolution of the structure and programme of the CoE towards more condemnations of countries that are targeted by the litigation undertaken by OSF.[2]

To achieve these goals, the OSF is in favour of an increase in the Court's budget that would allow the ECtHR's productivity to be enhanced. In this regard, more budget allocated to the ECtHR could give it the opportunity to recruit more judges and more staff in order to condemn reluctant member states in a more efficient way: 'We welcome current proposals to recruit additional judges and/or lawyers to help the Court deal with pending applications.'[3] According to an agent working for the European Commissioner for Human Rights, more budget to the ECtHR is achieved through lobbying certain member states, including those that contribute the most to the CoE (such as France, Germany, Italy and the UK). The process would be quite similar to the influence held by NGOs (which also ask for an increase in budget) on the ICC (Lohne 2017).

---

[1] OSJI, *Q&A: Protecting and Strengthening the ECHR*, 2012, available at www.justiceinitiative.org/uploads/a958f000-d342-49a4-b26a-cd53ee450d57/echr-reform-qanda-4-3-12-2.pdf, pp. 2–3.

[2] CoE, *Making a Difference. Voluntary Contributions. Facts and Figures*, 2011, available at www.coe.int/t/dgap/VC_DOC/Contributions_volontaires_EN.pdf, pp. 39, 42–43. For instance, the Open Society argues for the development of a more federalist EU, especially in terms of economic competences. See A. Richardson, 'European Treasury needed to avoid depression: Soros', *Reuters*, US edition, 15 September 2011, available at www.reuters.com/article/2011/09/15/us-eurozonesoros-idUSTRE78E0II20110915.

[3] Ibid.

4.1.1.2 The Brighton Conference on the Reform of the ECtHR

The OSJI, along with EHRAC, the HFHR, AI, HRW and Interights, notably managed to be invited by the CoE to participate and be heavily involved in the ongoing ECtHR reform process by filing submissions at each stage of the process.[4] Thanks to advocacy efforts, private foundations and the NGOs that they fund have contributed to the official discussions on the redesign and reform of the Strasbourg Court.

Following the Interlaken and the Izmir Conferences (at which the OSJI submitted its views to the Committee of Experts on the Reform of the Court, DH-GDR) on the necessity of improving states' implementation of ECtHR judgments, in particular in Italy, Poland, Russia, Hungary, the Czech Republic, Moldova and Ukraine,[5] the Brighton Conference was organised to reflect on the longer-term future of the system of the Convention. The AIRE Centre was then invited to represent the NGOs of Europe by attending and contributing to the Brighton Conference and by sharing its position on the reform of the ECtHR. AIRE relayed the proposals made by the OSJI, which consisted in backing the ECtHR with money and staff and reinforcing the effectiveness of the execution of its judgments against non-compliant states.[6] In this regard, and with a view to improving the ECtHR's effectiveness, the OSJI considered that the ECtHR should provide more public and detailed guidance to states on implementation, and in certain cases should fine states for non-compliance. According to the OSJI, such reforms would reduce the flow

---

[4] Council of Europe's European Committee for Human Rights, Report, 81st Meeting, CDDH(2014)R81 Strasbourg, 24–27 June 2014, available at www.coe.int/t/dghl/standard setting/cddh/CDDHDOCUMENTS/CDDH%282014%29R81_EN.pdf; Joint NGO Statement on Protocol No. 15 to the ECHR, 24 June 2013, available at www.interights.org/document/278/index.html; Joint NGO Statement on the Reform of the European Court of Human Rights as Negotiations on the Draft Brighton Declaration, 13 April 2012, available at www.interights.org/document/212/index.html; OSJI, 'An Open Society Justice Initiative concept note – short version, Human rights made real: establishing a Strasbourg-based presence to improve the implementation of ECHR judgments', September 2014, internal document.

[5] OSJI, National Implementation of the Interlaken Declaration. Perspectives of European Civil Society on National Implementation of the Interlaken Declaration and Action Plan: Czech Republic, Hungary, Italy, Poland, Republic of Moldova, Russian Federation and Ukraine. Submission to the Steering Committee for Human Rights (CDDH) and to the Committee of Experts on the Reform of the Court (DH-GDR), DH-GDR(2012)009, 23 October 2012, available at www.justiceinitiative.org/uploads/ed3e085c-3542-4267-a3bb-bc9226e9c536/echr-reform-implementation-10232012.pdf.

[6] OSJI, Q&A: Protecting and Strengthening the ECHR, 2012, pp. 2–3.

of new applications (some of which are repetitive cases) and the backlog of cases at the ECtHR.[7]

In response to the Brighton Declaration, the CM instructed the Steering Committee for Human Rights (CDDH)[8] at its 122nd Session to submit a report containing its opinions and possible proposals on the longer-term future of the system of the Convention and reform of the Strasbourg Court. Drafting Group 'F' (GT-GDR-F) was thus set up to conduct preparatory work on this topic.[9] It gathered representatives of the governments of the member states, ad hoc experts (including NGO representatives such as AIRE) and several NGOs backed up by private foundations (such as AI) and the OSJI as observers.[10] In particular, AIRE, through its nominated ad hoc expert Nuala Mole, who reflected the OSJI's views,[11] advocated against the principle of subsidiarity and for a narrower conception of the margin of appreciation enjoyed by national states, for a wider approach to third party interventions made by NGOs and private foundations, and for a reinforcement of the power exerted by the ECtHR (notably through a better execution of the ECtHR judgments).[12] Certain proposals submitted by AIRE were integrated into the final report on the longer-term future of the ECHR system, such as reinforced supervision of the execution and implementation of judgments.[13] The report was adopted by the CDDH at its 84th meeting (7–11 December 2015) and subsequently transmitted to the CM, which endorsed the CDDH report concerning (i) the authority of the Convention and its implementation at national level; (ii) the authority of the ECtHR; (iii) the authority of ECtHR judgments (execution of judgments

---

[7] Ibid.
[8] The Steering Committee for Human Rights, which was established by the Committee of Ministers in 1976 and whose task is to advise and give its legal expertise to the CM on all topics within its field of competence, is composed of experts representing the forty-seven member states of the CoE.
[9] See www.coe.int/en/web/human-rights-intergovernmental-cooperation/work completed/future-of-convention-system.
[10] Steering Committee for Human Rights (CDDH) Drafting Group 'F' on the Reform of the Court (GT-GDR-F) 8th Meeting, 14–16 October 2015 Strasbourg, Meeting Report, 16 October 2015; Drafting Group 'F' on the Reform of the Court 1st Meeting Strasbourg Wednesday 19 March–21 March GT-GDR-F(2014)R1, 21 March 2014.
[11] OSJI, *Q&A: Protecting and Strengthening the ECHR*, 2012, pp. 2–4.
[12] See https://docplayer.net/amp/9633446-Drafting-group-f-on-the-reform-of-the-court-gt-gdr-f.html.
[13] Ibid.

and its supervision) and (iv) the place of the ECHR mechanism in the European and international legal order.[14]

Following the Brighton Conference, the AIRE Centre also participated in a working group of European NGOs providing input on behalf of civil society to the development of Protocols No. 15 and No. 16 to the ECHR, which were drafted to improve the functioning of the Convention system.[15] This significant reform has involved changes to the judicial control mechanism influenced by NGOs (such as EHRAC) and funded by private foundations that made some amendments (see below).[16]

4.1.1.3 The Brussels Conference: Execution and Implementation of ECtHR Judgments

The Brighton Conference was followed by the Brussels Declaration, the purpose of which was to adopt a political declaration and an action plan for the reform process begun in 2010 with the Interlaken, Izmir and Brighton Declaration, while emphasising both the shared responsibility for implementation of the ECHR and the execution of the judgments of the ECtHR.[17] Indeed, while the Brussels Declaration emphasised recent progress and the fact that the ECtHR's backlog had been reduced, it underlined the sheer number of cases still pending at the Court. That is why, on 26 March 2015, the CoE member states met in Brussels for a high-level conference entitled 'Implementation of the European Convention on Human Rights (ECHR), our shared responsibility' to raise questions about the effectiveness of the implementation mechanism, given that over 11,000 judgments remained unimplemented by the member states at the end of 2013.[18] The draft Declaration proposed enhancing cooperation and bilateral dialogue amongst the CoE bodies and states parties with regard to implementation of the ECHR; to increase, at the level of both the CM and states parties, the effectiveness of the system of

---

[14] See www.coe.int/en/web/human-rights-intergovernmental-cooperation/work-completed/future-of-convention-system.

[15] AIRE Centre, *2012 Annual Report of the AIRE Centre*, p. 5.

[16] Ibid.

[17] High-level Conference on the Implementation of the European Convention on Human Rights, Our Shared Responsibility. Brussels Declaration 27 March 2015, available at https://justice.belgium.be/sites/default/files/downloads/Declaration_EN.pdf; See also Directorate General of Human Rights and Rule of Law, Council of Europe (2015) High-Level Conference on the Implementation of the European Convention on Human Rights, Our Shared Responsibility, Proceedings, Brussels, 26 and 27 March 2015.

[18] Ibid.

supervision of the execution of ECtHR judgments; to enhance the use, in a graduated manner, by the CM of 'all of the tools at its disposal' in the supervision process, as well as calling for it to hold 'thematic debates' on issues relating to the execution of judgments and to have national experts with 'sufficient authority and expertise' taking part in Committee meetings; to ensure better implementation of the ECHR at national level, including through the preparation of high-quality action plans and the involvement of national parliaments in the execution process; and to increase resources for the Department for the Execution of Judgments.[19]

Some important NGOs were given the opportunity by the Belgian Chairmanship to make comments on the draft Declaration. In response, on 26 February 2015, ten human rights NGOs (including EHRAC, the AIRE Centre, JUSTICE, the European Network of National Human Rights Institutions, the Law Society, the OSJI, the ICJ, the Dutch Section of the International Commission of Jurists, the HFHR, HRW and AI) signed a joint statement in response to the draft Brussels Declaration.[20]

The statement by the NGOs and private foundations recommended efforts to improve the implementation of ECtHR judgments, but it also expressed their concerns with the current draft, as well as making recommendations for improvement.[21] More specifically, the NGO statement put forward ten action points, including what kind of measures states should enact to improve their judgment execution process; what information they should transmit to the CM in a year's time; and the way the CM should publicly report on what specific measures have been adopted to increase the transparency of its working methods and the resources of the Department for the Execution of Judgments. The NGOs also promoted a more methodical and active follow-up on judgments related to systematic, systemic, widespread or gross human rights violations; removal of the invitation to the ECtHR to 'maintain its vigilance with regard to respect for the margin of appreciation'; and explicit acknowledgement of the role of civil society in the implementation of Convention rights, in the execution of ECtHR judgments and in supporting the efforts of states parties to better embed Convention rights at the national level.[22]

---

[19] Ibid.
[20] Joint NGO Statement on the draft Brussels Declaration on the Implementation of the European Convention on Human Rights, Our Shared Responsibility, March 2015.
[21] Ibid.
[22] Ibid.

The NGOs also took part in an official side event 'Implementation of Convention Rights and Judgments', notably to give their views on the implementation of judgments. For instance, EHRAC evoked specific issues with the implementation of the judgments of *Volkov v. Ukraine* (discussed in Chapter 3) and *Yuri and Klaus Kiladze v. Georgia*,[23] in which EHRAC sought redress over the malfunctioning of Georgian legislation concerning the granting of compensation to victims of Soviet-era repression. The ECtHR identified a 'legislative void', which led to the passing of new legislation by the Georgian authorities in 2011 in order to effect compensation payments for up to 20,000 victims.[24]

More importantly, in Brussels the OSJI was among the most important guests invited to share its opinion on the strengthening of the ECHR system and ECtHR judgments through their improved implementation at national level,[25] with a greater variety of graduated measures[26] to be used by the CoE against reluctant member states.[27] On this occasion, the OSJI argued for the reinforcement of the role played by NGOs and private foundations in terms of complaint, monitoring and assistance in the execution of judgments and communications with the CoE CM, with a view to transmitting more information to it and exerting more influence on it.[28]

This very active advocacy and agenda-setting on the part of private foundations and the NGOs they fund has continued and has even been intensified since the Brussels Declaration and meeting. For instance, the OSJI, the AIRE Centre, AI, EHRAC, the ICJ, Judgment Watch and JUSTICE sent comments together to the Ministers' Deputies' Ad Hoc Working Party on Reform of the ECHR system (GT-REF.ECHR)

---

[23] Case no 7975/06, *Klaus and Iouri Kiladze v. Georgia* [2 February 2010] ECtHR.
[24] Communication from M. Mamuka Longuraskvili, Georgian Ministry of Justice to Genevieve Mayer, Head of Department for Execution of Judgments, available at http://tinyurl.com/p8w9kyy.
[25] Directorate General of Human Rights and Rule of Law, Council of Europe (2015), High-Level Conference on the Implementation of the European Convention on Human Rights, Our Shared Responsibility, Proceedings, pp. 128–129.
[26] Including more rigorous forms of public scrutiny (such as the resumed use of press releases), public hearings, in situ missions, use of proceedings under Article 46(4), and more frequent meetings of the Committee of Ministers of Human Rights (CM-DH).
[27] Directorate General of Human Rights and Rule of Law, Council of Europe (2015), High-Level Conference on the Implementation of the European Convention on Human Rights, Our Shared Responsibility, Proceedings, p. 129.
[28] Ibid., p. 128.

focusing on implementation of Chapter C of the Brussels Declaration on the supervision of the execution of judgments.[29] In their submission, the NGOs advocated for more precise guidance as to the circumstances in which Article 46 §4, which set up an infringement proceeding, could be used (with more cooperation with NGOs), and for the development of graduated measures to be applied when a state refuses to abide by ECtHR judgments. The NGOs also promoted the enhancement of synergies between CoE stakeholders including the Parliamentary Assembly of the CoE, the CM, the Commissioner for Human Rights and the ECtHR. The NGOs recommended that their role should be more important and that they should have more influence at the Committee's Human Rights meetings.[30] Thanks to their advocacy efforts, the NGOs obtained an extension of Rule 9 and the possibility of international organisations and NGOs making written communications to the CoE.[31]

4.1.1.4 The Copenhagen Declaration

More recently, and following the Brussels Declaration, one private foundation (the OSJI) and seven NGOs (including EHRAC, Fair Trials, EIN, the AIRE Centre, the OMCT SOS-Torture Network, ICJ and AI) have been involved with the future of the ECHR system set out in the Copenhagen Declaration.[32] Some of the provisions of the Draft Copenhagen Declaration allow for rights to be relativised by reference to the importance of national considerations,[33] including the vagaries of political interest and influence,[34] and permitting diverse and varied implementation of the ECHR across national member states.[35] The NGOs

---

[29] AIRE Centre, AI, EHRAC, ICJ, Judgment Watch, JUSTICE and OSJI, Submission to Ambassador Šahović, 2015, available at http://ehrac.org.uk.gridhosted.co.uk/wp-content/uploads/2015/12/Brussels-Declaration-Chapter-C.11-12-15.pdf.

[30] Ibid.

[31] See www.coe.int/en/web/cm/april-2015/-/asset_publisher/FJJuJash2rEF/content/ad-hoc-working-party-on-reform-of-the-human-rights-convention-system-gt-ref-echr-14-04-2015-?desktop=false.

[32] Draft Copenhagen Declaration, 5 February 2018, available at https://menneskeret.dk/sites/menneskeret.dk/files/media/dokumenter/nyheder/draft_copenhagen_declaration_05.02.18.pdf.

[33] '... rights being protected predominantly at national level by State authorities in accordance with their constitutional traditions and in light of national circumstances' (§ 14).

[34] 'In matters of general policy, on which opinions in a democratic society may reasonable differ widely, the role of the domestic policy-maker should be given special weight' (§ 23).

[35] 'Consistency in the application of the Convention does not require that States Parties implement the Convention uniformly' (§ 57).

notably underlined, in a joint statement,[36] that the draft declaration made on 5 February 2018 by the Danish Chairmanship of the CM, which favours the principle of subsidiarity enjoyed by national states and some limitations on the jurisdiction of the Court,[37] is at risk of undermining the universality of human rights and the authority of the ECtHR and could even lead to the fragmentation of the European human rights system.[38] The NGOs also pointed out the lack of emphasis on national implementation of the ECHR and on the execution of judgments by national states.[39] The Parliamentary Assembly of the CoE and the NGOs both denounced the draft declaration, which according to them threatens (1) the universality of the rights protected by the ECHR,[40] (2) the independence of the ECtHR and its freedom from political influence,[41] (3) the very broad scope of the ECtHR's jurisdiction concerning interpretation and application of the ECHR, with some limitations specifically set up by the draft declaration on immigration and asylum,[42] and

---

[36] Joint NGO Response to the Draft Copenhagen Declaration, 13 February 2018, available at http://ehrac.org.uk/wp-content/uploads/2018/02/Joint-NGO-Response-to-the-Copenhagen-Declaration-13-February-2018.pdf. This NGO statement was further supported by the following organisations (status as of 22 February 2018): Committee on the Administration of Justice (CAJ), United Kingdom; DIGNITY, Danish Institute against Torture, Denmark; FIACAT –International Federation of Action by Christians for the Abolition of Torture; Foundation against the Violation of Law NGO, Armenia; Georgian Institute of European Values (GIEV); Georgian Young Lawyers' Association; Greek Helsinki Monitor, Greece; Memorial, Russian Federation; ILGA-Europe; Institute for Peace and Democracy, Azerbaijan/Netherlands; International Partnership for Human Rights; Justice and Peace Netherlands; Lawyers Committee for Human Rights, Serbia; Legal Resources Centres, Moldova; LGBT Denmark; Macedonian Young Lawyers Association (MYLA); Mass Media Defence Centre, Russian Federation; PINK Armenia; Promo-LEX Moldova; Redress; Danish Refugee Council; European Centre of Albania; Europe in Law Association, Armenia; Helsinki Foundation for Human Rights, Poland; Hungarian Helsinki Committee; Ukrainian Helsinki Human Rights Union; and Women's Initiatives Supporting Group (WISG), Georgia.

[37] 'The Court ... should not take on the role of States Parties whose responsibility it is to ensure that Convention rights and freedoms are respected and protected at national level' (§ 22).

[38] Joint NGO Response to the Draft Copenhagen Declaration, 13 February 2018; CoE Parliamentary Assembly (2018) Declaration on the Draft Copenhagen Declaration on the European Human Rights System in the Future Europe Adopted by the Standing Committee on 16 March 2018, AS/Per (2018) 03, available at http://assembly.coe.int/Communication/Declarations/AS_PER_2018_03_EN.pdf.

[39] Ibid., p. 2.

[40] Ibid.

[41] Ibid.

[42] 'The Court should not act as an immigration appeals tribunal, but respect the domestic courts' assessment of evidence and interpretation and application of domestic legislation,

CONTRIBUTION OF PRIVATE FOUNDATIONS AND NGOS 153

(4) the unconditional obligation of states parties[43] to implement the ECtHR's judgments.[44] Instead, the NGOs argued for the need to respect and preserve the independence of the ECtHR (albeit not from their own influence), ECtHR supervision of effective human rights protection at the national level, the enhancement of the role played by civil society in implementing the ECHR at the national level, the Court's authority to review human rights cases concerning asylum, immigration and cases arising from international conflicts, preservation of the Court from the influence of national states, better execution of judgments, and strengthening of national processes for the selection and election of European Court judges (see below).[45] A tension therefore exists between the claims by NGOs for an independent European Court and their own embeddedness in the Court.

More particularly, the monitoring of the implementation of judgments is part of broader efforts made by the OSJI to improve the effectiveness of the ECtHR through influence on the nominations of judges and the adoption of procedures and to increase the impact of its own strategic litigation.[46] Notably, in co-funding (along with the Human Rights Implementation Centre at Bristol University, the Human Rights Centre at the University of Essex, Middlesex University, and the Centre for Human Rights at the University of Pretoria) a project that aims to improve execution of judgments,[47] the OSF argued in a similar manner for a more efficient process of execution of the ECtHR rulings and for additional resources to be allocated to the Court:

unless arbitrary or manifestly unreasonable' (§ 25); 'When examining cases related to asylum and immigration, the Court should avoid intervening except in the most exceptional circumstances' (§ 26).
[43] 'The ensuing acceptance [of the Court's judgments] by all actors of the Convention system, including governments, parliaments, domestic courts, applicants and the general public as a whole, is vital for ensuring the authority and effectiveness of the Convention system' (§ 56)
[44] CoE Parliamentary Assembly (2018) Declaration on the Draft Copenhagen Declaration on the European Human Rights System in the Future Europe Adopted by the Standing Committee on 16 March 2018.
[45] Joint NGO Response to the Draft Copenhagen Declaration, 13 February 2018.
[46] OSJI, *Global Human Rights Litigation Report*, 2015, p. 4.
[47] The ESRC Human Rights Law Implementation Project (HRLIP), available at www.bristol.ac.uk/media-library/sites/law/documents/2016%2002%2005%20HRLIP%20Project%20Flyer%20(Eng).pdf. The aim of the project is to track selected decisions by the UN and regional human rights treaty bodies against nine countries in Africa, Europe and the Americas to see the extent to which states have implemented them and why.

> The CM should be encouraged and resourced to use their existing authority more robustly, transparently and effectively in overseeing the execution of judgements. We believe the answer lies in the enforcement and implementation of judgements. We welcome current proposals to recruit additional judges and/or lawyers to help the Court.[48]

In the context of ECtHR reform, the OSF considers its own role as an important factor of change and a significant contribution to a betterment of the execution of ECtHR judgments:

> ECtHR judgements that are not executed are a rebuke to the integrity of the Court, and frustrate the potential for positive change in Council of Europe countries. Council of Europe institutions offer unique tools to assist in protecting, respecting, and fulfilling the rights promised by ECHR judgements. The work carried out by OSJI over the past several years to improve the execution of ECHR judgements through strategic engagement of these tools – and OSJI's tangible contribution to strengthening the Committee of Ministers' capacity to supervise the execution of judgements – demonstrates the value of such strategic engagement on an ongoing basis.[49]

These efforts have resulted in increased participation by private foundations and the NGOs they fund in the reform of the ECtHR and the execution of ECtHR judgments by national governments, as seen above (Cliquennois and Champetier 2016), and in additional Protocols (notably Nos. 15 and 16) to the ECHR that reinforce the oversight of the execution of ECtHR judgments (see Chapter 1).

As a complement to litigation and to advocacy efforts oriented towards ECtHR reform, the OSF and EHRAC lobby the CM through regular meetings with officials including ministers, ambassadors and diplomats,[50] and the OSF provides information and expertise to the Committee through quarterly briefings.[51] These meetings allow the OSF plenty of opportunity to advocate a better execution of the cases that the foundations characterise as a priority, which turn out to be those brought against Russia, Azerbaijan and Greece.[52] The OSF lobbies other CoE

---

[48] OSJI, *Q&A: Protecting and Strengthening the ECHR*, 2012.
[49] Ibid.
[50] OSJI, 'An Open Society Justice Initiative concept note – short version, Human rights made real: establishing a Strasbourg-based presence to improve the implementation of ECHR judgments', internal document.
[51] Ibid.
[52] For instance, in 2014, cases considered as the most important by the Open Society were *Mahmudov and Agazade* v. *Azerbaijan* (No. 35877/04), and *Fatullayev* v. *Azerbaijan*

bodies, such as the Parliamentary Assembly, the Department of Execution of Judgments, the Commissioner for Human Rights (who recognises their influence by remaining very close to human rights defenders and NGOs),[53] and the European Commission against Racism and Intolerance, the General Rapporteur on the rights of the lesbian, gay, bisexual and transgender community, with a view to putting pressure either on the CM or on member states responsible for executing ECtHR judgments at the national level.[54]

In comparison, the influence of the OSF on the CJEU seems to be far less than that exerted on the ECtHR and is exercised more via advocacy and pressure on the European Parliament and the European Council than via direct participation in reform of the CJEU (McCown 2009; Sokur 2016). By 26 December 2020, the CJEU will have to report to the European Parliament, the Council and the Commission on the functioning of the General Court regarding its efficiency, the necessity and effectiveness of the increase to fifty-six judges, the use and effectiveness of resources, and the further establishment of specialised chambers and/or other structural changes.[55]

4.1.2 NGO Influence on the Rules of the ECtHR on the Treatment of Classified Documents

In 2018, the ECtHR's Standing Committee on the Rules of the Court organised a consultation on its report on the treatment of classified documents, published on 31 January 2018 with the view to introducing a new Rule of Court (Rule 44F) on classified documents. The aim of the Standing Committee's Report was to 'create a proper mechanism for

---

(No. 40984/07), Committee of Ministers Human Rights Meeting on 3–5 June 2014, Strasbourg; the *Namat Aliyev* v. *Azerbaijan* group of cases (No. 18705/06), 8 July 2010, CM Human Rights Meeting on 3–5 June 2014; *M. S. S.* v. *Belgium and Greece* (No. 30696/09), see Cliquennois and Champetier (2016).

[53] For instance, the European Commissioner for Human Rights stated in a third party intervention that 'the leading member of the NGO Memorial in Chechnya was a key partner of the Commissioner's Office', Third Party Intervention by the CoE Commissioner for Human Rights under Article 36 ECHR, Application no 42705/11, Svetlana Khusainovna Estemirova against the Russian Federation, CommDH(2016)18, 14 March 2016.

[54] OSJI, 'An Open Society Justice Initiative concept note – short version, Human rights made real: establishing a Strasbourg-based presence to improve the implementation of ECHR judgments', internal document.

[55] See Article 3(1) of Regulation (EU, Euratom) 2015/2422.

guaranteeing the parties, and in particular the Governments, adequate protection of confidential (sensitive/secret/classified) documents produced by them at the request of the ECtHR' following significant problems that had arisen, notably in extraordinary rendition cases such as *Al Nashiri v. Poland* (see Chapter 3). Some NGOs were consulted, including EHRAC, which submitted a response to such a consultation on 9 April 2018. In its response, EHRAC made a range of proposals about state authorities' non-disclosure of documents on the ground that they are 'classified' or otherwise confidential, or when the authorities claim not to have certain documents in the first place.[56]

The draft rule, which was proposed by EHRAC, imposes a new clear and specific obligation on states to disclose to the ECtHR any information which is claimed to be confidential and a full justification of such claims, which have to be scrutinised strictly by the ECtHR.[57] EHRAC advocated the drawing of adverse inferences by the ECtHR where a party falls short of the new procedures. EHRAC expects the Court's new practice to result in a higher level of disclosure (of documents which governments have previously refused to disclose), and clearer and more definitive consequences if a member state unjustifiably seeks to rely on claims of secrecy in refusing to provide disclosure.[58] Lastly, EHRAC proposed a concomitant right for applicants to the ECtHR to claim confidentiality, for instance in situations where there is evidence of intimidation and pressure exerted by state authorities.[59] These proposals remain pending.

4.1.3 Research Conducted by NGOs and Private Foundations on the ECtHR's Pilot Judgments Procedure and Fact-Finding Processes

Advocacy efforts combined with growing private participation in reform of the ECtHR could help to reinforce the growing influence of the Strasbourg Court. This might constitute one of the aims pursued by several private foundations, as it could give them more power. In addition, private foundations and some of the NGOs they fund conduct

---

[56] EHRAC submission to the European Court of Human Rights' Standing Committee on the Rules of Court – Report on the Treatment of Classified Documents (31 January 2018), 9 April 2018.
[57] Ibid.
[58] Ibid.
[59] Ibid.

research on several aspects of the European human rights judicial system with a view to reinforcing their influence on reforms of that system. For instance, EHRAC's research on the ECtHR's pilot judgment procedure (PJP) has informed and assisted the ECtHR in developing and codifying standards related to its use.[60] Upon completion of their research, Philippe Leach's team at EHRAC disseminated their findings at a collaborative seminar hosted at the ECtHR in Strasbourg in June 2010. Participants included ECtHR Judges (Lech Garlicki and Françoise Tulkens), registrars (Erik Fribergh, Michael O'Boyle), and Head of the Department for Execution of Judgments (Genevieve Mayer), as well as government representatives. Directly inspired by the EHRAC research, the Court announced in March 2011 the introduction of a new rule (Rule 61 of the Court Rules) to clarify and codify the PJP.[61]

In addition, EHRAC conducted a research on the ECtHR's fact-finding processes. This research is cited as a primary source by O'Boyle and Brady (ECtHR Deputy Registrar and Registry Lawyer) in their 2013 article in *European Human Rights Law Review* on the investigatory powers of the ECtHR (O'Boyle and Brady 2013), in which they discuss how the Court is likely to develop its approach to fact-finding. The approach applied by the ECtHR is consequently under the influence of EHRAC and a literature that is very close to the views expressed by NGOs financed by private foundations (see for instance Lambert Abdelgawad 2016). Such a phenomenon is reinforced by the direct participation of members of private foundations and NGOs in the scientific and legal literature on the ECtHR, its jurisprudence and strategic litigation they carry out (Goldston 2017).

More generally, the perspectives gained by private foundations and NGOs through their direct commitment and involvement in litigation are reflected and published in academic writing (see for instance Angelari et al. 2016, Leach 2005 and 2008, Leach et al. 2010a, Leach et al. 2010b) and academic presentations (see for instance Goldston 2001, 2018). The latter disseminate their achievement and advocate for implementing the new strategy and good practice they would like to be used by the European human rights justice system.

---

[60] See www.mdx.ac.uk/__data/assets/pdf_file/0018/145170/Human-Rights-Advocacy-and-Training-case-study3.pdf.
[61] ECtHR, Rule 61 of the Rules of Court, 18/03/2011. See www.strasbourgconsortium.org/content/blurb/files/Article_61_Pilot_judgment_procedure.pdf.

4.2 Private Influence on Nominations of European Judges

As a supplement to litigation and research activities,[62] and as part of their advocacy efforts, the OSJI and the ICJ have recently released an advocacy report on how to strengthen law and practice in the selection of human rights judges.[63] The report focuses on nominations at the national level, which it considers the critical point of entry for improving the selection process for regional human rights judges. The report notably points out the lack of a national legal framework for nominating judges; even though several European countries have created ad hoc processes for nominations, the report stresses that in practice only the Slovak Republic has an actual legal framework in place. The report also notes the lack of transparency on the processes for nominations, ranging from a lack of publicity for calls for applications to insufficient or non-existent consultation with civil society stakeholders, including national bar associations. Lastly, the report denounces the political aspect of nominations of European judges and makes in this regard five recommendations:

- the designation of a national independent body charged with conducting a national selection procedure with a view to ensuring a transparent and competitive process
- the development and publication of reasoned criteria order to check that all candidates meet the minimum qualifications for nomination
- the adoption of affirmative steps to make gender parity a reality
- the enhancement of the roles played by civil society, NGOs, and bar and civic associations in the dissemination of calls for application
- the establishment of an advisory committee/group.[64]

In recommending the integration of NGOs and civil associations and making them participate in the recruitment of judges, the OSJI and the ICJ are advocating for an increase in their own influence on the nomination of judges. In this regard, it is worth noting that one judge at the CJEU and some current judges at the ECtHR worked (before joining the ECtHR) either directly for private foundations (namely the OSF) or for NGOs financed by private foundations. A large majority of these judges come from Eastern countries and small countries that are easily

---

[62] See for instance the Volkov case analysed in Chapter 3.
[63] OSJI and ICJ, *Strengthening from Within: Law and Practice in the Selection of Human Rights Judges and Commissioners*, November 2017.
[64] Ibid.

influenced by private foundations.[65] Such influence is encouraged in part by the process of voting at the ECtHR, since each judge from any country has the same power to vote (according to Rule 23 of the ECtHR).[66] Judges who have previously worked for private foundations and NGOs participate on a regular basis in pilot and landmark judgments that are litigated by private foundations (such as those analysed in Chapter 3).

In this regard, at the ECtHR, the current Bulgarian judge and new President of section was member of the board of the OSJI (in New York) from 2011 to 2015, member of the board of the OSI (Sofia) from 2001 to 2004, member of the board of the Mental Disability Advocacy Center (Budapest) from 2002 to 2006, founding member of the Bulgarian Helsinki Committee from 1992 to 2013 and member of the Legal Advisory Committee of the European Roma Rights Centre from 1998 to 2010.[67] Similarly, the new Albanian judge was Director of Programs at the OSF for Albania (Tirana) from 2016 to 2017, Legal Officer and Senior Attorney at the OSJI (based in New York and Tirana) from 2003 to 2015,[68] and he worked for HRW from 2001 to 2003.[69] The current Croatian judge and the new president of the first section of the Strasbourg Court was member of the board of the Croatian Institute Open Society from 2005 to 2006 and worked with the International League for Human Rights and Helsinki Watch from 1991 to 1993 before becoming judge at the ECtHR in 2012.[70] She even participated from 2004 to 2007 in research conducted by Open Society Croatia on the creation and implementation of an 'index of open society' related to the rule of law.[71] The Ukrainian judge worked from 2008 to 2010 for the IPC,[72] which is

---

[65] Ibid.
[66] ECtHR (2019) Rules of the Court, Strasbourg, 9 September 2019.
[67] See www.echr.coe.int/Pages/home.aspx?p=court/judges&c=.
[68] In that position, he filed their party interventions to the ECtHR in *El-Masri v. Former Yugoslav Republic of Macedonia*, in *Yildirim v. Turkey*, in *Centro Europa 7 v. Italy*, in *Sanoma Uitgevers v. Netherlands*, in *Katya Kasabova v. Bulgaria*, in *Társaság a Szabadságjogokért v. Hungary* and in *Romanenko and Others v. Russia* (discussed in Chapter 3). See http://assembly.coe.int/nw/xml/XRef/Xref-XML2HTML-en.asp?fileid=25032&lang=en.
[69] See http://assembly.coe.int/nw/xml/XRef/Xref-XML2HTML-en.asp?fileid=25032&lang=en.
[70] Parliamentary Assembly (2012) Election of Judges to the European Court of Human Rights: List and Curricula Vitae of Candidates Submitted by the Governments of Bosnia and Herzegovina, Croatia, the Czech Republic, the Netherlands, Poland, the Russian Federation, Sweden and the United Kingdom, Doc. 12936, 22 May 2012, 35.
[71] Ibid., 36.
[72] See www.echr.coe.int/Pages/home.aspx?p=court/judges&c=.

financed by the OSF (see Chapter 2), and the Romanian judge was a member of the board of the ICJ before joining the ECtHR.[73] The current British judge was a member of the Board of Directors of the AIRE Centre from 2000 to 2008 and a trustee and member of the Board of Directors of Interights from 2004 to 2015.[74] Likewise, the Dutch judge was a member of the Advisory Committee of the Dutch Section of the ICJ from 2010 to 2017 and an expert to the ICJ mission on strengthening the judiciary in the Russian Federation from 2014 to 2016.[75] The current and well-known Portuguese judge (famous for his dissenting opinions in some cases in which the ECtHR notably decided to grant a certain margin of appreciation to the member states) worked for AI before joining the ECtHR.[76] The same applies to the former Hungarian judge who worked for the Central European University, which is fully financed by the OSF, and received an academic grant and fellowship from Soros.[77] At the CJEU, the Polish judge was a member of the Polish Helsinki Committee before joining the Luxembourg Court.[78]

More globally, a very recent report by the European Centre for Law and Justice asserts that at least 22 of the 100 European permanent judges between 2009 and 2019 are former officials or collaborators of seven NGOs that are highly active before the Strasbourg Court.[79] Twelve judges are linked directly to the OSF, seven to the Helsinki committees, five to the ICJ, three to AI, and one each to HRW, Interights and the AIRE Centre. Given the number of judges attached to it and its funding of the other six NGOs, the OSF is clearly the most influential of these. The report also tends to demonstrate that since 2009 judges have sat in a case that involved the NGO with which they were linked in 88 cases (of 185 cases in which at least one of these seven NGOs was officially involved in

---

[73] See www2.ohchr.org/english/bodies/hrc/membersCVs/motoc.htm.
[74] See www.echr.coe.int/Pages/home.aspx?p=court/judges&c=.
[75] Ibid.
[76] See CoE Parliamentary Assembly, Election de juges à la Cour européenne des droits de l'homme (conformément à l'article 22 de la Convention européenne des droits de l'homme) Liste et curricula vitae des candidats présentés par le gouvernement du Portugal, Doc. 12463 17 janvier 2011, p. 18, available at http://assembly.coe.int/nw/xml/XRef/X2H-Xref-ViewPDF.asp?FileID=12610&lang=fr.
[77] See https://people.ceu.edu/sites/people.ceu.hu/files/profile/attachment/1232/cvsajo2007.update-dec.pdf.
[78] See https://curia.europa.eu/jcms/jcms/Jo2_7026/en/.
[79] European Centre for Law and Justice (2020), *Report on NGOs, and the Judges of the ECtHR, 2009–2019*. Strasbourg, February 2020.

proceedings). Over the same period, a judge withdrew in only 12 cases, apparently because of a link with an NGO involved in the case.[80]

This professional background cannot be ignored and could be conducive, as neo-institutionalist theory puts it, to professional isomorphism, mimetic processes and normative pressures (DiMaggio and Powell 1983). These processes mean that professional experience and previous professional practices are not removed but regularly applied by judges to decide on the cases submitted to them, as analysis of their dissenting opinions reveals.[81] In this way, prior socialisation on the job tends to continue over time and to reinforce the conformities caused by having the same educational background (DiMaggio and Powell 1983), which includes fellowships, visiting scholarships and even having completed Master's degrees in American universities financed by private foundations.[82] Judges who have worked for these private donors and organisations are sensitive to the fields invested by private foundations (such as discrimination and rights of minorities) and generally share the same liberal (broad) approach to human rights as their former employers by defending a wider interpretation of the ECHR by the ECtHR and the dominance of the ECHR over the principle of subsidiarity and over the margin of appreciation enjoyed by national states. Such a view is notably expressed in some of the key cases in which the judges mentioned above have participated (and that we analysed in Chapter 3),[83] and also in dissenting opinions given by these judges as outlined above.

---

[80] Ibid., pp. 15–17.
[81] See for instance Case nos 26766/05 and 22228/06, *Al-Khawaja and Tahery* v. *United Kingdom* [15 December 2011] ECtHR, dissenting opinion of Judge Sajó; Case no 48876/08, *Animal Defenders International* v. *United Kingdom* [22 April 2013] ECtHR, dissenting opinion of Judge Sajó; Case no 57592/08, *Hutchinson* v. *United Kingdom* [17 January 2017] ECtHR, dissenting opinions of Judges Pinto de Albuquerque and Sajó. In this last case, Judge Pinto de Albuquerque was sharply critical of the idea that the margin of appreciation 'should be wider for those States which are supposed "to set an example for others" and narrower for those States which are supposed to learn from the example'. He explained that, '[t]his evidently leaves the door wide open for certain governments to satisfy their electoral base and protect their favourite vested interests. In my humble view, this is not what the Convention is all about.'
[82] See www.echr.coe.int/Pages/home.aspx?p=court/judges&c=.
[83] For instance, the Bulgarian judge was part of the decision making in the cases of *Denisov* v. *Ukraine*, *Fabian* v. *Hungary*, *Merabilishvili* v. *Georgia*, *Rasul Jafarov* v. *Azerbaijan*, *Mammadov* v. *Azerbaijan*, *Aliyev* v. *Azerbaijan* and *Mammadli* v. *Azerbaijan*. The Croatian judge notably took part in the following key cases: *Fabian* v. *Hungary*, *Roman*

Another way of partly capturing the internal organisation and the rules of the European Courts and of influencing European case law is for private foundations and NGOs to advocate for a broader approach to third party interventions that they regularly submit to the Courts.

4.3 A Broader Approach to Third Party Interventions Submitted by Private Foundations and NGOs

NGOs backed up by private foundations have also obtained over time a broader approach and an enlargement of the scope of litigation and of third party interventions and amicus curiae submitted by them to the ECtHR (see above). NGOs have notably asked for a right to third party intervention and the inclusion of parties to domestic proceedings without any condition or limitation by the ECtHR.[84] The case of *Cestaro v. Italy* illustrates this trend and the broader conception of amicus curiae (Bürli 2017).[85] In this judgment, while the Italian government promoted the view that the role of amicus curiae intervention is to provide new or additional information or arguments pertinent for the decision of a case,[86] the Italian Radical party and the NGO 'No Peace without Justice'[87] (funded by the OSF, the Sigrid Rausing Trust, the International Crisis Group, the UN, the World Bank and some national governments

---

Zakharov v. *Russia, Magyar Helsinki Bizottag* v. *Hungary, Blokhin* v. *Russia, Sargsyan* v. *Azerbaijan* and *Merabilishvili* v. *Georgia*. The Romanian judge participated in the judgment of *Magyar Helsinki Bizottag* v. *Hungary; Blokhin* v. *Russia, Fabian* v. *Hungary, Sargsyan* v. *Azerbaijan* and *Ilgar Mammadov* v. *Azerbaijan*. The Ukrainian judge appeared in the cases of *Denisov* v. *Ukraine, Kuric and Others* v. *Slovenia, S. A. S.* v. *France, Merabilishvili* v. *Georgia, Stanev* v. *Bulgaria, Sargsyan* v. *Azerbaijan, Navalnyy* v. *Russia, Janowiec and Others* v. *Russia, Magyar Helsinki Bizottag* v. *Hungary, Baka* v. *Hungary* and *Belane Nagy* v. *Hungary*. The British judge was involved in the judgments of *Navalnyy* v. *Russia* and *Karoly Nagy* v. *Hungary*. The Dutch judge participated in the cases of *Navalnyy* v. *Russia, Sargsyan* v. *Azerbaijan, Bayev* v. *Russia, Alekseyev* v. *Russia* and *Tsakoyevy* v. *Russia*. The Portuguese judge was involved in the judgments of *Câmpeanu* v. *Romania, Baka* v. *Hungary, Fabian* v. *Hungary, Mammadov* v. *Azerbaijan, Sargsyan* v. *Azerbaijan, Karoly Nagy* v. *Hungary* and *Merabilishvili* v. *Georgia*.

[84] Letter to the ECtHR on Behalf of OSJI, Human Rights Watch, the AIRE Centre, EHRAC, ICJ, Mental Disability Advocacy Centre, Justice, AI, Redress and European Roma Rights Centre, 30 November 2015, available at http://ehrac.org.uk.gridhosted.co.uk/wp-content/uploads/2015/12/Protocol-16-Letter-30-Nov-2015.pdf.

[85] Case no 6884/11, *Cestaro v. Italy* [7 April 2015] ECtHR.

[86] Ibid., §123.

[87] See www.npwj.org/About-NPWJ/Overview.html.

including the UK and the US)[88] considered in contrast that interventions proposing legal reforms or denouncing the lack of legislation in a certain area (as had been made by the three interveners in *Cestaro v. Italy*), are compatible with the role of amicus curiae intervention before the ECtHR.[89] The ECtHR, in admitting and considering such NGO interventions, disagreed with the Italian government and was obviously of the same opinion as the NGO that they were compatible with the role of amicus curiae.[90] Thus the ECtHR accepted from this moment an increasing influence on legislation and administrative reforms of NGOs through third party interventions.

The very high level of litigation carried out by private foundations and NGOs has also favoured the introduction of private-sector management techniques that advantage repeat litigants and thus private foundations and NGOs.

4.4 The Introduction of Private-Sector Management Techniques at the ECtHR and the CJEU Favouring NGOs and Private Foundations

Some management techniques coming from the private sector (synonymous with private foundations and the NGOs that they fund) such as cost-effectiveness evaluations, audit mechanisms and performance indicators have recently been introduced and implemented at both the ECtHR[91] and the CJEU,[92] with a view to reducing the number of pending cases and their backlog. The objective pursued by the European Courts is to reduce their costs and to improve their efficiency and productivity against a background of general reductions in public spending as part of the austerity measures. The origins of the backlog are considered by the whole literature on judicial management to lie in new membership, the enlargement of the CoE and the EU, additional protocols to the ECHR and new EU legislation, and the wider competences of both Courts (Chalmers 2012c; de Búrca 2013; Lambert Abdelgawad 2013).

However, although these factors tend to generate some judicial backlog, the role played by NGOs and private foundations, which litigate

---

[88] See www.npwj.org/About-NPWJ/Program-Partners.html.
[89] Case no 6884/11, *Cestaro v. Italy* [7 April 2015] ECtHR, §202.
[90] Ibid., §127.
[91] CoE, RBB(2012) Conclusions, Seminar on Results-Based Budgeting: Objectives, Expected Results and Performance Indicators, 25 September 2012.
[92] Court of Justice of the European Union, Annual Report 2014, Luxembourg.

thousands of cases to the European Courts (in particular pilot judgments, which often require more than a hundred applications, see Chapter 2) has been completely ignored by scholars. This role is significant, since the litigation activities conducted by NGOs and private foundations contribute alongside those other institutional factors to increasing the backlog and the number of pending cases. Even the wider scope of competences of the European Courts cannot be analysed without taking account of the advocacy efforts made by private foundations and NGOs (see above). Consequently, the latter have to be included in any analysis of the introduction of a management-based approach in both Courts resulting from a sharp rise in the number of individual applications and the backlog for which private foundations and NGOs are partly responsible.

Faced with this backlog, the ECtHR has been forced to improve its accountability and processes and to show to governments in economic difficulties that its policy is cost-efficient (Lambert Abdelgawad 2017). Even prior to the economic downturn, the CoE had decided in the 2000s to adopt a new budgetary management organisation by implementing the Results-Based Budgeting (RBB) strategy, as the increasing number of member states was putting strong pressure on the budget, with requests to cut costs coming from the German, Italian and UK governments in particular (Lambert Abdelgawad 2017). More precisely, RBB is defined as 'a results-driven budgeting process' with 'pre-defined objectives, expected results, outputs, inputs and performance indicators', which were initially the reduction of the backlog and full compliance with the backlog criteria. Several quantitative criteria were added in 2005 to integrate a minimal number of decisions and the introduction of a pilot procedure influenced by private foundations and NGOs (see above).[93] In 2007, an additional performance indicator emerged with 'the average number of finally disposed applications of per case-processing lawyer' supposed to measure the rise in productivity.[94]

This new policy oriented towards results was followed by the introduction of IT tools to accelerate the management of repetitive and easy cases,[95] of a priority policy focused on the most serious cases (see Chapter 1),[96] of Rule 47 with its stricter requirements for an application

---

[93] CM(2004)155 vol. 1, vote IV, 53.
[94] Budget 2007, CM(2006)146 vol. 1, title IV, 58.
[95] ECtHR, The Interlaken Process and the Court (2016 Report), 1 September 2016, 4, §8.
[96] The Court's priority policy is available at www.echr.coe.int/Documents/Priority_policy_ENG.pdf.

to be considered as valid,[97] and the establishment of specialised hubs at the Registry with a view to developing more standardised drafting on thematic issues such as immigration.[98] At the ECtHR, this managerial shift took place in several steps, with an internal audit in 2001,[99] a further internal audit in 2004 in response to requests for additional resources,[100] and an external audit in 2012.[101] The audit mechanism, defined as 'internal and external audits in conformity with generally accepted international auditing standards', was therefore an integral part of this managerial reform.

More generally, the CoE, but also the EU and many other international organisations, had used management strategies derived from the private sector, notably based on the UN's management model created in 2005 following the adoption of the Paris Declaration on Aid Effectiveness (founded on Ownership, Harmonisation, Alignment, Results and Mutual Accountability)[102] by more than a hundred countries in a context of austerity and a fight against government waste. This strategy was firmly grounded on a results-based approach and 'Results-Based Management' for programming and budgeting in order to get a real return on investment, to have a concrete, measurable effect on people and to demonstrate good performance.[103] Following the economic slump, the UN reinforced this approach,[104] and the EU improved its performance budgeting methods and audit mechanisms in 2010, followed by the CoE in 2011. This led to stronger links between activities, resources and results to

---

[97] ECtHR, Report on the Implementation of the Revised Rules on the Lodging of New Applications, 02.2015, 1, available at www.echr.coe.int/Documents/Report_Rule_47_ENG.pdf.
[98] ECtHR, The Interlaken Process and the Court (2016 Report), 1 September 2016, §12.
[99] Report no 02/2001, Report of the Audit of the European Court of Human Rights, Report No 02/2001 of 3 August 2001, Internal Audit Department, *Human Rights Law Journal* (2001) 22(5–8), pp. 335–337, at 336.
[100] The audit reported that average productivity could be increased by 20 per cent.
[101] CM(2012)100, §284.
[102] See www.oecd.org/dac/effectiveness/34428351.pdf; CoE, Budget Committee, 18–22 October 2004, Extracts on Performance Indicators, Extracts of the Meeting Report (CM(2004)192).
[103] European Union (2013), Performance Budgeting and Decentralized Agencies. Guidelines, December 2013, pp. 4–20; General Secretariat of the Council of Europe, Programme and Budget Service (2014) Review of the Programme and Budget Framework (RBM/RBB), Concept Paper, 15 April 2014.
[104] UNESCO, *Results-Based Programming, Management and Monitoring (RBM) – Guiding Principles*, January 2012; United Nations Development Programme, *Monitoring and Evaluating for Development Results*, 2009.

achieve short-term results and longer-term impact.[105] Quantitative indicators were refined by the ECtHR in 2011 to take into account the duration of proceedings, the number of cases a judge has decided, the increase in the number of cases decided according to court formation (with a focus on single-judge and priority cases in recent years) – and a decrease in the number of pending cases.[106]

For its part and in a similar manner, the CJEU has also had to cope with an increasing backlog of cases caused by the enlargement of the EU, the recent adoption of the ECFR, a large amount of new EU legislation and the new judicial review of EU criminal law (Chalmers 2012a; de Búrca 2013).[107] But unlike the ECtHR, the influence played on the CJEU by private foundations and NGOs is much weaker, since litigation activities are much less intense before the CJEU and the possibilities of intervening as third party are significantly fewer (see Chapters 2 and 5). The response to this backlog has been both constitutional and managerial. First, the constitutionalisation of the court has been considerably reinforced by the suppression of the EU's Civil Service Tribunal and by the doubling of the number of General Court judges in three successive stages up to 2019 in order to compensate for this suppression.[108] Second, the CJEU has taken significant organisational and procedural actions to increase its case handling and reporting.[109] In this regard, the CJEU has adapted the Rules of Procedure of both the Court of Justice and the General Court in order to accelerate the handling of cases.[110] It has also enhanced accountability, as the CJEU has decided to publish statistics and analysis on the outcomes of its judicial activity, including the average duration of proceedings, the time taken between the date on which the

---

[105] European Union (2013) Performance Budgeting and Decentralised Agencies. Guidelines, December 2013, p. 7; Commission Regulation (EC, EURATOM) No 2343/2002 on the Framework Financial Regulation for the Bodies Referred to in Article 185 of Council Regulation (EC, Euratom) No 1605/2002 on the Financial Regulation applicable to the general budget of the European Communities (see Article 27 in particular). Budget and Program of the Council of Europe, 2012–2013, pp. 53–56.
[106] ECtHR, The Interlaken Process and the Court (2016 Report), 1 September 2016, p. 3.
[107] During the period 2006–2016, some 1,500 cases were lodged on average each year at the CJEU, and the overall number of pending cases rose by around 20 per cent. See Special Report No 14/2017: Performance Review of Case Management at the Court of Justice of the European Union, 26 September 2017, available at www.eca.europa.eu/Lists/ECADocuments/SR17_14/SR_CJEU_EN.pdf.
[108] Court of Justice of the European Union (2015) Annual Report 2014, Luxembourg, p. 3.
[109] Special Report No 14/2017: Performance Review of Case Management at the Court of Justice of the European Union, p. 10.
[110] Ibid., p. 13.

case is lodged at the Registry and the date of the final judicial decision, and the ratio of the number of closed cases to the number of incoming cases and to the number of pending cases.[111] However, such accountability and the reinforcement of its political aspect over time could have a negative effect on judicial independence (Langbroek 2009; Langbroek et al. 2017).

Performance indicators have also been introduced at the CJEU to measure and enhance judges' 'productivity'.[112] More precisely, the indicators include length of proceedings, clearance rate (the ratio of the number of resolved cases to the number of incoming cases), the number of pending cases,[113] monitoring and evaluation of court activities (including satisfaction surveys, access to justice, and availability of electronic submission of claims), the training of judges, the availability of Information and Communication Technology, budget, human resources and the availability of alternative dispute resolution methods.[114] The CJEU has also monitored the progress of individual cases against indicative internal deadlines for the main stages of the judicial procedures. Lastly, it has introduced a case management approach and indicative time frames for key steps in the lifecycle of cases, as well as implementing progressive monitoring tools and reports to increase its focus on timeliness. However, according to an audit carried out in 2017 (itself part of the privatisation trend), the current case management approach is not focused on tailored time frames for individual cases, taking into account complexity, workload, resources needed and staff availability.[115] Up to now, the indicative time frames set for certain types of cases have served as an overall objective to be reached on average. Whilst this approach has led to some structural changes and has contributed to reducing the average time taken to adopt judicial decisions in both Courts,[116] as well as to reducing the significant backlog of cases that had built up at the General Court,[117] the average time taken to close certain

---

[111] Ibid.
[112] Court of Justice of the European Union (2015) Annual Report 2014, Luxembourg.
[113] Ibid.
[114] 2014 EU Justice Scoreboard, COM(2014)155 final, 6.
[115] Ibid.
[116] For example, in 2016 the overall average duration of proceedings was 14.7 months at the Court of Justice and 18.7 months at the General Court. This represents a reduction of 0.9 and 1.9 months respectively as compared to 2015. See Special Report No 14/2017, Performance Review of Case Management at the Court of Justice of the European Union, p. 13.
[117] Ibid., p. 10.

types of cases or procedures cannot be equated with the notion of reasonable time taken to deal with each individual case.[118] Consequently, this management approach tends to advantage litigating and well-funded organisations (such as the European institutions, private companies, trade unions, private foundations and NGOs) that are repetitive players before the Court and have much more time to litigate than individuals.

Beyond the need to evaluate audit mechanisms, performance indicators and outputs (Barzelay 2001), it is important to analyse their impact on the attitudes of NGOs and private foundations towards reform of the European judicial system and also on how the registrars of the European courts deal with cases on a daily basis. It is of particular interest to consider how the financial dimension, the performance indicators and the external audits have impacted judicial reforms and future reform proposals (see above). The impact of the external audits has certainly been to legitimise the new strategic approach adopted by the ECtHR and the CJEU towards the 'prioritisation' policy that is leading to the constitutionalisation of the European Courts. For instance, the first ECtHR audit report acknowledged that 'the transition to a results-based culture is a long and difficult process which requires new attitudes and practices to be adopted and, often, staff capacities to be increased'.[119] This new managerial policy has not only potentially impacted daily practices but has notably transformed the ECtHR into a new organisation partly inspired by the model of the US Supreme Court (Lambert Abdelgawad 2017) and characterised by its constitutionalism. In this way and since 2014, the definition of the ECtHR's mission has turned even more towards procedural choices and an acceleration of filtering, with the introduction of a single judge, a hierarchisation policy, and a communication policy suitable for deterring manifestly ill-founded applications.[120]

Therefore, the impacts of constitutionalisation, financial and management considerations on the protection of fundamental rights in Europe and on the influence played by private foundations and NGOs have to be scrutinised. The legitimacy and impacts of these mechanisms on the effective protection of fundamental rights have mostly been overlooked by scholars, with a few notable exceptions (Dehousse 2011) that have examined the relevance of this quantitative model to fundamental rights activities (for the UN, see Landman and Carvhalo 2009). In this regard,

---

[118] Ibid.
[119] Registry of the European Court of Human Rights (2013) Annual Report 2012, Strasbourg.
[120] CoE Programme and Budget 2014–2015, p.20.

the implementation of new managerial reforms seems to impact individual applicants who face financial obstacles when bringing their cases to the European courts (Lambert Abdelgawad 2011, 2016 and 2017), thus creating filters and distortions in guaranteeing fundamental rights through the European Courts. In this respect, the implementation of private-sector management techniques and quantitative criteria at the ECtHR and the CJEU has impacted their structures and their day-to-day handling of applications and complaints in such a way that the filtering and priority policy conducted by the Courts to fight their backlog and control the incoming flow of applications tends to favour repetitive and professional litigants (NGOs and private foundations) to the detriment of individual applicants.

In summary, the new constitutional designs of the European Courts and the development of a management approach applied by them (and caused in part by the litigation activities conducted by private foundations and NGOs) could enhance the influence of private foundations on the Courts' jurisprudence (and on the execution of judgments), since these management techniques tend to benefit professional, repetitive and well-funded litigants. In this perspective, private foundations could be encouraged to either engage or reinforce their involvement in litigation before the European Courts. They could also be motivated to increase their voluntary financial contributions to the EU and CoE organisations in return for more influence. It should be acknowledged that private foundations and NGOs not only litigate in but also advocate and lobby the European Courts, the CoE and the EU organs with the aim of influencing the design and the rules of the Courts and preparing a successful litigation. Such advocacy efforts contribute substantively to the growing influence of private foundations on European human rights justice. While their impact on the CJEU is rather limited, the influence of private foundations on the ECtHR consists in orienting and even capturing a significant portion of its jurisprudence, its execution of judgments, its evolutive structures and even its agenda-setting. Thus, rather than merely capturing the NGOs they finance, private foundations are partly able to capture not only the inputs of the ECtHR but also its outputs and its internal organisation. This process of capture has to be measured against the substantive dimension of the growing influence of private foundations on the European Courts. The creeping influence exerted by private foundations on the European justice system thus raises questions about the effectiveness of human rights protection in this specific context.

PART II

The Substantive Dimension of the Growing Influence of Private Foundations on European Human Rights Justice

The second part of the book studies the substantive aspect of the influence of private foundations by analysing its effects on the orientation of European jurisprudence towards specific countries (Eastern European countries and Russia) and domains (Chapter 5). In this perspective, the same chapter offers insight into countries and cases (notably related to austerity policies) neglected by private foundations and NGOs in their litigation activities. Chapter 6 emphasises the most important effect of the concentration of litigation on Russia and certain other Eastern European countries: the rise of tensions between the EU, the US and Russia. The orientation of European case law and these new political tensions therefore question the relationship between the litigation and advocacy carried out by private foundations and the political and economic agenda and interests they pursue (Chapter 7). In this regard, the main aim pursued by private foundations and NGOs is to influence the European Courts and make them deliver judgments that are priorised by the Courts and are in line with their interests and values. Finally, the Conclusion will consider whether the influence of private foundations in European human rights justice could be considered to be a private capture that could lead to the potential privatisation of human rights and their appropriation and ownership by private donors.

5

Effects of the Growing Influence of Private Interests on the Orientation of European Case Law

This chapter analyses the effects of the growing influence of private interests on the orientation of European case law. As discussed in Chapter 3, the cases in which the OSJI and NGOs intervene are selected in part through their potential prioritisation by the Courts (for a substantial part on the ground of the right to life, the right to dignity and the right to freedom and legal detention), for their potential to affect the Convention's effectiveness, or because they raise questions of general interest and pilot/leading judgments (which are considered by the ECtHR as an absolute priority in its own policy). Cases are also selected for their political and legal impacts on specific areas and countries, as we will see. In this regard, the first part of this chapter sheds light on the concentration of applications lodged by private foundations and NGOs in specific policy areas and specific countries, such as Eastern nationalist regimes including Russia. The second part of the chapter deals with countries and cases that are neglected or even ignored by private foundations and NGOs.

5.1 Orientation of Litigation towards Specific Policy Areas

As noted above, the legal cases in which the OSJI and some NGOs intervene are selected in part for their potential political and legal impacts on specific areas. In this respect, litigation priorities derive not only from the study of the case law of the European Courts but also from the current and future strategic goals set by private foundations and NGOs in their annual reports and their reports on their strategic litigation. For instance, EHRAC, one of the most active NGOs before the ECtHR, defines its current and future litigation priorities as follows:

> Our thematic foci in the coming 10 years will be to: Continue our focus on violations of the right to life, especially those arising from conflict situations and gross violations of human rights. This includes the right to

truth (1); Build on and expand our work around freedom of association and assembly (2); Explore and consider developing expertise on minority rights, freedom of religion, gender-based violence and environmental issues (3); Consider developing expertise in disability rights (4).[1]

More generally, the main policy and litigation areas invested by the OSJI and the NGOs financed by private foundations are discrimination against certain minorities (including ethnic and cultural minorities, refugees and LGTB persons); specific protection of certain ethnic, sexual and religious minorities (migrants, Roma, Muslims and LGTB persons) who are victims of state oppression; political opponents (who fight nationalist states) and human rights activists; penal and immigration policies and detention; changes to the judiciary; counterterrorism policies; political cases and fights over territories; and free election and media.

For example, the rulings which are brought by the OSJI (through direct litigation and third party intervention) concern heavily politicised issues, such as the Janowiec judgment delivered by the Grand Chamber of the ECtHR regarding the 1940 Katyn massacre (in which 21,000 Polish prisoners of war were killed by Soviet officials) and the inadequacy of the Russian authorities' investigation of the massacre.[2] The political tension culminated when the Russian government refused to disclose a copy of the decision made in 2004 to cease the investigation, on the ground that it was classified under domestic law,[3] following a third intervention submitted by the OSJI that 'the right to truth, seen in its individual dimension, presupposed access to the results of investigations, as well as to archived and open investigative files and that such disclosure was essential to prevent violations, fight immunity and maintain public faith in the rule of law'.[4] The case of *Bagdonavicius* v. *Russia*,[5] which was also litigated by the OSJI, involved an allegation of bulldozing and burning in

---

[1] EHRAC, *Strategic Plan 2013–2023*, p. 11, available at http://ehrac.org.uk/wp-content/uploads/2014/10/EHRAC-Strategy-2013.pdf#page=12.

[2] Case nos 55508/07 and 29520/09, *Janowiec and Others* v. *Russia* [21 October 2013] ECtHR, available at http://hudoc.echr.coe.int/eng?i=001-127684. Written comments were submitted by the OSJI as third party in the proceedings along with AI, the Public International Law and Policy Group, Memorial; the European Human Rights Advocacy Centre and the Transitional Justice Network. See also OSJI, *Global Human Rights Litigation Report 2015*, 1 July 2015, available at www.opensocietyfoundations.org/reports/global-human-rights-litigation-report, p. 35.

[3] Ibid., §§142–144.

[4] Ibid., §124.

[5] Case no 19841/06, *Leonas Iono Bagdonavicius and Others* v. *Russia* [11 October 2016] ECtHR, available at http://tinyurl.com/hykzkdc.

a discriminatory manner the Roma houses in the village of Dorozhoe. The Magnitskiy case against Russia is another politicised case brought by the OSJI, which obtained the condemnation of the Russian authorities (see Chapter 3).[6] The OSJI also took to the ECtHR the Makhashevy case,[7] which concerned racism, assault and ill treatment inflicted by the Russian police on Chechens on account of their ethnicity and the ensuing lack of proper investigation of the claims under Articles 3, 5, 13 and 14 ECHR.[8]

Other political cases taken by the OSJI to the CJEU and the ECtHR concern the way the Bulgarian authorities (including the police) stereotype Roma in a discriminatory manner,[9] and have convicted a reporter of defamation for a corruption story.[10] Similarly, the OSJI has obtained the condemnation of the Czech Republic for carrying out educational segregation of Roma children,[11] of Hungary for having violated the right to information of the NGO the Hungarian Civil Liberties Union,[12] of Macedonia and Poland for having hosted secret CIA prisons and inflicting torture,[13] and of Bosnia and Herzegovina for denying political and voting rights to ethnic minorities.[14]

Consequently, the specific policy areas litigated by private foundations and NGOs are also linked to the countries targeted by them, which are what some of them call 'nationalist regimes'.

5.2 Litigation against Specific Countries: Eastern Europe and Russia

The analysis of the European case law in Chapter 3 shows an overrepresentation of Eastern countries and Russia among the countries that

---

[6] Case nos 32631/09 and 53799/12, *Magnitskiy and Others* v. *Russia* [27 August 2019] ECtHR; see OSJI, 'Magnitskiy v. Russia: Summary of Application Filed before the European Court of Human Rights', October 2012, available at www.opensocietyfoundations.org/litigation/magnitsky-v-russia.

[7] Case no 20546/07, *Makhashevy* v. *Russia*, 31 July 2012, available at http://hudoc.echr.coe.int/eng?i=001-112535.

[8] Ibid.

[9] Case C-83/14, *Nikolova* v. *CEZ Electricity* [16 July 2015] CJEU; Case nos 43577/98 and 43579/98, *Nachova* v. *Bulgaria* [6 July 2005] ECtHR.

[10] Case no 22385/03, *Kasabova* v. *Bulgaria* [19 April 2011] ECtHR.

[11] Case no 57325/00, *D. H.* v. *Czech Republic* [13 November 2007] ECtHR.

[12] Case no 37374/05, *Társaság a Szabadságjogokért* v. *Hungary* [14 April 2009] ECtHR.

[13] Case no 39630/09, *El-Masri* v. *Macedonia* [13 December 2012] ECtHR; Case no 28761/11, *Al Nasrihi* v. *Poland* [24 July 2014] ECtHR; Case no 33234/12, *Al Nasrihi* v. *Poland* [31 May 2018] ECtHR.

[14] Case nos 27996/06 and 34836/06, *Sejdić and Finci* v. *Bosnia and Herzegovina* [22 December 2009] ECtHR.

are condemned by the ECtHR through litigation efforts made by private foundations and NGOs. Conversely, the roster of key repeated litigants against Eastern countries and Russia in particular allows us to assert that one private foundation (the OSJI) and a limited number of NGOs have played a key role in defining the input of the ECtHR case law against these countries (see Table 2.1). These NGOs have been able to play this role thanks to generous funding from a limited number of private donors. As discussed in Chapter 2, the influence exerted by donors is not purely informal; it is also formalised through calls for proposals, projects and grants explicitly aimed at 'enhancing' litigation and execution of judgments concerning nationalist regimes and Russia's involvement in regional and armed conflicts (such as in Chechnya and Georgia) and, in general, human rights violations in Eastern countries. Dependence on a limited number of private sources of funding may well result in a selection bias, as similar breaches of standards in other countries may not be brought before the ECtHR because of a lack of similar levels of private funding.

For instance, the cases in which the OSJI intervenes either as direct litigant or through third party interventions are notably selected for their potential political and legal impacts on specific countries. In this regard, the complaints which are brought by the OSJI (but also by NGOs more generally) mainly involve Eastern countries (Romania, Bulgaria, Poland, Hungary, Bosnia and Herzegovina, the Czech Republic, Lithuania, Slovenia and Macedonia) and Russia, countries which have been targeted by twenty-seven judgments out of forty-seven obtained by the OSJI between 2004 and 2018.[15]

What explains such an overrepresentation of Eastern countries undertaken by the OSJI and NGOs? One factor may be the structural flows of the constitutional systems of Eastern countries, their domestic remedies, and the sheer number of Conventions that they have recently adhered to and ratified. Another factor is the difference that private foundations and NGOs (which are experts in litigation against Eastern countries) make in litigation, since the number of cases litigated by private foundations and NGOs against Russia and Eastern countries (Table 5.1) exceeds proportionally the number of judgments rendered by the ECtHR against these countries (Tables 5.2 and 5.3). More precisely, around 40% of the judgments rendered by the ECtHR concerned three member states of

---

[15] OSJI, *Global Human Rights Litigation Report*, 2017, pp. 23–29.

Table 5.1 *NGOs and their litigation activities, 2000–2018*

NGO	Estimated number of cases against Russia and other Eastern countries brought before the ECtHR since 2000
Memorial	101 positive rulings, including 87 against Russia. Most rulings and complaints deal with Chechnya and violations by Russian security forces during the Chechen armed conflict and counterterrorism operations.
European Human Rights Advocacy Centre (EHRAC)	More than 300 positive judgments, including 150 rulings against Russia. Most cases concern the Beslan school siege and mass surveillance, the ongoing conflicts in Chechnya, Ukraine, Dagestan and in the contested region of South Ossetia, and the territorial dispute with Georgia.
International Protection Center (IPC)	450 cases, of which 420 concern Russia
Nizhny Novgorod Committee against Torture	93 cases against Russia. Most cases concern torture in police custody and police ill treatment.
Stichting Russian Justice Initiative (SRJI)	More than 450 cases against Russia. These cases are related to grave human rights abuse in Chechnya (following the Chechnya conflict), Ingushetia and other North Caucasus republics.
Open Society Foundations (OSF)	25 landmark cases, of which 17 concern Russia. These cases are entirely political (see above) and involve the Chechen conflict.
Interights	209 cases against Russia, not including sensitive cases. The most important cases are related to the political conflict between Russia and Moldova. Other cases concern torture, disability and sexual orientation.

Based on annual reports made by the NGOs and their cases taken to the ECtHR and the CJEU

the CoE: Turkey (17.13%), Italy (12.57%) and the Russian Federation (9.26%).[16] After these three countries, Romania (6.44%), Ukraine

---

[16] ECtHR (2018), Overview 1959–2017, available at www.echr.coe.int/Documents/Overview_19592017_ENG.pdf.

Table 5.2 *Total number of applications per country, 1959–2017*

Country	Number of applications decided (1959–2017)	Number of applications in which judgment was delivered (1959–2017)
Russian Federation (since 1998)	141,132	4,549
Turkey (since 1959)	89,079	5,272
Ukraine (since 1995)	82,514	17,369
Romania (since 1993)	66,180	2,132
Poland (since 1993)	65,973	1,159
Italy (since 1959)	37,882	3,350
France (since 1959)	31,652	1,104
Germany (since 1959)	29,620	357
United Kingdom (since 1959)	23,945	1,839
Hungary (since 1990)	17,875	592
Bulgaria (since 1992)	15,188	778
Czech Republic (since 1993)	12,588	266
Spain (since 1977)	11,729	225
Netherlands (since 1959)	10,209	184
Sweden (since 1959)	9,917	151
Greece (since 1959)	7,881	1,239
Switzerland (since 1963)	6,918	185
Portugal (since 1976)	3,540	512
Norway (since 1959)	1,733	53
Ireland (since 1959)	1,005	33

ECtHR (2018) Overview 1959–2017, available at www.echr.coe.int/Documents/Overview_19592017_ENG.pdf

(5.91%), Poland (5.67%), France (5.18%), Greece (4.74%), Bulgaria (3.10%) and the UK (2.83%) are the countries most often involved in ECtHR judgments.[17]

The very high number of cases against the Russian Federation and other Eastern countries seems to be the result of a combination of

[17] Ibid.

Table 5.3 *Numbers of ECtHR judgments and ECHR violations by Russia (1998-2017) and by main CoE member states (1959-2017)*

Country	Number of ECtHR judgments	Number of ECHR violations (at least one)
Turkey (since 1959)	3,386	2,988
Italy (since 1959)	2,382	1,819
Russian Federation (since 1998)	2,253	2,127
Romania (since 1994)	1,352	1,202
Ukraine (since 1995)	1,213	1,188
Poland (since 1993)	1,145	958
France (since 1959)	997	728
Greece (since 1959)	963	864
Bulgaria (since 1992)	653	588
United Kingdom (since 1959)	545	314
Hungary (since 1990)	472	448
Portugal (since 1976)	341	259
Germany (since 1959)	321	193
Czech Republic (since 1993)	230	186
Switzerland (since 1963)	182	106
Netherlands (since 1959)	160	90
Spain (since 1977)	157	103
Sweden (since 1959)	150	60
Norway (since 1959)	45	29
Ireland (since 1959)	34	22

ECtHR (2018) Overview 1959-2017, available at www.echr.coe.int/Documents/Overview_19592017_ENG.pdf

structural flows in their 'domestic' systems for protection of fundamental rights and the 'facilitating' role played by private foundations and NGOs in bringing a considerable amount of the set of potential cases before the ECtHR.

5.2.1 Structural Flows of the Constitutional Systems of Eastern Countries and Their Domestic Remedies

The impressive number of applications filed by private foundations and ECtHR judgments against Eastern countries and against Russia in particular may partly reflect the structural flows in the constitutional systems of these countries for protection of fundamental rights. A long line of cases taken to the Strasbourg Court shows Russia's failure to remedy persistent structural problems concerning the protection of fundamental constitutional rights. These structural problems boil down to three issues: first, a lack of domestic mechanisms to ensure compliance with rulings condemning Russia (and some other Eastern countries) for breaches of the ECHR; second, the fact that there is no genuine Russian supreme court; and third, the large number of conventions to which Russia is party.

In connection with the first point, a good many petitions are caused by a lack of domestic mechanisms to ensure that executive bodies comply with national judicial decisions. More than 200 rulings since 2002 have concerned the failure of the Eastern states (including Russia, Romania, Poland and Hungary, see above) to pay the amounts awarded by the ECtHR to litigants.[18] Similarly, the first pilot judgment against Russia concerned non-compliance with decisions of Russian courts by executive bodies.[19] As a result, the ECtHR has been acting vis-à-vis Eastern countries less as a subsidiary guardian of rights (as expected in the ECHR system) than as a de facto court of last instance. Thorbjørn Jagland, then secretary general of the CoE, claimed that this problem would be solved in due course through inter-ministerial coordination and the introduction of an effective domestic remedy. Indeed, there are now Eastern and particularly Russian laws that provide compensation to victims of unreasonably lengthy judicial and enforcement proceedings.[20]

In connection with the second point, structural problems with the institutional design of Eastern courts are the cause of another part of the mountain of cases against these countries that reach the ECtHR. For instance, in Russia a large portion of these cases are appeals against decisions taken by the regional courts of the eighty federal entities of the Russian Federation. This is a result of the limited jurisdiction of the Russian Constitutional Court. In particular, the Constitutional Court is not competent to review either legislation or administrative decisions by reference to the ECHR. Consequently, the Russian Federation, along with

---

[18] Council of Europe, ECtHR Violations by Each State 1959–2014, available at www.echr.coe.int/Documents/Stats_violation_1959_2014_FRA.pdf.

[19] Case no 33509/04, *Burdov* v. *Russia* [15 January 2009] ECtHR.

[20] Speech by Mr Thorbjørn Jagland, Secretary General of the Council of Europe, 'The Vertical of Justice', First Petersburg International Legal Forum, 20–21 May 2011, available at www.coe.mid.ru/doc/Jagland_20052011.htm.

other Eastern states, currently lacks a constitutional court or a genuinely supreme court, and this lack would explain a good number of the applications to the ECtHR.[21] The constitutional design of the Russian Constitutional Court is also problematic, because Article 125 of the 1993 Russian Constitution states that the Court is only able to review legislative acts enacted by the federal legislature, and only when the legislative normative act in question has been applied, or is about to be applied, to a concrete case (Hausmaninger 1995; Krug 1997). Section 4 of the said Article explicitly says that the Constitutional Court exercises abstract review of legislative normative acts in concrete cases; consequently, the Court is barred from considering the facts arising in concrete litigation (Hausmaninger 1995) and from reviewing normative or non-normative acts approved by the president and government (Kriazhkov and Lazarev 1998). Therefore, the rulings of Russian regional courts are quite often brought to the Strasbourg Court because there is no appeal possible to the Russian Constitutional Court.

In connection with the third point, the issues are compounded by the large number of human rights conventions to which Russia has recently become party. Russia is party to fifty-eight conventions.[22] Many of these conventions are considered and used by the Strasbourg Court as international relevant instruments and standards, although the only Convention monitored in principle by the court is the ECHR and its sixteen additional protocols (all of which have been ratified by Russia).[23] The

---

[21] Ibid.

[22] Including the European Social Charter, the Convention of the International Labour Organisation (ILO) on freedom of association and the protection of the right to organise and to bargain collectively, the framework for the protection of national minorities (which provides Russia with a monitoring system to assess how the treaty is implemented), the Convention on the Rights of Persons with Disabilities, the CoE Convention on the Protection of Children against Sexual Exploitation and Sexual Abuse, the Optional Protocol on the Sale of Children, Child Prostitution and Child Pornography, the 2002 General Policy Recommendation No. 7 on National Legislation to Combat Racism and Racial Discrimination Adopted by the CoE's European Commission against Racism and Intolerance (ECRI), the UN Convention on the Elimination of Racial Discrimination of 4 January 1969, and the MEDICRIME convention.

[23] See for instance Case nos 55762/00 and 55974/00, *Timishev* v. *Russia*, [13 December 2005] ECtHR, §33, litigated by the OSJI, which relies on the General Policy Recommendation No. 7 on National Legislation to Combat Racism and Racial Discrimination and the UN Convention on the Elimination of Racial Discrimination. See also Case no 67336/01, *Danilenkov and Others* v. *Russia*, 30 July 2009, available at http://hudoc.echr.coe.int/fre?i=00193855#{%22itemid%22:[%22001-93855%22]}, which applies Convention No. 87 of the International Labour Organisation (ILO) on Freedom of Association.

higher the number of normative commitments to the ECHR, the higher the number of potential breaches.

5.2.2 The Difference that Private Foundations and NGOs Make Concerning the Overrepresentation of Eastern Countries

The overrepresentation of Eastern countries could also be explained by the very high level of investment made by private foundations in these countries over time. As discussed in Chapter 2, the influence of private donors is not purely informal but has come to be formalised through calls for proposals, projects and grants explicitly aimed at 'enhancing' litigation to expand the influence of the human rights movement over the world through funding of international organisations dealing with human rights. A closer look at the profiles of directors and trustees chairing the boards of private foundations and the identities of the beneficiaries of litigation grants and funding launched by private foundations (see Chapter 7) shows, on the one hand, a free market and even neoliberal orientation adopted by private foundations (especially the Ford Foundation, the MacArthur Foundation and the OSF) and, on the other hand, a concentration of private investments in the monitoring of human rights in Eastern countries and especially Russia (and its involvement in regional and armed conflicts such as in Chechnya and Georgia). While historical factors such as the Helsinki Act might help explain this specific focus, private donors seem to reinforce this trend considerably and to be particularly interested by Eastern countries, as has been shown recently by their investments in specific grants and calls for proposals. For instance, in 2006 the OSF launched the call 'Chechnya Justice Project', which was granted to the SRJI.[24]

In this regard, although the Soros foundations have their headquarters in New York, Soros established his first non-US foundation in Hungary in 1984 and then foundations in Poland, Ukraine and Russia by the time of the fall of the Berlin Wall in 1989 (Porter 2015). After the collapse of communism, against which he fought along with other American foundations (such as the Carnegie Foundation, the Ford Foundation and the Rockefeller Foundation) through significant funding of NGOs (Tournès 2010), Soros created many foundations throughout Eastern Europe and

---

[24] See www.srji.org/files/reports/2004.doc.

Asia, also financing NGOs that seek change in the political regimes close to Russia (Giblin 2008; Pétric 2008).

The picture is quite similar for the Ford Foundation. The main grants from the Ford Foundation outside the US were made through the Eastern European Trust for Civil Society in Central and Eastern Europe (which was founded and financed by the German Marshall Fund of the United States, the OSF and the Rockefeller Brothers Fund) covering Bulgaria, Hungary, the Czech Republic, Poland, Slovakia, Slovenia and Romania.[25] The grants served to transfer donor assistance to active organisations and networks. In this way, the Ford Foundation supported and financed the HFHR (1982–2007),[26] which was composed of forty-six local Helsinki Committees, some of which are still active and continue to take cases to the ECtHR and the CJEU (see above). The local Helsinki Committees were the Eastern European Committees (see above), the Western European Committees (which were active in Denmark, Finland, the Netherlands, Norway and Switzerland) and Helsinki Watch in the US (which became HRW in 1993); these were also financed by the OSF to monitor the human rights practices of the signatory countries to the 1975 OSCE Helsinki Final Act.[27] This Ford funding continued in the next decades,[28] along with other financial supports from the Rockefeller Foundation[29] and the Mc Arthur Foundation,[30] before Eastern countries joined the CoE. Thus litigation undertaken by Eastern NGOs (including the European Human Rights Centre, the Polish Helsinki Foundation for Human Rights and the Russian Lawyers Committee for the Defense of Human Rights)[31] before the ECtHR was financed for the very first time by the Ford Foundation at the end of the 90s.[32]

---

[25] Ford Foundation, *Annual Report of 2007*.
[26] Ford Foundation records, Grants Helsinki Watch, Inc (0900307), 1 February 1979–31 March 1993.
[27] Ford Foundation records, Grants (FA732D), International Helsinki Federation for Human Rights (08600306), 1 March 1986–31 March 1998.
[28] Ibid. Ford Foundation records, Grants (FA732D) International Helsinki Federation for Human Rights (08600306), 1 March 1996–31 March 1998.
[29] Rockefeller Foundation, *Annual Report 1998–1999*.
[30] Ford Foundation records, Grants (FA732D), IHF (08350716) International Helsinki Federation for Human Rights, 1 August 1983–31 December 1985.
[31] Ford Foundation Grants, Russian Lawyers Committee in Defense of Human Rights, Grant 28119 for precedent-setting human rights litigation in Russia and at the European Court of Human Rights 2006, $240,000.
[32] Ford Foundation, *Ford Foundation Grantees and the Pursuit of Justice*, 2000, p. 19.

In 1992, the MacArthur Foundation opened a satellite office in Moscow that offered $173 million in grants to advance human rights in Russia. The Moscow Helsinki Group,[33] the Nizhny Novgorod Regional Non-Governmental Organisation Committee Against Torture and Public Verdict Fund (see above), the Kazan Human Rights Centre and the Independent Council of Legal Expertise were the main beneficiaries of the thematic grants launched by the Moscow office to develop their long-term strategy to promote police accountability, strengthen the rule of law, improve access to justice, and raise international human rights standards in Russia. The aim of such funding was to enhance the human rights movement by monitoring human rights in Russia and through the continued expansion of the regional monitoring network.[34] Nevertheless, the Moscow office was closed in 2015 because the Russian government continued to limit activities of NGOs considered as foreign agents (see below).

A new phase for the Oak Foundation began in the early 1990s, when its annual grant-making increased to 4,000 grants to organisations around the world through eleven programmes, including Environment, Child Abuse, Housing and Homelessness, International Human Rights, Issues Affecting Women and Learning Differences. Regarding human rights issues, through funding in the form of multi-year grants the Oak Foundation supports activist organisations involved in strategic litigation concerning gross violations of human rights, prohibition of arbitrary detention and torture, due process guarantees, discrimination faced by LGTB people and protection of human rights defenders at risk.[35] The Foundation directly funds human rights organisations in the EU (including the UK), the US, Russia, Brazil, India and Myanmar.[36] Several NGOs litigating the European Courts have benefitted from numerous thematic grants. Fair Trials received funding to protect fundamental rights and freedom from arbitrary detention and torture in Europe. Civic Rights Defenders, the Legal and Social Support Charity Foundation and Memorial received grants to provide legal support for victims of Russia's anti-immigration and anti-LGTB state law and protection from arbitrary

---

[33] The Moscow Helsinki Group was a recipient of the 2011 MacArthur Award for Creative and Effective Institutions and received $750,000. See www.macfound.org/maceirecipients/14/.
[34] http://macfound.org/media/article_pdfs/Russia_INFO_ENG.PDF See also www.macfound.org/maceirecipients/search/all?search_text=&program=11#recipients-search.
[35] See http://oakfnd.org/international-human-rights.html.
[36] Ibid.

arrest and detention. The Freedom of Information Foundation, the OSI (human rights and governance grants programme), the IPC, the Russian Justice Initiative, the Norwegian Helsinki Committee and the Nizhny Novgorod Committee against Torture have benefitted from grants to fight Russian human rights violations and implement ECtHR decisions. HRW has received funds to train a new generation of Russian human rights activists. EHRAC and the Public Verdict Foundation were funded to assist NGOs and lawyers in Russia in taking cases to the ECtHR to seek redress for gross human rights abuses committed by Russia (especially in Chechnya). The Bulgarian and Hungarian Helsinki Committees were financed to improve respect for human rights in Bulgaria and Hungary, with a particular focus on liberty and security and policing discrimination.[37]

The Sigrid Rausing Trust shares this approach of investing in programmes run in Eastern countries. For instance, EHRAC (through programmes for advocacy, research and litigation),[38] Redress and Fair Trials (both of them through programmes for detention, torture and the death penalty),[39] the HFHR and the Georgian Young Lawyers' Association (both of them through programmes for advocacy, research and litigation), the ICJ (through programmes for transparency and accountability),[40] and the HHC (through programmes for advocacy, research and litigation) have been financed since 2006, 2010, 2011, 2013, 2015 and 2017 respectively by the Sigrid Rausing Trust for their litigation and advocacy activities at the ECtHR.[41] This Eastern orientation is reflected in the history of the Rausing family; Hans Rausing, the father of Sigrid Rausing, became over the course of his career an expert in Russian affairs and made many investments in Russia and Ukraine.[42]

---

[37] See http://oakfnd.org/grant-database-ihr.html.
[38] See www.sigrid-rausing-trust.org/Grantees/Programmes/Advocacy-Research-Litigation.
[39] See www.sigrid-rausing-trust.org/Grantees/Programmes/Detention-Torture-and-Death-Penalty.
[40] See www.sigrid-rausing-trust.org/Grantees/Programmes/Transparency-and-Accountability.
[41] See https://www.sigrid-rausing-trust.org/Grantees/European-Human-Rights-Advocacy-Centre; www.sigrid-rausing-trust.org/Grantees/REDRESS; www.sigrid-rausing-trust.org/Grantees/Fair-Trials; www.sigrid-rausing-trust.org/Grantees/Helsinki-Foundation-for-Human-Rights; www.sigrid-rausing-trust.org/Grantees/Georgian-Young-Lawyers-Association; www.sigrid-rausing-trust.org/Grantees/International-Commission-of-Jurists; www.sigrid-rausing-trust.org/Grantees/Hungarian-Helsinki-Committee.
[42] He was responsible for Tetra Pak's Russian market and negotiated the first Tetra Pak machine export to the Soviet Union in 1959, eventually making Tetra Pak the largest foreign employer in Russia. See https://en.wikipedia.org/wiki/Hans_Rausing.

Lastly, the NED also has a specific focus on Eastern countries including Russia.[43] In this regard, the NED finances on quite a large scale NGOs taking cases to the ECtHR, especially against Russia (see above).[44] For instance, from 2014 to 2017, $457,089 was granted by the NED to several NGOs (including the Human Rights Center and the Helsinki Association) for their litigation activities in Russia.[45]

Globally, advocacy efforts made by private foundations are also concentrated on Eastern countries. Private foundations are very keen to see the CoE, and in particular the ECtHR, focus more on Eastern countries and especially on Russia.[46] For instance, the OSF has published a report calling for an improvement in the execution and enforcement of ECtHR judgments (through the recruitment of additional judges and lawyers) and an even stronger case law on Russia. It is worth quoting at some length:

> We and other civil society groups argue that the solution is to deal with the source of the problem: continuing fundamental rights violations in member countries which produce the greatest volume of applications, many of them so called repetitive applications. Five countries – Russia, Ukraine, Romania, Turkey and Italy – currently account for just over half of the cases before the Court, with Russia accounting for 27% of the applications last year. These problems can be fixed if the political will is there. The Council of Ministers of the Council of Europe should be encouraged and resourced to use their existing authority more robustly, transparently and effectively in overseeing the execution of judgements. We believe the answer lies in the enforcement and implementation of judgements. We favour measures that aim at improving implementation of the court judgments by enhancing national mechanisms and increasing the pressure from the Committee of Ministers.[47]

In the same way, EHRAC has recently fought through advocacy efforts the ECtHR rule that allows state authorities non-disclosure of documents on the ground that they are 'classified' or otherwise confidential, or when the authorities claim not to have certain documents in the first place.[48]

---

[43] See www.ned.org/region/eurasia/.
[44] Available from www.ned.org/wp-content/themes/ned/search/grant-search.php.
[45] Ibid.
[46] OSJI, *From Judgment to Justice Implementing International and Regional Human Rights Decisions*, 25 November 2010, available at www.opensocietyfoundations.org/reports/.
[47] OSJI, *Q&A: Reform of the ECtHR* (April 2012) Briefing paper 4, available at www.opensocietyfoundations.org/briefing-papers/q-reform-european-court-human-rights.
[48] EHRAC Submission to the European Court of Human Rights' Standing Committee on the Rules of Court – Report on the Treatment of Classified Documents (31 January 2018), 9 April 2018.

EHRAC argued that its proposal to the ECtHR (see Chapter 4) to prohibit such non-disclosure of documents was based on its extensive experience of litigating cases against Russia, Ukraine and the South Caucasus states, where access to certain documents was regularly denied to EHRAC on the basis that they are classified or that they do not (or no longer) exist.[49] EHRAC emphasised disclosure as an element of the redress sought and as a way to establish what has happened, especially as regards enforced disappearances and use of lethal force.[50] In a more general manner, EHRAC denounced the Russian authorities for their historical non-cooperation with the ECtHR.[51]

In summary, the selective bias against Eastern countries and Russia in particular does not entail that the rulings of the ECtHR condemning them are contrived, but rather that Eastern countries and Russia (but not other states that breach standards) are on the ECtHR 'radar'. The reasons for singling out some Eastern countries and Russia while not scrutinising breaches in other CoE states as closely are to be found not in standards of fundamental rights but in the overall goals pursued by private donors, some of which are highly problematic from the normative perspective internal to the ECHR system (a point raised by Philippe Leach, head of EHRAC, himself).[52]

Consequently, direct litigation conducted by one of the main private foundations (the OSF) and dependence on a limited number of private sources of funding may well result in a selection bias, as similar breaches of standards in other countries may not be brought before the ECtHR and the CJEU owing to lack of similar levels of private funding.

5.3 Reduced Protection of Human Rights in Certain Countries and Policy Areas: Countries and Cases Ignored by NGOs and Private Foundations

In contrast, some areas and fields are neglected or even ignored by private foundations and NGOs in their litigation. The second part of this chapter highlights the effects of the increased dependence of NGOs on economic finance and on some member states. In terms of issues ignored

---

[49] Ibid.
[50] Ibid., p. 2.
[51] Ibid., p. 8.
[52] P. Leach, 'EHRAC's litigation at the European Court of Human Rights', SAGE seminar, University of Strasbourg, 13 February 2014, on file with the author.

by private litigation, reduced protection of social and economic rights is not an area litigated by private foundations. This process could therefore seriously compromise the right of individuals to make complaints to the ECtHR and the CJEU and to obtain adequate redress when their economic and social rights are breached.

5.3.1 Countries Ignored by Private Litigation

If we take a closer look at the countries that are less often condemned by pilot and priority judgments delivered under Article 46 by the ECtHR, we note that most such countries are what some scholars have called 'the consolidated democracies' and the oldest CoE state members, starting with France, the UK and Germany (see Tables 5.2 and 5.3). While these old democracies have seldom been condemned by the European Courts and are litigated weakly by private foundations (see Table 5.1 and Chapter 3), the economic and social policies they conduct and the negative impacts of those policies on human rights have been denounced by the UN Committee on Economic, Social and Cultural Rights (CESCR).

For instance, the CESCR stated for the first time in 2016 that austerity measures, social security, healthcare and welfare reforms adopted by the UK constitute a breach of its international human rights obligations to respect, protect and fulfil economic, social and cultural rights progressively, to the maximum of its available resources. In particular, the CESCR denounced the disproportionate adverse impacts of these policies on inequalities, poverty, unemployment, homelessness, discrimination and restriction of access to social welfare, education and housing benefits, foodbanks, healthcare, childcare and justice, especially for disadvantaged and marginalised individuals and groups.[53] Such human rights violations have also been highlighted by scholars who point out a very significant rise in homelessness, foodbank usage and poverty under economic policies carried out by the UK (Adler 2018), Greece, Portugal, Spain and Ireland (Alesina et al. 2019; Kilpatrick and de Witte 2014; Walsh et al. 2015), which cut public services, including social and healthcare services (Bambra 2019; Jordan and Drakeford 2012), justice (Palmer et al. 2016) and local authority spending. Such policies particularly affect specific and vulnerable groups including disabled persons (Gedalof 2018), single

---

[53] See http://tbinternet.ohchr.org/_layouts/treatybodyexternal/Download.aspx?symbolno=E%2fC.12%2fGBR%2fCO%2f6&Lang=en.

parents, young people (Davies 2019), poor students, offenders and looked after children (Rushton and Donovan 2019). The UK has even introduced benefit sanctions and conditionality in accessing welfare benefits with a view to reducing claimants' ability to access state support (Adler 2018) and with negative impacts on mental health and living conditions (Jamieson 2020).

To a lesser extent, the Netherlands and Germany, which are also weakly condemned by the ECtHR compared to Eastern countries, have also applied public spending cuts and neoliberal policies (Biebricher and Vogelmann 2017) that reduce access to justice and negatively affect the protection of human rights, especially for vulnerable people including accused persons and prisoners (Jacobs 2018). France is not exempt from this policy trend, which among other things negatively impacts access to justice and legal aid (Guinchard and Wesley 2016).

5.3.2 Cases and Issues Neglected by Private Foundations: Absence of Real European Judicial Control over Austerity Policies and Their Effects

Some significant issues denounced by the UN, such as sexual offences, child pornography and human trafficking, are very poorly litigated by private foundations and their network of NGOs, although victims of such offences are protected by several conventions that offer solid legal grounds for litigation. Paradoxically, and although private foundations protect the rights of certain minorities as discussed above, other groups, such as Russian minorities in the Donbass, in Ukraine and in Georgia, are completely ignored by private foundations and NGOs. Moreover, the defence of certain minorities is characterised by contradictions. For instance, the protection of Muslims' rights leads to a clash of rights between the rights of Muslims and those of women and of LGTB people. More generally, in their litigation activities the OSF and the NGOs do not represent European people who are vulnerable, poor and affected by economic and social policies. Social and economic rights seem to be ignored by donors and litigators. For instance, although austerity policies deeply impact the economic and social rights of the most vulnerable citizens, they have never been litigated by private foundations.

Historically, many countries have been hit by deepening economic depression induced by the economic crisis of 2008, which had its origins in unregulated financial speculation operated by financiers including Soros himself, who carried out speculative operations on the

Greek,[54] Hungarian,[55] and Russian debts.[56] For instance, more than twenty London-based hedge funds (including Soros' Quantum Fund, Toscafund, Everest Capital and Abbeville Partners) were sanctioned in 2015 by the Hellenic Republic Capital Market Commission (which is the Greek market authority) to pay fines, as they had sought to profit from banks' falling share prices during the crisis.[57] The Greek regulator considered that these hedge funds had broken pan-European rules.[58] However, because national governments bailed out and recapitalised the broken banking system (Bieling 2014), they were blamed for the financial slump instead of speculators, and were asked by some international institutions to adopt austerity policies (Blyth 2013), with the support of certain financiers and creditors such as JP Morgan Chase, Deutsche Bank and Goldman Sachs.[59] Even though Soros currently criticises austerity policies and advises the EU and national governments to increase their borrowing capacities and to borrow more money from the private market and private lenders like him at 'a very advantageous rate',[60] he has never litigated and challenged austerity policies through the OSJI nor financed NGOs that fight austerity in the courts. On the contrary, Soros has in the past speculated on certain debts and austerity policies in the past to make more profit.[61]

Rather than seeking help from the private market, which already owned their debts, Portugal, Cyprus, Greece and Ireland requested financial assistance from the EU, the euro-area member states and the International Monetary Fund (IMF). In the aftermath of the economic

---

[54] D. Sicot, 'La Grèce, terre d'aventure privilégiée des spéculateurs', *L'Humanité*, 9–22 July 2015, pp. 29–30.

[55] Soros' firm was for instance involved in an attack against Hungary's largest lender, OTP Bank, in 2008. See P. Fischer, 'How Hungarian analysts see Soros' hedge fund lockdown', *Budapest Business Journal*, 27 July 2011, available at https://bbj.hu/business/how-hungarian-analysts-see-soros-hedge-fund-lockdown_59116.

[56] T. O'Brien, 'He's seen the enemy. It looks like him', *New York Times*, 6 December 1998, available at www.nytimes.com/1998/12/06/business/he-s-seen-the-enemy-it-looks-like-him.html.

[57] M. Johnson, 'Greek regulators battle with short-selling hedge funds', *Financial Times*, 18 June 2015, available at www.ft.com/content/09931350-15b8-11e5-be54-00144feabdc0.

[58] Ibid.

[59] M. Chossudovsky, 'Prime Minister Tsipras' bailout reform package: an act of treason against the Greek people', *Global Research*, 11 July 2015, available at www.globalresearch.ca/prime-minister-tsipras-bailout-reform-package-an-act-of-treason-against-the-greek-people/5461846.

[60] G. Soros, 'How to save Europe', ECFR (European Council on Foreign Relations) Annual Council Meeting, Paris, 29 May 2018.

[61] Sicot, 'La Grèce, terre d'aventure privilégiée des spéculateurs'.

downturn, an Economic Adjustment Programme was negotiated for these countries between the national authorities and officials from the European Commission, the European Central Bank (ECB) and the IMF, including a joint financing package from the European Financial Stabilisation Mechanism, the European Financial Stability Facility and the IMF. These national governments signed a Memorandum of Understanding (MoU) on Specific Economic Policy Conditionality with the EU, the ECB and the IMF, and two related documents, namely the Technical Memorandum of Understanding and the Loan Agreement. The MoU set out the economic and social policies, including tax and social security measures, that Portugal, Cyprus, Greece and Ireland should implement for the duration of the programme in order to improve their financial situation and receive financial support from the EU (Fischer-Lescano 2014).

In addition, on 2 February 2012, the Treaty establishing the European Stability Mechanism ('the ESM Treaty') was concluded in Brussels between Belgium, Germany, Estonia, Ireland, the Hellenic Republic, Spain, France, Italy, Cyprus, Luxembourg, Malta, the Netherlands, Austria, Portugal, Slovenia, the Slovak Republic and Finland. On the basis of a request by an ESM member, the Board of Governors may decide to grant stability support to that ESM member in the form of a financial assistance facility. In this proceeding, the Board of Governors shall entrust the European Commission (in liaison with the ECB and, wherever possible, together with the IMF) with the task of negotiating with the ESM member concerned an MoU that details the conditionality attached to the financial assistance facility. Such conditionality may range from a macro-economic adjustment programme to continuing respect of pre-established eligibility conditions.

This European policy involved draconian cuts in government budgets and spending, the privatisation of public sector organisations and administrations, and reductions in wages, pensions and prices to rescue financial and banking institutions that were deemed 'too big to fail'. For instance, in Greece, despite a popular referendum in which the Greek electorate refused the European debt and austerity package, austerity policies applied under the Troika by the government of Alexis Tsipras (who has been backed by Soros since 2013)[62] involve massive tax hikes, a

---

[62] For instance, Soros financed a trip to the US for Tsipras in February 2013 through a think tank he created in 2009, the New York-based Institute for New Economic Thinking. See G. Victor, 'Greece: George Soros' Trojan horse against Europe', *The American Spectator*, 24 May 2017, available at https://spectator.org/greece-george-soros-trojan-horse-against-europe/.

drastic reduction in public sector wages, cuts in pensions (including an increase in the retirement age to 67), and the privatisation of state assets including public utilities and infrastructure.[63] Even in Romania, Bulgaria, Lithuania and Georgia, austerity policies were adopted to face the public deficit.[64]

The main effects of these austerity policies have been described, studied and analysed in terms of the decline of welfare states, breaches of social rights, unemployment, rising social inequalities between the rich and the poor (Contiades and Fotiadou 2012; Kilpatrick and de Witte 2014; Vettori 2011) and a widening of differences in 'social Europe' (Martinsen and Vollaard 2014). In particular, the negative effects of austerity on the protection of fundamental rights have been monitored and denounced by several international and European institutions, including those responsible for protecting fundamental rights.[65] A critical approach to austerity policies was notably supported by the European Agency for Fundamental Rights (EAFR), the CoE Commissioner for Human Rights and the CoE Steering Committee for Human Rights.[66] Through reports, conferences and interactions with European judges, these offices are a source of influence and awareness about the social and economic consequences of austerity on the population, and in particular on vulnerable and poor people. However, scant academic attention has been paid to the way international and regional courts are dealing with some of the policies within the economic crisis as human rights violations (Salomon 2015).

While austerity policies are regarded as generating and increasing inequalities, poverty, unemployment, homelessness, discrimination and restriction of access to social welfare, to education and housing benefits,

---

[63] Chossudovsky, 'Prime Minister Tsipras' bailout reform package: an act of treason against the Greek people'.

[64] *Khoniakina v. Georgia* [19 June 2012] ECtHR; *Savickas v. Lithuania* [15 October 2013] ECtHR; *Mockienė v. Lithuania* [4 July 2017] ECtHR; Case no 1700/08 22552/08 6705/09, *Bakradze and Others v. Georgia* [8 January 2013] ECtHR; Case nos 45312/11, 45581/11, 45583/11, 45587/11 and 45588/11, *Frimu and Others v. Romania* [29 November 2012] ECtHR; *Panfile v. Romania* [20 March 2012] ECtHR; *Valkov and Others v. Bulgaria* [25 October 2011] ECtHR.

[65] See http://fra.europa.eu/en/publication/2013/european-union-community-values-safeguarding-fundamental-rights-times-crisis and https://wcd.coe.int/ViewDoc.jsp?p=&id=2130915&direct=truef.

[66] Council of Europe Steering Committee for Human Rights (2015) The Impact of the Economic Crisis and Austerity Measures on Human Rights in Europe – Feasibility Study, CDDH(2015)R84 Addendum IV, 11 December 2015.

to food banks, to healthcare, to childcare and to justice, especially for disadvantaged and marginalised individuals and groups,[67] the austerity cases taken to the European Courts have notably faced hurdles of admissibility and scope (Cliquennois 2017). Austerity cases have been filed only by individual litigants and not by private foundations or by NGOs, which are not interested in such matters.

In this regard, the ECtHR has rejected applications in a range of cases litigated by individual applicants concerning wages, welfare benefits and retirement pensions of public servants, which have been cut in the name of austerity. Applicants have used Article 1 of the first Protocol to the European Convention on the right to protection of property to claim that their right has been violated by austerity measures adopted by their government (notably through extraordinary solidarity contributions adopted by national authorities to comply with their international and European financial obligations). According to the ECtHR, compliance with Article 1 of Protocol No. 1 requires a measure of interference such as austerity measures to fulfil three basic conditions: it must be 'subjected to the conditions provided for by law',[68] which excludes any arbitrary action on the part of the national authorities; it must be adopted 'in the public interest'; and it must find a fair balance between the owner's rights and the interests of the community.[69] More precisely, in these austerity cases, the ECtHR, which found them inadmissible as manifestly ill-founded, relied on the principles of proportionality and subsidiarity and on the limited and temporary nature of austerity measures to underline that the right to property is not violated by such measures.[70]

---

[67] See http://tbinternet.ohchr.org/_layouts/treatybodyexternal/Download.aspx?symbolno=E%2fC.12%2fGBR%2fCO%2f6&Lang=en).

[68] See Case nos 62235/12 and 57725/12, *Da Conceição Mateus and Santos Januário v. Portugal* [8 October 2013] ECtHR, §20.

[69] See Case no 71243/01, *Vistiņš and Perepjolkins v. Latvia* [25 October 2012] ECtHR, §94.

[70] Case no 17767/08, *Khoniakina v. Georgia* [19 June 2012] ECtHR; *Savickas v. Lithuania* [15 October 2013] ECtHR; *Mockienė v. Lithuania* [4 July 2017] ECtHR; Case no 1700/08 22552/08 6705/09, *Bakradze and Others v. Georgia* [8 January 2013] ECtHR; Case nos 45312/11, 45581/11, 45583/11, 45587/11 and 45588/11, *Frimu and Others v. Romania* [29 November 2012] ECtHR; *Panfile v. Romania* [20 March 2012] ECtHR; *Valkov and Others v. Bulgaria* [25 October 2011] ECtHR; Case nos 62235/12 and 57725/12, *Da Conceição Mateus and Santos Januário v. Portugal* [8 October 2013] ECtHR; Case no 13341/14, *Da Silva Carvahlo Rico v. Portugal* [1 September 2015] ECtHR; Case nos 57665/12 and 57657/12, *Koufaki and Adedy v. Greece* [7 May 2013] ECtHR; Case nos 63066/14, 64297/14 and 66106/14, *Mamatas and Others v. Greece* [21 July 2016] ECtHR; *P. Plaisier B. V. v. Netherlands* [14 November 2017] ECtHR; *McDonald v. United Kingdom* [20 May 2014] ECtHR.

The ECtHR ruled that national states enjoy a large margin of appreciation concerning their social, economic and taxation policies and that they are better placed than an international court to assess local needs and conditions[71] and to use their power in these areas[72]. According to the ECtHR, when national states have to determine their priorities and to allocate limited resources in a context of economic crisis, the margin of appreciation must be as wide as possible.[73] In this respect, the ECtHR recalled that it had in the past recognised a wide discretion on the part of national states when they pass and enact laws in the context of a change of political or economic regime.[74] In addition, austerity measures adopted by many EU countries had been part of the country's goal of meeting obligations under EU budget rules,[75] and a way of avoiding the risk that the European Commission would take action against it for an excessive budget deficit.[76] The ECtHR also considers that austerity policies can be applied where they are necessary, not discriminatory and do not disproportionately affect the rights of disadvantaged and marginalised individuals and groups.[77]

The same line of reasoning is applied by the ECtHR concerning cuts by national governments to pensions and disability allowances in the name of the public purse.[78] The only ECtHR decisions that condemned a member state (Hungary, for ceasing to grant a disability allowance[79] and for imposing a 98 per cent tax on part of the applicant's severance pay under legislation that entered into force ten weeks before her dismissal)[80] were litigated by individuals with a third party intervention submitted by the European Trade Union Confederation, which pointed out that the overwhelming majority of CoE member states had agreed to provide

---

[71] Case nos 2033/04, 19125/04, 19475/04, 19490/04, 19495/04, 19497/04, 24729/04, 171/05 and 2041/05 *Valkov and Others* v. *Bulgaria* [25 October 2011] ECtHR.
[72] Case nos 57665/12 and 57657/12, *Koufaki and Adedy* v. *Greece* [7 May 2013] ECtHR.
[73] Ibid., §31.
[74] Case nos 2033/04, 19125/04, 19475/04, 19490/04, 19495/04, 19497/04, 24729/04, 171/05 and 2041/05 *Valkov and Others* v. *Bulgaria* [25 October 2011] ECtHR.
[75] Case nos 57665/12 and 57657/12, *Koufaki and Adedy* v. *Greece* [7 May 2013] ECtHR; Case no 46184/16, 47789/16 and 19958/17, *P. Plaisier B. V.* v. *Netherlands* [14 November 2017] ECtHR.
[76] Case no 27166/18 27167/18, *Aielli and Others and Arboit and Others* v. *Italy* [10 July 2018] ECtHR.
[77] Ibid.
[78] Case no 78117/13, *Fabian* v. *Hungary* [9 September 2017] ECtHR; Case no 53080/13, *Bélané Nagy* v. *Hungary* [13 December 2016] ECtHR.
[79] Case no 53080/13, *Bélané Nagy* v. *Hungary* [13 December 2016] ECtHR.
[80] Case no 66529/11, *N. K. M.* v. *Hungary* [14 May 2013] ECtHR.

protection against the risk of invalidity.[81] The condemnation of Hungary was justified by the fact that the denial of the applicant's eligibility for disability pension under the 2012 rules interfered with her property rights as protected by Article 1 of Protocol No. 1. With reference to the proportionality of that interference, the Grand Chamber of the ECtHR ruled that the applicant was subjected to a drastic change, namely the total removal of her entitlement to disability benefits, which constituted an excessive individual burden, with no possibility of remedying her situation once the new rules were enacted. The ECtHR underlined that the new 2012 legislation, although aimed at protecting the Hungarian public purse by overhauling and rationalising the scheme of disability benefits, consisted of measures which in the circumstances failed to strike a fair balance between the interests at stake, including the right to social assistance for disabled persons.[82] Such economic considerations cannot, in the ECtHR's view, justify legislating with retrospective effect and without transitional measures corresponding to the particular situation,[83] entailing as it did the effect of depriving the applicant of her legitimate expectation of receiving a disability pension.[84] The ECtHR thus found an absence of reasonable relation of proportionality between the objective pursued and the means used,[85] and a violation of the right to social assistance under Article 1 of Protocol No. 1.[86]

However and in a more general way, the ECtHR's refusal to take into account the negative effects of austerity on wages and pensions contrasts with a new awareness of the negative impacts of austerity measures that is reflected in the ECtHR's jurisprudence relating to access to justice. Although the ECtHR does not require that access to justice be completely free of charge, it has nevertheless recognised that state fees cannot be so high as to unreasonably obstruct people from bringing a case to court, especially in times of economic crisis.[87] According to the ECtHR, the size of a state fee should not be an obstacle to initiating proceedings, and excessive court fees (e.g. the equivalent of the average annual salary or

---

[81] Case no 53080/13, *Béláné Nagy* v. *Hungary* [13 December 2016] ECtHR, §69.
[82] Ibid., §124.
[83] See Case no 10373/05, *Moskal* v. *Poland* [15 September 2009] ECtHR, §§74 and 76; see also the ruling of the CJEU referred to in Case no 20261/12, *Baka* v. *Hungary* [23 June 2016] ECtHR, §69.
[84] Case no 53080/13, *Béláné Nagy* v. *Hungary* [13 December 2016] ECtHR, §124.
[85] Ibid., §126.
[86] Ibid.
[87] Case no 3111/10, *Mehmet and Suna Yiğit* v. *Turkey* [18 December 2012] ECtHR.

four times the minimum monthly wage) are manifestly in violation of the ECHR.[88] In addition, decisions delivered by courts must be executed within a reasonable time frame. In this regard, the ECtHR has rendered a number of pilot judgments (only obtained by individual litigants) requiring Greece to remedy the problem of delays by the courts in hearing administrative,[89] criminal,[90] and civil[91] cases caused by public cuts. The ECtHR stance echoes the opinion expressed by the Commissioner for Human Rights of the CoE and the EAFR, which have both pointed out the problems faced across Europe in the area of judicial protection in the context of economic downturn: high state fees, inaccessible legal assistance, inadequate alternative dispute resolution mechanisms, inconsistent judicial awards, drastic cuts to the budgets of the judiciary, and a low level of awareness among the population of rights and protection of rights.[92] In this regard, the ECtHR is aware of two important conclusions drawn at the annual conference of the European Union Agency for Fundamental Rights in December 2012, which addressed the issue of access to justice in times of austerity. First, despite the economic crisis or because of it, access to justice and the right to an effective legal remedy must be increased, however not so much quantitatively as qualitatively. Second, the Strasbourg Court outlined the necessity of developing legal awareness among poor citizens and ensuring that all people, especially vulnerable groups, are aware of their rights in times of economic crisis.[93] Nevertheless, this stance and awareness have been translated into ECtHR case law weakly up to now.

In the same way, the CJEU was only and exclusively seized by individual applicants (and not by private foundations or by NGOs supported by private foundations) to decide on austerity cases. For example, in the Mallis and Malli case,[94] actions for annulment were lodged with the CJEU by individuals concerning the restructuring of

---

[88] See www.riigikohus.ee/vfs/1054/G%20Gustavson_juurdepaas_oigusemoistmisele.pdf.
[89] Case no 50973/08, *Vassilios Athanasiou and Others* v. *Greece* [21 December 2010] ECtHR.
[90] Case no 54447/10, *Michelioudakis* v. *Greece* [3 April 2012] ECtHR.
[91] Case no 40150/09, *Glykantzi* v. *Greece* [30 October 2012] ECtHR.
[92] See http://fra.europa.eu/sites/default/files/fra_uploads/1520-report-access-to-justice_EN.pdf.
[93] See http://fra.europa.eu/en/speech/2012/closing-remarks-fundamental-rights-conference-2012.
[94] Case C-105/15 P, *Mallis and Malli* v. *Commission and ECB* [20 September 2016] CJEU; Case T-327/13 DEP, *Mallis and Malli* v. *Commission and ECB* [10 December 2018] CJEU.

the banking sector in Cyprus made by the Eurogroup. In its statement, the Eurogroup mentioned that it had reached an agreement with the Cypriot authorities on the main elements of a future macro-economic adjustment programme, which was supported by all the member states whose currency is the euro, as well as by the EU Commission, the ECB and the IMF. The CJEU held that the EU Commission and the ECB were not responsible for any such statement.[95] In addition, the CJEU considered that the Eurogroup is not an EU institution but an informal group of ministers of the member states and cannot be brought to justice.[96]

In the judgment of *Ledra Advertising Ltd and Others* v. *European Commission and ECB*,[97] an action for annulment was also taken to the CJEU relating to the MoU of 26 April 2013 on the Specific Economic Policy Conditionality concluded between the Republic of Cyprus and the European Stability Mechanism. The individual applicants argued that the EU should incur non-contractual liability for ordering banking measures that caused financial loss to the applicants. However, the CJEU ruled that the MoU is under international law and outside of the European Treaty. Meanwhile, and paradoxically, the CJEU underlined that both the European Commission and the ECB must comply with the EU Charter and promote it in all their remits and tasks, even when the European Commission acts outside the scope and procedures covered by the EU treaties. In a case of 13 June 2017, the CJEU confirmed that member states carry out the MoU measures and that austerity policies must comply with fundamental rights.

However, such an approach was not translated into a judicial decision that firmly condemned austerity measures, for several reasons. First, the complaint for annulment before the CJEU seems to be quite ineffective. Second, the locus standi is sometimes denied by the CJEU on the ground that the litigant had not shown his direct and personal interest in the complaint.[98] Third, the CJEU has rejected austerity cases (filed by Romania and some trade unions) by considering that the MoU and the conditionality measures were not within the EU law and the EU

---

[95] Case C-105/15 P, *Mallis and Malli* v. *Commission and ECB* [20 September 2016] CJEU, §§47 and 48.
[96] Ibid., §61.
[97] Case C-8/15 P, *Ledra Advertising* v. *Commission and ECB* [20 September 2016] CJEU.
[98] Case T-215/11, *Anotati Dioikisi Enoseon Dimosion Ypallilon (ADEDY) and Others* v. *Council of the European Union* [27 November 2012], CJEU.

Charter.[99] Fourth and finally, even when the CJEU decided that such conditionality measures and the MoU were part of the EU law in certain cases, owing to their recognition by the European Commission and the relationships between national measures and the European law, and the fact that they have to comply with the EU law, it ruled that fundamental rights were not violated by austerity measures[100] and that the MoUs regarding Cyprus[101] and Greece[102] were legal. Consequently, in a more restrictive way than the ECtHR, the CJEU has refused in its jurisprudence to condemn austerity measures and their negative effects on fundamental rights.

In summary, and although the potential impacts of austerity on fundamental and human rights are very significant, all the austerity cases, which are neither supported by private foundations nor certain member states, are litigated by individuals, trade unions and NGOs that are not financed by private foundations.[103] Although Soros has criticised austerity policies, his private foundation (the OSF) and the NGOs he finances have not challenged austerity policies before the European Courts. Of course, the absence of involvement of private foundations in austerity cases could be explained by negative expectations of austerity litigation, in particular before the CJEU, which is not the best judicial avenue for litigation of that kind. In this regard, the CJEU seems to be a rubber stamp for the European Commission and the European institutions rather than a real judicial censor (Chalmers 2012b). The absence of litigation in the field of austerity could also mean that private foundations refuse to challenge and interfere with austerity policies conducted by the EU, which co-funds some NGOs that litigate the European Courts. Furthermore, a private foundation could expect to lose austerity cases like these, and might therefore aim to avoid failures in litigation of this kind that could affect its reputation of being a successful litigant. The main effect of such phenomena is that the countries that are most

---

[99] Case C-128/12, *Sindicato dos Bancarios do Norte and Others* v. *BPN* [7 March 2013] CJEU; Case C-369/12, *Corpul Naţional al Poliţiştilor – Biroul Executiv Central, reprezentant al reclamanţilor Chiţea Constantin şi alţii* v. *Ministerul Administraţiei şi Internelor and Others* [15 November 2012] CJEU.

[100] Case C-258/14, *Eugenia Florescu and Others* v. *Casa Judeţeană de Pensii Sibiu and Others* [13 June 2017] CJEU.

[101] Case C-8/15 P, *Ledra Advertising* v. *Commission and ECB* [20 September 2016] CJEU.

[102] Ibid.

[103] For instance, the PAH movement was created in Spain in 2009 to work from grassroots to high levels to fight against housing eviction.

affected by austerity policies, including Greece, Spain, Portugal, the UK and even Eastern countries, are not challenged by private foundations. The lack of support given to the austerity cases and their rejection by the European Courts thus casts doubt on the real effectiveness of the protection of social and economic rights (especially for Greek, Spanish, Portuguese, Irish and British citizens) that are not covered by private foundations and their network of NGOs. Even austerity policies applied by some Eastern countries, such as Romania and Bulgaria, which are particularly targeted by private foundations through litigation efforts, have not been challenged by private donors or by NGOs.

Instead, private foundations undertake large-scale litigation against Eastern countries in other areas, such as minorities' rights, discrimination, political opposition, human rights activists, counterterrorism, prison policies and territories. This intense litigation impacts not only national policies but also international relations, and gives rise to a new cold war between Western countries and some Eastern nationalist regimes, including Russia, Poland, Hungary and Azerbaijan.

6

Effects of Private Litigation on Domestic Policies and International Relations: The Rise of Tensions between the EU, the US and Eastern Countries

This chapter stresses the most important effect of the concentration of litigation against some Eastern countries and Russia: politicisation of human rights and a rise in tensions between the EU, the US and nationalist regimes, in particular Russia. This chapter shows how the growing role played by private foundations impacts international relations and contributes to the birth and development of a new Cold War between these countries. We rely on Russian, Polish, Hungarian, Romanian and Azerbaijani legislation and documents related to foreign policy released by the EU, the CoE and the US over the last decade to analyse these political strains.

6.1 How ECtHR Judgments Transform National Policies, Are Politicised and Expose Nationalist Regimes in Eastern Countries

While the inputs of European jurisprudence reflect the litigation strategies and efforts made by private foundations and the NGOs funded by them, the analysis of the outputs tends to show how private foundations politicise certain European rulings. In this section we flesh out key elements in the litigation strategy of private foundations and the NGOs described in Chapter 2 by focusing on seven key cases that have resulted in rulings condemning Eastern countries, including Russia in particular.

The cases point to the main objectives being pursued by NGOs through litigation. The first and immediate objective is to obtain ordinary and, if possible, pilot rulings condemning nationalist regimes and Russia for breaches of ECHR rights (see Chapter 3). The second objective is to make use of single rulings or, even better, sets of rulings, to foster pressure on the nationalist and Russian governments to undertake substantial judicial and political reforms (again, see Chapter 3). The third objective is to weave sets of condemnations so as to project into public discourse the image of nationalist regimes (including Russia) as countries that engage in repeated breaches of the ECHR (thus using case law as the point of departure for a wider discourse on nationalist regimes and Russia) and that consequently are unreliable and aggressive states (see below). The fourth objective is to translate the ECHR's condemnations of political repression into a discourse that denounces Eastern authoritarian regimes that repress political opponents, human rights activists and minorities.

The six cases analysed below reflect not only the influence of private donors and litigants but also the large overlap between the agendas of certain private donors and the official foreign policy discourse of the US, the CoE and the EU about nationalist regimes and Russia. The Ananyev, Neshkov and Varga judgments have been turned into a symbol of the Russian, Hungarian and Bulgarian states as 'garrison states'; the Catan case has been made into a key plank in the characterisation of Russia as an 'aggressive, authoritarian and nationalist' power; and the Khashiyev and Akayeva ruling has played a key role in disseminating the image of Russia as a 'terrorist state' using violent means and breaching human rights against Chechens willing to exercise the right to self-determination. The Frumkin, Akimenkov and Navalnyy cases have contributed to exposing Russia as an oppressive and corruptive state that does not allow political opposition. The Al Nashiri and the Abu Zaybah cases have depicted Poland and Romania as secret states running illegal counterterrorist operations. Lastly, the Horváth and Kiss and D. H. judgments have tended to present Hungary and the Czech Republic as 'racist states' that violate the rights of minorities. In this regard, these ECtHR judgments (which were analysed in Chapter 3) do not only transform national policies conducted by condemned member states but are also politicised so as to expose nationalist regimes in Eastern countries to the international community and in particular to international and European sanctions.

6.1.1 *The Ananyev, Neshkov and Varga Cases: Bulgaria, Hungary and Russia as 'Garrison States'*

Litigation in the Ananyev, Neshkov and Varga cases was in line with the main priorities of the main donor of the NGOs involved, the OSF, which had made repeated claims against Russia characterising it as a 'closed society' by reference to its laws and its judicial and prison system.[1] The

---

[1] M. Van Riel, 'More than a decade after Kalashnikov, Russian prisons still abysmal', Open Society Foundations, 24 June 2015, available at www.opensocietyfoundations.org/voices/

outcome of these cases was immediately regarded as evidence that Russia, Hungary and Bulgaria were 'garrison states' and as proof of the need for substantial changes in their judicial systems and prisons.[2] Although this has been somewhat neglected, the fact of the matter is that Russia, Bulgaria and Hungary took a number of measures in direct response to the rulings (see above, Chapter 3). For instance, the detailed action plan provided by Russia to the CM in October 2012 in response to the pilot judgment entailed the following:

- measures to reduce the application of preventive measures for suspects and the accused
- measures to improve material conditions of detention
- measures setting up new domestic preventive and compensatory remedies and improving the existing ones

awareness-raising activities

closer cooperation with NGOs and civil society institutions.[3]

In August 2013, an additional action plan was submitted by the Russian authorities in which they provided updated information concerning the preventive and compensatory remedies.[4] A legislative reform was passed with a view to improving access to judicial remedies regarding conditions

---

more-decadeafter-kalashnikov-russian-prisons-still-abysmal; 'Foes see little good in Soros' activities in Russia', *The Moscow Times*, 11 October 1997, available at www.themoscowtimes.com/sitemap/free/1997/10/article/foes-see-little-good-in-soros-activities-in-russia/299140.html. In the same manner, Soros denounced the arrest of Khodorkovsky, the famous oil oligarch accused of laundering and fraud, as 'persecution' that would leave him in the hands of an oppressive Russian state. See 'Soros and Khodorkovsky', *The Tribune Review*, 16 November 2003, available at http://triblive.com/x/pittsburghtrib/opinion/columnists/datelinedc/s_165315.html#axzz3uOHIgaSG.

[2] Secretariat of the Committee of Ministers, Communication from a NGO (Association of Russian Lawyers for Human Rights) (29/11/2012) in the Cases of Mikheyev Group, Dedovsky and Others, Fedotov, Kalasnikov, Ananyev and Others against Russian Federation (Applications No. 77617/01, 7178/03, 5140/02, 4795/99 and 42525/07), DH-DD (2013)92, 4 February 2013, available at https://wcd.coe.int/ViewDoc.jsp?id=2027885&Site=CM&BackColorInternet=C3C3C3&BackColorIntranet=EDB021&BackColorLogged=F5D383.

[3] Communication from the Russian Federation, Action Plans Submitted to the Committee of Ministers DH-DD(2012)1009, 29 October 2012, available at https://wcd.coe.int/ViewDoc.jsp?id=1997391&Site=CM&BackColorInternet=C3C3C3&BackColorIntranet=EDB021&BackColorLogged=F 5D383.

[4] Action Plans DH-DD(2012)1072, 16 November 2012; DH-DD(2013)153, 13 February 2013, DH-DD(2013)936E, 6 September 2013, available at https://wcd.coe.int/ViewDoc.jsp?id=2098199&Site=CM&BackColorInternet=C3C3C3&BackColorIntranet=EDB021&BackColorLogged=F 5D383.

of detention in remand centres, police temporary detention facilities and prisons.[5] This reform will make it possible to decide on a civil claim for compensation in the framework of administrative law proceedings. In this respect, the Russian authorities seem to be considering amending the 1995 Law 'On Detention of Suspects and the Accused' and the Penitentiary Code to allow compensation for pecuniary and non-pecuniary damage inflicted as a result of poor conditions of detention, irrespective of any fault committed by the state.[6] On 30 April 2014, the Russian authorities updated their action plan,[7] submitting information concerning the resolution of 245 similar applications pending before the Court and following the delivery of the pilot judgment. In 201 applications, Russia admitted breaches of rights and expressed its readiness to pay compensation.[8]

Another major concern expressed by NGOs concerns the effectiveness of domestic investigation and the lack of independence of the Russian prosecutor's office. On 25 August 2016, the HFHR submitted comments describing the latest amendments to law changing the structure of the prosecutor's office. Since 4 March 2016 the office of Prosecutor General has been held by the Minister of Justice, who is an active politician and does not have to meet the requirements for the office of prosecutor (i.e. he can be a trainee prosecutor). According to the CoE Commissioner for Human Rights, these amendments raise important human rights concerns. The new law widened the competences of the Prosecutor General

---

[5] Ibid. The Draft Code provides for (1) the possibility that national courts order remedial measures (with clear identification of unlawful decisions, acts or omissions) in response to complaints related to poor conditions of detention; (2) a requirement that the authority having committed the violation should remedy it within a precise time-limit and report back to the Court regarding execution of the judgment; (3) an empowerment of the Court to undertake certain steps and to consider certain issues ex officio; (4) penalties to sanction unjustified failure to submit evidence to the Court; (5) a new imposition on the state body to prove the lawfulness of particular actions, omissions and decisions and to evidence their arguments; (6) the participation of all competent authorities in the proceedings; (7) the possibility of the Court submitting a judgment for immediate execution, to order interim measures and to speed up proceedings and (8) lastly a mechanism allowing reduction of court fees and other costs for the complainants.
[6] Ibid.
[7] Action Plan (DH-DD(2014)580E), 5 May 2014, available at https://wcd.coe.int/ViewDoc.jsp?id=2189699&Site=CM&BackColorInternet=C3C3C3&BackColorIntranet=EDB021&BackColorLogged=F 5D383.
[8] Ibid; CoE, Round Table on the Setting Up of Effective Domestic Remedies to Challenge Conditions of Detention, Strasbourg, 8–9 July 2014, available at www.coe.int/en/web/execution/setting-up-of-effective-domestic-remedies-conditions-of-detention.

and did not establish any safeguards against undue political influence on each investigation or against abuse of his/her power.

In themselves, these decisions by the Russian, Bulgarian and Hungarian governments (except the one on the new Prosecutor General) seem to prove that litigation has been successful beyond symbolic condemnation, as it has resulted in changes to the Russian, Bulgarian and Hungarian judicial and administrative systems (see also Chapter 3 for penal and prison changes in Bulgaria and Hungary).[9] In particular, opponents to the Russian government, especially those suffering in their own person the consequences of expressing their opposition, now have access to better and faster means of executing judgments. These changes may still be highly insufficient, but they constitute evidence of the influence of the NGOs involved in litigating and executing this ruling and previous and subsequent related rulings. Nevertheless, the NGOs have tended to play down the extent to which the ruling has led to improvements, and have continued to denounce Russia and Hungary as authoritarian states.[10] This has played a far from irrelevant role in mainstream media portrayals of Russia as a 'garrison state', a country well known for its infamous prison system and its scandalous conditions of detention.[11]

But while there seems to be a great deal of room for improvement in Russian, Bulgarian and Hungarian prisons, it is somehow odd that the narrative is thoroughly impervious to the fact that litigation does actually deliver some results. It is hard not to ask whether reluctance to acknowledge any improvement actually contributes to improving matters, or whether it might instead foster further political and cultural tension between Russia, Hungary and the EU, reinforcing discourses that characterise these countries as garrison states that inflict torture and other inhumane abuses resulting from bad conditions of detention. Such narratives rely on the implicit assumption that the EU's prison systems are in full compliance with ECHR standards. However, such an assumption

---

[9] See for instance SRJI, *Ten Years 2001–2011*, available at www.srji.org/en/about/annual/, p. 3.

[10] M. Van Riel, 'More than a decade after Kalashnikov, Russian prisons still abysmal', Open Society Foundations, 24 June 2015, available at www.opensocietyfoundations.org/voices/more-decadeafter-kalashnikov-russian-prisons-still-abysmal.

[11] See for instance M. Gessen, 'Latitude: views from around the world. Life in a Russian prison', *The New York Times*, 23 September 2013, available at http://latitude.blogs.nytimes.com/2013/09/23/life-in-arussian-prison/?_r=0; A. Rosen, 'Inside Russia's prison system', *The Atlantic*, 18 October 2012, available at www.theatlantic.com/international/archive/2012/10/inside-russias-prison-system/263806/.

might underestimate the extent of the structural problems that exist in no small number of EU prison systems (Cliquennois and Snacken 2018; Cliquennois and de Suremain 2018; Daems and Robert 2017).

6.1.2 The Catan Case: Russia as an 'Aggressive, Authoritarian and Nationalist' State that Oppresses Minorities

All the claims exposed by Promo-Lex and Interights in the Catan case (see Chapter 3) resonate with the public discourse of the OSF in their Asian and Russian programmes, in particular to the extent that such discourses highlight the need to uphold ethnic and linguistic diversity (Porter 2015). However, while the ECtHR found Russia responsible for the violation of the applicants' right to education under Article 2 of Protocol No. 1 of the Convention as it was de facto the effective holder of power in the territory, the ECtHR did not find evidence of either any direct participation by Russian agents in the measures taken against the applicants or of Russian involvement in or endorsement of MRT's language policy. This seems to weaken the claim that there is a causal link between the set of specific human right breaches and Russian imperialism per se.

Nevertheless, regarding the execution of the Catan judgment, the CM was very concerned with continuous violation of the applicants' right to education on the basis of a report made by Promo-Lex[12] and Moldova[13] and with no reference to the general and individual measures taken by Russia to execute the Court's judgment. Russia's failure[14] was both denounced by Interights and Promo-Lex[15] and deplored by the CM.

The Catan judgment becomes even more controversial and politicised when the breach of such rights is woven into a narrative that establishes a

---

[12] Committee of Ministers, Communication from the Applicants' Representatives (17/09/2014) in the Case of Catan and Others against Russian Federation, DH-DD(2014)1107, 18 September 2014, available at https://wcd.coe.int/ViewDoc.jsp?id=2236117&Site=CM&BackColorInternet=C3C3C3&BackColorIntranet=EDB 021&BackColorLogged=F5D383.

[13] Ibid.

[14] Committee of Ministers, Decision on Case No 17 (Catan and Others) against Russia, 1214th Meeting, 4 December 2014, available at https://wcd.coe.int/ViewDoc.jsp?id=2267425&Site=CM&BackColorInternet=C3C3C3&BackColorIntranet=EDB021&BackColorLogged=F5D383.

[15] Committee of Ministers, Submission from Promo-Lex and Interights (04/03/13) in the Case of Catan and Others against Russian Federation, DH-DD(2013)287, 15 March 2013, available at https://wcd.coe.int/ViewDoc.jsp?id=2045689&Site=CM&BackColorInternet=C3C3C3&BackColorIntranet=EDB021&BackColorLogged=F5D383.

necessary and unequivocal causal link between the poor protection of human rights in territories such as Transdniestria and 'Russian imperialism and nationalism' that threatens the EU's values and principles. According to the founder of the OSF:

> Vladimir Putin's aggressive nationalism challenges values and principles on which the EU was founded ... Now Russia is presenting an alternative that poses a fundamental challenge to the values and principles on which the European Union was originally founded. It is based on the use of force that manifests itself in repression at home and aggression abroad, as opposed to the rule of law ... The collapse of Ukraine would be a tremendous loss for NATO, the European Union and the United States. A victorious Russia would become much more influential within the EU and pose a potent threat to the Baltic states with large ethnic Russian populations ... [Putin] may then revert to the smaller victory that would still be within his reach: he could open by force a land route from Russia to Crimea and Transdniestria (a pro-Moscow breakaway state in Moldova) before winter.[16]

Then, the CM firmly called upon Russia several times to put an end to the violation of the applicants' right to education resulting from acts of intimidation and pressure affecting the functioning of the Latin-script schools in the Transdniestrian region and to submit a global action plan describing measures taken by Russia in response to the Court's judgment.[17] The lack of response on the Russian side led to an escalation of political conflict with the CoE and in particular with the Parliamentary Assembly, which called on Russia to 'promptly implement ... the ruling of the ECtHR ..., and refrain ... from boycotting Moldovan products with the objective of unduly influencing the Republic of Moldova's foreign policy choices'.[18]

---

[16] J. Borger, 'George Soros: Russia poses existential threat to Europe. Investor says Vladimir Putin's aggressive nationalism challenges values and principles on which the EU was founded', *The Guardian*, 23 October 2014, available at www.theguardian.com/world/2014/oct/23/george-soros-russiathreat-europe-vladimir-putin.

[17] Committee of Ministers, Interim Resolution CM/ResDH(2015)157. 1236th Meeting, Execution of the Judgment of the European Court of Human Rights Catan and Others against Russian Federation 22–24 September 2015, available at https://wcd.coe.int/ViewDoc.jsp?id=2362779&Site=CM&BackColorInternet=C3C3C3&BackColorIntranet=EDB021&BackColorLogged=F5D383.

[18] Parliamentary Assembly of the Council of Europe 52015, Challenge, on Substantive Grounds, of the Still Unratified Credentials of the Delegation of the Russian Federation, Resolution 2034 (2015), 28 January 2015 and Resolution 1990 (2014), available at http://assembly.coe.int/nw/xml/XRef/ Xref XML2HTML-en.asp?fileid=21538&lang=en.

Thus, the Catan case renders explicit not only the structural problems with Russian cultural and linguistic policy but also the extent to which such policies are intertwined with geopolitical concerns, both on the Russian and on NGO side. On the one hand, repeated litigant NGOs are strategically interested in pursuing these cases (but not those against other states in which similar violations take place) so as to have a lever with which to influence Russian policy and to establish a connection between Russian cultural and linguistic policy and Russian imperialism and nationalism. It is not an overstatement to say that they have been quite successful in that regard, since the European Parliament and the CoE Parliamentary Assembly have established a connection between Russian cultural policy and the conflict in Ukraine.[19] More precisely, the Parliamentary Assembly has, as part of its justification for sanctions on the Russian authorities, called for them

> to promptly implement ... the ruling of the European Court of Human Rights in the case of Catan and others v. the Republic of Moldova and Russia related to the right to education in Latin-script schools in Transdniestria, and refraining from boycotting Moldovan products with the objective of unduly influencing the Republic of Moldova's foreign policy choices.[20]

On the other hand, Russia has deemed the ECtHR ruling as a 'political decision' that threatens Russian cultural influence on its vicinity.[21] This has resulted in what is a rather exceptional Russian stance: total non-compliance with the ruling. The CM has publicly denounced this non-compliance. Therefore, through this case, NGOs have contributed to an escalation in the conflict between Russia, the EU and the CoE, and to the sanctions decided by the latter and strongly encouraged by some NGOs, including the OSF.[22]

---

[19] European Parliament Resolution of 6 February 2014 on Transnistria (2014/2552(RSP)), Right to Education in the Transnistrian Region P7_TA-PROV(2014)0108, available at www.europarl.europa.eu/document/activities/cont/201402/20140219ATT79600/20140219ATT79600EN.pdf.

[20] Parliamentary Assembly of the Council of Europe 52015, Challenge, on Substantive Grounds, of the Still Unratified Credentials of the Delegation of the Russian Federation, Resolution 2034 (2015), 28 January 2015.

[21] Comment of the Ministry of Foreign Affairs of the PMR on the Decision of the European Court of Human Rights in the Case of Catan and Others Versus Moldova and Russia, 23 October 2012, available at http://mfa-pmr.org/en/xbG.

[22] Sputniknews, 'It's been fund: Russia sends Soros speculating his way out the door', 30 November 2015, available at http://sputniknews.com/russia/20151130/1030990303/

6.1.3 The Khashiyev and Akayeva and Tagayeva Cases: Russia as a 'Terrorist and Violent State'

The Khashiyev and Akayeva case directly echoes the role played by the OSF's support of the case for Chechen independence since 1995 and with no reference to the general and individual measures taken by Russia. Support for Chechen independence by the OSF was made concrete through the establishment of a humanitarian aid fund (USD 5 million given in 1995 as a humanitarian aid effort in the refugee camps of Ingushetia, in schooling and hospitals, and in legal counselling) for the victims of the war in Chechnya,[23] and through several calls for proposals relating to Chechnya (such as the Justice Project granted to the SRJI in 2006, see Chapter 2).[24] The ECtHR largely followed the NGOs (EHRAC and Memorial) and condemned Russia on the basis of an enquiry conducted by HRW into human rights violations committed in Grozny between December 1999 and January 2000.[25]

Condemnation in the Khashiyev and Akayeva case led to some changes in Russian practice. Following this ruling (and the one in *Aslakhanova and Others* v. *Russia*, championed by the SRJI),[26] Russia adopted general measures and several action plans to comply with the obligations imposed by the ECtHR and its commitment to bringing those responsible for human rights violations in Chechnya to justice under the monitoring of the CM[27] and of several NGOs, including EHRAC,

---

foundation-list-prosecutorsrussia.html#ixzz3uTex8cdq and http://sputniknews.com/russia/20151130/1030990303/foundation-list-prosecutors-russia.html.

[23] G. Babakian, 'Soros starts aid fund for Chechnya', *The Moscow Times*, 18 January 1995, available at www.themoscowtimes.com/news/article/soros-starts-aid-fund-for-chechnya/343959.html.

[24] Indeed, support for Chechen independence is a characteristic part of movements that favour strengthening links with the EU and the US while weakening those with Russia, despite the latter being a traditional economic partner. Similarly, economic 'liberalism', including privatisation and unleashing of capital movements, is depicted as a geostrategic if not 'cultural' choice to be fostered, rather than as a controversial socio-economic policy to be assessed by reference to its concrete contextual implications.

[25] Case nos 57942/00 and 57945/00, *Khashiyev and Akayeva* v. *Russia* [24 February 2005] ECtHR, §§36 and 150.

[26] Case nos 2944/06 and 8300/07, 50184/07, 332/08, 42509/10, *Aslakhanova and Others* v. *Russia* [18 December 2012] ECtHR.

[27] Action Plans Submitted by Russia to the CM, DDH-DD(2012)488 part 1, DH-DD(2012) 757, DH-DD(2013)935E and DH-DD(2014)1117E, available at http://tinyurl.com/zqsrnte;http://tinyurl.com/zw3ubjk;http://tinyurl.com/zw3ubjk.

Memorial and the Russian Justice Initiative.[28] In particular, Russia set up a programme to combat abductions and created an integrated independent body in charge of searching for persons missing as a result of counterterrorism operations in Chechnya.[29] Russia also adopted organisational and methodological measures to assist the criminal investigation subdivisions of the Ministry of Internal Affairs in bringing perpetrators before the courts. A Federal Law on Citizens' Participation in Maintaining Public Order was also passed to facilitate working with the victims (including specific recognition of their status) and to increase cooperation with civil society institutions and NGOs.[30]

Under the pressure exerted by EHRAC, Memorial and the Russian Justice Initiative, the CM has remained largely unpersuaded that these changes are sufficient. Russia has been reproached for its lack of effective and independent investigation and prosecution of the perpetrators of crimes in Chechnya.[31] For its part, Russia has outlined that effective investigation is impossible for 'objective' reasons, including the long time between the events and the passing of judgment, the loss and destruction of substantial evidence and archival documents during combat operations, and the participation of officials ascribed to different bodies in counterterrorist operations on a temporary basis.[32] Russia has also

---

[28] CM, Communications from Russian Justice Initiative, The European Human Rights Advocacy Centre, The Centre for International Protection and The Memorial Human Rights Centre) (18/04/2013)DH-DD(2013)491, 2 May 2013, available at https://wcd.coe.int/ViewDoc.jsp?id=2060631&-Site=CM&BackColorInternet=C3C3C3&BackColorIntranet=EDB021&BackColorLogged=F5D383; Communication From Russian Justice Initiative, Astreya and The Human Rights Centre 'Memorial' (Moscow) (10/01/2014) DH-DD (2014)154, 4 February 2014, available at https://wcd.coe.int/ViewDoc.jsp?id=2155089&Site=CM&BackColorInternet=C3C3C3&Back-ColorIntranet= EDB021&BackColor Logged=F5D383.

[29] Action Plan Submitted by Russia to the CM, DH-DD(2014)1431E/21 November 2014, available at https://wcd.coe.int/ViewDoc.jsp?id=2263705&Site=CM&BackColorInternet=C3C3C3&BackColorIntranet=EDB021&BackColorLogged=F5D383.

[30] Updated Action Plan Submitted by Russia to the CM, 17/07/2015, DH-DD(2015)773E/24 July 2015, available at https://wcd.coe.int/ViewDoc.jsp?id=2345055&Site=CM&BackColorInternet=C3C3C3&BackColorIntranet=EDB021&BackColorLogged= F5D383.

[31] CM, Decision Cases No. 17 Khashiyev and Akayeva Group against Russian Federation / Del/OJ/DH(2014) 1208/17 / 26 September 2014, available at https://wcd.coe.int/ViewDoc.jsp?id=2237871&Site=CM&BackColorInternet=C3C3C3&BackColorIntranet= EDB021&BackColorLogged=F 5D383.

[32] Ibid and Action Plan Submitted by Russia to the CM, DH-DD(2014)892E/31, July 2014, available at https://wcd.coe.int/ViewDoc.jsp?id=2219993&Site=CM&BackColorInternet=C3C3C3&BackColorIntranet=EDB021& BackColorLogged=F5D383.

stonewalled behind the claim that it regards some information as a state secret.[33]

Condemnations on 'Chechen' cases have been used as a 'smoking gun' to request international organisations, including the IMF, to sever ties and suspend cooperation with Russia. The OSF have argued in particular that the IMF should 'pull out of Russia' with regard to the illegal counter-terrorist actions in Chechnya and in Beslan.[34] This request was seconded by the then US Treasury Secretary Lawrence Summers, who called on the Russian government to rebuild its economy around the 'rule of law' (a far-from-oblique reference to the situation in Chechnya) and to enhance confidence among both local and international investors.[35]

The more recent Tagayeva case also amplified these international effects, exposing Russia to international tensions and US critics. Although the case was litigated by EHRAC, Beslan Mothers and Voice of Beslan also took part as grassroots NGOs and advocacy groups established in the aftermath of the 2004 North Ossetian Beslan school siege. Both groups have set out a version of events that is in complete contradiction with the official narrative that militants linked to the Chechen separatist movement took more than 1,000 people hostage in Beslan's School Number One. According to the groups, the attack was an inside job committed by school employees and town and army officials, who made use of weapons and bombs that had been placed inside the Beslan school and detonated.[36] This is why Voice of Beslan, which is financed by the NED,[37] asked for an international investigation into the Beslan terrorist attack. In November 2005, it urged the EU and the European Parliament to set up their own inquiry into the event with a view to uncovering the truth about the Beslan attack,[38] as well as urging

---

[33] Action Plan Submitted by Russia to the CM, DH-DD(2012)757E/31, August 2012, available at https://wcd.coe.int/ViewDoc.jsp?id=1969337&Site=CM&BackColorInternet=C3C3C3&BackColorIntranet=EDB021&BackColorLogged=F 5D383.

[34] P. Jennings, 'IMF should pull out of Russia', *Global Policy Reform*, 30 January 2000, available at www.globalpolicy.org/component/content/article/221/47048.html; Associated Press, 'Soros: IMF should not help Russia', 30 January 2000, available at http://olympia.gr/2013/04/19/soroschechnya-boston-beslan-greece/.

[35] Ibid.

[36] See AFP, 'Relatives want Europe to probe Beslan tragedy', 30 November 2005 available at www.globalsecurity.org/military/library/news/2005/11/mil-051130-rferl06.htm; see also Voice of Beslan www.golosbeslana.ru/english.htm.

[37] NED, *Annual Report 2011*, p. 50.

[38] AFP, 'Relatives want Europe to probe Beslan tragedy', 30 November 2005.

the US to publish satellite pictures taken of the school during the siege.[39] In 2006, members of Voice of Beslan met with the UN High Commissioner for Human Rights, Louise Arbour,[40] and with the CoE Commissioner for Human Rights.[41] In response, criminal charges were brought against Voice of Beslan for 'slander of public officials' and 'humiliating national pride' in their statement accusing President Putin of refusing to launch an independent investigation into the Beslan siege.[42] Although the charges were dismissed by the Pravoberezhny District Court of North Ossetia,[43] the position adopted by the Russian authorities was denounced to the UN by the ICJ and Memorial.[44] In particular, Memorial and EHRAC accused Russia of using threats, suits, harassment and threats of death, abduction or other ill treatment against victims or their families and lawyers attempting to seek justice and obtain reparations for violations of human rights either in the domestic courts or before the ECtHR.[45] Such accusations were brought to the CoE Parliamentary Assembly, which issued a report on them,[46] denouncing 'a lack of willingness (from Russian authorities) to carry out full and effective investigations [that] in some cases are even indicative of whitewashing'.[47]

---

[39] Voice of Beslan, www.golosbeslana.ru/english.htm.
[40] Ibid.
[41] Commissioner for Human Rights of the Council of Europe (2011) Report by Thomas Hammerberg Following His VSisit to the Russian Federation from 12 to 21 May 2011. CommDH(2011)21, Strasbourg, 6 September 2011, p. 8, §23.
[42] ICJ (2008), *E-bulletin on Counter-Terrorism and Human Rights*, January 2008, available at www.icj.org; the charges were dismissed by the Pravoberezhny District Court of North Ossetia, ICJ, *E-bulletin*, May 2008.
[43] ICJ (2008), *E-bulletin*, May 2008.
[44] ICJ Submission to the Universal Periodic Review of the Russian Federation, United Nations Human Rights Council, 4th Session of the Working Group on Universal Periodic Review, 2-13 February 2009, pp. 2 and 4.
[45] Memorial and EHRAC, Memorandum on Threats to Applicants to the EctHR in Cases from Chechnya, November 2006, Annex III to EHRAC Written Evidence to Eminent Jurists Panel, available at http://ejp.icj.org.
[46] Parliamentary Assembly of the Council of Europe (2007), Report on Member States' duty to Co-operate with the European Court of Human Rights by the Committee on Legal Affairs and Human Rights, Rapporteur: Mr Christos Pourgourides (Group of the European People's Party), Doc. 11183, 9 February 2007.
[47] Ibid, §35.

6.1.4 Russia and Azerbaijan as 'Oppressive and Corruptive States that Do Not Allow Political Opposition'

Some ECtHR cases litigated by private foundations have been politicised to such an extent that they depict Russia and Azerbaijan as oppressive states.

6.1.4.1 The Frumkin, Akimenkov and Navalnyy Cases: Russia as an 'Oppressive and Corruptive State'

The cases of Frumkin, Akimenkov, Navalnyy and Ofitserov, and Navalnyy against Russia litigated by EHRAC, Memorial, IPC and Article 19 all concern the right of political opponents to Putin's regime to demonstrate. These cases notably involve Alexei Navalnyy, who is the most famous political activist, opposition leader, anti-corruption campaigner and popular blogger in Russia. Navalnyy is very close to Khodorkovsky (they are co-chairs of RPR-PARNAS),[48] who is fully supported by Soros.[49] Navalnyy has organised demonstrations on a regular basis to promote reform and attack political corruption in Russia, for which he has been sentenced several times. The Frumkin and Navalnyy cases were considered by the ECtHR to be a retaliation for his political activity and as violations of Navalnyy's right to a fair trial. In this regard, some NGOs, including Memorial, AI and HRW, have relayed the ECtHR judgments by considering Navalnyy to be a political prisoner and even a prisoner of conscience.[50] In a more general way, HRW accused Russian police and ultra-nationalist and pro-government groups of harassing, intimidating and interfering with Navalnyy's presidential campaign.[51]

The ECtHR judgments were also followed by some critical responses from the European and CoE institutions. For instance, on 21 September 2017 the CM of the CoE invited the Russian authorities, in connection

---

[48] 'Parnas party envisions Navalnyy, Khodorkovsky as future leaders', *The Moscow Times*, 5 July 2015, available at www.themoscowtimes.com/2015/07/05/parnas-party-envisions-navalny-khodorkovsky-as-future-leaders-a47908; see also https://khodorkovsky.com/navalny-and-i-are-allies-khodorkovsky/.

[49] TribLive (2003), 'Soros and Khodorkovsky', 16 November 2003, available at https://archive.triblive.com/news/soros-and-khodorkovsky. See also https://khodorkovsky.com/an-evening-with-george-soros-at-open-russia-club/.

[50] Human Rights Watch, 'Russia: nationwide assaults on political opposition campaign', 6 September 2017.

[51] Ibid.

with the Navalnyy and Ofitserov case, to erase and stop the prohibition on Mr Navalnyy's standing for election.[52] The EU Parliament and the EU external action department asserted that Navalnyy's removal cast 'serious doubt' on the Russian election and the independence of Russian justice.[53] These reactions to the Navalnyy case tend to present Russia as an oppressive and corruptive state that prohibits political opposition and manipulates both elections and justice to obtain condemnations of the most prominent political opponents who denounce Russian corruption. In response, Russia has recently labelled Navalnyy's Anti-Corruption Foundation a 'foreign agent' (historically financed by NED)[54] that will be subject to increased state monitoring.[55]

6.1.4.2 The Mammadov Case: Azerbaijan as a 'Repressive Regime that Censors Political Opposition'

The same process of labelling an Eastern country as a 'repressive regime' that tends to fight and strike against the political opposition applies to Azerbaijan, traditionally an ally of Russia. The Court ruled in the Mammadov case that the arrest and detention of the famous Azerbaijani opposition politician Ilgar Mammadov was unlawful, and that the actual aim of his detention was 'to silence and punish' him for criticising the Azerbaijani government. On 11 October 2017, the CoE Parliamentary Assembly in its Resolutions 2184 (2017) and 2185 (2017) considered that the legislative framework for the activities of NGOs contravened European standards and denounced the legal proceedings brought against NGO leaders and the fact that some of them are held in custody. The Parliamentary Assembly called on Azerbaijan to cease reprisals against human rights activists and to repeal all laws restricting freedom of

---

[52] CM, 1294th Meeting on Navalnyy and Ofitserov v. Russian Federation (Application No. 46632/13), 19–21 September 2017 (DH) H46–25.
[53] European Parliament, Resolution 2015/2503(RSP) on Russia, in Particular the Case of Alexei Navalnyy, 15 January 2015; EU External Action, Decision of the Russian Central Election Commission to Bar Alexei Navalnyy from Running in the 2018 Presidential Election, 26 December 2017, available at https://eeas.europa.eu/headquarters/headquarters-homepage/37894/decision-russian-central-election-commission-bar-alexei-navalny-running-2018-presidential_en.
[54] 'Navalny's private e-mails leaked', *The Moscow Times*, 26 October 2011.
[55] 'Russia declares opposition leader Alexei Navalny's anti-corruption group "foreign agent"', *The Daily Telegraph*, 9 October 2019, available at www.telegraph.co.uk/news/2019/10/09/russia-declares-opposition-leader-alexei-navalnys-anti-corruption/.

association.[56] On 5 December 2017, for the very first time in the CoE's history, the CM launched 'infringement proceedings' against Azerbaijan in relation to the Mammadov case. In view of Azerbaijan's failure to respond to its repeated calls to release Ilgar Mammadov, and following some warning communications from the HFHR, Freedom Now and the Public Association for Assistance to Free Economy (which defends free trade and property rights and is notably financed by the OSF and the Friedrich Naumann Foundation),[57] the CM referred the case back to the Court, under Article 46(4) ECHR, for it to legally determine whether Azerbaijan has failed to abide by the judgment.[58] In particular, Freedom Now made a submission to the CM stating that Azerbaijan had failed to execute the Court's judgment by failing to release Mr Mammadov or to stop domestic judicial proceedings against him and by failing to provide any workable plan to curtail political prosecutions. The NGO urged the CM to initiate proceedings under Article 46(4).[59]

In response, the ECtHR, which was required to make a definitive legal assessment of the question of compliance, decided that Azerbaijan had failed to fulfil its obligation under Article 46(1) to abide by the Mammadov judgment.[60] While the ECtHR noted that Azerbaijan did take some steps towards executing the first Mammadov judgment, such as the just satisfaction awarded by the Court at the applicant's disposal, an Action Plan setting out some measures capable of executing the judgment, and the judgment delivered by the Shaki Court of Appeal, which released the applicant, it emphasised that release was conditional and imposed a number of limitations on the applicant for a period of nearly eight months.[61]

---

[56] PACE, Resolution 2184 on the Functioning of Democratic Institutions in Azerbaijan, 11 October 2017; Resolution 2185 on Azerbaijan's Chairmanship of the Council of Europe: What Follow-Up on Respect for Human Rights? 11 October 2017.
[57] See www.freeeconomy.az/who-we-are/haqq-m-zda/?language=english.
[58] CM (2017), Interim Resolution CM/ResDH(2017)429, Execution of the Judgment of the European Court of Human Rights Ilgar Mammadov against Azerbaijan Adopted by the CM on 5 December 2017 at the 1302nd Meeting of the Ministers' Deputies, CM/ResDH (2017)429, 7 December 2017.
[59] Communication from Freedom Now to the CM, DH-DD(2015)844, 26 November 2014.
[60] Case no 15172/13, *Ilgar Mammadov* v. *Azerbaijan* [29 May 2019] ECtHR.
[61] Ibid., §216.

6.1.5 The Al Nashiri and Abu Zaybah Cases: Poland and Romania as 'Secret States Running Illegal Counterterrorist Operations'

Although several states, including Italy, Macedonia, France and Sweden, set up secret prisons in close cooperation with the US and the CIA to run secret prison programmes in Europe, it was Poland and Romania that were particularly targeted and blamed though litigation undertaken by private foundations (namely the OSJI). Secret prison programmes were denounced by AI,[62] HRW,[63] and the HFHR,[64] which drew up and released several reports on secret detention facilities. These reports were scrutinised by both the European Parliament and the CoE, which decided to make additional reports of their own to document secret prisons. Several recommendations and resolutions on the alleged transportation and illegal detention of prisoners in European countries by the CIA were adopted by the Parliamentary Assembly of the CoE[65] and two

---

[62] See for instance the AI report, *Unlock the Truth: Poland's Involvement in CIA Secret Detention*, June 2013.

[63] HRW, 'Statement on US secret detention facilities in Europe', 6 November 2005.

[64] International Helsinki Federation for Human Rights Report, *Anti-Terrorism Measures, Security and Human Rights: Developments in Europe, Central Asia and North America in the Aftermath of September 11*, April 2003.

[65] Report of 12 June 2006 on Alleged Secret Detentions and Unlawful Inter-state Transfers Involving Council of Europe Member States, Parliamentary Assembly, Committee on Legal Affairs and Human Rights, Rapporteur: Dick Marty, PACE doc. 10957, 12 June 2006; Second Report of 11 June 2007 on Secret Detention and Illegal Transfers of Detainees Involving the Council of Europe Member States, Parliamentary Assembly, Committee on Legal Affairs and Human Rights, Rapporteur: Dick Marty, PACE Doc. 11302, 11 June 2007; Information Documents of the Council of Europe, Report of 28 February 2006 by the Secretary General on the Use of His Powers under Article 52 of the European Convention on Human Rights in the Light of Reports Suggesting that Individuals, Notably Persons Suspected of Involvement in Acts of Terrorism, May Have Been Arrested and Detained, or Transported while Deprived of Their Liberty, by or at the Instigation of Foreign Agencies, with the Active or Passive Co-operation of States Parties to the Convention or by States Parties Themselves at Their Own Initiative, without Such Deprivation of Liberty Having Been Acknowledged, SG/Inf (2006) 28 February 2006; Resolution 1562 (2007)1, Secret Detentions and Illegal Transfers of Detainees Involving Council of Europe Member States: Second Report, Parliamentary Assembly of the Council of Europe (PACE); Recommendation 1801 (2007)1, Secret Detentions and Illegal Transfers of Detainees Involving Council of Europe Member States: Second Report, PACE; Opinion on the International Legal Obligations of Council of Europe Member States in Respect of Secret Detention Facilities and Inter-state Transport of Prisoners, European Commission for Democracy through Law (Venice Commission), No. 363/2005, 17 March 2006.

committees of the European Parliament,[66] alleging breaches of human rights in the secret detention facilities and during the secret transfer of prisoners inside and outside Europe. The cases mentioned by the CoE and the EU were subsequently reported to the ECtHR, which had also issued hostile judgments against Italy, Poland, Romania, Lithuania and Macedonia based on reports by AI and the OSJI in addition to those by the European institutions.[67]

Thanks to litigation efforts made by the OSJI, Poland and Romania were condemned by the ECtHR in the Al Nashiri and the Abu Zaybah cases (litigated by the OSJI). Such condemnations publicly exposed Poland and Romania to certain European critics, who saw them as the main states in Europe that had hosted secret prisons, endorsed illegal counterterrorist policies and contravened the rule of law,[68] although other countries, including France, Sweden, Finland, Denmark and the UK were also involved in such secret programmes without being condemned or even being brought to justice.[69]

6.1.6 *The Horváth and Kiss and D. H. Judgments: Hungary and the Czech Republic as 'Racist States'*

The very first policy change in Hungary and Czech Republic forged through the Horváth and Kiss and D. H. cases litigated by the OSJI on racial discrimination was the adoption of state policy mandating the collection of ethnically disaggregated data in schools. For years, the

---

[66] Resolution of 6 July 2006 on the Alleged Use of European Countries by the CIA for the Transportation and Illegal Detention of Prisoners (2006/2027(INI)), P6_TA (2006)0316) European Parliament; European Parliament, Directorate General for Internal Policies, Policy Department's Citizen Rights and Constitutional Affairs, Justice, Freedom and Security, Note on the Results of Inquiry into the CIA's Programme of Extraordinary Rendition and Secret Detention in European States in Light of the New Legal Framework Following the Lisbon Treaty, 2012, PE 462-456; Final Report of 30 January 2007 on the Alleged Use of European Countries by the CIA for the Transportation and Illegal Detention of Prisoners (2006/2200 (INI)), doc. A6–0020/2007), European Parliament, Resolution of 10 October 2013 on Alleged Transportation and Illegal Detention of Prisoners in European Countries by the CIA (2013/2702(RSP)).

[67] OSJI, *Globalising Torture: CIA Secret Detention and Extraordinary Rendition*, February 2013; AI, *Unlock the Truth: Poland's Involvement in CIA Secret Detention*, June 2013.

[68] European Parliament, Resolution 2016/2573(RSP) on Follow-up to the European Parliament Resolution of 11 February 2015 on the US Senate Report on the Use of Torture by the CIA, 8 June 2016.

[69] European Parliament; Resolution of 10 October 2013 on Alleged Transportation and Illegal Detention of Prisoners in European Countries by the CIA (2013/2702(RSP)).

HOW ECTHR JUDGMENTS TRANSFORM NATIONAL POLICIES   217

Czech and Hungarian authorities had refused to collect, or even condone independent collection of, ethnic data and had impeded efforts to document practices related to Roma due to their constitutional tradition. Nevertheless, almost immediately after the ECtHR rulings, the Czech[70] and Hungarian[71] governments decided for the first time to collect disaggregated data about the ethnic background of all pupils to provide a quantifiable measure of the placement of ethnic Roma students in schools where the curriculum caters to students with intellectual disabilities.[72] In Hungary, specific issues arose with the collection of ethnic data (including the potential participation of NGOs in the data collection process) despite the establishment of a voluntary declaration of the ethnic identity of the child by the parents in proceedings before the expert committees since November 2014.[73] In this regard, following discussion with the CoE's Department for the Execution of ECtHR Judgments, the Hungarian government will submit an updated action plan by 31 December 2020.[74]

In reaction to its condemnation by the ECtHR in *Horváth and Kiss v. Hungary* and following several communications sent to the CM by the ERRC (which notably pointed out a significant number of misdiagnoses on ethnic grounds to the detriment of Roma children and the negative role played by religious institutions in school segregation),[75] the

---

[70] Communication from the Czech Authorities to the CM of the Council of Europe, *Comprehensive Evaluation of the Reform of Inclusive Education in Relation to Roma Pupils*, 5 April 2019, DH-DD(2019)391, available at https://search.coe.int/cm/Pages/result_details.aspx?ObjectId=090000168093de28.

[71] In July 2014, the Hungarian parliament amended its main education legislation to mandate that expert panels, which diagnose pupils with disability, collect and record ethnically disaggregated data in a centralized database. A Ministry of Human Resources official confirmed that this database was adopted in reaction to the Horváth and Kiss judgment.

[72] OSJI, *Strategic Litigation Impacts. Insights from Global Experience*, 2018, p. 50.

[73] Communication from the Hungarian Authorities, Action Plan, 5 April 2019, DD(2019) 384, available at https://search.coe.int/cm/Pages/result_details.aspx?ObjectID=09000016804a2ccd, pp. 2-3; Communication from Hungary Concerning the Case of HORVATH and KISS v. Hungary (Application No. 11146/11) to the CM of the CoE, 1302nd Meeting (December 2017) (DH), Action Plan, 25 September 2017, available at https://search.coe.int/cm/Pages/result_details.aspx?ObjectId=0900001680751d0e.

[74] Ibid., p. 4.

[75] Communication from NGOs (Chance for Children Foundation (CFCF) and European Roma Rights Centre (ERRC)), DD(2015)1292, 20 November 2015, available at https://search.coe.int/cm/Pages/result_details.aspx?ObjectID=09000016804a82d3. Communication from NGOs (Chance for Children Foundation (CFCF), European Roma Rights Centre (ERRC)), DD(2014)368, 4 March 2014, available at https://search.coe.int/cm/

Hungarian government also adopted a policy aimed at decreasing the disproportionate number of Roma people put in disadvantaged schools and at bringing its practices into compliance with the ECtHR judgment.[76] In particular, institutional and procedural guarantees were established by the Hungarian authorities to ensure fairness and to guard against any misdiagnosis in the testing and examination process. These measures were further reinforced in 2013, and the entire system of pedagogical expert services (including the expert committees) was fully reorganised in 2013.[77] Since 2017, domestic remedies have been in place, as the administrative authorities can be seized to challenge the findings of the expert committees, and their decisions (as to both the diagnosis and the designation of the educational institution) can be challenged before the judicial authorities.[78] More generally, global efforts have been made by Hungary to implement an inclusive education policy.[79]

Under pressure exerted by the D. H. ruling and the follow-on civil society advocacy by the OSJI[80] and AI,[81] which sent very critical communications to the CM regarding the execution of the D. H. judgment, in September 2016 the Czech government passed new amendments to the Czech Education Act designed to provide more support for children with 'disabilities or with social disadvantage' and with special educational needs.[82] The new legislation limited the number of children with special

---

Pages/result_details.aspx?ObjectID=090000168063d97e. See also Communication from ERRC, DH-DD(2019)935, 10 September 2019, available at https://search.coe.int/cm/Pages/result_details.aspx?ObjectId=0900001680973351.

[76] Communication from the Hungarian Authorities, Action Plan, 5 April 2019, DD(2019) 384.

[77] Ibid., p. 1.

[78] See Act No. CL of 2016 on the General Rules of Administrative Proceedings and Act No. I of 2017 on the Rules of the Proceedings before the Administrative Courts.

[79] Communication from the Hungarian Authorities, Action Plan, 5 March 2019, p. 2.

[80] The OSJI sent no fewer than fourteen communications to the Committee of Ministers of the Council of Europe in the case of *D. H. and Others* v. *Czech Republic*, available at www.coe.int/en/web/execution/submissions-czech-republic#{%2215012143%22:[1]}.

[81] Communication from Amnesty International to the Committee of Ministers of the Council of Europe: D. H. and Others v. Czech Republic, 71/009/2013, available at www.amnesty.org/en/library/info/EUR71/009/2013/en; Communication from Amnesty International to the Committee of Ministers of the Council of Europe: D. H. and Others v. Czech Republic, 6 May 2010, available at https://search.coe.int/cm/Pages/result_details.aspx?ObjectID=09000016804a2816.

[82] Amendment to Article 16 of Act No. 561/2004 on Pre-school, Primary, Secondary, Tertiary, Professional and Other Education(the Schools Act), Effective since 1 September 2016; Regulation No. 27/2016 on the Education of Pupils with Special Educational Needs and of Gifted Pupils.

educational needs to five per class and abolished separate schools and classes for children with mild mental disabilities.[83] In 2017, two amendments to Regulation No. 27/2016 on the education of pupils with special educational needs and of gifted pupils were also passed with a view to alleviating the excessive administrative burden in relation to inclusive education and to clarifying the rules for using support measures based on findings from the functioning of the system in practice.[84] In effect, the Czech government adopted a policy that requires schools to accept any reasonable proxy as identity papers for Roma and to prohibit denial of school access for lack of documents.[85] The factual findings and legal conclusions reached by the ECHR in the D. H. case were used and applied by the European Commission, in 2014, as factual basis, legal support, and political cover to launch for the very first time unprecedented infringement proceedings against the Czech government for alleged failure to comply with the EU Racial Equality Directive.[86] The pre-litigation mechanism allows the European Commission to hold the Czech government accountable, and to put pressure on it publicly and politically to end the systemic and unlawful practice of discrimination against Roma children in Czech schools as underlined by the ECtHR.

In November 2014, as a first reaction to the infringement, the Czech government cast doubt on the Commission's competence to trigger an infringement procedure in the context of education. The Czech government argued that the organisation of educational systems remains the competence of individual member states. The Czech government has therefore been engaging in a strained and conflictual dialogue with the

---

[83] The content of the new legislation is detailed in the Revised Action Plan for the Enforcement of the Judgment of the European Court of Human Rights in the Case of D. H. and Others v. Czech Republic submitted to the CM of the CoE, DH-DD(2016)161, 5 February 2016, available at https://search.coe.int/cm/Pages/result_details.aspx?ObjectID=09000016805ad0ba; see also Communication from the Czech Authorities, Action Plan Submitted to the CM, DD(2018)194, 15 February 2018, available at https://rm.coe.int/1310th-meeting-march-2018-dh-action-plan-15-02-2018-communication-from/168078e57f.

[84] Communication from the Czech Authorities to the CM of the Council of Europe, Comprehensive Evaluation of the Reform of Inclusive Education in Relation to Roma Pupils, 5 April 2019, DH-DD(2019)391, p. 4.

[85] Communication from the Czech Authorities to the CM of the Council of Europe, Comprehensive Evaluation of the Reform of Inclusive Education in Relation to Roma Pupils, 5 April 2019, DH-DD(2019)391, p. 3.

[86] See European Commission, Justice, Fundamental Rights and Citizenship. Non-conformity with Directive 2000/43 on Racial Equality: Discrimination of Roma Children in Education. Formal Notice 258 (ex226).

Commission, particularly on the legal reform of the School Amendment Act. Nevertheless, even though ethnic discrimination in Czech schools is still denounced by both the OSJI[87] and AI,[88] and the Czech government is exposed to European critics on this issue, some gradual improvements have been made in the placement of Roma in programmes for children with mild mental disability, according to the OSJI itself[89] and the Czech Public Defender of Rights.[90]

In summary, our point is not that there are no serious or even very serious problems with rights protection in Eastern countries and in Russia, but that (a) the picture has been distorted, because Eastern countries and Russia are subjected to excessive focus and monitoring, while the state of protection of human rights may be even worse in some other states, including 'Western' CoE states that conduct austerity policies (see Chapter 5); and (b) the extent to which nationalist regimes and Russia have paid fines (except in one very specific case) and adopted measures to correct the breaches tends to be not only minimised but largely placed out of focus. In other words, our claim is not that Eastern countries and Russia are innocent victims of legal tricks. Most of the ECtHR rulings can only be welcomed when considered in isolation. The point is a very different one, namely that it is not only Eastern countries and Russia that make problematic decisions in trying to minimise the extent to which political discretion is limited by the substantive constitutional yardstick enshrined in the ECHR. There is also a political agenda behind the litigation undertaken by private foundations and NGOs, and even more, a policy surrounding what that litigation entails, and both litigation and policy are very much influenced by the set of private donors that make the litigation and politicisation of rulings possible.

In other words, through a combination of litigation and advocacy, NGOs can increase pressure on the European human rights system and on certain national states, maximise the extent to which the CoE

---

[87] OSJI, *Strategic Litigation Impacts: Insights from Global Experience*, p. 50, available at www.justiceinitiative.org/uploads/fd7809e2-bd2b-4f5b-964f-522c7c70e747/strategic-litigation-impacts-insights-20181023.pdf.
[88] AI, *Must Try Harder. Ethnic Discrimination of Roma Children in Czech Schools*, pp. 50–55, available at www.amnestyusa.org/files/musttryharder_embargoed_report.pdf.
[89] OSJI, *Strategic Litigation Impacts. Insights from Global Experience*, 2018, p. 50.
[90] Communication from NHRI (the Czech Public Defender of Rights) to the Committee of Ministers of the Council of Europe in the Case of D. H. v. Czech Republic, 23 May 2019, available at https://search.coe.int/cm/Pages/result_details.aspx?ObjectId=090000168094d830.

monitors certain Eastern countries (such as Russia), and in the process bring judicial and political changes, which may lead in the medium and longer run to regime change in Russia and in other Eastern countries. A possible lack of compliance by certain Eastern countries (including Russia) with reinforced monitoring can be used by the OSF to stigmatise these member states as rogue, unreliable, and responsible for the ECtHR backlog and, in general, for the malfunction of the ECHR system that must be reformed.[91] Thus Russian and Eastern reactions to this private scrutiny need to be analysed to obtain a broader view of the whole process.

6.2 The Eastern and Russian Reactions to European Judicial Condemnations

How do Eastern countries and Russia react to ECtHR judgments and to the litigation undertaken by private foundations and NGOs? The nature of their reactions is of interest since it documents the strength of the impacts of such litigation on these countries. We argue that the tensions that arise between Eastern nationalist regimes (including in particular Russia, Hungary, Poland and Azerbaijan), on the one hand, and the ECtHR and the CoE, on the other hand, are partly caused by a politicisation of certain ECtHR judgments litigated by private foundations and the NGOs funded by them. These strains can be observed in the Russian, Polish, Hungarian and Azerbaijani reactions to these judgments and to this kind of litigation. To a certain extent, their reactions take the form of political backlash (a potential reaction associated with intense litigation, see Klarman 2013) against NGOs, which risks a deterioration in the protection of human rights in these countries over a longer period of time.

6.2.1 Bans on Foreign Private Foundations and NGOs in Russia, Hungary and Azerbaijan and Control over NGOs in Poland

In response to the political litigation undertaken by private foundations and NGOs, Russia and Hungary have banned them. On 20 July 2012 the Russian parliament adopted amendments to the laws on NGOs,

---

[91] OSJI, *From Judgment to Justice: Implementing International and Regional Human Rights Decisions*, 25 November 2010, available at www.opensocietyfoundations.org/reports/judgment-justice-implementing-international-and-regional-human-rights-decisions.

collectively known as the Foreign Agents Act. The Act defined as follows the concept of a 'foreign agent' in Section 2 of the Law on Non-Commercial Organisations (hereinafter referred to as the NCOs Act): a Russian non-commercial organisation which gets funds and other property from foreign states, their governmental bodies, international and foreign organisations, foreign nationals, stateless persons or persons authorised by any of the above, or a Russian legal entity receiving funds and other property from the above-mentioned sources, and which is involved in political activity, including political activity in the interests of foreign providers of funds, in the territory of the Russian Federation. Of particular interest is the concept of 'political activity' carried out by foreign agents and NGOs, which is defined by Section 2 of the NCOs Act as participation (including financial participation) in the organisation and implementation of political actions with a view to influencing state authorities' decision-making and affecting state policy and public opinion. The main focus of the statute is thus NGOs that receive funding or other material resources from 'foreign' sources. The law characterises such NGOs as 'foreign agents' in order to subject them to a set of specific rules.

First, the Foreign Agents Act gives power to the Russian state to control such organisations through registration, inspections, accounting and publications, and Section 32 of the NCOs Act, as amended on 20 July 2012, obliges all non-commercial organisations exercising the functions of a 'foreign agent' to seek registration with the Ministry of Justice. Such a requirement existed prior to the NCOs Act and was set up by Section 29 of the 1995 Public Associations Act,[92] which requires an NGO qualifying as a foreign agent to register with a competent body. Nevertheless, compared to the 1995 Public Associations Act, the Foreign Agents Act added new provisions,[93] which contained specific grounds for unscheduled inspections of non-commercial organisations exercising the functions of a foreign agent.[94] Second, routine inspections of a non-commercial organisation exercising the functions of a foreign agent have to be carried out once a year.[95] Third, organisations registered as

---

[92] Federal Law No. 82-FZ of 19 May 1995; Russian Federal Law No. 7-FZ On Non-Profit Organizations (January 12, 1996), Adopted by the State Duma on December 8, 1995 available at http://legislationline.org/download/action/download/id/4380/file/Fed_Law_Non profit_Associations_1996_am2009_en.pdf.
[93] A new subsection was added to Section 32 of the NCOs Act.
[94] Section 32(4.6) of the NCOs Act.
[95] Section 32 of the NCOs Act.

foreign agents are required to label their publications to indicate that they have been issued or distributed by a non-commercial organisation exercising the functions of a foreign agent.[96] Fourth, the Foreign Agents Act introduced new accounting requirements, such as compulsory audits for financial reports of foreign agents, which must keep separate records of income or expenses coming from foreign sources (which have to be published) and income or expenses obtained from other sources.[97] They also have to comply with stricter accounting requirements.[98] Fifth, the Foreign Agents Act created new specific criminal offences to punish the violation of human rights and deliberate non-compliance with the legislation on foreign agents. A subsequent law of 12 November 2012 introduced sanctions for violation of the legal provisions on foreign agents into the Code of Administrative Offences (CAO) and set up new administrative sanctions (fines) for failure to provide information to the state authorities. Although the new provisions also defined administrative sanctions for failure to register as a foreign agent and for violation of the duty to label publications as originating from a foreign agent,[99] these were considered to be unlawful by the Constitutional Court,[100] which underlined that the administrative fines did not allow proper consideration of the nature of the offence, the degree of guilt of the person held responsible, his or her property and financial status, and other circumstances significant for the individualisation of punishment.[101] On 4 June 2014, the Federal Parliament amended the Ministry of Justice's power to register an NGO on the list of foreign agents on its own initiative.

The definition of a 'foreign agent' was thus enlarged on 2 June 2016 to include organisations that are engaged in activities in the fields of statehood, the protection of the Russian constitutional system, federalism, the protection of the Russian Federation's sovereignty and territorial integrity, the rule of law, public security, national defence, external policy, the Russian Federation's social, economic and national development, development of the political system, state and local authority activities, and human rights, for the purpose of influencing state policy, state and local authority structure, or their decisions and actions.

---

[96] Section 24 of the NCOs Act.
[97] Section 32(1) of the NCOs Act.
[98] Section 32(3) and (3.2) of the NCOs Act.
[99] Article 19.34 of the Law of 12 November 2012.
[100] Although the Constitutional Court upheld the provisions of the Foreign Agents Act as being compatible with the Constitution.
[101] Case no 10-P, Russian Constitutional Court, 8 April 2014.

Theoretically, litigation financed by foreign funds is included in these activities, which cover actions affecting public authorities and officials, such as actions encouraging the adoption, amendment or repeal of laws or other legal acts and the dissemination, including via information technology, of views on the decisions and policy of state authorities.

The organisations banned by the Russian authorities are notably the OSF and the IPC, which were included in the list of 'undesirable NGOs' drawn up by the Russian Prosecutor General's Office and by the Federation Council in July 2015, following an allegation that the OSF posed a threat to 'Russia's constitutional system, defence capability and national security'.[102] This ban has been particularly criticised by some European states and NGOs (backed up by private foundations) and has led to an escalation of the conflict between on the one hand the EU and the CoE and on the other hand Russia (see below).

In response, forty-eight NGOs (including Memorial, Public Verdict and the Sakharov Center, see below) banned by the Russian authorities have recently lodged a complaint with the ECtHR against the law on foreign agents.[103] In their applications, the NGOs notably cite two reports by the Human Rights Resource Centre[104] and AI[105] that analyse cases of forcible inclusion on the list of foreign agents, standardised grounds for classifying an NGO's activities as political, and a wide interpretation of the term 'political activity' applied by the domestic courts and the Russian authorities. Both reports came to the conclusion, which was shared by the European Commissioner for Human Rights,[106] that the legislation on foreign agents had negative impacts on the situation of NGOs, including obliging some of them to close down. The NGOs have also relied on the opinions of the Venice Commission[107] and

---

[102] Sputniknews, 'It's been fund: Russia sends Soros speculating his way out the door', 30 November 2015, available at http://sputniknews.com/russia/20151130/1030990303/foundation-list-prosecutorsrussia.html#ixzz3uTex8cdq and http://sputniknews.com/russia/20151130/1030990303/foundation-list-prosecutors-russia.html.

[103] Case nos 9988/13 14338/14 59787/14 ... [forty-eight applications], *Ecodefence and Others* v. *Russia* [23 March 2017] communicated case to the ECtHR.

[104] Human Rights Resource Centre, 'Foreign agents: mythical enemies and Russian society's real losses', March 2015.

[105] AI, 'Agents of the people: four years of 'Foreign Agents' Law in Russia', November 2016.

[106] The Commissioner for Human Rights of the Council of Europe (2015) Opinion on Legislation and Practice in the Russian Federation on Non-Commercial Organisations in Light of Council of Europe Standards: Update, 9 July 2015, pp. 4–5.

[107] European Commission for Democracy through Law (2014) Opinion No. 716-717/2013, 27 June 2014.

the European Commissioner for Human Rights,[108] both of which denounced the definitions of the terms 'political activities' and 'foreign agent', and argued that the Russian legislation on foreign agents should be amended with the aim of establishing a clear, coherent and consistent framework in line with applicable international standards.[109] Both institutions also stated that reporting and accounting requirements should be transparent, coherent and the same for all NGOs, regardless of the sources of their income.[110] While all the NGOs alleged in their applications that the Russian authorities have violated Articles 10 and 11 ECHR with regard to the quality of the Foreign Agents Act, persecuting them for failing to register as foreign agents, and excessive state control,[111] thirty-nine NGOs complained that their rights under Articles 10, 11 and 14 ECHR have been breached in that they are subjected to discrimination and to restrictions and excessive reporting obligations (unlike other NGOs, which are exempt from such duties).[112] Lastly, three NGOs alleged that under Articles 10, 11 and 18 their freedom of expression and association was limited for purposes other than those prescribed by the ECHR.[113]

The Russian Foreign Agent Act has inspired some other Eastern countries to pass similar laws. In the summer of 2013, the OSF, AI, HRW and other NGOs (including the HHC) funded by foreign private foundations denounced a statement made by the Hungarian prime minister about human rights NGOs being 'paid political activists who are trying to help foreign interests'[114] through their US funding.[115] Administrative and criminal investigations were then applied against a number of NGOs financed through the EEA/Norway Grants (NGO

---

[108] The Commissioner for Human Rights of the Council of Europe (2013) Opinion on the Legislation of the Russian Federation on Non-Commercial Organisations in Light of Council of Europe Standards, 15 July 2013.
[109] Ibid.
[110] Ibid.
[111] Case nos 9988/13 14338/14 59787/14 ... [forty-eight applications], *Ecodefence and Others v. Russia* [23 March 2017] communicated case to the ECtHR.
[112] Ibid.
[113] Cases nos. 9988/13, 15098/16 and 26303/16, *Ecodefence and Others v. Russia* [23 March 2017] communicated case to the ECtHR.
[114] HRW, *Dispatches: The End of Liberal Democracy in Hungary?* 29 July 2014, available at www.hrw.org/news/2014/07/29/dispatches-end-liberal-democracy-hungary.
[115] HHC, *Timelines of Governmental Attacks against NGOs*, 7 April 2017, available at www.helsinki.hu/en/timeline-of-governmental-attacks-against-ngos/.

Fund) scheme.[116] These accusations have even been levelled at foreign governments, including that of the US and most notably that of Norway, which has been accused of interfering in Hungarian politics by giving grants to NGOs that challenge or are critical of certain actions and decisions of the Hungarian Fidesz government.[117] The latter labelled George Soros as an enemy of the state, denouncing his humanitarian and political involvement in the European refugee crisis,[118] and taking measures to limit the influence played by private foundations and NGOs. In this respect, on 4 April 2017 the Hungarian parliament adopted a new Act that amended the Higher Education Act of 2011. The changes added new requirements concerning the names of foreign higher education institutions, the need for bilateral agreements between Hungary and non-European Economic Area countries of origin of higher education institutions, the requirement to provide higher education services also in the country of origin, and additional requirements for the registration and authorisation of higher education services in Hungary. In this way, the Hungarian government attacked the OSF and tried to revoke the licence of the Central European University. Similarly, on 13 June 2017 it passed a law on foreign-funded NGOs with a view to overseeing activities in Hungary carried out by several international NGOs funded by foreign funds and to deterring private foundations from making donations from abroad to civil society organisations in Hungary.[119] Like the Russian Foreign Agents Act, the Hungarian law introduced new obligations for certain categories of NGOs receiving annual foreign funding above HUF 7.2 million (approx. €24,000) to register and label themselves in all their publications, websites and press material as 'organisations supported from abroad'.[120] These NGOs are also obliged to provide the Hungarian authorities with specific information about the funding they receive from abroad (including donations of more than HUF 500,000 in a given year) along with detailed data concerning the donor and each donation (which is included in a special registry and thus made publicly accessible). The NGOs face sanctions if they do not comply with the new registration,

---

[116] United States Mission to the OSCE, Statement on Intimidation of Civil Society and Media in Hungary, June 2014.
[117] Ibid.
[118] S. Adl-Tabatabai, 'Hungary joins Israel and labels Soros "Enemy of the State"', News-Punch, 18 July 2017, available at https://newspunch.com/hungary-soros-enemy/.
[119] Act LXXVI Hungarian Law of 13 June 2017 on the Transparency of Organisations Receiving Support from Abroad.
[120] Ibid.

reporting and transparency obligations.[121] On 18 January 2018, the Hungarian government established the first 'Stop Soros' package consisting of three laws that target NGOs, requiring those that receive foreign funding and that allegedly 'propagate mass migration' or 'support illegal migration' to register as such and to pay a 25 per cent tax on any foreign funding given for 'supporting illegal migration'. On 13 February 2018 this package was replaced by the second 'Stop Soros' package, another set of three bills that require, amongst other things, NGOs carrying out activities in the field of migration to apply for a licence from the Interior Ministry to continue their work. Failure to apply for a licence could ultimately lead to dissolution by a court. Licensed groups are required to pay a 25 per cent tax on any foreign funding. Such legislation goes so far as to criminalise activities (including giving legal advice) that support asylum and residence applications, and it further restricts the right to request asylum with a view to preventing private foundations and NGOs from acting in this field.[122]

In response to this Hungarian legislation, the OSF decided on 16 May 2018 to move its office from Budapest to Berlin, blaming the move on an 'increasingly repressive' climate in Hungary.[123] In parallel, the OSF also lodged a complaint with the ECtHR arguing that that Hungary's 'Stop Soros' legislation violates its rights to freedom of expression, association, and assembly guaranteed by Articles 10 and 11 ECHR.[124] On 19 September 2018, HHC filed two applications before the ECtHR to fight the Hungarian legislation. In these applications, HHC stressed the concerns raised by the OSF over the threat posed by Article 353/A of Hungary's Act C of 2012 on the Criminal Code (Criminal Code) as inserted into the Criminal Code by Act VI of 2018 on the Amendment of Certain Laws Related to Measures against Illegal Migration in Hungary. In this regard, HHC raised violations of Articles 10, 11 and 18 (regarding illegitimate aims pursued by the legislation).[125]

---

[121] Ibid.
[122] Hungarian Criminal Code, Act VI of 2018 on the Amendment of Certain Laws Related to Measures against Illegal Migration in Hungary.
[123] 'Soros Foundation to close office in Budapest over Hungarian government's "repressive" policies', *The Daily Telegraph*, London, 15 May 2018, available at www.telegraph.co.uk/news/2018/05/15/soros-foundation-close-office-budapest-hungarian-governments/.
[124] *OSI-Budapest v. Hungary* [12 September 2018] ECtHR.
[125] *Hungarian Helsinki Committee v. Hungary* [19 September 2018] ECtHR, available at www.helsinki.hu/wp-content/uploads/Application_HHC_SS3.pdf.

Azerbaijan has also passed strict legislation on NGOs financed by foreign private donors. On 28 December 2015, the Ministry of Justice adopted new 'rules on studying the activities of NGOs, branches or representative offices of foreign NGOs', which came into force in February 2016. These new rules attributed to the Minister large powers to conduct 'regular' or 'extraordinary' inspections on NGOs. Moreover, the President of Azerbaijan signed a decree on 21 October 2016 that puts grants by foreign donors to NGOs under the influence of national authorities. In this regard, the new rules establish a 'one-stop shop' (or 'single window') for this procedure as of 1 January 2017. NGOs that receive funds from foreign donors are obliged to obtain authorisations from the authorities.[126]

To a much lesser extent, Poland has tried to take control of funding for NGOs. In October 2017, it created a National Freedom Institute in charge of administering EU cohesion funds and national funds for NGOs,[127] thereby increasing government control over EU funding.[128] Like the Hungarian government, the Polish authorities have the express aim of controlling the distribution of the Norwegian NGO Fund grants.[129] Both in Hungary and Poland, public funding for NGOs is decreasing (Kapronczay 2017), and this process is having a negative effect on the protection of human rights in these countries. Lastly, and inspired by the Russian and Hungarian legislation on foreign agents, Romania and Ukraine have recently proposed draft laws imposing additional financial reporting obligations on NGOs.

6.2.2 New Powers Given to the Russian Supreme Court

In reaction to many condemnations pronounced by the ECtHR and litigated by private foundations and NGOs, amendments to the

---

[126] Monitoring Committee's Co-rapporteurs Messrs Schennach and Preda, Information Note on a Fact-finding Visit to Baku (12–14 January 2017) AS/Mon (2017)06 declassified, 19 February 2017.

[127] 'Poland's President signs divisive Bill on funding NGOs', *The Washington Post*, 14 October 2017.

[128] M. Dunai, 'Hungarians protest against crackdown on education, NGOs', *Reuters*, 12 April 2017, available at https://uk.reuters.com/article/uk-hungary-soros-protests-education/hungarians-protest-against-crackdown-on-education-ngos-idUKKBN17E279?il=0.

[129] EEA Grants, *Active Citizens Fund 2014–2021*, 12 January 2017, available at https://eeagrants.org/What-we-do/Programme-areas/Civil-society/Active-Citizens-Fund-2014-2021.

Constitutional Law of the Constitutional Court of Russia (the 'Constitutional Law') were passed to limit the influence of the ECtHR on Russia. According to the new law, a ruling from an international body (including the ECtHR) that is in conflict with the Russian Constitution can be declared impossible to implement by the Russian Constitutional Court.[130] The First Deputy Chairperson of the Legal Affairs Committee of the Parliamentary Assembly of the CoE then conveyed the Committee's decision to request an opinion of the Venice Commission on the 'draft legislation pending before the Russian Parliament which would empower the Constitutional Court to determine whether findings by international bodies on protection of human rights and freedoms (including those of the ECtHR) are to be implemented or not'. In its analysis, the Venice Commission addressed the main points of the Russian Constitutional Court's judgment, as well as the constitutional amendments of 2015, concluding that the new system established by Russia may breach a number of norms of international law and of the ECHR.[131] The Commission therefore recommended that Russia adopt a number of measures, including the removal of two of the key amendments that give new powers to the Constitutional Court. Notwithstanding the Commission's interim opinion, the Russian authorities have not amended the Constitutional Law.

In April 2016, the Russian Constitutional Court stressed that the Russian constitutional legal order is not subordinate to the European conventional system and, for the sake of the effectiveness of the ECHR norms, the ECtHR should respect the national constitutional identities.[132] However, the Russian Court 'recognised the fundamental significance of the European system of protection of human and civil rights

---

[130] Federal Law of the Russian Federation No. 7-KFZ (CDL-REF(2016)006, introducing amendments to the Federal Constitutional Law No. 1-FKZ of 21 July 1994 on the Constitutional Court of the Russian Federation (CDL-REF(2016)007, 4 December 2015.

[131] European Commission for Democracy through Law, Interim Opinion on the Amendments to the Federal Constitution Law on the Constitutional Court of the Russian Federation Adopted by the Venice Commission at its 106th Plenary Session, CDL-AD (2016)00, Venice, 11–12 March 2016, available at www.venice.coe.int/webforms/documents/default.aspx?pdffile=CDL-AD(2016)005-e; European Commission for Democracy through Law, Russian Federation: Final Opinion on the Amendments to the Federal Constitution Law on the Constitutional Law on the Constitutional Court Adopted by the Venice Commission at its 107th Plenary Session, Venice, 10–11 June 2016, available at www.venice.coe.int/webforms/documents/default.aspx?pdffile=CDL-AD(2016)016-e.

[132] Case no 12-P/2016, Constitutional Court of the Russian Federation [19 April 2016] CDL-REF(2016)033.

and freedoms, judgments of the European Court of Human Rights being part of it' and was 'ready to look for a lawful compromise for the sake of maintaining this system, reserving the determination of the degree of its readiness for it, so far as it is the Constitution of the Russian Federation which outlines the bounds of the compromise in this issue'.[133] The Constitutional Court, as the final judicial institution in charge of making it possible to execute judgments of the ECtHR, must find

> a reasonable balance in carrying out this power, so that the decision taken by it should on the one hand answer the letter and spirit of the judgment of the ECtHR, and on the other not come into conflict with the fundamental principles of the constitutional order of the Russian Federation and the legal regulation of human and civil rights and freedoms established by the Constitution of the Russian Federation.

Such a compromise means that whereas certain ECtHR judgments are in adequacy with the Russian constitutional and legal order, other judgments delivered by the ECtHR contravene the Russian legal system and cannot be executed. In this regard, the Russian Constitutional Court ruled that the 2013 ECtHR judgment regarding prisoners' voting rights (see above)[134] could not be implemented in the Russian legal order.[135] The Russian Constitutional Court, on the basis of the previous Soviet/Russian constitutions and of the travaux préparatoires of the current one, stated that the will of the constituent legislator was without any doubt that all convicted persons deprived of liberty under a court sentence be disenfranchised.[136] In parallel, and according to the Russian Constitutional Court, interpretation of Article 3 of Protocol No. 1 ECHR was evolutive rather than a well-established one that allowed a certain margin of appreciation.[137] Consequently, the ECtHR judgment was in conflict with the Russian constitutional order,[138] which took precedence.

In summary, the political litigation undertaken by private foundations and NGOs and the politicisation of European judgments achieved by such organisations (following the litigation process) have pushed the

---

[133] Ibid., p. 5.
[134] Case nos 11157/04 and 15162/05, *Anchugov and Gladkov* v. *Russia* [4 July 2013] ECtHR.
[135] Case no 12-P/2016, Constitutional Court of the Russian Federation [19 April 2016].
[136] Ibid.
[137] Article 3 of Protocol No. 1 ECHR reads as follows: 'The High Contracting Parties undertake to hold free elections at reasonable intervals by secret ballot, under conditions which will ensure the free expression of the opinion of the people in the choice of the legislature'.
[138] Case no 12-P/2016, Constitutional Court of the Russian Federation [19 April 2016].

Russian and Hungarian authorities to respond legally and judicially with a view to significantly increasing their control over the foreign funding and activities conducted by organisations defined as foreign agents. In return, some NGOs financed by private donors have very recently litigated and challenged before the ECtHR this control and oversight of their litigation activities regarded as political by the Russian and Hungarian governments. The Russian reaction has the effect of demonstrating the political role played by such litigation and the great influence exerted by foreign funds. Undoubtedly, these double litigation efforts have contributed to an increase in political tensions between the Russian authorities and the CoE institutions, including the European Commissioner for Human Rights and the Venice Commission, which have both criticised the Russian reaction to the influence of NGOs. Litigation, which must be analysed as a double process with spill-over effects over time, is thus also used by NGOs to counteract the negative effects and even the political backlash of litigation initially conducted by them (and which tends to cause a deterioration in the protection of human rights in Russia, Hungary, Azerbaijan and Poland).

6.3 The Rise of Political Tensions between Russia and the EU Backed by the US

Through a combination of litigation and advocacy, private foundations and NGOs can increase pressure on Russia, maximise the extent to which the CoE monitors Russia, and in the process bring judicial and political changes, which may lead in the medium and long run to regime change in Russia. Russia's lack of compliance with reinforced monitoring serves to stigmatise it as a rogue and unreliable state responsible for the ECtHR backlog and the general malfunctioning of the ECHR system.[139] The objectives pursued by the OSF and other US and UK private foundations in terms of support for advocacy and litigation against Russia seem to be in line with US and European foreign policy objectives towards Russia.

In this regard, the European Commission has expressed its concerns not only about the levels of corruption in the public administration, the lack of genuinely independent media or the numerous attempts to compromise the independence of bureaucracy, but also (and perhaps

---

[139] OSJI, *From Judgment to Justice. Implementing International and Regional Human Rights Decisions*, 25 November 2010, available at www.opensocietyfoundations.org/reports/judgment-justice-implementing-international-and-regional-human-rights-decisions.

mainly) about the (strong) role of the state in the economy. This is why the Commission claims that Russia has to seek stability, security and prosperity through the development of accountable institutions, an independent judiciary and a free-market system integrated into the European economy. Indeed, the Commission moves from this conclusion to the assertion that only if democracy, the rule of law and the protection of fundamental rights and liberties are entrenched in Russia can EU–Russian relations develop satisfactorily. A very strong civil society is regarded as fundamental.[140] The murder of the extremely well-respected and highly critical journalist Anna Politkovskaya, shot at point-blank range in Moscow in circumstances that are still far from clear, and the law on NGO registration discussed above are taken as evidence of the unwillingness of the Russian government to allow civil society a breathing space.[141]

Nevertheless, EU–Russia human rights consultations were established in 2005 and have been held biannually since. The result has been a substantial dialogue on the state of human rights in Russia and the EU and on EU–Russian cooperation on human rights issues and matters concerning international NGOs in international forums. Many issues have been discussed: the human rights situation in Chechnya and the rest of the North Caucasus (including torture and ill treatment); freedom of expression and assembly, including freedom of the media; the state of civil society in Russia, notably in light of the laws on NGOs and extremist activities; the functioning of the judiciary, including independence issues; observation of human rights standards by law enforcement officials; racism and xenophobia; and legislation relating to elections.[142]

In this perspective, the main instrument the EU has used vis-à-vis Russia has been the European Initiative for Democracy and Human Rights (EIDHR).[143] This instrument has allowed the EU to work with the CoE and NGOs in fields such as penal reform, improving the ability of lawyers and law enforcement officials to apply the ECHR, combatting human rights violations in the North Caucasus and in Chechnya,

---

[140] European Commission Country Strategy Paper 2007–2013 on Russian Federation, available at http://eeas.europa.eu/russia/docs/2007-2013_en.pdf.
[141] Ibid.
[142] EU–Russia Common Spaces, available at https://web.archive.org/web/20110124130605/http://eeas.europa.eu/russia/common_spaces/fsj_en.htm.
[143] See http://ec.europa.eu/europeaid/how/finance/eidhr_en.htm.

protecting the human rights of conscripts in the armed forces, and promoting children's rights and the rights of indigenous peoples.[144]

US foreign policy also aims to reform the Russian judicial and political systems, strengthening civil society, promoting human rights, supporting the fight against corruption and bolstering the rule of law and democratic political processes.[145] The USAID programme established in 1992 (with the OSF as a partner) provides assistance and financial aid (amounting to USD 160 million between 2009 and 2014) to Russian NGOs focused on human rights,[146] and to independent regional media that find themselves in a difficult economic situation.[147] The programme is supposed to transform previously authoritarian, centrally planned societies into Western-style market-led democracies with liberal economies, open political systems (through monitoring of elections, political parties and local government), democratic judicial systems (through workshops, training and exchanges on a broad number of issues related to legal reform, including introduction of the jury system) and a strong civil society.[148] To this end, it provides technical assistance and institutional development support to the Sakharov Center in helping to improve the coordination between the activities of disparate human rights NGOs operating within Russia.[149]

In response, Russia put an end to the USAID programme, claiming that the actual goal of the programme was to give cover to US interference in Russian internal affairs.[150] The response of the Obama

---

[144] Ibid.
[145] Department of State, 'The Obama administration's strategy for supporting democracy and human rights in Russia', Washington, DC, 4th January 2014, available at www.humanrights.gov/factsheet-the-obama-administrations-strategy-for-supporting-democracy-and-human-rights-in-russia.html.
[146] USAID, *Strategic Objective Close-Out Report. 2001. Strengthened Rule of Law and Respect for Human Rights*, available at http://pdf.usaid.gov/pdf_docs/Pdach458.pdf; see also Department of State, 'The Obama administration's strategy for supporting democracy and human rights in Russia'; OSI, *Partnerships and Donor Partners Report*, 20 July 2009, 1, available at www.opensocietyfoundations.org/sites/default/files/partners_20090720_0.pdf+&cd=1&hl=fr&ct=clnk&gl=be.
[147] Ibid.
[148] See https://web.archive.org/web/20010216073455/ and www.usaid.gov/regions/europe_eurasia/.
[149] USAID, *Strategic Objective Close-Out Report. 2001. Strengthened Rule of Law and Respect for Human Rights*.
[150] US Foreign Policy Department, 'Statement on Russian decision to end USAID activities in Russia, Spokesperson Victoria Nuland', Washington DC, 18 September 2012, available at www.state.gov/p/eur/ci/rs/c49686.htm.

administration was to favour the enactment by Congress of the so-called 'Magnitskiy Act'[151] of 2012 on behalf of William Browder (the former head of Hermitage Capital Management and a client of Magnitskiy, who was also condemned by the Russian Courts) and in response to the Magnitskiy judgment litigated by the OSJI (and analysed in Chapter 3). The UK and Canada did the same. The US, Canadian and UK Acts denounce Russia for serious human rights violations and corruption,[152] and enable their respective governments to impose targeted sanctions on perpetrators and beneficiaries of serious human rights violations. This legislative reaction (which has not been called into question or amended by the Trump administration) constitutes further evidence of the key role played by private foundations and NGOs and of the influence that litigation strategies can have on the shaping of foreign and domestic policy (and perhaps also vice versa). In April 2014, the CoE Parliamentary Assembly unanimously passed a resolution urging the competent Russian authorities to investigate fully the circumstances and background of the death in pre-trial detention of Sergei Magnitskiy and to hold the perpetrators to account.[153] It was the first time in the Parliamentary Assembly's history that a vote was used to establish a public sanctions list.[154] A new resolution on Sergei Magnitskiy fighting impunity by targeted sanctions was adopted in 2019 against Russia by the CoE Parliamentary Assembly.[155] Although the Magnitskiy case had not yet been judged by the ECtHR, it had already impacted and damaged US, EU and Russian relations (see below) and contributed to the portrayal of Russia as a corrupt state that represses political opponents and whistle blowers. In addition, the US administration stepped up its support to the US Russia Foundation for Economic Advancement and the Rule of Law (USRF), which states that its objective is to support the development of civil society in Russia. In return, the reinforcement of NGOs through this official support potentially nurtures litigation that supports specific foreign policy options.

The affinity between US and European foreign policy towards Russia and the objectives pursued by the OSF and other US and UK private

---

[151] US Congress-Senate, Bill, 112TH 2nd Session, 19 July 2012, available at www.gpo.gov/fdsys/pkg/BILLS-112s3406pcs/pdf/BILLS-112s3406pcs.pdf. The Foundation has spent over USD 13 million in the last two years toward building a broad-based civil society.
[152] See http://nhc.no/filestore/Dokumenter/Magnitskydocuments.pdf.
[153] CoE Parliamentary Assembly, Resolution 1966 (2014) 28 January 2014.
[154] Ibid.
[155] CoE Parliamentary Assembly, Resolution 2252 (2019) 22 January 2019.

foundations in terms of support for advocacy and litigation against Russia can be explained by the fact that several members of private foundations funding NGOs litigating the ECHR against Russia belong to the Council on Foreign Relations, including George Soros himself and Aryeh Neier, president emeritus of the OSF.[156] If we admit that the Council on Foreign Relations (CFR) is a very powerful think tank, able to influence and even significantly orient US foreign policy (which seems to be attested by the fact that many leaders of the US State Department have been or are CFR members), the connections between private foundations and the most powerful think tank in US foreign policy could explain the fact that the priorities pursued by private foundations are fully in line with US foreign policy towards Russia (Shoup 2015). In addition, there are connections between NGOs and officials who are very close to the US (and who work in foreign policy affairs). For instance, the OSJI has recruited 'the former Deputy to the Permanent Representation from Sweden, Sara Finnigan, to assist in the development of a strategic plan for the establishment of a sustainable NGO presence in Strasbourg'.[157]

The EU and the CoE denounce the lack of respect for human rights by countries that refuse and condemn these critics. Overall, the conflict finds its origin in Chechnya, Crimea and Ukraine (which have all been the focus of ECtHR judgments condemning Russia) and has resulted in political and economic sanctions taken by the EU and the Parliamentary Assembly of the CoE against Russia (see Cliquennois and Champetier 2016). In response, and despite being one of the main contributors to the CoE budget along with France, the UK, Italy and Germany, Russia decided to suspend payment of its contribution to the CoE since 2017, when, following the annexation of Crimea, Russia's voting rights in the

---

[156] Council on Foreign Relations, 'Board list', available at www.cfr.org/about/membership; for the OSF, 'People', available at www.opensocietyfoundations.org/people/george-soros. CFR members who are also members of the NED are Vin Weber (vice-chair of the NED and CFR board director), Elliott Abrams, Francis Fukuyama, Zalmay Khalilzad, Moisés Naím, Melanne Verveer and Robert B. Zoellick (all on the board of directors of the NED), see https://web.archive.org/web/20011211190008/ and www.oakfnd.org/governance_&_staff.htm; for the Oak Foundation see https://web.archive.org/web/ and www.oakfnd.org/governance_&_staff.htm; for the MacArthur Foundation (Jamie Gorelick, Drew Saunders Days III and John P. Holdren) see www.macfound.org/about/our-history/past-board-members/.

[157] OSJI, 'An Open Society Justice Initiative concept note – Short version, Human rights made real: establishing a Strasbourg-based presence to improve the implementation of ECHR judgments', September 2014.

PACE (and its participation in decision-making bodies of the Assembly and its monitoring missions to observe elections in the space of the CoE) were revoked.[158] Russia might even leave the CoE if its voting rights continue to be suspended.[159] Even if Moscow does not withdraw from the CoE, it may no longer be able to work with the ECtHR, because the CoE's regulations stipulate that a country that does not pay membership fees can be denied representation in the CoE body.[160] However, and after much turmoil, Russia has finally decided to pay its contribution to the CoE in 2019 after a voted decision adopted by the CoE Parliamentary Assembly (a decision mainly supported by France and Germany) to maintain Russia's membership in the CoE.[161]

6.4 Towards a New Cold War?

Not only are cases against some Eastern countries (including Russia) very relevant in quantitative terms, but also a considerable set of pilot judgments and landmark decisions have resulted from actions against these states. There are objective reasons why the Eastern case law is decisive. But if the number of actions (and of successful actions) against some Eastern countries is disproportionately high, this is also because private donors with deep pockets and specific political and social agendas are keen to provide funding to the NGOs that play a key role in the litigation. Here, instead of downplaying the role of donors and NGOs, regarding them as mere facilitators of individual actions aimed at redressing injustices in individual cases, we take seriously the need to identify which NGOs are key players, which donors provide them with the bulk of their funding, and how the preferences of those donors coalesce with foreign policy priorities. This leads us to conclude that litigation before the ECtHR has become one of the fields, perhaps one of the key fields, in which a 'new Cold War' is unfolding between Russia and other Eastern countries (especially Hungary and Poland) on one side, and the European Union and the United States on the other. Our point, quite

---

[158] M. Bushuev and M. Ostapchuk, 'Russia withholds payments to the Council of Europe', *DW*, 1 March 2018, available at www.dw.com/en/russia-withholds-payments-to-the-council-of-europe/a-42792673.
[159] Ibid.
[160] Ibid.
[161] J. Rankin (2019) 'Council of Europe votes to maintain Russia's membership', *The Guardian*, 17 May 2019, available at www.theguardian.com/world/2019/may/17/council-of-europe-votes-to-maintain-russia-membership-crimea.

obviously, is not to take sides, but to show how the two parties actively try to instrumentalise the ECHR and the ECtHR.

Consider the US and EU statements on policy vis-à-vis Russia. With the exception of a brief interlude during which some Eastern countries and Russia were regarded as a necessary partner in the 'war on terror'[162] (leading, for example, to the NATO Partnership for Peace programme), relations have been constantly conflictual and have thus led to a 'new Cold War' (Cohen 2011; Menon and Rumer 2015). Cohen gives insight into US policy towards post-Soviet Russia by tracing its origins in the Clinton and Obama administrations, both of which were influenced by the doctrine of Zbigniew Brzeziński dating back to the first Cold War (Cohen 2011). In this context, the US has constantly referred to human rights violations in the conflicts in Chechnya, Crimea, Georgia, Moldova and Ukraine, with more than occasional reference to rulings of the ECtHR serving as evidence that Russia has become a 'rogue state'. ECtHR case law (heavily shaped by repeated litigation by private foundations and NGOs) has thus fuelled a public discourse supportive of an escalation of conflict between Russia on the one hand and the US and the EU on the other. Applications to the ECtHR concerning the Georgian, Crimean and Ukrainian armed conflicts prove not only that human rights have been breached but also that they have been turned into evidence in public discussions of the impossibility of normal relations with Russia.[163]

On the Russian side of the equation, the combination of a growing number of condemnatory rulings and the role played by NGOs funded by private donors in bringing and arguing the underlying cases has been regarded by the Russian Federation as aggression waged by judicial

---

[162] Council on Foreign and Defense Policy Working Group on Russia and Globalization, World News Connection, FBIS-SOV-2001-1113, 8 October 2001, available at www.cfr.org; V. Georgiyev, 'The Club', *Nezavisinay Gazeta*, 22 November 2001, on file with the author.

[163] See for instance European Parliament, Resolution on Georgian occupied territories ten years after the Russian invasion (2018/2741(RSP): 'Members noted that 10 years after the Russian military aggression in Georgia of August 2008, the Russian Federation still continues its illegal occupation of these Georgian territories, reinforcing its illegal military presence in Georgia's occupied territories by constructing new bases, bringing in new troops and equipment, and conducting military exercise. The 2008 invasion was Russia's first major open attack on the European order, and was later followed by others, including the annexation of Crimea and the war in Eastern Ukraine. Parliament reiterated that Russia continues to be in breach of its international obligations and refuses to fully implement the EU-mediated ceasefire agreement of 12 August 2008.'

proxy. As underlined above, this is clearly revealed by the 2006 Russian law governing 'foreign agent' NGOs and, perhaps even more so, by the way in which this Act has been implemented (as analysed above). After the statute entered into force, the Russian government concluded that certain NGOs had failed to respect several of the requirements. It claimed that a number of NGOs, including that of Navalnyy (the major political opponent, see above), were interfering with the Russian political process.[164] More than ninety other organisations (many US-based), including not only AI and HRW but also the National Democratic Institute, the International Republican Institute and the Netherlands-based Russian Justice Initiative, were expelled from Russia.[165] The law and its implementation led to a clear deterioration in relations between Russia on the one hand and the EU and the US on the other. The latter denounced the new Russian law and the decision to expel or suspend NGOs. On the ground, the Russia law on NGOs acting as 'foreign agents' has not completely prevented NGOs from continuing to litigate (van der Vet 2018). Likewise, Hungary has been subject to several infringement procedures initiated by the European Commission concerning its NGO law (which controls foreign funding).[166] In response to Eastern legislation that either bans or limits foreign private funds given to NGOs, the CoE Parliamentary Assembly has adopted several resolutions to condemn new restrictions on NGO activities in certain Eastern countries.[167] In particular, the Assembly denounced 'restrictive laws and regulations concerning registration requirements or funding, administrative harassment, smear campaigns against certain groups and threats and intimidation against NGO leaders and activists' in these Eastern countries.

Similarly, Russia has claimed explicitly that the ECtHR has become exceedingly politicised,[168] setting up Russia as its target. This will have been facilitated by the structural reforms to the ECtHR (discussed earlier) and perhaps most especially by the larger role of the CM when it comes

---

[164] 'Vladimir Putin's declaration', 21 October 2006, *The Irish Times*, available at www.irishtimes.com/ news/russia-suspends-activities-of-ngos-in-clampdown-on-dissent-1.1018608.

[165] Ibid.

[166] European Commission, Infringement Proceeding against Hungary and Its NGO Law, 7 December 2017.

[167] PACE, Resolution 2226 (2018) on New Restrictions on NGO Activities in Council of Europe Member States, 27 June 2018; Recommendation 2134 on New Restrictions on NGO Activities in Council of Europe Member States, 27 June 2018.

[168] Comment of the Ministry of Foreign Affairs of the PMR on the Decision of the European Court of Human Rights in the Case of Catan and Others versus Moldova and Russia, 23 October 2012, available at http://mfa-pmr.org/en/xbG.

to the execution of judgments (where Russia is bound to be on the minority side). To quote then Russian Foreign Minister Sergey Lavrov on the Catan case,[169]

> The changing reality when the European Court of Human Rights, functioning for more than 50 years as a supreme body defending human rights, becomes instrument of pressure is perceived with worry in the Ministry of Foreign Affairs of the PMR (and Russia). It is regrettable that rights of people are cynically used for political goals by certain countries. We believe such situation does not promote improvement of authority of the Council of Europe as an organisation able to work out European standards in humanitarian sphere.[170]

Similar concerns were raised when Russia (rather reluctantly) ratified Protocol No. 14, which clearly results in a further empowerment of Strasbourg judges.[171] The 'troika' of judges would be applying double standards: one set to pass judgment on Russia, another (less demanding) set when deciding cases involving other countries. Lack of receptiveness on the part of the ECtHR to the Russian invocation of the 'secrets of state' exception when being asked to provide documents on Chechnya has also been peddled as a matter of the 'politicisation' of judges.

Both the US/EU and Russian reconstructions of litigation before the ECtHR aim to present the case-law-making process in openly political and strategic terms. This facilitates a radically one-sided reconstruction and assessment of new events, as facts and arguments that reflect the legal and political complexities are disregarded in public discourse, and strong pressure is applied to render them irrelevant when the ECtHR and CoE structures in general have to take decisions. This 'filtering' has clearly been at play regarding the conflict in Ukraine. The US and the EU characterised Russian actions as an unlawful invasion and blamed Russians for the conflict in eastern Ukraine, which rapidly escalated into a war. For its part, Russia described its actions as a response to encirclement by new

---

[169] The Ministry of Foreign Relations of the Russian Federation, Transcript of Response by Russian Minister of Foreign Affairs Sergey Lavrov to Questions from Parliamentarians After Speech at PACE 61st Session, Strasbourg, April 29, 2010, available at http://archive.mid.ru/brp_4.nsf/0/ADC25496E4B0957AC325771B002B0874.

[170] Comment of the Ministry of Foreign Affairs of the PMR on the Decision of the European Court of Human Rights in the Case of Catan and Others Versus Moldova and Russia, 23 October 2012, available at http://mfa-pmr.org/en/xbG.

[171] Legal Informatics Blog, 'Interlaken Conference on the future of the European Court of Human Rights', 25 December 2009, available at https://legalinformatics.wordpress.com/2009/12/25/conference-on-thefuture-of-the-european-court-of-human-rights/.

NATO countries belonging to the Commonwealth of Independent States, subject to 'colour revolutions' that were more or less explicitly said by the Russian authorities to be funded and supported by the US and the EU (Krickovic 2015; Menon and Rumer 2015), notably through private foundations (and in some cases, relying on the very same donors that provided resources to litigating NGOs).

An economic embargo against Russia was then adopted by both the US and the EU,[172] a resolution condemning Russia was adopted by the European Parliament,[173] and the Parliamentary Assembly of the CoE decided to suspend the voting rights of the Russian representative, as well as their right to be represented in the Bureau, Presidential Committee and Standing Committee of the Assembly to participate in the election of observation missions.[174] As discussed above, these tensions led Russia to threaten to withdraw from the CoE Parliamentary Assembly for a further year if its powers were not restored,[175] and possibly even to withdraw from the CoE.[176]

Beyond the escalated conflict between some Eastern countries, the EU, the CoE and the US, to which the litigation and advocacy activities carried out by private foundations and NGOs contributed, litigation funding calls into question more generally the existence, nature and content of economic and political interests pursued by private foundations.

---

[172] Regulation (EU) No 833/2014 Concerning Restrictive Measures against Russia, OJ L 229, of 31 July 2014, 1–11; Council Regulation (EU) No 1351/2014 of 18 December 2014 Amending Regulation (EU) No 692/2014 Concerning Restrictive Measures in Response to the Illegal Annexation of Crimea and Sevastopol, OJ L 365 of 19 December 2014, 46–59; Statement by the President of the European Council Herman Van Rompuy and the President of the European Commission in the Name of the European Union on the Agreed Additional Restrictive Measures against Russia, EUCO 158/14 PRESSE 436 PR PCE 140, Brussels, 29 July 2014, available at www.consilium.europa.eu/uedocs/cms_data/docs/pressdata/en/ec/144158.pdf.

[173] European Parliament Resolution on the Invasion of Ukraine by Russia (2014/2627 (RSP)), 13 March 2014, available at www.europarl.europa.eu/sides/getDoc.do?type=TA&language=EN&reference=P7-TA-2014-0248.

[174] Parliamentary Assembly of the Council of Europe, Challenge, on Substantive Grounds, of the Still Unratified Credentials of the Delegation of the Russian Federation, Resolution 2034 (2015), 28 January 2015 and Resolution 1990 (2014), available at http://assembly.coe.int/nw/xml/XRef/Xref-XML2HTML-en.asp?fileid=21538&lang=en.

[175] TASS Russian News Agency, 'Russian delegation to leave PACE for one more year if sanctions prolonged – lawmaker', 11 June 2015, available at http://tass.ru/en/ukraine.

[176] Interfax, 'Russia's withdrawal from CoE would not be conducive to Russia–EU dialogue', 22 January 2015, available at www.interfax.com/newsinf.asp?pg=5&id=566296.

7

The Relationships between Litigation Funded by Private Foundations and the Economic and Political Interests They Pursue

Of course, private foundations and NGOs that take test cases to the European Courts seek to set a useful judicial precedent that others can follow. But beyond this traditional aim, we argue that the main objective pursued by private foundations through direct litigation and their funding of NGOs is to spur social changes connected with and close to their interests (Collins 2018). In this regard, private foundations and NGOs can transform national policies that cause human rights violations. As discussed in Chapter 2, legal cases are conceived by the OSJI as a way not only of 'obtaining individual redress but also as a means of achieving a broader effect by setting an important precedent or otherwise reforming official policy and practice'.[1] The concentration of applications and complaints against specific countries and in specific policy areas raises questions about the economic and political interests pursued by private foundations. This is why this chapter examines the relationships between litigation undertaken and funded by foreign private foundations and their economic and political interests.

The economic interests of private foundations can be traced and identified through the identities and CVs of their board members and through the economic investments made by their heads. Judgments litigated and delivered by the ECtHR that favour and promote a free market and free trade are analysed. Litigation documents and archives collected and gathered in 2016 at the Rockefeller Foundation archives in New York and at the OSF archives in Budapest are also used to show the international and liberal perspective endorsed by private foundations.

7.1 The Fight against Nationalism as Part of the Promotion of Borderless Neoliberalism and Free Trade

We demonstrate in this first section that the composition of the founders and the boards of the private foundations involved in the funding of

---

[1] OSJI, *Global Human Rights Litigation Report*, October 2013, p. 1.

litigation is dominated by US capitalists with neoliberal profiles who are mostly strangers to the realm of philanthropy and by people with excellent knowledge of Eastern countries and Russia in particular. Our second aim is to show that human rights help private donors to do business and make economic speculation in a more discreet way.

7.1.1 The Identity and Profile of Board Members of Private Foundations: Businessmen, Not Philanthropists

The founders and owners of the main private foundations we have studied (the OSF, the Ford Foundation, the MacArthur Foundation, the Oak Foundation and the Sigrid Rausing Trust) are very wealthy businessmen who are not in general experts in philanthropy and human rights. Georges Soros, a billionaire investor and speculator (the twenty-ninth richest person in the world and the world's richest hedge fund manager),[2] exemplifies this trend. In 1969, Soros founded the Double Eagle hedge fund based in Curaçao. In 1970, he created Soros Fund Management and became its chair. In 1973, he resigned from the management of the Double Eagle fund and established the Soros Fund, which was later renamed Quantum (Arnold 2011). Since its inception in 1973, the Quantum fund has generated no less than $40 billion. Soros' speculative activities were so intense that they were condemned in 2002 by a French penal court for insider trading against the Société Générale bank in 1988.[3] Soros appealed the French judgment to the ECtHR on the ground that under Article 7 ECHR no person may be punished for an act that was not a criminal offence at the time that it was committed.[4] However, the ECtHR rejected his appeal, considering that Soros had been aware of the risk of breaking insider trading laws and that France did not violate his rights in punishing him criminally for trading on inside information about Société Générale.[5] The Quantum fund, based in the Cayman islands for tax purposes, has also made headlines after its speculation against sterling, the German mark, the Thai baht and the Malaysian ringgit and further successful speculative operations, allegedly

---

[2] Forbes 2017 Billionaires List: 'Hungarian-American George Soros is the richest hedge fund manager, 29th richest person on Earth', 22 March 2017.
[3] Case *Soros v. France* [20 December 2002] French Penal Court. See also M. Morano, 'Soros conviction for insider trading upheld in French court', *CSNNews.com*, 7 July 2008.
[4] Case no 50425/06, *Soros v. France* [6 October 2011] ECtHR, §42.
[5] Ibid., §§54–62.

including those on Hungarian,⁶ Russian,⁷ and Greek debts (see above, Chapter 5), for which Soros was recently condemned.⁸ Some famous economists, including Paul Krugman, have been critical of Soros' effect on financial markets (Krugman 1999, 160):

> Nobody who has read a business magazine in the last few years can be unaware that these days there really are investors who not only move money in anticipation of a currency crisis, but actually do their best to trigger that crisis for fun and profit. These new actors on the scene do not yet have a standard name; my proposed term is 'Soroi'.

Through his funding of certain NGOs, Soros is also considered to have contributed notably to the revolutions and changes in political regimes in Eastern countries such as in Georgia (the Rose Revolution)⁹ and in Ukraine (the Orange Revolution),¹⁰ as Soros himself admits.¹¹

A closer look at the identity of the board members of the main influential private foundations that finance litigation before the European Courts shows that the average profile is that of a businessperson rather than of a pure philanthropist or litigator. This profile indicates that the realm of human rights could constitute a real business run by business-people and politicians endorsing a free-market and neoliberal views rather than a pure philanthropic domain dominated by idealists, utopians, NGO activists and cause lawyers (Israël 2009; Sarat and Scheingold 2006). The issue of private interests and public policy really counts, therefore, and cannot be ignored at this stage.

While the OSF remains the property of Georges Soros (global board chair) and Andrea and Alexander Soros, his two sons,¹² the new president is Patrick Gaspard (who served as US ambassador to South Africa

---

[6] Soros' firm was for instance involved in an attack against Hungary's largest lender, OTP Bank, in 2008. See P. Fischer, 'How Hungarian analysts see Soros' hedge fund lockdown', *Budapest Business Journal*, 27 July 2011, available at https://bbj.hu/business/how-hungarian-analysts-see-soros-hedge-fund-lockdown_59116.

[7] T. O'Brien, 'He's seen the enemy. It looks like him', *The New York Times*, 6 December 1998, available at www.nytimes.com/1998/12/06/business/he-s-seen-the-enemy-it-looks-like-him.html.

[8] D. Sicot, 'La Grèce, terre d'aventure privilégiée des spéculateurs', *L'Humanité*, 9–22 July 2015, pp. 29–30.

[9] For instance, Alexander Lomaia, who is currently Secretary of the Georgian Security Council and former Minister of Education and Science, is a former Executive Director of the Open Society Georgia Foundation (O'Beachain and Polese 2010: 21).

[10] CNN, interview with George Soros, 25 May 2014.

[11] Ibid.

[12] See www.opensocietyfoundations.org/about/boards/open-society-global-board.

from 2013 to 2016 and was formerly assistant to President Obama and director of the White House Office of Political Affairs). The vice president is Leonardo Benardo, who was previously regional director for Eurasia and oversaw the Russia programme's full range of grant-making activities, as well as those in Poland and Hungary.[13] The composition of the global board shows that a very significant number of members carry out capitalist and economic activities and that others work in Eastern countries. Global board members include Anatole Kaletsky, who is co-chair and chief economist of Gavekal Dragonomics (an investment research and asset management group based in Hong Kong and Beijing) and a director of JPMorgan Emerging Markets Investment Trust; Mark Malloch Brown, who served as number two at the United Nations, in the UK cabinet and foreign office, and as vice president at the World Bank and is currently chairman of SGO (a leading elections technology company) and on the boards of Investec and Seplat (stock markets) and Kerogen (an oil and gas private equity fund); Daniel Sachs, who is CEO and a member of the boards of Proventus AB (a family-owned investment company) and Proventus Capital Management, and a council member of the European CFR; Maria Livanos Cattaui, who was secretary general of the International Chamber of Commerce and managing director at the World Economic Forum; Michael Ignatieff, who is the rector and president of Central European University in Budapest and a former member of the Canadian parliament and leader of the Liberal Party; Ivan Krastev, who is chairman of the Centre for Liberal Strategies in Bulgaria and a founding board member of the European CFR; and Istvan Rev, who is a professor of history and political science at Central European University in Budapest.[14]

Like the Rockefellers, who funded some of the most important universities in the US (Fischer 1983; Mazon 1985), including the University of Chicago and Stanford University (Chernow 1998), and the London School of Economics in the UK (Scot 2010), Soros founded the Central European University, which generates new forms of 'policy knowledge' and social sciences convergent with the economic interests of the elite (Guilhot 2004). Soros also contributes through oriented training of new leaders at the Central European University to the institutionalisation and

---

[13] See www.opensocietyfoundations.org/people/patrick-gaspard and www.opensocietyfoundations.org/people/leonard-benardo.

[14] See www.opensocietyfoundations.org/about/boards/open-society-global-board.

spread of the economic globalisation and free trade promoted by him and the elite (Guilhot 2004, 2007).

As regards the Ford Foundation, its current president is Darren Walker, who used to be vice president of the Rockefeller Foundation. He had a long career in international law and finance at Cleary Gottlieb Steen & Hamilton and UBS.[15] He notably succeeded people who had endorsed a free-market perspective while being strangers to the philanthropic realm, such as Louis Ubiñas (McKinsey), Susan Berresford (formerly at the Manpower Career Development Agency and on the board of Chase Manhattan Bank), Franklin Thomas (Bedford-Stuyvesant Restoration Corporation), who established Ford Foundation programmes in Russia and China, and McGeorge Bundy, who was national security advisor to Kennedy and Johnson.[16] In the same way, the successive boards of the foundations have been composed of former presidents of Xerox, Alcoa, Levi Strauss & Co and Reuters Holdings, vice presidents of Texaco and an executive vice president of Coca-Cola. Other companies represented at the Ford Foundation include Time Warner, Ryder System, CBS, AT&T, the Adolph Coors Company, Dayton-Hudson, the Bank of England, JPMorgan, Marine Midland Bank, Southern California Edison, KRCX Radio, the Central Hudson Gas & Electric Corporation, DuPont, Citicorp and the New York Stock Exchange.[17] Business leaders are also very well represented on the board of trustees, with Kofi Appenteng, investment banker and board director at Panbros Salt Industries; Afsaneh Mashayekhi Beschloss, president and chief executive officer of the Rock Creek Group (formerly Carlyle Asset Management Group) and former director of investments at the World Bank, JPMorgan and Shell; Ursula M. Burns, who was executive chair of the board of directors at Veon after serving as president and director at Xerox, Exxon Mobil and American Express; Amy C. Falls, chief investment officer and vice president for investments at Rockefeller University after serving as a managing director and global fixed income strategist for Morgan Stanley; J. Clifford Hudson, president of Sonic Corp (a drive-in fast-food restaurant chain); Robert S. Kaplan, CEO and president of the Federal Reserve Bank of Dallas; Thurgood Marshall, a partner at Morgan Lewis Consulting and at the law firm Morgan, Lewis & Bockius; N. R. Narayana

---

[15] www.thenonprofittimes.com/news-articles/darren-walker-promoted-to-president-at-ford-foundation/.
[16] www.fordfoundation.org/about/about-ford/our-origins/.
[17] Ford Foundation records.

Murthy, who co-founded Infosys (an international software services firm) and was its CEO; Peter A. Nadosy, managing partner of East End Advisors and former vice chair at Morgan Stanley; Gabrielle Sulzberger, a general partner and investment manager of the private equity fund Rustic Canyon/Fontis Partners LP and former principal at several private funds, such as Citigroup, HPB Associates and the Commonwealth Enterprise Fund.[18]

The board members of the MacArthur Foundation also share this characteristic and have important positions in business, finance and politics. Succeeding presidents were strangers to the philanthropy domain and all held top positions at universities and in governmental and international agencies and business.[19] Julia Stasch, prior to being the current president of the MacArthur Foundation, was president and chief executive officer of ShoreBank Chicago Companies and of Stein & Company, and served as chief of staff for the City of Chicago (with deep ties to the city's elite business clubs) and deputy administrator of the General Services Administration in Washington during the first Clinton administration.[20] With the exceptions of Elizabeth McCormack, who directed the Rockefeller philanthropy offices,[21] and Margaret E. Mahoney, who had leadership roles at the Carnegie Corporation, the Robert Wood Johnson Foundation and the Commonwealth Fund from 1980 until 1995,[22] most board chairs and board members had no real experience in the philanthropy realm, having worked in the bank, insurance and business sectors with a clear free-market and free-trade orientation.[23] For instance, board chairs have included Paul Dwight Doolen, a retired vice chairman of the board at Bankers Life and Casualty Company, who had suggested that MacArthur establish his foundation; Thornton F. Bradshaw, who was a leader in US business as president of the RCA

---

[18] www.fordfoundation.org/about/people/board-of-trustees/.
[19] They are Robert L. Gallucci (2009–2014), who served as dean at Georgetown University and in various US governmental and international agencies as diplomat and ambassador; Jonathan F. Fanton (1999–2009), who was former president of the New School for Social Research in New York City and provided assistance to dissident scholars in Eastern and Central Europe, most of whom were leaders of human rights organisations in their home countries; Adele S. Simmons (1989–1999); and John E. Corbally (1979–1989), who led Syracuse University before becoming president of the University of Illinois. See www.macfound.org/about/our-history/past-presidents/.
[20] See www.macfound.org/about/people/president/.
[21] See https://littlesis.org/person/71192-Elizabeth_J_McCormack#.
[22] See https://nyam.org/awards-grants/student-grants/margaret-e-mahoney-fellowships/.
[23] See www.macfound.org/about/our-history/past-board-members/.

corporation (which he sold to General Electric) and the oil company Atlantic Richfield; Robert E. Denham, a partner at Munger, Tolles & Olson, who notably worked for Bank of America, Citigroup and Goldman Sachs; William Kirby, a partner in the Chicago law firm of Hubachek, Kelly, Rauch and Kirby; Marjorie Scardino, former CEO of PLC and the Economist Group. Again, the current board of directors shares the same business profile and the free-market philosophy that it entails: Daniel Huttenlocher is vice provost of Cornell Tech and currently serves as a director of Amazon and Corning; Julie T. Katzman was managing director at Lehman Brothers before joining the Inter-American Development Bank as executive vice president; Paul Klingenstein is founder and managing partner of Aberdare Ventures after a period at the Rockefeller Foundation, where he advised on the initial public–private partnerships and impact investment funds; and James Manyika is a director of the McKinsey Global Institute and a senior partner and board member at McKinsey & Company. Board members have notably included Louis Feil, a billionaire businessman in the fur business and in real estate; Robert E. Ewing, president and CEO of Van Nostrand Reinhold; Gaylord A. Freeman, former chair and chief executive of the First National Bank of Chicago and former president of Bankers Life and Casualty Company, in addition to being advisor to Jimmy Carter and member of the Kennedy Commission on Money and Credit and the Williams Commission on International Trade and Investment Policy under Nixon; William E. Simon, secretary of treasury under Nixon and Ford and a businessman who worked for Salomon Brothers bank and served on the boards of over thirty companies including Xerox, Citibank, Halliburton, Dart & Kraft and United Technologies; Weston Robert Christopherson, who was CEO of the bank Northern Trust Corporation; Alan Hallene, president of Montgomery Elevator and director of the Moline National Bank; Adele S. Simmons, independent director at Marsh & McLennan, who has served on the boards of directors at Ceres, Marsh & McLennan, Chicago Metropolis 2020, the Synergos Institute, Metropolis Strategies, the Economic Club of Chicago, the Chicago Council on Global Affairs and ShoreBank; Walter E. Massey, who served as director and chairman of the board at Bank of America Corporation and BankAmerica Corp and as director of the University of Chicago and the Commonwealth Fund; George Ranney, who was president and CEO of Metropolis Strategies and served in various capacities for Inland Steel Industries; Thomas Theobald, who served as the chief executive officer at Continental Bank Corporation and worked at Xerox and at Citicorp/Citibank (including in a vice chairman position); John Seely Brown, who is an independent co-chairman of the Deloitte Center for the Edge and former chief scientist at Xerox; and Alan B. Krueger, who is professor of economics at the University of Princeton and a member of the advisory panel at the Federal Reserve Bank of Chicago.[24]

The Oak Foundation is directed by a six-member board of trustees that includes only members of the Parker family with a background in business and economics: as chair, Caroline Turner, daughter of Alan Parker, who works for the Oak Foundation in the US; as vice chair, Kristian Parker, son of Alan Parker, who has directed the Oak Foundation's environment programme since its inception; as vice chair, Natalie Shipton, daughter of Alan Parker, who is an advisor at Oak; other members are Christopher Parker, Jette Parker and Alan Parker (the founder).[25] An advisory panel also supports the Foundation's work on its main programmes. Unlike the OSF, the Ford Foundation and the MacArthur Foundation, some of the Oak Foundation's current members have a general background in philanthropy and civil litigation: Kathleen Cravero, president of the Oak Foundation since 2009, was director of the Bureau for Crisis Prevention and Recovery at the United Nations Development Programme and deputy executive director of the Joint United Nations Programme on HIV/AIDS, and also worked for the UN Children's Emergency Fund and the World Health Organization; William Norris works as a barrister and litigator at Essex Chambers in the field of large loss insurance claims and personal injury; Julie Sandorf has served as president of the Charles H. Revson Foundation since January 2008 and was formerly a consultant to the Rockefeller Foundation and a co-founder and executive director of Nextbook;[26] and Barbara Rothschild[27] is an art collector.

At the Sigrid Rausing Trust, the current board, whose profile is quite similar to that of the Oak Foundation, includes Sigrid Rausing (see above, Chapter 2); Andrew Puddephatt, who is executive chair of the advisory board at Global Partners Digital (GPD) and leads the secretariat for the intergovernmental Freedom Online Coalition;[28] Margo Picken, who is a

---

[24] See www.macfound.org/about/people/board-directors/.
[25] See http://oakfnd.org/meet-the-team.html.
[26] Nextbook is a national organization dedicated to the creation and promotion of Jewish literature, culture and the arts.
[27] See http://oakfnd.org/meet-the-team.html.
[28] See www.gp-digital.org/board/andrew-puddephatt/.

visiting fellow at the London School of Economics and an associate of its Centre for the Study of Human Rights (having directed the office of the UN High Commissioner for Human Rights in Cambodia from 2001 to 2007 and the office of AI from 1976 to 1987, and having worked for the Ford Foundation from 1988 to 1995, where she was responsible for the Foundation's international human rights programme);[29] Chris Stone, who is an independent advisor on justice reform and organisational strategy, having served as president of the OSF from 2012 to 2017 and as director of the Vera Institute of Justice (1994–2004);[30] Sir Jeffrey Jowell, who is an advocate in public and regulatory law, in offshore and in public international law,[31] and who has also served as professor in public law and as non-executive director of the Office of Rail Regulation and as chair of the Ombudsman Committee of British Waterways; Joshua Mailman, who is managing director of Serious Change Investments (a $70 million sole LP impact investment vehicle started in 2006) and is currently a founding or key investor in many member companies (including Indigenous Designs, Lotus Foods, Emerge Financial, Social Imprints, Ice Stone, Red Rabbit, Equilibrium Capital, RSF Mezzanine Fund, Icon Wheelchair, Everyone Counts, Giving Assistant, Napo Pharmaceutical and Sustain Condoms);[32] Princess Mabel of Orange-Nassau, who is the widow of Prince Friso and sister-in-law of King Willem-Alexander of the Netherlands, co-founder of War Child Netherlands and member of the European CFR, having served as an advisor to the OSF (as former director of international advocacy and director of EU affairs) and as an expert in Balkan diplomacy and international relations.[33]

Lastly, the board of the NED has the same economic profile as the boards of the OSF, the Ford Foundation and the MacArthur Foundation. The main members are Andrew Card, who serves on the board of directors of public corporation Union Pacific and on the business advisory board of BrainStorm Cell Therapeutics, having been acting dean of the Bush School of Government and Public Service;[34] David Skaggs, who holds positions as co-chair of the board of the Office of Congressional

---

[29] See www.c-r.org/who-we-are/people/author/margo-picken.
[30] See www.law.ox.ac.uk/people/chris-stone.
[31] See www.blackstonechambers.com/barristers/sir-jeffrey-jowell-qc-hon/.
[32] www.hrw.org/about/people/joshua-mailman.
[33] See https://en.wikipedia.org/wiki/Princess_Mabel_of_Orange-Nassau.
[34] See www.ned.org/experts/andrew-h-card-jr-chairman/.

Ethics and is currently a senior advisor with Dentons US LLP (a company that specialises in banking and finance transactions);[35] Marilyn Carlson Nelson, who is co-CEO and former chair of Carlson Holdings (one of the largest privately held companies in the world);[36] Robert Holmes Tuttle, who is a businessman with extensive experience in the private sector (including as co-managing partner of Tuttle-Click Automotive Group, one of the largest retail automotive companies in the US) after serving as US ambassador to the UK from 2005 to 2006;[37] James Boland, who is on the board of directors of ULLICO (an intermodal transportation business serving waterways) and was president of the International Union of Bricklayers and Allied Craftworkers from 2010 to 2015;[38] Marlene Colucci, who is executive director of the Business Council (an elite group of CEOs);[39] Eileen Donahoe, who is executive director of the Global Digital Policy Incubator at Stanford University's Center for Democracy and a board member of the Benetech advisory board, having served as director of global affairs at HRW;[40] Daniel Fried, who was special assistant and senior director of the National Security Council for Presidents Clinton and Bush, ambassador to Poland and assistant secretary of state for Europe (2005–2009), as well as an expert in Russia and in the policy of NATO enlargement to Central European nations and, in parallel, NATO–Russia relations;[41] Barry Jackson, who serves as strategic advisor at Brownstein Hyatt Farber Schreck and managing director of the Lindsey Group;[42] Mel Martínez, who serves as chair of the Southeast & Latin America for JPMorgan Chase & Co. and is on the board of Marriott Vacations Worldwide as lead director;[43] Victoria Nuland, who is senior counsellor at the Albright Stonebridge Group (a global strategic advisory and commercial diplomacy firm), former CEO of the Center for a New American Security (a bipartisan national security think tank in Washington),[44] former US ambassador to NATO and a top State Department official charged with overseeing US

---

[35] See www.ned.org/experts/david-e-skaggs/.
[36] See www.ned.org/experts/marilyn-carlson-nelson/.
[37] See www.ned.org/experts/ambassador-robert-h-tuttle-treasurer/.
[38] See www.ned.org/experts/james-boland/.
[39] See www.ned.org/experts/marlene-colucci/.
[40] See www.ned.org/experts/eileen-donahoe/.
[41] See www.ned.org/experts/ambassador-daniel-fried/.
[42] See www.ned.org/experts/barry-jackson/.
[43] See www.ned.org/experts/mel-martinez/.
[44] See www.ned.org/experts/victoria-nuland/.

policy toward Russia; Dayton Ogden, who is the global leader of Spencer Stuart's CEO Succession advisory services and a member of the board and industrial practices[45]; Ileana Ros-Lehtinen, who is a senior advisor at the law firm Akin Gump Strauss Hauer & Feld;[46] Elise Stefanik (the daughter of industry leader Ken Stefanik), who worked for Premium Plywood Products before becoming a congresswoman;[47] Linda Thomas-Greenfield, who is a senior counsellor at Albright Stonebridge Group;[48] Richard Verma, who is vice chairman and partner at the Asia Group;[49] and Melanne Verveer, who is the executive director of the Georgetown Institute for Women, Peace and Security at Georgetown University and a founding partner of Seneca Point Global, a global strategy firm for the advancement of women.[50]

Consequently, many board members of the private foundations involved in the funding of litigation in the European Courts have a clear neoliberal (and sometimes neoconservative) orientation.[51] They often work for private companies and are board members of international companies that are complete strangers to the realm of philanthropy. These neoliberal and capitalist profiles call into question whether and what kind of economic and speculative goals are being pursued by private foundations through their litigation and advocacy activities.

7.1.2 *Litigation Impacts in Terms of Economy and Market: Making Business in a More Discreet Way through Policy and Regime Change*

As outlined above, litigation priorities are self-defined by private foundations and NGOs, notably with regard to the potential impacts of cases taken to the European Court and in guiding their choice of cases, which in turn orients the issues dealt with in the European Courts. In this regard, the selection of cases is operated by private foundations and

---

[45] See www.ned.org/experts/dayton-ogden/.
[46] See www.ned.org/experts/the-honorable-ileana-ros-lehtinen/.
[47] See www.ned.org/experts/the-honorable-elise-stefanik/.
[48] See www.ned.org/experts/ambassador-linda-thomas-greenfield/.
[49] See www.ned.org/experts/ambassador-rich-verma/.
[50] See www.ned.org/experts/melanne-verveer/.
[51] One former NED board member is Elliott Abrams, who is a senior fellow of Middle Eastern studies at the CFR and a US diplomat who served in foreign policy positions for Presidents Ronald Reagan, George W. Bush and Donald Trump. He was involved in the Iran-Contra scandal during the Reagan administration, which led to his conviction in 1991. See www.ned.org/experts/elliott-abrams/.

NGOs with an eye to the litigation impacts they can generate in line with their advocacy policies. Litigation activities funded by US and UK private foundations and the NGOs they fund are concentrated on alleged human rights violations by countries that are considered (by private foundations and the NGOs) to be political and economic enemies of free trade, private markets and borderless capitalism; these include nationalist states such as Russia, Poland and Hungary and new Eastern regimes such as Ukraine. In this way (as discussed Chapter 2), the goal of the grants distributed by the NED to 'local, and independent organisations and litigants (that are opponent to nationalists regimes) is to promote political and economic freedom'. In particular, substantial changes in the policy conducted by Eastern countries could be obtained by private foundations through judgments pronounced by the European Courts. As the OSJI puts it, litigation serves less to address individual claims than to change societies, policies, legislations, administrations and practices by furthering 'open societies' and economic liberalism.[52]

For instance, the case of *Zelenchuk and Tsytsyura v. Ukraine* was litigated by EarlyBusiness,[53] an NGO that is backed by the OSF and works closely with the International Renaissance Foundation (founded by the OSF and part of the OSF international network),[54] the Centre for Economic Strategy,[55] which is partly financed by the OSF and the International Renaissance Foundation, the Atlas Network,[56] the Friedrich Naumann Foundation and the World Bank. EarlyBusiness aims to create a better competitive business-enabling environment and to develop a free market (including a free farmland market) and free trade in Ukraine through advocacy and litigation.[57] In *Zelenchuk and Tsytsyura v. Ukraine*, EarlyBusiness submitted a third party intervention in which the NGO promoted the creation of a free land market in Ukraine with a view to reducing the amount of land owned by Ukrainian farmers and to increasing the price of land and thus of houses. In this regard, Early Business advocated for a rise in the value of land (with reference to international experience that refers to a Western neoliberal model) and

---

[52] OSJI, *Global Human Rights Litigation Report*, 2015, p. 5; OSJI, *Global Human Rights Litigation Report*, 2017, p. 2.
[53] Case no 846/16 1075/16, *Zelenchuk and Tsytsyura v. Ukraine* [22 May 2018] ECtHR.
[54] See www.irf.ua/en/about/.
[55] See https://ces.org.ua/en/our-sources-of-funding/.
[56] The Atlas Network and in particular the Atlas societies promote the capitalist ideas of Ayn Rand, who in her books praised the virtues of individual capitalism and selfishness.
[57] See www.easybusiness.in.ua/who-we-are/.

an increase in its attractiveness to foreign investors in order to avoid low rents and cheap land prices.[58] The ECtHR was sensitive to this argument, condemning the Ukrainian authorities for violation of Article 1 Protocol No. 1.[59] In particular, the ECtHR held that the repeated extensions of the moratorium on the creation of a free land market, which had been established by the Ukrainian authorities with the aim of finding alternatives to the liberalisation of the land market, had itself contributed to legal uncertainty and to the burden imposed on the applicants.[60] According to the ECtHR, realisation of one of the key elements of the applicants' ownership, the right to dispose of one's property, became subject to the passage of legislation of indefinite content, passage which has been postponed in a way that appears unpredictable and insufficiently explained.[61] Thus, in practical terms, the moratorium rendered their ownership rights precarious and defeasible.[62] The ECtHR concluded that the Ukrainian state had overstepped its wide margin of appreciation in this area and had not struck a fair balance between the general interest of the community and the property rights of the applicants.[63] Furthermore, the ECtHR outlined that the issue underlying this violation concerns the legislative situation itself. The ECtHR considered that the Ukrainian state should take appropriate legislative and/or other general measures to find a fair balance between the interests of agricultural landowners, on the one hand, and the general interests of the community, on the other hand, in adequacy with the principles of protection of property rights under the ECHR.[64] The Zelenchuk and Tsytsyura case echoes the Hutten-Czapska judgment,[65] in which the ECtHR sanctioned the Polish state for having tried to regulate the free land market and to limit the price of rent through rent-control schemes in favour of tenants recognised as vulnerable; these measures were considered by the ECtHR to be excessive.[66] In this kind of case, the protection of the right to property spurs property to its highest-valued

---

[58] Ibid., §96.
[59] Ibid., §§104–149.
[60] Ibid., §§114–121.
[61] Ibid., §§118, 119 and 122.
[62] Ibid., §146.
[63] Ibid., §148.
[64] Ibid., §150.
[65] Case no 35014/97, *Hutten-Czapska* v. *Poland* [19 June 2006] ECtHR.
[66] Ibid., §198.

end use and quickly converts the local economy to a neoliberal model that is open to foreign investors and thus to potential speculation.

Litigation undertaken against nationalist countries could thus allow private foundations to obtain more liberalism and free trade. In particular, nationalist regimes such as Russia are opponents of political figures (such as Alexei Navalnyy, one of the main political opponents of the Putin regime and applicant in the case of *Frumkin* v. *Russia* litigated by EHRAC and Memorial, see Chapter 6) and businessmen (such as Vladimir Potanin, Viktor Chernomyrdin, Vladimir Gusinsky and Mikhail Khodorkovsky, who himself litigates the ECtHR against the Putin regime, Chapter 6) who are fully backed by the heads of private foundations such as Georges Soros.[67] For example, Soros denounced the arrest of Mikhail Khodorkovsky, the famous oil oligarch accused of laundering and fraud, as 'persecution' that left him in the hands of an oppressive Russian state,[68] having co-founded several of the programmes conducted by Open Russia (an NGO established by Khodorkovsky).[69]

In addition, Soros, who participated directly in decision-making concerning Russian privatisation programmes, benefitted from the privatisation plan that was implemented in the early 1990s in Russia and in other Eastern countries (which in return obtained significant loans from international and US institutions) under the supervision of the World Bank, the IMF and USAID (Chussodovsky 1997). In this context of privatisation and liberalisation programmes run by the World Bank and the IMF that caused massive poverty, impoverishment of the middle class, public spending cuts in healthcare and welfare and many human rights violations (Chussodovsky 1997; Stiglitz 2002), Soros contributed by investing massively in Russian and Eastern companies that were privatised. For instance, he became a significant shareholder in Novolipetsk, Russia's second-largest steel mill, and Sidanko Oil, whose reserves exceed those of Mobil. Soros also invested in Russia's high-yielding, IMF-subsidised domestic bond market (Wedel 1996; Williamson 1998), and in July 1997 he purchased 24 per cent of Svyazinvest, the telecommunications giant, in partnership with Uneximbank's Vladimir Potanin (Williamson

---

[67] See 'Soros and Khodorkovsky', *The Tribune Review*, 16 November 2003, available at http://triblive.com/x/pittsburghtrib/opinion/columnists/datelinedc/s_165315 .html#axzz3uOHIgaSG. See also https://khodorkovsky.com/an-evening-with-george-soros-at-open-russia-club/.
[68] Ibid.
[69] Ibid.

1998). Thanks to these investments made under the privatisation scheme, Soros made and gained money.

Soros and other founders of private foundations therefore have an interest in changes of political regime that could favour their private interests and businesses. Such changes in government and economic policy require 'nationalist', 'populist' regimes and their closed societies (in contrast to the open societies that, according to Soros [who adheres to Karl Popper's ideas on open society, see below] characterise the consolidated Western democracies) to be exposed and denounced, notably in terms of the gross human rights violations they commit. According to Soros himself: 'Right now, Putin is the embodiment of a certain form of nationalism, and this nationalism resonates in Russia, so Putin has managed extremely well in gathering the support of the country for his brand of nationalism',[70] and 'Now Russia is presenting an alternative that poses a fundamental challenge to the values and principles on which the European Union was originally founded. It is based on the use of force that manifests itself in repression at home and aggression abroad, as opposed to the rule of law'.[71] Transforming such 'closed societies' into 'open societies' would allow the Eastern economies to be opened up to the private interests pursued by the heads of private foundations. This process is echoed in recent research conducted by Winkler on how corporations in the US have carried out extensive, and often successful, strategic litigation campaigns to create, preserve, protect and expand their rights to do business, and to promote their interests and causes, free from government regulation (Winkler 2018).

Alongside financial and political means, litigation is not only an effective and practical way of bringing some openness to the economies of Eastern countries but also of shaming Russia, Azerbaijan and Hungary and destabilising their governments, which are opponents of some US private foundations and speculators and of Soros in particular (see for instance the Russian and Hungarian bans on foreign agents, discussed in Chapter 6). A change in regime and economic orientation, or at least a destabilisation of nationalist regimes, could allow their economic policies to fit into the neoliberal agenda set up and pursued by private foundations.

---

[70] Ibid.
[71] J. Borger, 'George Soros: Russia poses existential threat to Europe', *The Guardian*, 23 October 2014, available at www.theguardian.com/world/2014/oct/23/george-soros-russia-threat-europe-vladimir-putin.

7.2 How and Why Private Foundations Promote Cultural Liberalism and Globalism

Individual freedom as part of the rights of individuals and groups is conceived by private foundations as the translation and equivalent of the economic globalism and free market endorsed by private foundations. In this regard, we have shown that the right to property enshrined in Article 1 of Protocol No. 1 has been used by private foundations to speed up the trade liberalisation of the farmland market in Ukraine and in Poland. Certain minorities' rights (those of Roma and Muslims in particular) and especially the rights of immigrants and refugees who are victims of the state's refusal to welcome and recognise them, are also a translation of borderless capitalism, which is characterised by freedom of movement for both products and individuals. This is why the rights of certain minorities constitute one of the main areas in which private foundations are engaged through their litigation activities against conservative values, nationalism, and traditional religions including Christianity. In this regard, one of the main aims pursued by private foundations is to orient national states that are opposed to immigration towards being multi-ethnic countries that accept large-scale immigration and minorities' rights.[72] For private foundations, fighting ethnic discrimination has also been a consequence of the transformation of national countries into the international and multi-ethnic states they want. These multi-ethnic states could be defined as open societies (to use Karl Popper's term) in contrast to closed societies, which are attached to their borders and to their own populations. What is therefore at stake for private foundations is the defeat of closed societies and their national sovereignty through advocacy and litigation efforts. For instance, the Soros Foundation states that

> [t]he goal of the Soros foundations network in more than 50 countries throughout the world is to transform closed societies into open ones and to protect and expand the values of existing open societies. In pursuit of this common mission, the foundations established and supported by George Soros fund and operate a range of programs and activities. These initiatives deal with arts and culture; the strengthening of civil society; economic development and reform; education at all levels; human rights, with special attention to the rights of marginalized groups; legal reform and public administration; media and information, including publishing, electronic communication, and libraries; and public health. A priority in

---

[72] OSJI, *Global Litigation Report, 2017*, p. 9.

all these areas is to establish public policies and practices that advance open society values.[73]

In this regard, the transformation of nationalist states into multi-ethnic globalist countries and 'open societies', as the main task carried out by private foundations, both involves and contributes to a reduction in the strength of strong states (such as Russia) and to a homogenisation and reduction in the historical and background differences between states. For instance, states that present cultural differences are particularly targeted by private foundations. This is the case for countries marked by their Christian and Orthodox legacies and traditions, which are fought against by private foundations and subject to litigation by them in the fields of freedom of religion and thought (and in particular the right for Muslim women to wear the veil or burqa), the right to abortion, the right to sexual education, homosexual rights and euthanasia (see Chapter 3). The defence of the rights of certain minorities is also an efficient way to expand the globalist model and to make economies of scale and cost-savings for multinational and international companies. This model, the world society, is also necessary for economic purposes, as economic globalisation relies on cultural globalisation.

More generally, the expansion of a globalist world that is organised and regulated by several international institutions (including the IMF, the World Bank, the UN, the ICJ and the ICC) is needed by Soros and other heads of private foundations to increase their economic power. For instance, Soros is in favour of the creation of a world government, a world currency and a central world bank whose task would be to coordinate and regulate access to loans and to fight the economic instability (Soros 2005) that is partly caused by his speculation (along with that of other speculators and hedge funds) on financial markets. Such an international order, which according to its proponents will also avoid national conflicts and wars (although the UN was totally unable to prevent wars in Iraq, Afghanistan, Libya, Syria and the former Yugoslavia), requires fighting national states to reduce their strength and to make them accept the authority of the international order and its institutions. The question of compliance with international institutions partly reflects the degree of acceptance by national states of an international order that is influenced

---

[73] See www.opensocietyfoundations.org/uploads/5e4f2b5f-075a-4190-ad2f-25bc95f64255/a_complete_8.pdf.

by private foundations, notably through their funding and their advocacy.

There is no doubt that international law has been one of the key instruments used by private foundations to propagate their globalist model. More precisely, private foundations, including the MacArthur and Ford Foundations and the OSF, have played an important role in building a constituency for universally enforceable international law. In this regard, private foundations have fully financed the development of international law and the creation of the ICC.[74]

7.3 The Interests of Certain CoE Member States

As discussed in Chapter 2, the privatisation of litigation is also backed up by certain member states that participate through their embassies in the co-funding of NGOs that litigate against Eastern countries. The Netherlands, UK, Norway, Sweden and Switzerland are the main countries that finance this oriented litigation. The financial scheme to which these governments contribute is thus a mix of private and public funds, although private funding remains the more important source. The scheme constitutes a convenient way for these states to avoid being directly involved in inter-state cases that are no longer considered by the ECtHR to be a priority and that could be risky in terms of political and diplomatic relations. Such funding is also a way for states to escape the censure of the European Courts and to avoid being condemned for human rights violations committed on their national soil. For instance, we noted in Chapter 5 that the UK has never been condemned by the European Courts for its policy of austerity, despite the policy being denounced by the UN Council on economic and social rights.

These states not only try to divert the European Courts' attention away from their own human rights violations but also obtain judicial condemnations of their political and economic enemies, who are the same wealthy financiers that finance and participate in litigation before the European Courts. Public and certain private interests collude and thus boost the effects of public–private litigation discussed in previous chapters. The politicisation of certain judicial complaints and condemnations financed by the UK, the Netherlands, Sweden, Norway and Switzerland

---

[74] John D. and Catherine T. MacArthur Foundation, 'Background on MacArthur support for the International Criminal Court', memo; Ford Foundation, *Annual Report of 1998*, available at www.ford-found.org/.

has sometimes resulted in economic sanctions against Russia and other Eastern nationalist countries (see Chapter 6). These economic sanctions could benefit European countries that are engaged in an economic battle against Russia, especially in times of increasing economic competition between states. The fight between states over territories is another area in which geopolitical interests and competition prevail. Political sanctions against countries (such as Russia) that annex other countries could also be of interest to states engaged in an economic battle.

In sum, we have identified some relationships between the litigation undertaken and funded by foreign private foundations (and some national countries) and their economic and political interests. The economic interests of private foundations have been traced through the identities and CVs of the board members of these private foundations and through the economic investments made by their heads. Some judgments litigated and delivered by the ECtHR that favour the free market and free trade promoted by private foundations have been also analysed to demonstrate how the litigation and economic interests pursued by private foundations coincide and intersect.

Conclusion: Towards a Privatised Capture of Human Rights?

Through repeated litigation and advocacy, private foundations and some NGOs funded by them are influencing not only the actual content of each individual decision of the ECtHR, but also the overall shape of the case law of the Strasbourg Court through inputs (applications brought before the ECtHR and evidence used by the Court) and outputs (active participation in the execution of ECtHR judgments). While some US socio-legal scholars have assumed that NGOs are captured by their private funders (Vincent 2019) in their litigation efforts before the US Supreme Court, we have demonstrated that private foundations (in particular the OSF) do not only finance some litigating NGOs but also take cases to the European Courts directly. In doing so, they partly capture the Courts' jurisprudence by orienting them towards highly political cases (territories and political topics) and the defence of the rights of certain minorities (such as Muslims, Roma, migrants, LGTB persons, prisoners, terrorists, human rights activists and political opponents supported by some private foundations), especially in Eastern countries and in Russia. In particular, repeated litigation plus public policy advocacy by NGOs specialising in litigation before the ECtHR and the CJEU shape the way in which the conflicts underlying cases are selected, discussed and resolved.

Nonetheless, the impacts of private foundations are not limited to the case law of the European Courts; they encompass their evolving architecture, their nomination of judges, and the new public management approach they have applied to handle applications and to clear the backlog generated by the adhesion of new member states to the CoE and the EU and the litigation carried out by private foundations. Although the capture phenomenon also covers the influence of private donors on NGOs, the process of capture is thus more related to the way private foundations and NGOs capture the European Courts, and especially the ECtHR, through many dimensions (architectural, the management of applications, the execution of ECtHR judgments, and so on).

While this capture phenomenon could be limited and even broken by the politicisation of European judgments that intervene at the last stage (but sometimes prior to new litigation efforts undertaken by private foundations and some NGOs to counterbalance and fight against the political backlash caused by their former litigation and advocacy activities), the interests of private foundations seem to coincide to a large extent with those promoted and pursued by the European and CoE institutions and those of the US. If private foundations and NGOs were not pushing specific issues onto the agenda of the ECtHR and the CJEU and playing a repeat game until they obtain rulings from the ECtHR (which they can then try to amplify or minimise depending on the ruling), it is not improbable that the underlying social conflicts would be settled differently.

We might wonder whether the capture phenomenon that has been demonstrated throughout this book contributes to a privatisation of European human rights justice, and why such a process is regulated neither by the European Courts nor by the CoE and the EU institutions. The absence of regulation might be explained by the participation of the EU institutions in the process of NGO funding and litigation, and by the fact that the European Courts increase their judicial activities and power through the investments made by private foundations on which they have become dependent. While administration and decision-making stays in the hands of public judicial institutions, the absence of real regulation of this private influence raises issues about a potential privatisation of European and national human rights justice. In this regard, some politicians have very recently called for the integrity of the Strasbourg Court to be restored and for potential conflicts of interest of judges at the ECtHR to be remedied.[1]

Similarly, we would question not only the impact of the growing private influence on the potential privatisation of European human rights justice, but its effects on the content of human rights. The question is whether this process is leading to a privatisation and even to a commodification of human rights. In other words, to what extent could human

---

[1] The absence of regulation has very recently been denounced by certain politicians, including Isabel Mereilles from the Parliamentary Assembly of the Council of Europe, who addressed the issue to the CM: 'How to remedy potential conflicts of interest of judges at the European Court of Human Rights?', Written Question No. 747 to the Committee of Ministers, Doc. 15095, 23 April 2020. See also Milan Knezevic, again from the Parliamentary Assembly: 'Restoring the integrity of the European Court of Human Rights', Written Question No. 748 to the Committee of Ministers, Doc. 15096, 24 April 2020.

rights become the property of the private sector? We have shown that through the growing influence of monetarism and the free play of market forces human rights are being managed through market mechanisms (privatisation of the inputs and outputs of the jurisprudence delivered by the ECtHR) and are being progressively transformed into private issues that coincide with private interests and neoliberal policies pursued by private donors. Consequently, European law is under the influence of economic interests that are also partly ruled by European jurisprudence to such an extent that law and economy are intertwined (Bessy et al. 2011). From this perspective, the privatisation of human rights (by private foundations) and their commodification, which could be a new approach to human rights applied by the European Courts under the influence played by private foundations, contribute to a blurring of the boundaries between public and private spheres. The intervention of private lawyers in the process tends to reinforce this blurring phenomenon, which is also found at a national level (France and Vauchez 2017)

It is certain that in this capture phenomenon, private foundations and NGOs are participating in the juridification and the judicialisation of the underlying issues. They are influencing the specific type of politics that is being played out. We have argued that litigation against Eastern countries and Russia before the ECtHR and the CJEU proves our point. We have identified the patterns underlying the input to the Courts and the shape of the case-law-making process. In particular, we have seen that litigation before the Strasbourg Court has been turned into a field of what social scholars have called a 'new cold war' between the EU/US and Russia. We have tried to show that judicial decisions are transformed in political terms and that they foster the escalation of conflict. This is problematic not only when contrasted with the philanthropic public mission that NGOs and private foundations claim to have, but also when contrasted with the purpose of the ECHR and the EU Charter of Fundamental Rights, especially with regard to the effective protection of human rights. In particular, such private orientation appears to be especially detrimental to the protection of economic and social rights, which are notably affected by austerity policies but have so far never been challenged by private foundations and NGOs. This trend undermines and thwarts the legitimacy of the European Courts, which already lack democratic control (Alter 2014; Vauchez 2016).

In terms of a contextual research agenda on the international and European system of human rights, this proves that the analysis of the jurisprudence of international and regional courts must keep very much in mind that normative aspirations may cloak the instrumental use of rights, and that a proper assessment requires setting the case-law-making process in the context of the politics of NGO funding and of international relations per se. To a certain extent, European case law is also the result of a struggle between the liberal and Christian forces that both litigate worldwide (the latter have not really been investigated in this book but will be scrutinised in a future book). This phenomenon certainly deserves to be part of a new research agenda on international and regional human rights justice. It would not be the first time that powerful interests (private concentrations of wealth, powerful governments including European, US or Russian ones, or international organisations) have bent rights to serve their own agenda (Moyn 2012, 2014). We should not underestimate the extent to which rights have been a rallying cry, so to speak, of 'neoliberal' policies (Guilhot 2005), and most especially, the means by which neoliberal policies have been expanded to new territories, including European human rights justice.

SELECT BIBLIOGRAPHY

Adler M. (2018) *Cruel, Inhuman or Degrading Treatment? Benefit Sanctions in the UK*. London: Palgrave Macmillan.

Ahmed S. (2011) 'The impact of NGOs on international organizations: complexities and considerations'. *Brooklyn Journal of International Law*, 36, 817–840.

Albiston C. (1999) 'The rule of law and the litigation process: the paradox of losing by winning'. *Law & Society Review*, 33(4), 869–910.

Alesina A., Favero C. and Giavazzi F. (2019) *Austerity: When It Works and When It Doesn't*. Princeton, NJ: Princeton University Press.

Alkema E. A. (2000) 'The European Convention as a Constitution and its Court as a constitutional court', in P. Mahoney, F. Matscher, H. Petzold and L. Wildhaber (eds.) *Protecting Human Rights: The European Perspective: Studies in Memory of Rolv Ryssdal*. Cologne: Karl Heymanns Verlag, 41–63.

Alter K. (2014) *The New Terrain of International Law: Courts, Politics, Rights*. Princeton, NJ: Princeton University Press.

Andenas M. and Bjorge E. (2013) 'National implementation of ECHR rights', in A. Føllesdal, B. Peters and G. Ulfstein (eds.) *Constituting Europe: The European Court of Human Rights in a National, European and Global Context*. Cambridge: Cambridge University Press, 181–262.

Angelari M., Berger V., Borkowski G., Culhin I., Hopma A., Khurshudyan A., Kuijer M., Murdoch J. and Tibbits F. (2016) *ELP Guidebook on Human Rights Training Methodology for Legal Professionals*. Strasbourg: Council of Europe Publishing.

Arai-Tahakashi Y. (2013) 'The margin of appreciation doctrine: a theoretical analysis of Strasbourg's variable geometry', in A. Føllesdal, B. Peters and G. Ulfstein (eds.) *Constituting Europe: The European Court of Human Rights in a National, European and Global Context*. Cambridge: Cambridge University Press, 62–104.

Arnold G. (2012) *The Great Investors: Lessons on Investing from Master Traders*. London: Pearson.

Arnove R. F. (1980) *Philanthropy and Cultural Imperialism: The Foundations at Home and Abroad*. New Delhi: Indiana University Press.

Bambra C. (2019) *Health in Hard Times: Austerity and Health Inequalities*. Bristol: Policy Press.

Barzelay M. (2001) *The New Public Management*. Berkeley, CA: University of California Press.

Bates E. (2010) *The Evolution of the European Convention on Human Rights: From Its Inception to the Creation of a Permanent Court of Human Rights*. Oxford: Oxford University Press.

Berman E. (1983) *The Influence of the Carnegie, Ford and Rockefeller Foundations on American Foreign Policy*. New York, NY: New York University Press.

Bertoni E. A. (2009) 'The Inter-American Court of Human Rights and the European Court of Human Rights: a dialogue on freedom of expression standards'. *European Human Rights Law Review*, 12(3), 332–352.

Bessy C., Delpeuch T. and Pélisse J. (2011) *Droit et regulations des activités économiques: perspectives sociologiques et institutionnalistes*. Paris: LGDJ.

Biebricher T. and Vogelmann F. (2017) *The Birth of Austerity: German Ordoliberalism and Contemporary Neoliberalism*. London: Rowman & Littlefield International.

Bieling H.-J. (2014) 'Shattered expectations: the defeat of European ambitions of global financial reform'. *Journal of European Public Policy*, 21(3), 346–366.

Blyth M. (2013) *Austerity: The History of a Dangerous Idea*. New York, NY: Oxford University Press.

Bond M. (2012) *The Council of Europe: Structure, History and Issues in European Politics*. Abingdon: Routledge.

Bouwen P. and McCown M. (2007) 'Lobbying versus litigation: political and legal strategies of interest representation in the European Union'. *Journal of European Public Policy*, 14, 422–443.

Bremner R. (1988) *American Philanthropy*. Chicago, IL: University of Chicago Press.

Bringedal Houge A. and Lohne K. (2017) 'End impunity! Reducing conflict-related sexual violence to a problem of law: end impunity!' *Law & Society Review*, 51(4), 755–789.

Brown R. (1979) *Rockefeller Medicine Men: Medicine and Capitalism in America*. Berkeley, CA: University of California Press.

Bürli N. (2017) *Third-Party Interventions before the European Court of Human Rights: Amicus Curiae, Member-State and Third-Party Interventions*. Cambridge: Intersentia.

Calligaro O. (2018) 'Une organisation hybride dans l'arène européenne: Open Society Foundations et la construction du champ de la lutte contre les discriminations'. *Politix*, 121(1), 151–172.

Cameron I. (2013) 'The Court and the Member States: procedural aspects', in A. Føllesdal, B. Peters and G. Ulfstein (eds.) *Constituting Europe: The European Court of Human Rights in a National, European and Global Context*. Cambridge: Cambridge University Press, 25–61.

Carrera S., de Somer M. and Petkova, B. (2012) 'The Court of Justice of the European Union as a fundamental rights tribunal: challenges for the effective delivery of fundamental rights in the area of freedom, security and justice'. *CEPS Papers in Liberty and Security in Europe*, 49.

Chahim D. and Prakash A. (2013) 'NGOization, foreign funding, and the Nicaraguan civil society'. *International Journal of Voluntary and Nonprofit Organizations*, 25, 487–513.

Chalmers D. (2015) 'Judicial performance, design and membership at the Court of Justice', in M. Bobek (ed.) *Selecting Europe's Judges*. Oxford: Oxford University Press, 51–78.

(2012a) 'Introduction: the conflicts of EU Law and the conflicts in EU law'. *European Law Journal*, 18 (5), 607–620.

(2012b) 'The European Court of Justice is now little more than a rubber stamp for the EU. It should be replaced with better alternative arrangements for central judicial guidance'. LSE European Politics and Policy (EUROPP) Blog, 8 March.

(2012c) 'The European Court of Justice has taken on huge new powers as "enforcer" of last week's Treaty on Stability, Coordination and Governance. Yet its record as a judicial institution has been little scrutinized'. LSE European Politics and Policy (EUROPP) Blog, 7 March.

Chernow R. (1998) *Titan: The Life of John D. Rockefeller*. New York, NY: Vintage.

Christoffersen J. and Madsen M. R. (2011) *The European Court of Human Rights between Laws and Politics*. Oxford: Oxford University Press.

Cichowski R. (2007) *The European Court and Civil Society Litigation, Mobilization and Governance*. Cambridge: Cambridge University Press.

Choudry A. and Kapoor D. (2013) *NGOization: Complicity, Contradictions and Prospects*. New York, NY: Zed Books.

Chussodovsky M. (1997) *The Globalisation of Poverty: Impacts of IMF and World Bank Reforms*. New York, NY: Zed Books.

Cliquennois G. (2017) 'The impact of austerity policies on international and European courts and their jurisprudence'. *European Journal of International Law* Talk blog, www.ejiltalk.org/author/gcliquennois/, 3 March.

Cliquennois G. and Champetier B. (2016) 'The economic, judicial and political influence exerted by private foundations on cases taken by NGOs to the European Court of Human Rights: inklings of a new Cold War?' *European Law Journal*, 22 (1), 92–126.

Cliquennois G. and de Suremain H. (2018) *Monitoring Penal Policy in Europe*. Abingdon: Routledge.

Cliquennois G. and Lambert Abdelgawad E. (2016) 'The development of the European system of human and fundamental rights in the current economic and political context'. *European Law Journal*, 22(1), 2–8.

Cliquennois G. and Snacken S. (2018) 'European and United Nations monitoring of penal and prison policies as a source of an inverted panopticon?' *Crime, Law and Social Change*, 70(1), 1–18.
Cohen S. (2011) *Soviet Fates and Lost Alternatives: From Stalinism to the New Cold War*. New York, NY: Columbia University Press, 2011.
Collins P. M. (2018) 'The use of amicus briefs'. *Annual Review of Law and Social Science*, 14, 219–237.
Conant L. (2002) *Justice Contained: Law and Politics in the European Union*. New York, NY: Cornell University Press.
Condliffe Lagemann E. (1999) *Philanthropic Foundations, New Scholarship, New Possibilities*. Bloomington, IN: Indiana University Press.
Contiades X. and Fotiadou X. (2012) 'Social rights in the age of proportionality: global economic crisis and constitutional litigation'. *International Journal of Constitutional Law*, 10(3), 660–686.
Cordes J. J. and Steuerle C. E. (2009) *Nonprofits and Business*. Washington, DC: Urban Institute Press.
Cummins S. and Rhode D. (2009) 'Public interest litigation: insights from theory and practice'. *Fordham Urban Law Journal*, 36, 603–651.
Curti M. and Nash R. (1965) *Philanthropy in the Shaping of American Higher Education*. New Brunswick, NJ: Rutgers University Press.
Daems T. and Robert L. (2017) *Europe in Prisons: Assessing the Impact of European Institutions on National Prison Systems*. Cham: Palgrave Macmillan.
Davies B. (2019) *Austerity, Youth Policy and the Deconstruction of the Youth Service in England*. London: Palgrave Macmillan.
De Búrca G. (2013) 'After the EU Charter of Fundamental Rights: the Court of Justice as a human rights adjudicator?' *Maastricht Journal of European and Comparative Law*, 20(2), 168–184.
De Búrca G. and Weiler J. (2001) *The European Court of Justice*. Oxford: Oxford University Press.
De Feyter K. and Gómez Isa F. (2005) *Privatisation and Human Rights in the Age of Globalization*. Cambridge: Intersentia.
Dehousse F. (2011) 'The reform of the EU Courts, the need of a management approach'. Trans-European Policy Studies Association, Egmont Paper 53, http//aei.pitt.edu/33464/Reform-EUCourts.PDF.
Devaux C. (2019) *La fabrique du droit du commerce international. Réguler les risques de capture*. Brussels: Bruylant.
De Wolf A. H. (2011) *Reconciling Privatization with Human Rights*. Cambridge: Intersentia.
DiMaggio P. J. and Powell W. (1983) 'The iron cage revisited: institutional isomorphism and collective rationality in organizational fields'. *American Sociological Review*, 48, 147–160.

Dowie M. (2002) *American Foundations: An Investigative History*. Cambridge, MA: MIT Press.

Duffy H. (2018) *Strategic Human Rights Litigation: Understanding and Maximising Impact*. Oxford: Hart Publishing.

Epp R. (1998) *The Rights Revolution: Lawyers, Activists and Supreme Courts in Comparative Perspective*. Chicago, IL: University of Chicago Press.

Farrow T. (2014) *Civil Justice, Privatization, and Democracy*. Toronto: University of Toronto Press.

Ferguson K. (2013) *Top Down: The Ford Foundation, Black Power, and the Reinvention of Racial Liberalism*. Philadelphia, PA: University of Pennsylvania Press.

(2007) 'Organizing the ghetto: CORE, the Ford Foundation, and American Pluralism, 1967–1969'. *Journal of Urban History*, 34 (1), 67–100.

Fischer D. (1983) 'The role of philanthropic foundations in the reproduction and production of hegemony: Rockefeller foundations and the social sciences'. *Sociology*, 17(2), 206–233.

Fischer-Lescano A. (2014) *Human Rights in Times of Austerity Policy: The EU Institutions and the Conclusion of Memoranda of Understanding*. Baden-Baden: Nomos.

Føllesdal A., Peters B. and Ulfstein, G. (2013) *Constituting Europe: The European Court of Human Rights in a National, European and Global Context*. Cambridge: Cambridge University Press.

France P. and Vauchez A. (2017) *Sphère publique, intérêts privés. Enquête sur un grand brouillage*. Paris: Presses de Sciences Po.

Francis M. M. (2018) 'The price of civil rights: black lives, white funding, and movement capture'. *Law and Society Review*, 53(1), 275–309.

Galanter, M. (1974) 'Why the 'haves' come out ahead: speculations on the limits of legal change'. *Law & Society Review*, 9, 95–160.

Gedalof I. (2018) *Narratives of Difference in an Age of Austerity*. London: Palgrave Macmillan.

Giblin B. (2008) 'Editorial'. *Hérodote*, 129(2), 3–5.

Glasius M. (2006) *The International Criminal Court: A Global Civil Society Achievement*. London: Routledge.

Goldston J. A. (2018) 'The impacts of strategic human rights litigation: a view from the field'. Presentation given at the International and Interdisciplinary Symposium on the Use of Law by Social Movements and Civil Society, Free University of Brussels, 23 March.

(2017) 'The unfulfilled promise of educational opportunity in the United States and Europe: from *Brown v. Board* to *D. H.* and beyond', in J. Bhabha, A. Mirga and M. Matache (eds.) *Realizing Roma Rights*. Philadelphia, PA: University of Pennsylvania Press, 163–184.

(2001) 'A future for Roma rights?' Presentation given at the Central European University, 8 April.
Goulden J. (1971) *The Money-Givers*. New York, NY: Random House.
Guilhot N. (2007) 'Reforming the world: George Soros, global capitalism and the philanthropic management of the social sciences'. *Critical Sociology*, 33(3), 447–477.
(2005) *The Democracy Makers: Human Rights and International Order*. New York, NY: Columbia University Press.
(2004) 'George Soros, les sciences sociales et la régulation du marché mondial'. *Actes de la Recherche en Sciences Sociales*, 151–152(1), 36–48.
Guinchard A. and Wesley S. (2016) 'The French approach to access to justice', in E. Palmer, T. Cornford, Y. Marique and A. Guinchard (eds.) *Access to Justice: Beyond the Policies and Politics of Austerity*. Portland, OR: Hart Publishing, 259–287.
Haddad H. N. (2018) *The Hidden Hands of Justice: NGOs, Human Rights, and International Courts*. Cambridge: Cambridge University Press.
Haines H. (1984) 'Black radicalization and the funding of civil rights'. *Social Problems*, 32, 31–43.
Hausmaninger H. (1995) 'Towards a "new" Russian constitutional court'. *Cornell International Law Journal*, 28, 349–391.
Hellman J., Jones G. and Kaufmann D. (2003) 'Seize the state, seize the day: state capture and influence in transition economies'. *Journal of Comparative Economics*, 31, 751–773.
Hershkoff H. and McCutcheon A. (2000) 'Public interest litigation: an international perspective', in M. McClymont and S. Golub (eds.) *Many Roads to Justice: The Law-Related Work of Ford Foundation Grantees around The World*. New York, NY: The Ford Foundation, 283–296.
Hitoshi Mayer L. (2011) 'NGO standing and influence in regional human rights courts and commissions'. *Brooklyn Journal of International Law*, 36, 911–946.
Hodson L. (2011) *NGOs and the Struggle for Human Rights in Europe*. Oxford: Hart.
Holcombe R. G. (2018) *Writing Off Ideas: Taxation, Philanthropy and America's Non-Profit Foundations*. New York, NY: Routledge.
Howell J. and Pearce J. (2001) *Civil Society and Development*. Boulder, CO: Lynne Rienner Publishers.
Israël L. (2009) *L'arme du droit*. Paris: Presses de Sciences Po.
Jacobs P. (2018) 'Austerity measures and their effects on penal litigation'. Paper given at the conference on Overcoming the Obstacles to Access of Detained Persons to Rights and to Court: European Perspectives, European Court of Human Rights, Strasbourg, 7 December.

Jamieson M. (2020) *The Austerity Cure: The Impact of Benefit Sanctions on Mental Health*. Edinburgh: Luna Press Publishing.

Jenkins C. and Eckert C. (1986) 'Channeling Black insurgency: elite patronage and professional social movement organizations in the development of the Black movement'. *American Sociological Review*, 51, 812–829.

Jordan B. and Drakeford M. (2012) *Social Work and Social Policy under Austerity*. Basingstoke: Palgrave Macmillan.

Kamat S. (2002) *Development Hegemony*. New York, NY: Oxford University Press.

Kapronczay S. (2017) 'War on NGOs in Eastern countries: coalition building as a possible answer'. *International Journal on Human Rights*, 26, available at https://sur.conectas.org/en/war-on-ngos-in-eastern-europe/.

Kelemen R. D. (2011) *Eurolegalism: The Transformation of Law and Regulation in the European Union*. Cambridge, MA: Harvard University Press.

Kilpatrick, C. and de Witte, B. (2014) 'Social rights in times of crisis in the Eurozone: the role of fundamental rights' challenges'. European University Institute, Department of Law, *EUI Working Paper Law*, 2014/05.

Klarman M. J. (2013) *From the Closet to the Altar: Courts, Backlash and the Struggle for Same-Sex Marriage*. Oxford: Oxford University Press.

Kriazhkov V. and Lazarev L. (1998) *Konstitutsionnaia iustitsiia v Rossiiskoi Federatsii*. Moscow: BEK.

Krickovic A. (2015) 'When interdependence produces conflict: EU–Russia energy relations as security dilemma'. *Contemporary Security Policy*, 36(1), 3–26.

Krige J. and Rausch H. (2012) *American Foundations and the Coproduction of World Order in the Twentieth Century*. Gottingen/Bristol, CT: Vandenhoeck & Ruprecht.

Krug P. (1997) 'Departure from the centralized model: the Russian Supreme Court and constitutional control of legislation'. *Virginia Journal of International Law*, 37(3), 725–778.

Krugman P. (1999) *The Accidental Theorist and Other Dispatches from the Dismal Science*. New York, NY: W. W. Norton.

Lambert Abdelgawad E. (2017) 'Measuring the judicial performance of the European Court of Human Rights'. *International Journal for Court Administration*, 8(2), 20–29.

(2016) 'The economic crisis and the evolution of the system based on the ECHR: is there any correlation?' *European Law Journal*, 22(1), 74–91.

(2013) 'The Court as part of the Council of Europe: the Parliamentary Assembly and the Committee of Ministers', in A. Føllesdal, B. Peters and G. Ulfstein (eds.) *Constituting Europe: The European Court of Human Rights in a National, European and Global Context*. Cambridge: Cambridge University Press, 263–300.

(2011) *Preventing and Sanctioning Hindrances to the Right of Individual Petition before the European Court of Human Rights*. Cambridge: Intersentia.
Landman T. and Carvalho E. (2009) *Measuring Human Rights*. Abingdon: Routledge.
Langbroek P. M. (2009) *Administering Courts and Judges: Rethinking the Tension between Accountability and Independence of the Judiciary*. Utrecht: Universiteit Utrecht.
Langbroek P. M., Dijkstra R. I., Bozorg Zadeh K. and Türk Z. (2017) 'Performance management of courts and judges: organizational and professional learning versus political accountabilities', in F. Contini (ed.) *Handle with Care: Assessing and Designing Methods for Evaluation and Development of the Quality of Justice*. Bologna: Lappeenranta University of Technology, 297–325.
Leach P. (2014) 'EHRAC's litigation at the European Court of Human Rights'. Intervention at the SAGE workshop, Université de Strasbourg, Strasbourg, 13 February.
   (2013) 'No longer offering fine mantras to a parched child? The European Court's developing approach to remedies', in A. Føllesdal, B. Peters and G. Ulfstein (eds.) *Constituting Europe: The European Court of Human Rights in a National, European and Global Context*. Cambridge: Cambridge University Press, 142–180.
   (2008) 'The Chechen conflict: analysing the oversight of the European Court of Human Rights'. *European Human Rights Law Review*, 6, 732–761; also published in Russian in 2010, *Comparative Constitutional Review*, 1 (74), 143–168.
   (2005a) *Taking a Case to the European Court of Human Rights*. Oxford: Oxford University Press.
   (2005b) 'Beyond the Bug River: a new dawn for redress before the European Court of Human Rights'. *European Human Rights Law Review*, 148, also published in Russian in 2005, *Sravnitelnoe Konstitutsionnoe Obozrenie* (Comparative Constitutional Review), 3(52), 94–104, Institute for Law and Public Policy, Moscow.
Leach P., Hardman H. and Stephenson S. (2010a) 'Can the European Court's pilot judgment procedure help resolve systemic human rights violations? Burdov and the failure to implement domestic court decisions in Russia'. *Human Rights Law Review*, 10(2), 346–359.
Leach P., Paraskev C. and Uzelac G. (2010b) 'Human rights fact-finding: the European Court of Human Rights at a crossroads'. *Netherlands Quarterly of Human Rights*, 28(1), 41–77.
Levine M. and Forrence J. (1990) 'Regulatory capture, public interest, and the public agenda: toward a synthesis'. *Journal of Law, Economics, and Organization*, 6, 167–198.

Lohne K. (2019) *Advocates of Humanity: Human Rights NGOs in International Criminal Justice.* Oxford: Oxford University Press.
  (2017) 'Global civil society, the ICC, and legitimacy in international criminal justice', in N. Hayashi and C. M. Bailliet (eds.) *The Legitimacy of International Criminal Tribunals.* Cambridge: Cambridge University Press, 449–472.
Margolis J. and Walsh J. (2003) 'Misery loves companies: rethinking social initiatives by business'. *Administrative Science Quarterly*, 48, 268–305.
Martinsen D. and Vollaard H. (2014) 'Special issue. Implementing social Europe in times of crises: re-established boundaries of welfare?' *West European Politics*, 37(4), 677–692.
Marquez B. (2003) 'Mexican–American political organizations and philanthropy: bankrolling a social movement'. *Social Service Review*, 77, 329–346.
Mayerfeld J. (2011) 'A Madisonian argument for strengthening international human rights institutions: lessons from Europe', in L. Cabrera (ed.) *Global Governance, Global Government: Institutional Visions for an Evolving World System.* New York, NY: State University of New York Press, 211–251.
Mazon B. (1985) 'La Fondation Rockefeller et les sciences sociales en France, 1925-1940'. *Revue française de sociologie*, 26(2), 311–342.
McAdam D. (1982) *Political Process and the Development of Black Insurgency, 1930-1970.* Chicago, IL: University of Chicago Press.
McCann M. (1994) *Rights at Work: Pay Equity Reform and the Politics of Legal Mobilization.* Chicago, IL: University of Chicago Press.
McCarthy, J. and Zald, M. (1977) 'Resource mobilization and social movements: a partial theory'. *American Journal of Sociology*, 82, 1212–1241.
McCown, M. (2009) 'Interest groups and the European Court of Justice', in D. Coen and J. Richardson (ed.) *Lobbying the European Union: Institutions, Actors and Issues.* Oxford: Oxford University Press, 89–104.
McCrudden C. (2015) 'Transnational culture wars'. *International Journal of Constitutional Law*, 13(2), 434–462.
McGregor L. (2015) 'Alternative dispute resolution and human rights: developing a rights-based approach through the ECHR'. *European Journal of International Law*, 26(3), 607–634.
McIntosh Sundstrom L. (2014) 'Russian NGOs and the European Court of Human Rights: a spectrum of approaches to litigation'. *Human Rights Quarterly*, 36, 844–868.
Menon R. and Rumer E. B. (2015) *Conflict in Ukraine: The Unwinding of the Post-Cold War Order.* Cambridge, MA: MIT Press.
Mertus J. (1999) 'From legal transplants to transformative justice: human rights and the promise of transnational civil society'. *American University International Law Review*, 14, 1335–1389.

Meyers S. (2016) 'NGO-ization and human rights law: the CRPD's civil society mandate'. *Laws*, 21(5), available at www.mdpi.com/2075-471X/5/2/21.

Morgan R. and Evans M. (2002) *Combating Torture in Europe: The Work and Standards of the European Committee for the Prevention of Torture*. Strasbourg: Council of Europe Publishing.

Moyn S. (2014) *Human Rights and the Uses of History*. New York, NY: Verso.

(2012) *The Last Utopia: Human Rights in History*. Cambridge, MA: Harvard University Press.

Nazneen S. and Sultan M. (2009) 'Struggling for survival and autonomy: the NGOisation of women's organizations in Bangladesh'. *Development*, 52, 193–199.

Nielsen W. A. (2002) *Golden Donors: A New Anatomy of the Great Foundations*. Abingdon: Routledge.

Nowak M. (2017) *Human Rights or Global Capitalism: The Limits of Privatization*. Philadelphia, PA: University of Pennsylvania Press.

O'Beachain D. and Polese A. (2010) *The Colour Revolutions in the Former Soviet Republics: Successes and Failures*. London and New York, NY: Routledge.

O'Boyle M. and Brady N. (2013) 'Investigatory powers of the European Court of Human Rights'. *European Human Rights Law Review*, 6(4), 378–391.

Palmer E., Cornford T., Guinchard A. and Marique Y. (2016) *Access to Justice: Beyond the Policies and Politics of Austerity*. Oxford: Hart.

Parmar I. (2015) 'The "Big 3" foundations and American global power'. *American Journal of Economics and Sociology*, 74(4), 676–703.

(2014) 'American power and philanthropic warfare: from the war to end all wars to the democratic peace'. *Global Society*, 28(1), 54–69.

(2012) *Foundations of the American Century*. New York, NY: Columbia University Press.

(2011) 'American hegemony, the Rockefeller Foundation, and the rise of academic international relations in the US', in N. Guilhot (ed.) *The Invention of International Relations Theory*. New York, NY: Columbia University Press, 182–209.

Parmar I., Miller, L. B. and Ledwidge, M. (2014) *Obama and the World: New Directions in US Foreign Policy*. London: Routledge.

Pétric B. (2008) 'À propos des révolutions de couleur et du soft power américain'. *Hérodote*, 129(2), 7–20.

Piven F. F. and Cloward R. A. (1977) *Poor People's Movements: Why They Succeed, How They Fail*. New York, NY: Pantheon Books.

Popelier P., Heyning C. and Nuffels, P. V. (2011) *Human Rights Protection in the European Legal Order: The Interaction between the European and the National Courts*. Cambridge: Intersentia.

Porter A. (2015) *Buying a Better World: George Soros and Billionaire Philanthropy*. Roanoke, VA: TAP Books.

Reckhow, S. (2012) *Follow the Money: How Foundation Dollars Change Public School Politics*. New York, NY: Oxford University Press.

Rietzler K. (2014) 'Fortunes of a profession: American foundations and international law, 1910–1939'. *Global Society*, 28(1), 8–23.

Roelofs J. (2003) *Foundations and Public Policy: The Mask of Pluralism*. New York, NY: State University of New York Press.

Ron J., Pandya A. and Crow D. (2016) 'Universal values, foreign money: funding local human rights organizations in the Global South'. *Review of International Political Economy*, 23(1), 29–64.

Rosenberg G. (1991) *The Hollow Hope: Can Courts Bring About Social Change?* Chicago, IL: University of Chicago Press.

Rushton P. and Donovan C. (2019) *Austerity Policies: Bad Ideas in Practice*. London: Palgrave Macmillan.

Sadurski W. (2009) 'Partnering with Strasbourg: constitutionalisation of the European Court of Human Rights, the accession of Central and East European states to the Council of Europe, and the idea of pilot judgments'. *Human Rights Law Review*, 9, 397–453.

Salomon M. (2015) 'Of austerity, human rights and international institutions'. *European Law Journal*, 21(4), 521–545.

Samuel A. (2004) 'Arbitration, alternative dispute resolution generally and the European Convention on Human Rights'. *Journal of International Arbitration*, 21(5), 413–438.

Sarat A. and Scheingold S. (2006) *Cause Lawyers and Social Movements*. Stanford, CA: Stanford University Press.

(2001) *Cause Lawyering and the State in a Global Era*. New York, NY: Oxford University Press.

(1998) *Cause Lawyering: Political Commitments and Professional Responsibilities*. New York, NY: Oxford University Press.

Scot M. (2010) '"Rockefeller's Baby": la London School of Economics et la recherche économique dans l'Angleterre de l'entre-deux-guerres', in L. Tournès (ed.) *L'argent de l'influence. Les fondations américaines et leurs réseaux européens*. Paris: Autrement, 84–104.

Scott-Smith G. (2014) 'Maintaining transatlantic community: US public diplomacy, the Ford Foundation, and the successor generation concept in US foreign affairs, 1960s–1980s'. *Global Society*, 28(1), 90–103.

(2012) 'Expanding the diffusion of US jurisprudence: the Netherlands as a 'beachhead' for US foundations in the 1960s', in J. Krige and H. Rausch (eds.) *American Foundations and the Coproduction of World Order in the Twentieth Century*. Gottingen/Bristol, CT: Vandenhoeck & Ruprecht, 210–231.

Sharpe J. (2010) *The Conscience of Europe: 50 years of the European Court of Human Right*. London: Third Millennium Publishing.

Shoup L. H. (2015) *Wall Street's Think Tank: The Council on Foreign Relations and the Empire of Neoliberal Geopolitics, 1976-2014*. New York, NY: Monthly Review Press.

Slater, C. (2009) *Soros: The World's Most Influential Investor*. New York, NY: McGraw Hill.

Sokur, S. (2016) *Political Problems of International Systems and Global Development*. PhD in Political Sciences, National University of Kiev, 29 September.

Soros, G. (2005) *Georges Soros on Globalization*. New York, NY: Public Affairs.

Spano, R. (2014) 'Universality or diversity of human rights? Strasbourg in the age of subsidiarity'. *Human Rights Law Review*, 14(3), 487-502.

Stigler G. (1971) 'The theory of economic regulation'. *Bell Journal of Economics and Management Science*, 2, 3-21.

Stiglitz J. (2002) *Globalization and Its Discontents*. New York, NY: W. W. Norton.

Susanu, S. (2016) *Costs and Expenses before the European Court of Human Rights through the Lens of Ethics*. Master's thesis, University of Strasbourg.

Teles, S. (2008) *The Rise of the Conservative Legal Movement: The Battle for Control of the Law*. Princeton, NJ: Princeton University Press.

Torres Pérez, A. (2009) *Conflicts of Rights in the European Union: A Theory of Supranational Adjudication*. Oxford: Oxford University Press.

Tournès L. (2010) *L'argent de l'influence. Les fondations américaines et leurs réseaux européens*. Paris: Autrement.

Tulkens, F. (2014) 'Les prisons en Europe. Les développements récents de la jurisprudence de la Cour européenne des droits de l'homme'. *Déviance et Société*, 38(4), 425-448.

(2007) 'The European Convention on Human Rights between international law and constitutional law', in European Court of Human Rights, *Dialogue between Judges*. Strasbourg: Council of Europe, 8-15.

Tushnet M. (1987) *The NAACP's Legal Strategy against Segregated Education, 1925-1950*. Chapel Hill, NC: University of North Carolina Press.

Vajic, N. (2005) 'Some concluding remarks on NGOs and the European Court of Human Rights', in T. Treves, A. Fodella, A. Tanzi and M. Frigessi di Rattalma (eds.) *Civil Society, International Courts and Compliance Bodies*. The Hague: Springer, 93-106.

Van den Eynde L. (2013) 'An empirical look at the amicus curiae practice of human rights NGOs before the European Court of Human Rights'. *Netherlands Quarterly of Human Rights*, 31(3), 271-313.

Van der Vet F. (2018) '"When they come for you": legal mobilization in new authoritarian Russia'. *Law & Society Review*, 52(2), 301-336.

Van Zyl Smit D. and Snacken S. (2009) *Principles of European Prison Law and Policy*. Oxford: Oxford University Press.

Vauchez A. (2016) *Democratizing Europe*. New York, NY: Palgrave Macmillan.

Vauchez A. and Willemez, L. (2006) *La justice face à ses réformateurs*. Paris: Presses Universitaires de France.

Vettori G. (2011) 'Fundamental social rights: a discussion between two crises'. *European Journal of Social Law*, 1(4), 232–243.

Vincent M. (2019) 'The price of civil rights: Black politics, White money, and movement capture'. *Law and Society Review*, 53(1): 275–309.

Walsh K., Carney G. M. and Léime A. N. (2015) *Ageing through Austerity*. Bristol: Bristol University Press.

Wedel J. R. (1996) 'Clique-run organizations and US economic aid: an institutional analysis'. *Demokratizatsiya: The Journal of Post-Soviet Democratization*, 4 (4), 571–602.

Weiler, J. H. H. (2016) 'A Faustian deal?' *International Journal of Constitutional Law*, 14(2), 321–324.

(2009) 'Fundamental rights and fundamental boundaries: common standards and conflicting values in the protection of human rights in the European legal space', in R. Kastoryano (ed.) *An Identity for Europe: The Relevance of Multiculturalism in EU Construction*. The Hague: Springer, 73–101.

Weiler, J. H. H and Lockhart, N. J. S. (1995) '"Taking rights seriously" seriously: the European Court and its fundamental rights jurisprudence – part I'. *Common Market Law Review*, 32(1), 51–94.

Williamson A. (1998) *How America Built the New Russian Oligarchy*, unpublished manuscript.

Willoughby-Herard T. (2015) *Waste of a White Skin: The Carnegie Corporation and the Racial Logic of White Vulnerability*. Berkeley, CA: University of California Press.

Winkler A. (2018) *We the Corporations: How American Businesses Won Their Civil Rights*. New York, NY: W. W. Norton.

Witt J. F. (forthcoming) *The American Fund: A Story of Money and Politics in America*. New York, NY: Simon & Schuster.

Zunz, O. (2012) *Philanthropy in America: A History*. Princeton, NJ: Princeton University Press.

INDEX OF AUTHORS

Adler, Michael, 188–189, 264
Ahmed, Shamima, 10, 264
Albiston, Catherine, 13, 264
Alesina, Alberto, 188, 264
Alkema, Evert Albert, 16, 264
Alter, Karen, 262, 264
Andenas, Mads, 20, 264
Angelari, M., 157, 264
Arai-Tahakashi, Yutaka, 22, 264
Arnold, Glen, 242, 264
Arnove, Robert F., 13–14, 264

Bailliet, Cecilia M., 272
Bambra, Clare, 188, 265
Barzelay, Michael, 168, 265
Bates, Ed, 16, 265
Berger, V., 264
Berman, Edward, 13–14, 265
Bertoni, Eduardo Andrés, 22, 265
Bessy, Christian, 262, 265
Bhabha, Jacqueline, 268
Biebricher, Thomas, 189, 265
Bieling, Hans-Jürgen, 190, 265
Bjorge, Eirik, 20, 264
Blyth, Mark, 190, 265
Bond, Martyn, 18, 265
Borkowski, G., 264
Bouwen, Pieter, 144, 265
Bozorg Zadeh, Kyana, 271
Brady, Nathalia, 157, 273
Bremner, Robert H., 13, 265
Bringedal Houge, Anette, 10, 265
Brown, Richard, 13–14, 265
Bürli, Nicole, 10, 13, 16, 162, 265

Calligaro, Oriane, 33, 265
Cameron, Iain, 18, 265

Carney, Gemma M., 276
Carrera, Sergio, 28, 266
Carvalho, Edzia, 271
Chahim, Dean, 11, 266
Chalmers, Damian, 163, 166, 198, 266
Champetier, Brice, 16, 31, 40, 154, 235, 266
Chernow, Ron, 244, 266
Chossudovsky, Michel, 190, 192
Choudry, Aziz, 11, 266
Christoffersen, Jonas, 16–17, 266
Cichowski, Rachel, 10, 12, 266
Cliquennois, Gaëtan, 16, 21, 31, 40
71, 154–155, 193, 205, 235, 266–267
Cloward, Richard A., 11, 273
Coen, David, 272
Cohen, Stephen, 237, 267
Collins, Paul M., 10, 241, 267
Conant, Lisa, 29, 267
Condliffe Lagemann, Ellen, 13, 267
Contiades, Xenophon, 192, 267
Contini, Francesco, 271
Cordes, Joseph J., 14, 267
Cornford, Tome, 269, 273
Crow, David, 274
Culhin, I., 264
Cummins, Scott, 10, 267
Curti, Roderick, 13, 267

Daems, Tom, 205, 267
Davies, Bernard, 189, 267
De Búrca, Gráinne, 23, 27, 29, 163, 166, 267
De Feyter, Koen, 3, 9, 267
De Somer, Marie, 266
De Witte, Bruno, 188, 192, 270

De Wolf, Antenor Hallo, 3, 9, 267
Dehousse, Franklin, 168, 267
Delpeuch, Thierry, 265
Devaux, Caroline, 2, 11, 267
Dijkstra, Rachel I., 271
DiMaggio, Paul J., 160–161, 267
Donovan, Catherine, 189, 274
Dowie, Mark, 13, 268
Drakeford, Mark, 188, 270
Duffy, Helon, 13, 268

Eckert, Craig M., 11, 270
Epp, Charles R., 11, 31, 268
Evans, Malcolm, 21, 273

Farrow, Trevor, 9, 268
Favero, Carlo, 264
Ferguson, Karen, 11, 42, 268
Fischer, Donald, 13–14, 244, 268
Fischer-Lescano, Andreas, 191, 268
Føllesdal, Andreas, 18, 264–265, 268, 270–271
Forrence, Jennifer, 2, 11, 271
Fotiadou, Alkmene, 192, 267
France, Pierre, 262, 268
Francis, Megan Ming, 2, 11–13, 268

Galanter, Marc, 11, 268
Gedalof, Irene, 188, 268
Giavazzi, Francesco, 264
Giblin, Béatrice, 183, 268
Glasius, Marlies, 10, 268
Goldston, James A., 157, 268
Golub, Stephan, 269
Gómez Isa, Felipe, 3, 9, 267
Goulden, Joseph, 13, 269
Guilhot, Nicolas, 13–14, 16, 244–245, 263, 269, 273
Guinchard, Audrey, 189, 269, 273

Haddad, Heidi N., 12–13, 269
Haines, Herbert, 11, 269
Hardman, Helen, 271
Hausmaninger, Herbert, 181, 269
Hayashi, Nobuo, 272
Hellman, Joseph, 2, 11, 269
Hershkoff, Helen, 40, 269
Heyning, Catherine (Van de), 273

Hitoshi Mayer, Lloyd, 10, 269
Hodson, Loveday, 12, 17, 19, 269
Holcombe, Randall G., 13, 269
Hopma, A., 264
Howell, Jude, 11, 269

Israël, Liora, 243, 269

Jacobs, Pauline, 189, 269
Jamieson, M., 189, 270
Jenkins, Craig, 11, 270
Jones, Geraint, 269
Jordan, Bill, 188, 270

Kamat, Sangeeta, 11, 270
Kapoor, Dip, 11, 266
Kapronczay, Stefánia, 228, 270
Kaufmann, Daniel, 269
Kelemen, R. Daniel, 29, 270
Khurshudyan, A., 264
Kilpatrick, Claire, 188, 192, 270
Klarman, Michael J., 221, 270
Kriazhkov, Vladimir, 181, 270
Krickovic, Andrej, 240, 270
Krige, John, 13, 270, 274
Krug, Peter, 181, 270
Krugman, Paul, 243, 270
Kuijer, M., 264

Lambert Abdelgawad, Elisabeth, 17–18, 20–21, 157, 163–164, 168–169, 266, 270
Landman, Todd, 168, 271
Langbroek, Philip M., 167, 271
Lazarev, Leonid, 181, 270
Leach, Philip, 19–20, 43, 157, 271
Ledwidge, Mark, 273
Léime, Aine Ni, 276
Levine, Michael, 2, 11, 271
Lockhart, N. J. S., 26, 276
Lohne, Kjersti, 10, 145, 265, 272

Madsen, Michael Rask, 16–17, 266
Mahoney, Paul, 246, 264
Margolis, Joshua, 12, 272
Marique, Yseult, 269, 273
Marquez, Benjamin, 11, 272
Matache, Margareta, 268

INDEX OF AUTHORS

Matscher, Franz, 264
Mayerfeld, Jamie, 22, 272
Mazon, Brigitte, 244, 272
McAdam, Doug, 11, 272
McCann, Michael, 10–11, 272
McClymont, Mary, 269
McCarthy, John, 11, 272
McCown, Margaret, 28, 144, 155, 265, 272
McCrudden, Christopher, 1, 3, 13, 15, 272
McCutcheon, Audrey, 40, 269
McGregor, Lorna, 9, 272
McIntosh Sundstrom, Lisa, 10, 272
Menon, Rajan, 237, 240, 272
Mertus, Julie, 10, 272
Meyers, Stephen, 11, 273
Miller, Linda B., 273
Mirga, Andrzej, 268
Morgan, Rod, 21, 273
Moyn, Samuel, 263, 273
Murdoch, J., 264

Nash, Merle, 13, 267
Nazneen, Sohela, 273
Nielsen, Waldemar A., 13, 273
Nowak, Manfred, 3, 9, 273

Palmer, Ellie, 188, 269, 273
Pandya, Archana, 274
Parmar, Inderjeet, 13–14, 273
Pearce, Jenny, 11, 269
Pélisse, Jérôme, 265
Peters, Birgit, 264–265, 268, 270–271
Petkova, Bilyana, 266
Pétric, Boris, 183, 273
Petzold, Herbert, 264
Piven, Frances Fox, 11, 273
Popelier, Patricia, 20, 273
Porter, Anna, 182, 205, 273
Powell, Walter, 161, 267
Prakash, Aseem, 11, 266

Rausch, Helke, 13, 270, 274
Reckhow, Sarah, 13–14, 274
Rhode, Deborah, 10, 267
Richardson, Jeremy, 145, 272
Rietzler, Katarina, 13, 274

Robert, Luc, 205, 267
Roelofs, Joan, 13–15, 274
Ron, James, 12, 274
Rosenberg, Gerald, 10, 274
Rumer, Eugene B., 237, 240, 272
Rushton, Peter, 189, 274

Sadurski, Wojciech, 17, 274
Samuel, Adam, 2, 9, 274
Sarat, Austin, 10, 243, 274
Scheingold, Stuart, 10, 243, 274
Scot, Marie, 244, 274
Scott-Smith, Giles, 13, 274
Sharpe, Jonathan L., 17, 274
Shoup, Laurence H., 235, 275
Slater, Roberts, 34, 275
Snacken, Sonja, 21, 71, 205, 267, 275
Sokur, S., 155, 275
Soros, George, 28, 257, 275
Spano, Robert, 22, 275
Stephenson, Svetlana, 271
Steuerle, C. Eugene, 14, 267
Stigler, George, 2, 11, 275
Stiglitz, Joseph E., 254, 275
Sultan, Maheen, 273
Susanu, S., 31, 275

Teles, Steven, 11, 275
Tibbits, F., 264
Tournès, Ludovic, 13, 182, 274–275
Tulkens, Françoise, 20, 157, 275
Türk, Zübeyir, 271
Tushnet, Mark, 11, 275

Ulfstein, Geir, 264, 268, 270–271
Uzelac, Gordana, 271

Vajic, Nina, 10, 275
Van den Eynde, Laura, 10, 275
Van der Vet, Freek, 275
Van Zyl Smit, Dirk, 21, 275
Vauchez, Antoine, 4, 262, 268, 275
Vettori, Giuseppe, 192, 276
Vogelmann, Frieder, 189, 265
Vollaard, Hans, 192, 272

Walsh, James P., 12, 272
Walsh, Kieran, 188, 276

Wedel, Janine R., 254, 276
Weiler, Joseph H. H., 23–24, 26, 28, 267, 276
Wildhaber, Luzius, 264
Willemez, Laurent, 4, 276
Williamson, Anne, 254, 276
Willoughby-Herard, Tiffany, 13, 276
Winkler, Adam, 255, 276
Witt, John Fabian, 13, 276

Zald, Mayer, 11, 272
Zunz, Olivier, 13–14, 276

GENERAL INDEX

A., B. and C. v. *Ireland* [16 December 2010] ECtHR 112–113
Abakarova v. *Russia* [15 October 2015] ECtHR 89
abortion 15, 59, 111–112, 142, 257
Abu Zaybah cases 201, 214, 216
Abuyeva and Others v. *Russia* [2 December 2010] ECtHR 69
ACCEPT (NGO) 107, 110
access to justice 128, 273
accountability 52, 92, 164–166, 184–185, 271
action plan 70, 73, 75, 93, 96, 99, 116–117, 146, 202–203, 208–210, 214, 219
adjudication 27, 29, 275
Adrian Coman, Robert Clabourn Hamilton and NGO Accept v. *Romania* [5 June 2018] CJEU 205 107
advocacy 1, 3–4, 11, 13, 15, 24, 31 34, 36, 38, 43, 50, 53–55, 60, 62, 64, 81, 96, 99, 117, 140, 143–144, 146, 150, 154–156, 158–159, 162, 164, 169, 171, 174, 176–177, 185–186, 209–210, 218, 220, 231, 235, 240, 249, 251–252, 256, 258, 260–261
AIRE Centre 51, 62, 116, 148, 150, 162
Akayeva case 44, 69–70, 138, 201, 208–209
Akimenkov v. *Russia* [6 February 2018] ECtHR 98, 201, 212
Al Nashiri cases 35, 39, 121–122, 138, 156, 201, 215–216
Al Nashiri v. *Poland* [24 July 2014] ECtHR 39, 121, 138

Al Nashiri v. *Romania* [31 May 2018] ECtHR 35, 39, 121–122, 138
Alekseyev v. *Russia* [21 October 2010] ECtHR 45, 99, 162
Alexei Navalnyy and Peter Ofitserova v. *Russia* [23 February 2016] ECtHR 97
Aliyev v. *Azerbaijan* [8 April 2010] ECtHR 83–84, 155, 161
Allen &Overy Foundation 41, 50, 62
amicus curiae briefing 10, 13, 29–30, 41, 54, 141, 154, 162, 186, 267, 275
Amnesty International (AI) 51–52, 79, 119, 133, 139, 146, 149, 174, 215, 218, 224–225, 249
Amsterdam Treaty 23
Ananyev case 71–73, 75, 142, 201–202
Ananyev and Others v. *Russia* [10 January 2012] ECtHR 71, 75
annual reports 23–24, 32, 41–44, 47, 51, 54–57, 59–60, 65, 67, 73, 81, 95, 105, 112, 137, 139, 148, 163, 166, 168, 173, 183, 210, 258
applications 1, 3, 5, 17, 19, 23, 27–28, 35–37, 43–44, 48–49, 51, 54, 58, 69, 73, 80, 83–85, 88, 90, 92–93, 95, 101, 108–109, 113, 118, 130–132, 145, 147, 151–152, 155, 158, 164, 168–169, 173, 175, 178–179, 181, 186, 193, 202–203, 213, 217, 224–225, 227, 237, 241, 260
architecture of the Courts 1
archives
  Ford Foundation 5
  Rockefeller 5, 65, 241
Article 19 (NGO) 54, 63, 65, 98, 212, 223

281

Article 46 ECHR 30, 66–67, 76–79, 81, 84–88, 96–99, 143, 150–151, 188, 214
Askhabova v. *Russia* [18 April 2013] ECtHR 69
Assenov and Others v. *Bulgaria* [28 October 1998] ECtHR 119
Association of Russian Lawyers for Human Rights 53, 76, 142, 202
asylum 27, 51–53, 56, 80, 109, 116, 118, 152, 227
Atlantic Philanthropies 53
audit mechanisms 163, 165, 168
austerity policies 1, 31–32, 171, 189–190, 192, 194, 197–198, 220, 262, 266, 274
Azerbaijan 2, 35–36, 42–43, 59, 81–84, 126, 133, 137–138, 143, 152, 154, 161, 199–200, 212–214, 221 228, 255

backlog 19, 23, 147–148, 155, 163, 166–167, 169, 221, 231, 260
Baka v. *Hungary* [23 June 2016] ECtHR 129, 162, 195
ban on foreign private foundations 221
Baring Foundation 50, 62
barristers 19, 31, 39, 41, 43, 248–249
Bayev and Others v. *Russia* [20 June 2017] ECtHR 45, 99, 162
board members 242
board members of private foundations 242
Brighton Conference 146, 148
Brighton Declaration 146–147
Brussels Declaration 148–151
Bulgaria 35–36, 40, 52, 55, 63–64, 72, 94–95, 102, 114, 118–119, 124 139, 159, 162, 175–176, 178–179, 183, 185, 192–193, 199, 201–202, 244
Bulgarian Helsinki Committee (BHC) 55
business 14, 46, 59–60, 131, 190, 242–243, 245–246, 248–249, 251–252, 255, 267, 272
businesspeople 64, 242–243, 247, 250, 254

capitalism 4, 14, 252, 256, 265, 269, 273
capture 2, 4–5, 7, 11, 67, 143–144, 169, 171, 260, 262, 267–269, 271
 movement capture 2, 11, 268
 private capture 7, 171
 state capture 269
case law of the European Court of Human Rights (ECtHR) 1, 4, 9, 22
caseload 23–24
Catan and Others v. *Moldova and Russia* [19 October 2012] ECtHR 134
Catan case 53, 201, 205, 207, 239
cause lawyers, lawyering 2, 11, 243 274
Cebotari v. *Moldova* [13 November 2007] ECtHR 82
Centre for Legal Resources on behalf of Valentin Câmpeanu v. *Romania* [17 July 2014] ECtHR 95
Centro Europa 7 v. *Italy* [7 June 2012] ECtHR 125, 159
Cervenka v. *Czech Republic* [13 October 2016] ECtHR 94–95
Charles Stewart Mott Foundation 60, 63
Charter of Fundamental Rights of the European Union 24, 27
Ciorap v. *Moldova* [19 June 2007] ECtHR 75
CJEU *see* Court of Justice of the European Union
classified documents, treatment of 155–156, 186
Committee for Human Rights (CDDH) 65, 146–147, 152, 192
Committee of Ministers (CM), Council of Europe 20, 141, 218, 220
Commonwealth Office Human Rights Project Fund 60, 63
competition 4, 23, 26, 28, 125, 259
complaints 1, 3, 18–19, 29, 31–32, 34, 36, 39–40, 43, 46–48, 73, 75, 96, 100, 114, 126, 169, 176–177, 188, 203, 241, 258
constitutional systems 179, 223
control over NGOs 221
Copenhagen Declaration 151–153

cost-effectiveness evaluations 163
costs and expenses 9, 30-31, 36,
  163-164, 203, 223, 257, 275
Council of Europe (CoE)member states
  20, 65, 115, 148, 194, 258
counterterrorism 46, 49, 88, 121, 174,
  177, 199, 211
counterterrorism policies 121, 174
Court of Justice of the European Union
  (CJEU) 1-5, 9-12, 15-16, 22-29,
  32-38, 41, 51-53, 56, 64-67,
  102-104, 107-110, 118, 130, 136,
  144, 155, 158, 160, 163, 166-169,
  175, 177, 183, 187-188, 195-198,
  260-262, 266-267, 272
criminal investigations 132, 225
crisis 3, 12, 16, 30-31, 137, 162, 189,
  192, 194, 196, 226, 243, 248, 267,
  270
  economic 3, 12, 16, 30-31, 189, 192,
    194-195, 267, 270
cultural liberalism 256
cuts in public spending 188, 196
Czech Republic 35, 59, 94-95, 146, 159,
  175-176, 178-179, 183, 201, 216,
  219-220

D. G. v. Poland [12 February 2013]
  ECtHR 78
D. H. v. Czech Republic [13 November
  2007] ECtHR 35, 94, 175
decision-making process 2, 4-5, 16, 89,
  222, 236, 261
Denisov v. Ukraine [25 September
  2018] ECtHR 128-129, 161
detention 18, 35, 39, 46, 51, 56, 58-59,
  64, 68, 71-83, 85, 98, 102,
  115-116, 118-119, 121-122, 126,
  133, 135, 138, 173-174, 184-185,
  202-204, 213, 215-216, 234
detention conditions 58, 71-74, 76,
  80-81, 117, 126
discrimination 15, 35, 38-39, 46, 51-53,
  55, 60, 63, 68, 99, 102-107, 110,
  118-119, 134, 161, 174, 181, 184,
  188, 192, 199, 216, 219-220, 225,
  256, 265
  economic 103

ethnic 110
police 35, 102
sexual 39
domestic policies 200
domestic remedies 3, 20, 39, 56,
  71-76, 90, 94, 126, 132, 179
  203, 218

Eastern constitutional systems 176, 179
Eastern countries 175, 178, 182, 200,
  270
Ecodefence and Others v. *Russia* 44
ECtHR *see* European Court of Human
  Rights
EHRAC (European Human Rights
  Advocacy Centre) 38, 40-44, 46,
  62, 65, 70, 81, 84, 87-90, 93, 97,
  100-101, 114-116, 126-128,
  132-133, 136, 138, 143, 146,
  148-151, 154, 156-157, 162,
  173-174, 177, 184, 186-187,
  208-210, 212, 215, 254, 271
election of judges 4, 90, 93
El-Masri v. *Macedonia* [13 December
  2012] ECtHR 35, 95, 175
Embassy of Great Britain 45
Embassy of the Netherlands 45
empirical data 5
Equal Rights Trust 68
Esmukhambetov and Others v. *Russia*
  [29 March 2011] ECtHR 44, 87
European Union (EU)
  Charter of Fundamental Rights 109,
    262, 267
  institutions 268
  legislation 23, 163, 166
European Arrest Warrant(EAW) 52
European Commission 16, 22, 25, 27,
  42, 45, 47, 50, 55-57, 62, 107, 130,
  141, 145, 155, 181, 191, 194,
  197-198, 215, 219, 224, 229, 231,
  238, 240
European Commissioner for Human
  Rights, Council of Europe 50, 145,
  155, 224, 231
European Convention on Human
  Rights (ECHR) 26, 30, 139,
  148-150, 215, 265, 274

European Council 22, 51, 117, 155, 190, 240, 244, 249
European Court of Human Rights (ECtHR) 1, 16–18, 31, 44, 46–47, 59, 119, 146, 156, 159, 165, 168, 175, 183, 186–187, 206–207, 211, 214, 219, 230, 238–239, 261, 264–266, 268, 275
  budget 144–145
  rules 155–156
European Courts 1–5, 7, 10, 15–16, 33, 35–36, 39–41, 54, 64, 66, 136, 140, 143–144, 162–163, 168–169, 171, 173, 184, 188, 193, 198, 241, 243, 251, 258, 260–262, 266
European human rights justice 171
European judicial control 189
European Parliament 22, 24–25, 27–28, 155, 207, 210, 213, 215–216, 237, 240
European Roma Rights Centre (ERRC) 40, 60, 63, 105
Evan Cornish Foundation 40, 50, 62
execution of judgments 144, 149–150, 155, 157
extradition 132, 137

F. v. Bevándorlási és Állampolgársági Hivatal [25 January 2018] CJEU 56, 109
Fadeyeva v. Russia [9 June 2005] ECtHR 46, 100
failure 25, 30, 90, 94–95, 112–113, 126–127, 140, 180, 203, 205, 214, 219, 223, 227, 271
fair trials 51–53, 128, 151, 184
Filatenko v. Russia [6 December 2007] ECtHR 124
filtering 18, 21, 29, 168–169, 239
fiscal emergencies 1, 32
Ford Foundation 37, 40, 53–54, 60–61, 75, 105, 112, 138–139, 183, 242, 245, 249, 258, 268–269, 274
foundations 5, 34, 37, 40, 42, 47, 50, 54–57, 59–62, 64, 73, 75, 78, 81, 99, 105, 107, 112, 137–139, 145, 152, 183–185, 203, 213–214, 217, 233–235, 242–243, 245–246, 248–249, 252, 258, 268–269, 273–274; see also Ford Foundation, Heinrich Böll Foundation, MacArthur Foundation, Oak Foundation, Solon Foundation
France 3, 35, 38, 45, 62, 145, 162, 178–179, 188–189, 191, 215–216, 235, 242, 262, 268, 272, 276
Frasik v. Poland [5 January 2010] ECtHR 136
free market 4, 182, 233, 241, 243, 245–246, 252, 256, 259
free trade 241
Freedom Now (NGO) 81, 83–84, 143, 214
freedom
  of expression 54, 126–127, 265
  of the press 123
  of religion 106
Frumkin v. Russia [5 January 2016] ECtHR 97–98, 201, 212, 254
funders, private 2, 11, 40, 260

Genderdoc-M v. Moldova [12 June 2012] ECtHR 99
Georgian Young Lawyers' Association 43–44, 49
German Marshall Fund of the United States 55
Germany 3, 145, 178–179, 188–189, 191, 235
globalism 256

healthy environment 100
Heinrich Böll Foundation 59
Helsinki Act 55, 182
Helsinki Committees 55, 63, 65, 183; see also Bulgarian Helsinki Committee, Hungarian Helsinki Committee, Norwegian Helsinki Committee, Romanian Helsinki Committee
Helsinki Committee for Human Rights 65
Helsinki Foundation for Human Rights (HFHR) 59, 78, 81, 83–84, 111, 121, 129, 136, 141, 146, 149, 152, 183, 203, 214

GENERAL INDEX 285

Hirsi Jamaa and Others v. *Italy* [23 February 2012] ECtHR 52, 79
Hirst v. *United Kingdom*[6 October 2005] ECtHR 51, 122
Horváth and Kiss v. *Hungary* [29 January 2013] ECtHR 105, 217
human rights 16–18, 21–22, 26, 30–32, 34–36, 41–50, 53–54, 57, 59–60, 62–64, 69, 75–76, 78–79, 81, 83–84, 96, 105–106, 119, 121, 126–127, 129, 131–132, 135, 137–141, 143, 145–153, 156–159, 162, 165, 168, 171, 174–176, 183–184, 186–187, 192, 196 203, 206–209, 211–212, 214–215, 219, 221, 224, 230–233, 235, 238–239, 241, 249–250, 264–267, 269–276
human rights activists 81, 126
Human Rights House Foundation 59, 81, 83–84
Human Rights Watch (HRW) 34, 38, 48, 52, 64, 69, 79, 96, 105–106, 132, 137–138, 146, 149, 162, 183, 212, 225, 251
human trafficking 113
Hungarian Helsinki Committee (HHC) 56, 73, 77, 117, 137, 152, 185, 225, 227
Hungary 2–3, 35–36, 51, 54, 56, 63, 73, 77, 105, 116–117, 126–130, 137, 146, 159, 161, 175–176, 178–180, 182, 185, 190, 194–195, 199, 201–202, 204, 211, 216–218, 221, 225, 227–228, 231, 236, 238, 243–244, 252, 255
Husayn (Abu Zubaydah) v. *Poland* [24 July 2014] ECtHR 121, 138

Iacov Stanciu v. *Romania* [24 July 2012] ECtHR 74
Idalov v. *Russia* [22 May 2012] ECtHR 76
Ilgar Mammadov v. *Azerbaijan* [22 May 2014] ECtHR 81, 83, 162, 214
Ilias and Ahmed v. *Hungary* [14 March 2017] ECtHR 51, 56, 116, 137
ill treatment 117

immigration 27–28, 79, 102, 115, 117, 152, 165, 174, 184, 256
implementation of ECtHR judgments 148
independence 4–5, 37
individual 1, 17–19, 34, 50, 81, 94 104, 108–109, 116, 119, 129, 164, 167, 169, 174, 193, 195–197, 205, 208, 219, 236, 241, 252, 256 260, 271
individual, redress 34, 241
inputs of the ECtHR 1, 3–5, 7, 33 61, 65, 143, 164, 169, 200, 260 262
intepretation 1, 9, 19–21, 27, 103, 110, 152, 161, 224, 230
interest groups 2–3, 11, 29, 33
interests, economic 5, 241, 244, 259, 262
political 240–241, 259
Interights 32, 38, 60, 62, 65, 99, 102, 105–106, 111, 113–114, 121, 133–134, 136, 138, 146, 160, 177, 205
Interlaken Conference 18, 239
International Helsinki Federation for Human Rights 50, 139, 183, 215
International Protection Center (IPC) 47, 177
international relations 200, 273
interveners 30, 52, 163
interviews 5
Intigam Aliyev v. *Azerbaijan* [20 September 2018] ECtHR 84
Isayeva v. *Russia* [24 February 2005] ECtHR 69
Ismoilov v. *Russia* [24 April 2008] ECtHR 51, 132–133
Israilova and Others v. *Russia* [23 April 2009] ECtHR 69
Italy 3, 22, 35, 39, 51–52, 71–72, 79, 106–107, 125, 145–146, 159, 162–163, 177–179, 186, 191, 194, 215, 235
Izmir Conference 146

Joseph Rowntree Charitable Trust 40, 50, 62, 105
Judgment Watch 81, 142, 150

judgments
  obtained under Article 46 ECHR 30, 66–67, 76–79, 81, 84, 87–88, 97–99, 143, 188
  politicisation of 1, 200, 221, 230, 239, 258, 261
  pilot 18–19, 21, 29, 33, 52, 56, 58, 61, 66–67, 122, 138, 143, 156–157, 164, 180, 196, 202–203, 236, 271, 274
  quasi-pilot 19, 76
judicial results 66
Jugheli and Others v. *Georgia* [13 July 2017] ECtHR 101
jurisprudence 266, 274
  of the ECtHR 2, 9, 32
  and national human rights 5

Kadzoev v. *Bulgaria* [1 October 2013] ECtHR 117–118
Kaprykowski v. *Poland* [3 February 2009] ECtHR 78
Kasabova v. *Bulgaria* [19 April 2011] ECtHR 36, 124, 159, 175
Kehayov v. *Bulgaria* [18 January 2005] ECtHR 70, 72, 208
Khashiyev and Akayeva v. *Russia* [24 February 2005] ECtHR 44, 69, 138, 208
Khodorkovsky Mikhail 53, 254
Kiss judgment 105, 201, 216–217
Kudeshkina v. *Russia* [26 February 2009] ECtHR 39, 130–132
Kulykov and Others v. *Ukraine* [19 January 2013] ECtHR 93
Kurić and Others v. *Slovenia* [12 March 2014] ECtHR 68

landmark judgments 102
László Magyar v. *Hungary* [20 May 2014] ECtHR 77
Lawyers for Human Rights 53, 76, 82, 135, 142, 202
legal aid 31, 189
Legal Information Centre of Non-Governmental Organisations 68
legal precedent 28, 32
length of proceedings 31, 167
LGTB people 97

liberalism 11, 14, 208, 252, 254, 256, 268
liberty of expression 123
life sentences 77, 117
Lisbon Treaty 23, 27–28
literature 1, 3, 9, 11, 13–14, 16, 157, 163, 248
  legal 5, 9–10, 157
  socio-legal 5, 9–10
litigants, repeated 32, 61, 176
litigation 1–5, 7, 9–15, 17, 19, 24, 26–30, 32–38, 40–45, 47, 49, 51–56, 59–61, 64–69, 71, 81, 90, 93, 101–104, 106, 110–111, 115, 117, 121, 124–126, 139–141, 143–145, 153–154, 157–158, 162–164, 166, 169, 171, 173–177, 181–187, 189, 198, 200–201, 204, 215–217, 219–221, 224, 230–231, 234–237, 239–241, 243, 248, 251, 254–260, 262, 264–269, 271–272
  funding 5, 30, 240
  impacts 34, 36, 199, 220, 251
  private 28, 33, 67, 71, 188, 200, 258
  strategic 2, 34, 36, 53, 56, 60–61, 66, 153, 157, 173, 184, 217, 220, 255
  teams 3, 33, 67
Luxembourg Court 32, 160
Lyapin v. *Russia* 48

M. A. and Others v. *Poland* 51
M. C. and A. C. v. *Romania* [12 April 2016] ECtHR 95
M. C. v. *Bulgaria* [4 December 2003] ECtHR 114
Magnitskiy and Others v. *Russia* [27 August 2019] ECtHR 35, 85, 175
Magyar Helsinki Bizottság v. *Hungary* [8 November 2016] ECtHR 128
Mammadli v. *Azerbaijan* [19 April 2018] ECtHR 83, 161
Mammadov case 81, 83, 143, 161, 213–214
management techniques 163, 169
margin of appreciation 19, 22, 70, 100, 107, 124, 136, 147, 149, 160–161, 194, 230, 253, 264

Matra programme 55
MacArthur Foundation 41, 54, 63, 112, 183, 242, 246
Medova v. *Russia* [15 January 2009] ECtHR 132, 136
member states 16–18, 20–23, 27, 29, 65–66, 70, 76, 115, 121, 140, 148, 150, 160, 164, 187, 190, 194, 197–198, 215, 258
Merabishvili v. *Georgia* [28 November 2017] ECtHR 115
method, socio-legal 4
migration 50, 53, 75, 77, 227
military conflicts 133
minorities 205
  religious 174
Moldova 31, 53, 75, 82, 93, 99, 134–135, 146, 152, 177, 205–207, 237–238
money 3, 9, 34, 41, 146, 190, 243, 247, 269, 274, 276
  foreign 274
  private 3, 9
monitoring 16, 21, 35, 48, 50, 57, 59, 66, 76, 82, 96, 101, 139–140, 142, 145, 150, 153, 165, 167, 181–182, 184, 203, 208, 213, 220, 228, 231, 233, 236, 266
  of the execution of judgments 66
Moscow Helsinki Group 50, 120, 184

Nachova v. *Bulgaria* [6 July 2005] ECtHR 35, 102, 139, 175
National Endowement for Democracy (NED) 59
nationalism 206–207, 241, 255–256
nationalist regimes 200–201, 252
Navalnyy v. *Russia* [15 November 2018] ECtHR 97–98, 162, 201, 212–213, 238
Neier, Aryeh 34, 54, 235
neoliberalism 16, 241, 265
Neshkov and Others v. *Bulgaria* [27 January 2015] ECtHR 72–73, 201
Netherlands Ministry of Foreign Affairs 54
NGOs 1, 3–5, 10–17, 19, 26, 28–34, 36, 40–45, 47, 51, 55, 61, 64, 66–67, 69–71, 76–79, 81–82, 84, 87, 89, 94, 96–103, 105–107, 110–111, 113–118, 121–123, 126–128, 130, 135–136, 139–151, 154–156, 158, 162–164, 168–169, 171, 173, 175–177, 179, 182–184, 186–187, 189–190, 193, 196, 198, 200–204, 207–208, 210, 212–213, 217, 220–221, 224–225, 227–228, 230–237, 240–241, 243, 251–252, 260, 262–263, 265–266, 269–270, 272, 275
Nikolova v. *Romanian CEZ Electricity* [16 July 2015] CJEU 35, 103–104
Nizhny Novgorod Committee against Torture 47, 50, 62, 185
non-execution of judgments 31
Norwegian Helsinki Committee 43, 45, 185

O. M. v. *Hungary* [5 July 2016] ECtHR 56, 116
Oak Foundation 40, 42, 47, 54–56, 60–61, 64, 81, 138–139, 184, 235, 242, 248
offences, sexual 10, 113, 189
Oleksandr Volkov v. *Ukraine* [9 January 2013] 90
Open Russia (NGO) 53, 254
open society 3, 5, 33–34, 36, 42, 49, 57, 62, 137–138, 145–146, 154, 159, 174, 176–177, 185–186, 201, 204, 213, 217, 220–221, 231, 233, 235, 243, 265
Open Society Foundation (OSF) 5, 33–34, 40, 42, 47–48, 50, 53, 55–57, 60–62, 65–66, 68, 75–76, 81, 99, 105, 112, 117, 128, 137, 139, 142, 144–145, 153–155, 158–159, 162, 177, 182–183, 186–187, 189, 201, 204–208, 210, 214, 221, 224–225, 227, 231, 233–234, 241, 243, 249, 252, 258, 260, 265
Open Society Justice Initiative (OSJI) 3, 30, 34, 36, 41, 52, 62, 66, 68, 76, 82, 85, 102–104, 111, 117, 121, 123, 125, 127, 136, 138, 140–141, 146–147, 149–151, 153–154,

158–159, 162, 173–176, 181, 186, 190, 215–216, 218, 221, 224, 231, 234–235, 238, 241, 252, 256
orientation of European case law 175
Orlov and Others v. *Russia* [14 March 2017] ECtHR 127
Orsus and Others v. *Croatia* [16 March 2010] ECtHR 105
outputs of the ECtHR 65–66
overrepresentation of Eastern countries 182

Parliamentary Assembly, Council of Europe 206, 215, 224, 239
penal policies 69, 83
performance indicators 163–165, 167–168
philanthropists 242
Piechowicz v. *Poland* [17 April 2012] ECtHR 78
Pilgrim Trust 50, 63
pilot judgments 18–19, 21, 29, 33, 52, 56, 58, 61, 66–67, 122, 138, 143, 156–157, 164, 180, 196, 202–203, 236, 271, 274
players, repeated 1, 4, 17
Poland 3, 35, 39, 51–52, 54–55, 59, 63, 71, 78–79, 111–112, 121, 129, 136, 138–139, 141, 146, 152, 156, 159, 175–176, 178–180, 182, 199, 201, 214–215, 221, 228, 231, 236, 244, 250, 252–253, 256
political opponents 81, 97, 174, 201, 213, 234, 260
political opposition 35, 199, 201, 211–213
political tensions 171, 231
politicisation of judgments 1, 200, 221, 230, 239, 258, 261
prison
  custody 27
  policies 70, 199, 267
  sentences 73
prisoners 122
private actors 4, 32, 65
private donors 2, 5, 9, 14–16, 22, 28, 32–33, 36, 61, 67, 161, 171, 176, 182, 187, 199, 201, 220, 228, 231, 236–237, 242, 262

private foundations 1–5, 7, 9, 12–14, 16, 19, 32–33, 36–37, 40–41, 54, 61–62, 65–72, 76, 79, 81, 89, 94, 100, 102, 105–106, 110–111, 113, 115, 118, 121–123, 126, 136, 139–141, 143–148, 150, 155, 157–158, 161–164, 168–169, 171, 173, 176, 179, 182, 186–187, 189, 193, 196, 198–200, 212, 215, 220–221, 224–225, 228, 230–231, 234–235, 237, 240–241, 243, 251, 254–262, 266
private funding 4–5, 14, 40, 65, 176, 187, 258
private influence 3, 5, 7, 15, 33, 261
private interests 3–4, 15, 173, 243, 255, 258, 262
private sector 42, 67, 144, 163, 165, 250, 262
professional isomorphism 161
Promo-Lex 53, 65, 134, 205
protection 1, 5, 16–18, 22, 28, 43–44, 46–47, 50–51, 55, 57, 85, 87, 92, 96, 99, 101, 103, 109, 113–114, 119–120, 123, 126, 130–131, 140, 153, 156, 168–169, 174, 177, 180–181, 184, 188–189, 192–193, 195–196, 199, 206, 209, 220–221, 223, 228–229, 231–232, 253, 262, 273, 276
  of fundamental rights 22, 168, 179, 232
  of human rights 4–5, 17–18, 43, 45, 47, 57, 126, 131, 140, 184, 187, 189, 206, 220–221, 228–229, 231, 262, 276
protocols 17–18, 21, 24–25, 28, 47, 80, 87, 105–106, 122, 127, 134–135, 146, 162, 181, 193, 195, 205, 230, 239, 253, 256
public funding 1, 3–4, 32, 228
public spending 163, 191, 254
Public Verdict Foundation 53, 73

quasi-pilot judgments 19, 76

Rantsev v. *Cyprus and Russia* [7 January 2010] ECtHR 52 113, 136

Rasul Jafarov v. *Azerbaijan* [17 March 2016] ECtHR 81–82, 161
Rechters voor Rechters 53
reform of the CJEU 155
reform of the ECtHR 46, 142, 144, 146, 154, 156, 186
regime change 221, 231, 251
repressive regimes 213
respect for private life 93, 106, 129
Results-Based-Budgeting (RBB) 163–165
Rezmives and Others v. *Romania* [25 April 2017] ECtHR 58, 74–75
rights
  to demonstrate 38, 44, 97, 212
  to dignity 22, 39, 52, 74, 79, 173
  to education 105, 135, 205–207
  to a fair trial 44, 77, 93, 129, 132, 136, 212
  to freedom 44, 57–58, 98–99, 108, 123, 128, 130–131, 136, 173
  to health 81, 126
  to information 36, 126–127, 175
  to liberty and security 58
  to life 18, 37–38, 49, 58, 87–89, 95, 173
  to marry 106
  to property 54, 193, 253, 256
Rockefeller Archives 5, 65
Rockefeller Brothers Fund 37, 60, 63, 183
Roman Zakharov v. *Russia* [4 December 2015] ECtHR 44, 97, 162
Romanenko and Others v. *Russia* [8 October 2009] ECtHR 123, 159
Romania 30, 35, 39, 54–55, 57–58, 60, 63, 74, 95–96, 101, 107–108, 110, 121–122, 135–138, 162, 176–180, 183, 186, 192, 197, 199, 201, 216, 228
Romanian Helsinki Committee (APADOR-CH) 57–58, 74, 95, 122, 135, 137
rules of the ECtHR 155
Russia 2, 26, 31, 35, 39, 42–49, 52–55, 59, 61, 69–71, 75–76, 85, 87–89, 97–100, 113–115, 117–118, 120, 122–124, 126–127, 130, 132–139, 141–143, 146, 154, 159, 162, 171, 173–177, 180–185, 187, 194, 200–210, 212–213, 220–221, 224–225, 229–235, 237–240, 242, 244–245, 250, 252, 254–255, 257, 259–260, 262, 270–271, 275
Russian NGO Lawyers for Constitutional Rights and Freedoms (JURIX) 53, 76, 123

S. N. v. *Russia* [20 November 2018] ECtHR 114
Sargsyan v. *Azerbaijan* [16 June 2015 and 12 December 2017] ECtHR 133–134, 162
scholars
  legal 2, 5, 10, 260
  socio-legal 2, 10, 260
Sejdić and Finci v. *Bosnia and Herzegovina* [22 December 2009] ECtHR 52, 111
Sergei Ryabov v. *Russia* [17 July 2018] ECtHR 120
Shamayev and Others v. *Georgia and Russia* [12 April 2005] ECtHR 133
Sigrid Rausing Trust 40, 50, 53, 55, 59–61, 63–64, 75, 99, 105, 107, 162, 185, 245, 248
Solon Foundation 55
Soros, George 33–34, 137, 182, 189–191, 198, 202, 206–208, 212, 226–227, 235, 242–244, 254–257, 269, 273, 275
Spain 3, 35, 51–52, 178–179, 188, 191, 198–199
specific policy areas 173, 175, 241
Stanev v. *Bulgaria* [17 January 2012] ECtHR 94, 162
Stichting Russian Justice Initiative (SRJI) 48, 62, 65, 137, 177, 185, 208–209, 238
Strasbourg Court 13, 16, 20–22, 65, 74–75, 102, 105, 128, 146–147, 156, 159, 180–181, 196, 260, 262
strategic funding 2, 32
subsidiarity, principle of 19, 22, 95, 147, 152, 161, 193, 275
Suleymanov v. *Russia* [22 January 2013] ECtHR 127

Suso Musa v. *Malta* [23 July 2013] ECtHR 39, 79
Sweden 42–43, 49, 57, 64–65, 142

T. P. and A. T. v. *Hungary* [4 October 2016] ECtHR 117
Tagayeva and Others v. *Russia* ECtHR 43, 88, 208, 210
Társaság a Szabadságjogokért v. *Hungary* [14 April 2009] ECtHR 36, 128, 159, 175
Tatar v. *Romania* [27 January 2009] ECtHR 101
third party litigation 4, 29
third party interventions 16, 29, 32, 77, 99, 119, 122, 125, 174
torture 18, 21, 35, 39, 44, 46–49, 58, 62, 64–65, 69–70, 80, 102, 115, 117, 119–121, 127, 133, 137, 151–152, 175, 177, 184–185, 204, 216, 232, 273
tribunals 3, 24, 26, 28, 41, 90–91, 130, 152, 166, 266
Tsechoyev v. *Russia* [15 March 2011] ECtHR 132
Tymoshenko v. *Ukraine* [30 April 2013] ECtHR 82

Ukraine 26, 31, 42–43, 45, 59, 82, 90, 92–93, 129, 146, 150, 162, 177–179, 182, 185–187, 189, 206–207, 228, 235, 237, 239–240, 243, 252, 256, 272
Ukrainian Helsinki Human Rights Union 43–44, 152

Unbound Philanthropy (NGO) 50, 63
United Kingdom 3, 30, 36–37, 39 48, 51–52, 54, 60, 62–65, 77, 93, 106, 119, 122, 133, 136, 139, 142, 145, 152, 159, 163, 178–179, 184, 188, 193, 216, 234–235, 244 258, 264
United Kingdom Foreign and Commonwealth Office 48, 51, 54, 60, 62–63
unlawful detention 82–83, 115–116
United States 3, 10, 13–15, 18, 34, 37, 42, 53–54, 57, 59, 61, 64–65, 139, 145, 163, 168, 171, 182, 184, 191, 200–201, 206, 208, 210, 215–216, 225, 231, 233–234, 236, 238–240, 244, 246, 248, 250, 255, 260–263, 268, 273–274
United States Agency for International Development (USAID) 32, 42 55, 59–60, 62–63, 233, 238–239, 254

Varga and Others v. *Hungary* [10 March 2015] ECtHR 56, 72–73, 84, 201

watchdogs 81, 126
watching states 97, 135
William and Flora Hewlett Foundation 54, 63

Yukos 53
Yunusova and Yunusov v. *Azerbaijan* [2 June 2016] ECtHR 126

Made in the USA
Columbia, SC
27 November 2024